WOMEN IN RUSSIA, 1700–2000

Original in its range and analysis, *Women in Russia, 1700–2000*, fills an enormous gap in the field. It is the first book to provide a lively and compelling chronological narrative of women's experiences from the eighteenth century to the present. Synthesizing recent scholarship with her own work in primary and archival sources, Barbara Alpern Engel skillfully evokes the voices of individuals to enliven the account. The book captures the diversity of women's lives, detailing how women of various social strata were affected by and shaped historical change. Adopting the perspective of women provides fresh interpretations of Russia's past and important insights into the impact of gender on the ways that Russians defined themselves and others and imagined political change. Designed for a scholarly as well as undergraduate readership, the book integrates women's experience into broader developments in Russia's social, economic, cultural, and political history.

Barbara Alpern Engel is Professor of History at the University of Colorado. Her books include *Mothers and Daughters: Women of the Intelligentsia in Nineteenth-Century Russia* (1983) and *Between the Fields and the City: Women, Work, and Family in Russia, 1861–1914* (1993), both published by Cambridge. She has served on the editorial board of *Slavic Review* and has been a consulting editor for *Feminist Studies*.

ADVANCE PRAISE FOR *WOMEN IN RUSSIA, 1700–2000*

"In richly textured and graceful prose, the premier historian of Russian women, Barbara Engel, has given us the story of the burdens and conflicts, triumphs and defeats of women in tsarist Russia and the Soviet Union. Bringing in both elite and ordinary women, Russians and the non-Russian peoples, their everyday lives as well as political achievements, she tells a tale, not of steady progress, but of constant struggle against traditional patriarchy, unfulfilled promises of reformers and revolutionaries, and great and small victories always vulnerable to reversal. Here Russia's history is rounded out by the voices of those too often left silent."

—Professor Ronald Grigor Suny, University of Chicago

"Ranging from Peter the Great to the present, from tsarina to peasant, and from village to city, Barbara Engel's sweeping synthesis presents, for the very first time, the full panorama of Russian women's history. Her stories of women and their struggles through the centuries will prove essential to every student and teacher of Russian history."

—Wendy Z. Goldman, Professor, Department of History,
Carnegie Mellon University

"This extraordinary survey combines astute synthesis and telling, sometimes searing, detail. The clear and thoughtful narrative carries the reader through three centuries of riveting history, including the critical events of the past fifteen years. Engel is at the top of her form and has written another top-notch book."

—Bonnie G. Smith, Rutgers University, author of *Changing Lives: Women in European History since 1700* (1989)

BARBARA ALPERN ENGEL

University of Colorado

WOMEN IN RUSSIA, 1700 – 2000

PUBLISHED BY THE PRESS SYNDICATE OF THE UNIVERSITY OF CAMBRIDGE
The Pitt Building, Trumpington Street, Cambridge, United Kingdom

CAMBRIDGE UNIVERSITY PRESS
The Edinburgh Building, Cambridge CB2 2RU, UK
40 West 20th Street, New York, NY 10011-4211, USA
477 Williamstown Road, Port Melbourne, VIC 3207, Australia
Ruiz de Alarcón 13, 28014 Madrid, Spain
Dock House, The Waterfront, Cape Town 8001, South Africa

http://www.cambridge.org

First published 2004

Printed in the United States of America

Typefaces Ehrhardt 10$\frac{1}{2}$/12$\frac{1}{2}$ pt. and Bodoni   *System* LaTeX 2ε [TB]

A catalog record for this book is available from the British Library.

Library of Congress Cataloging in Publication Data
Engel, Barbara Alpern.
Women in Russia, 1700–2000 / Barbara Alpern Engel.
p.   cm.
ISBN 0-521-80270-9 (hc.) – ISBN 0-521-00318-0 (pbk.)
1. Women – Russia – History.   2. Women – Soviet Union – History.
3. Women – Russia (Federation)   I. Title.
HV1662.E54   2003
305.4′0947 – dc21   2003043017

ISBN 0 521 80270 9 hardback
ISBN 0 521 00318 0 paperback

CONTENTS

LIST OF ILLUSTRATIONS

ACKNOWLEDGMENTS

To acknowledge all the intellectual debts that I have incurred in the course of conceiving and writing this book is literally impossible. The product of countless interactions as well as my own reading of secondary and primary sources, it draws on decades of conversations with colleagues and friends, on scholarly papers heard at conferences and responses to papers of my own, and on colleagues' insightful critiques over the years of works I have circulated for their commentary. My thinking has also been affected in innumerable ways by more than three decades of stimulating scholarship on Russian women's history, on the history of other women, and in women's studies.

For reasons of space as well as the failings of memory, I acknowledge here only those who contributed to this particular book. For their assistance in obtaining documents and illustrations, I thank the staffs of the Slavonic Division of the New York Public Library, the Photographic Division of the Library of Congress, the Slavonic Collection of the Helsinki University Library, the Russian State Historical Archive, the State Historical Archive of the Russian Federation, and the Central State Archive of the city of Moscow. For their immensely helpful readings of the manuscript in part or as a whole, I am very grateful to Lindsey Hughes, Gail Warshovsky Lapidus, LeRoy Moore, Ronald Grigor Suny, Nina Tumarkin, William Wagner, and Christine Worobec. Thanks also to Victoria Bonnell for graciously allowing me to reproduce several posters. Finally, I thank the students in History 3713, spring term 2002, and in particular, Christopher Asbury, William Haberfeld, Matthew Hicks, and Mike Kreps for responding as honestly and thoughtfully as they did to this book at an earlier stage. Their responses have improved the final product and, I hope, made it more accessible to readers such as themselves. Any errors of fact or interpretation are, of course, my own responsibility.

NOTE ON TRANSLITERATION AND DATES

Transliterating Russian into English is a tricky business. Scholars in the United States use the Library of Congress system of transliteration, which differs from the one in use in popular literature (Tolstoi rather than the familiar Tolstoy; Aleksandra rather than the more familiar Alexandra; Tver' incorporating the Russian soft sign, rather than simply Tver and the like). In this book, I have adopted a mixed approach. I use names that are familiar to the reader for well-known historical actors and places (Tsars Peter, Nicholas, and Alexander; Catherine; and Moscow, for example) and adopt a modified Library of Congress system (minus soft signs and diacriticals) in other cases (Maria instead of Mariia, Evgenia instead of Evgeniia, Olga instead of Ol'ga, etc.). For the notes and for Russian terms transliterated in the text (*skhod, bol'shak*), I adhere to the Library of Congress system.

Until February 1918, the Russian calendar was thirteen days behind the Western and modern Russian calendar. I give dates according to the system in place at the time.

TIMELINE

1675	Arrest of Boiarynia Feodosia Morozova
1682–9	Regency of Sophia Ivanovna
1689–1725	Reign of Peter (Peter I), the Great
1689	Peter's marriage to Evdoksia Lopukhina
1699	Evdoksia forced into a nunnery
1701	Law mandating "German" dress
1702	Law requiring six-week betrothal
1712	Peter marries his mistress, the future Catherine I, formerly Marfa Skavronska
1712, 1714, 1715	Creation of shelters for illegitimate children
1716	"Loose women" ordered away from regiments
1718	Decree mandating mixed sex assemblies
1721	Divorce becomes a formal procedure
	Spiritual Regulations forbid women under fifty years of age to take the veil
	Women convicted of "loose behavior" are condemned to industrial labor
1722	Law forbids forced marriages
1725–7	Reign of Empress Catherine I
1727–30	Reign of Emperor Peter II
1730–40	Reign of Empress Anna Ivanovna
1731	Abolition of Law of Single Inheritance, increasing noblewomen's property rights and, over time, the rights of other women
1736	Empress Anna orders "debauched women" beaten
1740–1	Reign of Emperor Ivan VI
1741–61	Reign of Empress Elizabeth Petrovna, daughter of Peter the Great
1750s	Midwifery courses are introduced

1753	Senate decision secures noblewomen's control of property
1761–2	Reign of Emperor Peter III
1762	Decree abolishes requirement that nobles serve the state
1762–96	Reign of Empress Catherine the Great
1764	Church lands are confiscated, curtailing the number of nunneries and monasteries
	Smolnyi Institute is founded
	Imperial Foundling home established in Moscow
	Hospital designated to confine women of "debauched behavior"
1771	Imperial Foundling home established in St. Petersburg
1779	First journal for women, the *Monthly Fashion Essay*, begins publication
1783	Catherine Dashkova becomes Director of the Academy of Sciences and founds and becomes President of the Russian Academy
1785	The St. Petersburg Obstetrical Institute is founded
1786	Decree issued founding primary and high schools, admitting girls
1787	M. M. Shcherbatov publishes *On the Corruption of Morals*
1793	Reduction of military service to 25 years
1796–1801	Reign of Emperor Paul I
1796	Empress Maria Feodorovna assumes guardianship of Smolnyi Institute
1797	Emperor Paul issues new law of succession, excluding women from the throne
1800	Emperor Paul orders that prostitutes be condemned to forced labor in factories
1801–25	Reign of Emperor Alexander I
1801	Moscow Obstetrical Institute founded
1810	Natalia Dolgorukova autobiography published, the first autobiography by a woman in Russian
1812	Napoleon invades Russia
	Foundation of Women's Patriotic Society
1825	Decembrist uprising
	Elite wives and sisters follow the rebels into exile
1825–55	Reign of Emperor Nicholas I
1834	Reduction of military service to 20 years
1843	Orthodox Church establishes primary schools for clerical daughters
1853–6	Crimean War; women volunteer as nurses
1855–81	Reign of Emperor Alexander II

1856	Nikolai Pirogov publishes *Questions of Life*
	Nikolai Dobroliubov publishes *A Realm of Darkness*
1858	Girls *gimnazia* and *progimnaziia* approved
1859	Anna Filosofova, Nadezhda Stasova, and Maria Trubnikova launch Society for Inexpensive Lodgings
	Women begin to audit university lectures
1859–62	Publication of *Daybreak* (*Razsvet*), the first "thick journal" for women
1861	Emancipation of the serfs
	Scientists at Medical-Surgery Academy open laboratories to women
1863	Nikolai Chernyshevskii publishes *What Is to Be Done?*
	Women banned from university lecture halls following student demonstrations
1864	Zemstvo reform
	Judicial reform
	Women expelled from Medical-Surgery Academy
1867	Nadezhda Suslova earns medical degree in Zurich
1868	Varvara Kashevarova-Rudneva earns medical degree in Russia, having promised to serve Muslim women
1869	Alarchinskii and Liubianskii higher courses open
1871	Government decree defines parameters of educated women's work
1872	Guerrier higher courses open
	Courses for "Learned Midwives" open at the St. Petersburg Medical-Surgery Academy
1873	Government decree orders women studying abroad to return
1874	Sofia Kovalevskaia becomes first woman in Europe to earn the degree of Doctor of Philosophy
	Movement "To the People"
1876	Courses for Learned Midwives become "Women's Medical Courses"
	Higher courses for women open in Kazan
1878	Higher courses for women open in Kiev and St. Petersburg (the Bestuzhev courses)
	Vera Zasulich shoots Governor Trepov
1881	Sofia Perovskaia leads assassination of Alexander II and is hanged
	Gesia Gelfman's death sentence is commuted because she is pregnant
1881–94	Reign of Emperor Alexander III
1882	Women's Medical Courses cease to admit new students
1883	Sofia Kovalevskaia becomes first woman to occupy a university position (in Stockholm)

1885	Prohibition of night work for women industrial workers
1886	Women's higher courses close, except for the Bestuzhev courses, which reopen in 1889
1887	Women's Medical Courses close
1892	Publication of Maria Bashkirtseva's diary
1894–1917	Reign of Emperor Nicholas II
1894	Establishment of Municipal Guardianships for the Poor
1895	Establishment of Women's Mutual Philanthropic Society
1895–8	Major strikes by women tobacco and textile workers
1897	Women's Medical Institute opens
	St. Petersburg city government forbids women teachers to marry
1899	Foundation of the Society for the Protection of Women
1900	First women's *Hromada* formed
1900–1	Guerrier courses reopen
1903	Pedagogical Institute opens in Odessa
1903–10	Publication of *Alem-i-Nisvan* (*Women's World*), a Muslim women's journal
1904–17	Publication of *The Women's Herald* (*Zhenskii vestnik*)
1905	"Bloody Sunday" initiates massive unrest
	Women's organizations emerge: The All Russian Union for Women's Equality; the Women's Progressive Party; The League of Equal Rights for Women
	The first women's political meeting is held
	The October Manifesto grants the vote to men
1906	Finnish women gain the right to vote
	Formation of Women's Leagues among Baltic Germans
1906–10	New women's courses open in cities across the empire
1908	All-Russian Congress of Women convenes
1911	Women gain right to matriculate in institutions of higher education and graduates of higher courses gain the right to qualify for a university degree
1911–3	Publication of *Ishigh* (*Light*), a Muslim women's journal
1914	Law grants married women the right to their own internal passport
1914	World War I breaks out
	The Bolshevik journal *The Working Woman* (*Rabotnitsa*) is founded
1915	Subsistence riots begin
1917	Women's Day demonstrations set off revolution
	Tsar Nicholas II abdicates throne
	Provisional government is established

	Women gain the right to serve as attorneys and obtain equal rights with men in civil service
	Women over age twenty are enfranchised
	Women join the military in record numbers
	Soldiers' wives demonstrate and form unions
	Domestic servants unionize
	Laundresses and dyeworkers strike
	Bolsheviks seize power, led by Vladimir I. Lenin
1918–21	Civil War
1918	New Family Code issued
	Central Asian women gain right to divorce under Soviet law
	First All-Russian Congress of Working Women convenes
1919	The Women's Bureau (*Zhenotdel*) approved; Inessa Armand becomes its first director
1920	Abortion becomes legal if performed by a physician
1921	New Economic Policy (NEP) initiated
1921–3	Polygamy, brideprice, and marriage without bridal consent are banned in Muslim regions
1922	Land Code equalizes women's legal position in peasant households
1923	Contraception legalized
1924	Lenin dies
	Joseph Stalin begins his climb to power
1926	New Family Code is implemented, further simplifying divorce
1927	*Khudzhum* campaign initiated
1929	Rationing introduced
	First Five Year Plan adopted
	Collectivization and de-kulakization begin
1930	Zhenotdel abolished
1932	Nadezhda Allilueva, Stalin's second wife, commits suicide
1932–3	Famine
1933	Second Five Year Plan adopted
	Azeri women's clubs closed
1934	Sergei Kirov is assassinated
	Homosexuality becomes a criminal offense
1934–41	*Obshchestvennitsa* movement
1935	Coalminer Aleksei Stakhanov sets production record
	Rationing ends
1936	New Family Code restricts divorce; prohibits abortion except to save the mother's life; offers incentives to mothers; contraceptives are withdrawn from the market
	Opening of First Soviet House of Fashion

1936–8	Mass arrests and repression from which party members and intellectuals suffer disproportionately
1938	Valentina Griazodubova, Marina Raskova, and Polina Osipenko set world flying record
1939	Nazi-Soviet "Non-Aggression" Pact
1940	War with Finland
1941	Germany invades Soviet Union on June 22; Leningrad besieged; Moscow threatened Draconian labor laws introduced Rationing reintroduced All-female air regiments created
1942	Women formally accepted into military
1943	800,000 women serve in armed forces and partisan units Coeducation ends in urban schools
1944	New Family Law further restricts divorce, stigmatizes illegitimate children, and penalizes single women and childless couples; motherhood medals are introduced
1945	War ends Most women soldiers demobilized
1947	Rationing ends
1953	Stalin dies Nikita Khrushchev begins his climb to power
1954–61	Publications devoted to family and private life quintuple in number
1955	Abortion becomes legal
1956	Khrushchev makes "Secret Speech," revealing some of Stalin's crimes
1957	Ekaterina Furtseva appointed Minister of Culture Sputnik, world's first earth-satellite, is launched
1959	American National Exhibit opens in Moscow
1960	Abortions begin to outnumber live births in European Russia
1961	Ekaterina Furtseva removed from office Soviets send Iurii Gagarin into space
1963	Valentina Tereshkova becomes first woman in space
1964	Fall of Khrushchev Leonid Brezhnev begins his climb to power
1965	Divorce becomes easier
1968	New Family Law opens door to paternity suits
1969	Natalia Baranskaya publishes *A Week Like Any Other*
1979	*Samizdat* publication of *An Almanac: Women and Russia*

1982	Brezhnev dies, succeeded briefly by Iurii Andropov and Konstantin Chernenko
1985–91	Mikhail Gorbachev becomes head of U.S.S.R., implements *glasnost'* and *perestroika*
1986	Chernobyl nuclear power plant explodes
1987	Soviet Women's Committee critiques party policy
	Foreign fashion magazines appear on newsstands
1988	Miss Moscow contest held, Soviet Union's first beauty pageant
1989	Formation of Committee of Soldiers' Mothers
	Publication of "How We Solve the Woman Question" in *Kommunist*
1990	Yearbook *Women in the USSR* reports on difficult conditions
	Formation of Moscow Center for Gender Studies
1991	Rationing reintroduced
	The Soviet Union collapses
1991–2000	Female unemployment grows; life expectancy for men and women declines; infant mortality increases
	New opportunities emerge for organizing
	Images of women diversify

GLOSSARY

baba: Peasant woman, often used pejoratively to indicate ignorance or backwardness

babka: Village midwife, without professional training

boiar: Head of one of pre-Petrine Russia's leading clans

boiarynia: Female form of boiar

bol'shak: The male head of the peasant household

bol'shukha: The female head of the peasant household

byt: Everyday life

chachvan: A waist-length black horsehair veil worn by some Muslim women

feld'sher: Medical assistant

glasnost': Literally, "openness," the policy adopted by Mikhail Gorbachev soon after he assumed power

kladka: Brideprice

komsomol: League of Young Communists

kolkhoznitsa: Female collective farm member

kulak: Allegedly prosperous peasant

nigilistka: Female nihilist

obshchina: Women's religious community

parandzha: A cloaklike garment, concealing the face and body

perestroika: The restructuring policy adopted by Mikhail Gorbachev

proletkul't: The Proletarian Culture movement, a mass organization that sought to shape proletarian artistic forms and create a proletarian morality and way of life

rabfak: School designed to prepare workers and peasants for university entrance

skhod: The assembly of male heads of households governing peasant villages

snokhachestvo: The sexual relationship of father-in-law and daughter-in-law

soldatka (plural, soldatki): A soldier's wife

soska: Chewed bread or gruel, wrapped in a rag and used by peasants as a pacifier

stakhanovite: A norm-busting movement that began in 1935

terem: The separate quarters in which elite women dwelled

tsaritsa: Female member of the tsar's immediate family

zemstvo: Following 1864, an elected organ of local self-government, enjoying limited authority

zhenotdel: Women's Bureau of the Communist party, authorized in 1919

Map 1. Russia, early twentieth century.

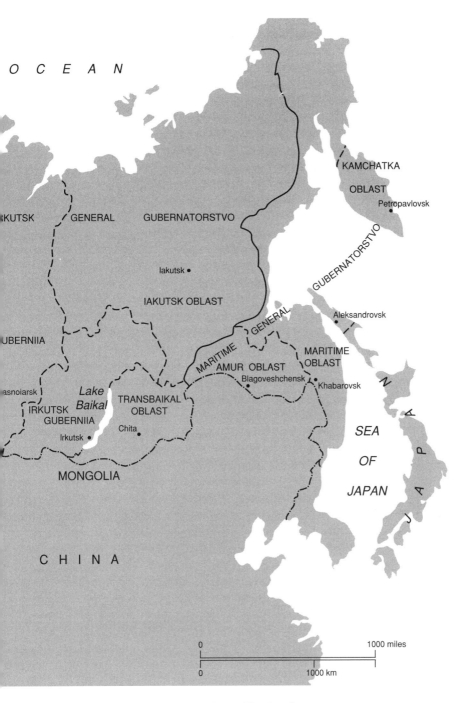

Map 1. (*Continued*)

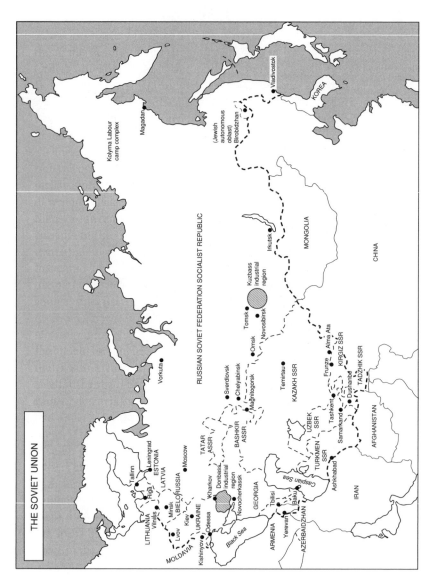

Map 2. The Soviet Union, in 1979.

INTRODUCTION

The revival of the women's movement in the late 1960s sparked a resurgence of interest in women in Russia and the Soviet Union, prompting historians to try to find information about women, who were omitted from previous accounts of Russian and Soviet history. In 1978, Richard Stites published his monumental and pioneering study that maps vast portions of the terrain that other historians would later explore in greater detail and from different perspectives.[1]

Some members of this cohort of scholars, myself among them, were personally and politically as well as intellectually motivated. Feminism encouraged women historians to seek "our" past, to tell "herstory." To correct the masculine bias of earlier accounts, we hunted through archives and published sources, looking for traces of women's experience, trying to hear women's hitherto silent voices. To the usual questions of historians, this feminist cohort added new ones, questions concerning the power that men exercised over women and its impact on women's ideas and experience. We questioned the nature and sources of patriarchal power and asked how being female shaped a woman's choices and activities. Much of this initial scholarship focused either on women of the intelligentsia or on the Bolsheviks' attempt to liberate women after 1917, not only because of the intrinsic importance of these topics but also because they left a relatively accessible paper trail.

However, as the field matured and the focus broadened, the questions became more multifaceted and the methodologies more diverse. The collapse of the Soviet Union has prompted new questions, for example about the uniqueness of the Russian and Soviet experience, and the opening of formerly Soviet archives has made more accessible the evidence that scholars need to address these new questions. The rich body of scholarship that has appeared over the past three decades has enabled me to write this book.

---

[1] Richard Stites, *The Women's Liberation Movement in Russia: Feminism, Nihilism and Bolshevism, 1860–1930* (Princeton, N.J.: Princeton University Press, 1978).

Nevertheless, I have found the task daunting. This is mainly because of the extraordinary diversity of the Russian empire's peoples, making it difficult to speak of *Russian women*, a term I usually avoid. Some of the distinctions were imposed from above. From the reign of Peter the Great (1689–1725) until 1917, Russia was a society formally organized according to estate (*soslovie*), rather than class. To the nobility (called gentry by some historians), social origins brought privileges, such as the right to own land and until 1861, peasant serfs, plus freedom from the poll tax and corporal punishment. For peasants and ordinary townspeople, social origins brought liabilities, among them the obligation to pay the poll tax, to provide recruits to the army and labor services to the state, and to suffer corporal punishment for crimes and misdemeanors. There were other estates, too, among them merchants, clergy, and the category of *raznochintsy*, educated and semi-educated people whose numbers would burgeon as Russia modernized. Even as Russia's social structure grew more complex and class became increasingly meaningful in shaping peoples lives and identities, these formal distinctions persisted. Other differences arose from Russia's imperial conquests, which drew into the empire's orbit peoples of diverse ethnicities, religions, and modes of life. By the end of the eighteenth century, Russia's women included animistic reindeer herders of the north, nomadic Muslim women of the Central Asian steppes, Jewish women of the *shtetl*, Tatar women of villages and towns along the Volga, German women of the Baltic region, and many, many more. The Soviet state, which sought completely to reconfigure the social order, left the empire's ethnic diversity largely intact. For much of the period examined in this book, the identity of most women derived at least as much from membership in their particular social and ethnic group as from their gender.

No one book can do justice to such a multi-faceted story. I decided not try. In part, the research interests of scholars in the field prompted my decision. Much has been written, for example, on women of the elites, the educated, and the peasantry during the imperial period, whereas very little has been published to date on the lives of women of imperial Russia's urban estates (merchants and townswomen) and clergy. Scholarship has just begun on women's religious experience and culture, a profoundly important element in many women's lives. Research on women of the empire's minority peoples is even less developed, the Jewish people being something of an exception. We know little about women's life in small towns and regions far from Moscow and St. Petersburg. Historians of the Soviet period have only recently turned their attention to the post-war era and the period following Stalin's death. The preoccupations of recent scholarship as well as its lacunae inevitably affect the shape of this book. So, however, do my own predilections and interests as a scholar. Using the same body of evidence, another author might write a very different book.

In this book, I set out to capture some of the diversity of women's experience and identity and to show how these changed over time and in response to broader economic, social, cultural, and political developments. Because women lived in families and communities, this book explores their social and familial world. The history of gender constitutes an important part of the story. The social construction of masculinity and femininity, that is, what it means to *be* a woman, and what it means to *be* a man, both reflects and contributes to the ways that societies structure power. Gender shapes how people define themselves and others, and it affects the ways that people imagine change. But to me, most important of all was to tell a compelling story, drawing on women's own words to the extent that sources allow.

The emphasis is on change and on difference. I begin the book with Tsar Peter the Great's "revolution from above," which aimed to reshape the lives of elites, elite women as well as men, in pursuit of broader goals and according to models derived from the West. The Petrine revolution had profound repercussions for women. Rigidifying and intensifying social distinctions, reconfiguring the lines between public and private, Peter's innovations at the same time provided new opportunities for social mobility. Eventually, Peter's introduction of criteria for advancement other than by birth and his privileging of education and "civilization" brought benefits to women as well as men. For elites, Peter's innovations also opened the door to new understandings of what it was to be a wife and mother, altering but not eliminating the hierarchical relationship of the sexes in family and society. By transforming elite lifestyles and attitudes toward women's domestic roles, the Petrine revolution deepened the social and cultural differences between noble and peasant women. Yet in some respects, Russia's women had much in common. Until well into the nineteenth century, if not later, the lot in life of almost all of Russia's women – not only nobles and peasants but also merchants, townswomen, clergy, and the rest – remained virtually identical: first a marriage arranged to suit others' needs, then childbearing, childrearing, and the labor of maintaining the home and provisioning the family. Beneath the developments traced in the chapters to follow, the everyday duties of marriage, motherhood, and housekeeping continued to govern most women's lives.

For much of the imperial era, the benefits of the Petrine revolution accrued primarily to the educated or propertied elites. For the vast majority, Russia's peasant women and men, Peter's innovations brought new burdens rather than benefits. Eking a living from the soil with implements like those of their parents and grandparents before them, living in self-contained communities, peasants adopted cautiously at best to the ways of the larger world even after the emancipation of the serfs in 1861. Most peasant women continued to marry by the age of twenty, bear on the average six or seven children with the assistance of a peasant midwife, and lose almost half of their offspring before they reached the age of five. Although the growth of commerce and industry in the late nineteenth century offered opportunities unavailable in the village and access to new ideas and ways of life, these developments touched the lives of comparatively few. Even as the Bolsheviks sought to reconfigure the political, social, and cultural order, their seizure of power in 1917 brought surprisingly little alteration to the peasant way of life. Only in the late 1920s did change really reach the peasantry in the form of collectivization of agriculture and even then, the change was only partial. Although the narrative to follow focuses on transformation rather than continuity, bear in mind that during the first two and a quarter centuries covered by the narrative, life changed remarkably little for Russia's peasant women.

Every writer writes for an imagined audience. In writing this book, I have envisioned two. The first audience consists of college students such as those I teach at the University of Colorado, who enjoy a good story and who find the past most accessible when approached through its human dimension. To keep the narrative moving, as well as to contain the length of the manuscript, I footnote only those sources from which I quote or on which I draw substantively for information or interpretation. For similar reasons, I limit discussion of differing historical interpretations but have sought to represent the range of historical views in footnotes, in the suggested readings that conclude each chapter, and sometimes in both. The suggested readings refer only to the small portion of our burgeoning field most relevant to the particular chapter. Fortunately for readers interested in exploring more widely, M. E. Sharpe will soon publish: *Bibliography on Women and Gender in Russia, the Successor States of the Former Soviet Union and East Central Europe*, 2 volumes, compiled by Mary Zirin, Irina Livezeanu, June Pachuta Farris and Christine Worobec.

The second audience consists of my colleagues and future colleagues, other historians and graduate students, for whom this book is intended as an introduction to the field of Russian women's history or as an encouragement to supplement, perhaps even rethink what they already know. Covering a lengthy period of time, three centuries, enables me to trace themes and identify continuities that would otherwise be easy to overlook. Although it is no longer necessary to defend the study of women's history, there remains much to be said about its centrality to Russia's history. This book is intended as a contribution to that conversation.

1

·

THE PETRINE REVOLUTION: NEW MEN, NEW WOMEN, NEW IDEAS

Women in Public and the New Domesticity

This book begins with dramatic changes – in some ways a revolution – initiated from above by Tsar Peter the Great (1689–1725) that eventually transformed the existence of almost everyone, women and men alike. In 1689, when Peter ousted his half-sister Sophia, who acted as regent, and took the throne, Russia was just gradually emerging from her medieval ways. Governed by religious values, largely isolated from the cultural and intellectual changes transforming the worldview of Western elites, most Russians remained wary of the outside world. In order to secure Russia's imperial status, Peter sought to reshape Russian society, culture, and politics according to models that he had seen and admired in Moscow's foreign community and during his travels to the West. The state became far more dynamic and prone to intervene in the lives of its subjects under Peter's leadership. Vastly accelerating changes already underway, Peter deployed decrees and legislation like weapons in a war against Russia's traditional order and meted out harsh punishments, even to elites who dug in their heels. Shock waves from the Petrine revolution reverberate to this day.

Like many contemporary European societies, Russia was divided into *orders*: those who fought (servicemen), those who worked (taxpayers), and those who prayed (churchmen). Peter's Westernizing revolution was aimed primarily at the service elites, members of aristocratic *boiar* clans and Russia's service nobility. New political institutions began the transformation of the Muscovite system of rule into a modern bureaucracy, formalizing and augmenting the power of the autocrat. Peter revamped Russia's army and founded its navy. To administer new or reformed institutions, Peter required new kinds of individuals, men who looked, behaved, and even thought differently than had their fathers and grandfathers. Peter needed new kinds of women, too, fit consorts for the new men. Revealing their flesh in Western-style clothing, enjoying the pleasures of mixed society, rearing their sons in the appropriate Petrine spirit, elite women would serve the state as men did, but in a different fashion. To ensure elite participation in the new order, Peter sought to reshape their public and personal lives.

Gender and the Pre-Petrine Order

Transforming the elite family order was essential to Peter's efforts to formalize political authority. Behind the facade of Muscovite autocracy, leading *boiar* clans maneuvered for power and patronage, with marital and kinship ties among the major determinants of success. To advance their families' interests, elites arranged the marriages of their offspring. The practice of secluding women and segregating the sexes helped to sustain this political system. Women of the most elite families lived in their own special quarters, known as the *terem*. They might receive visitors there or interact with men while managing their household, but they did not socialize with men, even members of their family. "I was born a recluse, raised within four walls," Princess Daria Golitsyna (1668–1715) told a young foreign friend. Before Peter the Great forced her to alter her lifestyle, Princess Daria ventured forth only two or three times a year, including visits to church and the cemetery, and even rarer were visits to female relatives. She always traveled in a closed or curtained carriage so as to remain hidden from view.[1] This sexually segregated social life prevented the personal attachments between men and women that might interfere with arranged marriages.

Even as it restricted their movement and contacts, women's separate sphere may also have provided women a source of independent authority. This authority was exercised by the tsar's wife, the *tsaritsa*, and her daughters, who dwelled in the royal *terem*. As in many medieval courts, in Muscovite Russia, the personal and private realm was inextricably intertwined with public affairs of the state. In Russia, a pious *tsaritsa* served as spiritual intercessor, an intermediary between the tsar and his subjects and God. As spiritual helpmate to her husband, she ensured both the tsar's salvation and that of his realm by performing pious deeds, dispensing charity, and ensuring social justice. She also exercised more mundane but no less significant authority in her separate realm. In the royal *terem*, the *tsaritsa* supervised noble attendants and servants, arranged weddings, and bestowed dowries that might include sizeable grants of land. *Tsaritsy* (plural of *tsaritsa*) also enjoyed independent status in the law. They managed their own properties and exercised judicial authority over their subjects. As facilitators of peace and justice, *tsaritsy* received numerous petitions from Russian subjects requesting intervention in relatives'

---

[1] Quoted in Daniel Schlafly, "A Muscovite *Boiarynia* Faces Peter the Great's Reforms: Dar'ia Golitsyna Between Two Worlds," *Canadian-American Slavic Studies* 31, no. 3 (Fall 1997), 255.

legal affairs, even in affairs of state. As autocracy grew more bureaucratized and the tsar acquired a tougher image, the *tsaritsa* appeared to offer a kinder and gentler form of authority and an alternate route to the throne.[2]

Other elite women likely played a similarly active role in their own gendered sphere. They, too, administered large and complex households and often took the initiative in arranging the marriages of their children, including marriages that might provide access to political power. Women held the power to veto or approve the marital alliances of male kin, sometimes entering the women's quarters of other families to evaluate a prospective bride.[3] Tsars' mothers were no exception. Natalia Naryshkina, Peter the Great's mother, selected his first wife Evdoksia, to whom Peter was quite indifferent. In the countryside, elite women managed estates when their husbands served in the army. Wealthy widows enjoyed still greater freedom of action.

Gender segregation and the concealment of women's hair and bodies also upheld the collective and clan-oriented Muscovite system of honor and shame. Elite women wore high necklines, long sleeves, and long skirts, and their clothing fit loosely so as to hide the body's contours. The more important the occasion and the wealthier the woman, the more layers she would wear. Because religion taught that it was sinful for a man to gaze upon a married woman's hair, her hair was hidden by the appropriate headdress and by capacious scarves, which sometimes covered the shoulders as well (Fig. 1). Women who observed dress and behavioral codes preserved their own and their family's honor; women who violated honor codes harmed not only themselves but also their kin. Family honor held enormous importance for the servitor class. It provided the measuring stick that determined their status in the social hierarchy.[4] The system of honor also granted social esteem and power to defend their dignity to women who lived up to honor's dictates. If a woman followed the rules, she could obtain legal compensation from men who violated those rules by, for example, pulling her braid or peering into her carriage. In the words of Nancy Shields Kollman, "Patriarchy served itself by serving women well."[5]

The teachings of Russian Orthodoxy, the official religion, supported this gender segregation, offering women a profoundly dualistic message. It

---

[2] Isolde Thyret, *Between God and Tsar: Religious Symbolism and the Royal Women of Muscovite Russia* (DeKalb, Ill.: Northern Illinois University Press, 2001), 119–23.

[3] Nancy Shields Kollman, "The Seclusion of Elite Muscovite Women," *Russian History* 10, pt. 2 (1983), 184.

[4] Nancy Shields Kollman, "Muscovite Patrimonialism," in James Cracraft (ed.), *Major Problems in the History of Imperial Russia* (Lexington, Mass.: D.C. Heath, 1994), 45.

[5] Nancy Shields Kollman, "Women's Honor in Early Modern Russia," in Barbara E. Clements, Barbara A. Engel, and Christine Worobec (eds.), *Russia's Women: Accommodation, Resistance, Transformation* (Berkeley, Calif.: University of California Press, 1991), 72.

1. Portrait of M. Apraksina, from *The Female Portrait in Russian Art* (Leningrad, 1974)

condemned women as sinful – wanton, deceitful instigators of lust and pollution. "What is a woman like on earth?" rhetorically inquired an eighteenth
century sermon. "A slanderer of saints, a serpent's resting place, the Devil's
consolation, an incurable sickness, a treasure that inflames, a temptation for
the saved, an incalculable evil, a whore by day, an inn where one cannot rest,

the Devil's accomplice."[6] Such views encouraged men to fear and distrust women and to control their sexuality in order to protect the family from dishonor and society from disorder. But Russian Orthodoxy also offered a positive model, the good woman, whose qualities were diametrically opposite those of her sinful sister. The *good woman* was modest and hardworking, pious and chaste, devoted to her household and children, and submissive to her husband. The good woman gave generously to the needy and used her access to figures of authority to champion the powerless and downtrodden. The *Domostroi*, a household guide penned in the sixteenth century for an elite readership, idealized the wife who managed her household while living a semicloistered life. "Who can find a capable wife? Her worth is far beyond coral," begins the section entitled "In Praise of Women," employing a quotation from Proverbs.[7] The church also contributed to the spiritualizing of the *tsaritsy*, associating them with famous Orthodox women saints rather than with sinfulness.

Female saints who endured martyrdom for their faith offered devout women the most exalted model of all. The most commonly read books in pious households, the lives of the saints, presented images of spiritual strength and self-denying asceticism. Devoted to a higher ideal, saints held to their convictions even in the face of persecution and torment. Such images, intended to celebrate piety, could encourage women's rebellion as well as their submission. These images inspired the extraordinarily wealthy widow, the *boiarynia* Feodosia Morozova (1632–75), to become a martyr for her beliefs. In the 1660s, the Russian Orthodox Church instituted modernizing reforms that revised and standardized liturgical practices, provoking fierce opposition. Morozova became the most well-known female opponent of reform. In her struggle to preserve long-standing religious practices, she defied both religious and secular authorities and ignored the appeals of her family to capitulate. Her enormous wealth and relative freedom as a widow enabled Morozova to transform her Moscow mansion into a kind of refuge for religious dissidents and center for the production and distribution of dissident writings. Eventually she became a nun. Arrested with two other leading female schismatics and tortured in 1672, Morozova refused to recant her beliefs. Together with her two companions, she was sent to a distant monastery, where the three were starved to death in a punishment pit.[8] Old Believers, as

---

[6] Robin Bisha, Jehanne M. Gheith, Christine Holden, and William Wagner (eds.), *Russian Women 1698–1917: Experience and Expression – An Anthology of Sources* (Bloomington, Ind.: Indiana University Press, 2002), 22.

[7] Carolyn Johnston Pouncy (ed. and trans.), *The Domostroi: Rules for Russian Households in the Time of Ivan the Terrible* (Ithaca, N.Y.: Cornell University Press, 1994), 102.

[8] Margaret Ziolkowski (ed.), *Tale of Boiarynia Morozova: A Seventeenth-Century Religious Life* (Lanham, Md.: Lexington Books, 2000), 5–12.

the schismatics were known, considered Morozova a saint. Her biography, written around 1674–5, was widely disseminated in manuscript and served as a key text in Old Believer ideology.

Peter the Great's half sister, Sophia, offers another example of a rebel, but in a different religious key. First as regent for her underage brothers (Ivan and the future tsar, Peter), then increasingly in her own right, Sophia ruled Russia from 1682 until 1689. Sophia's authority was portrayed in feminine terms in order to demonstrate her worthiness for the throne. Emphasis on her piety and asceticism, for example, drew on myths and rituals connected with the royal *terem*. This extension of the authority that *tsaritsy* had enjoyed as spiritual helpmates into the secular political realm strengthened Sophia's claim to govern directly.[9] Then, in 1689, Peter the Great's forces ousted her from power. For the remainder of her life, Sophia was incarcerated in a nunnery, a common fate for uppity or unwanted women.

Few women launched such overt challenges to the religious or political order, as far as we know. Instead, they accepted their assigned place or at least gave the appearance of accepting it. However highly prized, good women functioned within a fundamentally patriarchal order. The Old Believer leader, Archpriest Avvakum, who eulogized the *boiarynia* Morozova as one of "Christ's martyrs," was capable of chastising her harshly when she crossed him: "You did not listen to us, you acted according to your own will – and truly the devil has led you to complete degradation.... Stupid, witless, disgraceful woman, *put out your eyes with a weaving shuttle, as did the famous Mastridia!*" [italics in original][10]

In letters surviving from Peter's time, women refer to themselves with self-deprecation. They sign their letters, "thy unworthy sister," or "your unworthy daughter," or as Morozova did in a letter to Avvakum, "a most sinful and unworthy woman." They refer to themselves in this fashion even when, or perhaps especially when, they were themselves *tsaritsy*. Self-deprecating phrasing appears in the surviving letters of Peter the Great's first wife, Evdoksia. Raised conventionally, Evdoksia wrote to her husband following their marriage in 1689: "Your unworthy wife Dun'ka greets you;" and in a separate letter "Write to me, my light, about your health, and make poor wretched me happy in my sadness."[11] Such verbal self-deprecation failed to protect Evdoksia from a fate identical to her sister-in-law Sophia's.

[9] Thyret, *Between God and Tsar*, 139–69.

[10] "Archpriest Avvakum Describes His Struggle for the Lord, ca. 1673," in Cracraft, *Major Problems*, 71; For the condemnation of Morozova, see Ziolkowski, *Tale*, 91.

[11] Ziolkowski, 90; Quoted in Lindsey Hughes, "Peter the Great's Two Weddings: Changing Images of Women in a Transitional Age," in Rosalind Marsh (ed.), *Women in Russia and the Ukraine* (New York: Cambridge University Press, 1996), 32.

The Petrine Revolution

Peter the Great reconfigured Russia's patriarchal order. His modernizing reforms that aimed at strengthening the bureaucracy and institutionalized forms of authority inevitably affected the informal authority that women exercised in their separate sphere. Initially, the transformation of political life along Western European lines was symbolized by new dress and facilitated by new demeanor. Peter forced men to shave their beards and abandon their caftans and women to wear foreign clothing. A law of 1701 mandated "German clothes, hats and footwear" for men and women of all ranks of the service nobility, as well as for leading merchants, military personnel, and inhabitants of Moscow and other towns; only clergy and peasants were exempted.[12] Henceforward, women who failed to wear dresses, German overskirts, petticoats, hats, and shoes of foreign design became subject to fines.

In order to give his court a Western appearance, Peter breached the walls of the *terem*, forcing elite women to leave its seclusion in order to socialize in public at European-style evening parties. Squeezed into corsets and displaying their bodies in low-cut gowns, they were expected to perform Western dances, to display appropriate social skills, and to converse with men in French. This was, as Lindsey Hughes put it, "a female version of service to the state, albeit in ballroom and assembly hall rather than regiment or chancellery."[13] In his 1718 decree on assemblies, Peter attempted to extend such entertainments beyond the court, where they had already become customary. Peter even proposed to send noblewomen abroad to learn languages and social graces. But in this case, fierce parental opposition forced him to retreat. An edict of 1722 required basic literacy of women by forbidding a woman to marry if she could not sign her name.[14] No one appears to have paid attention.

Peter's second marriage exemplified the Petrine combination of high-handedness and Western-style modernity. Dissatisfied with his first wife, Evdoksia, in 1699 he forced her into a nunnery. In 1712, Peter married for a second time to a woman of common birth, who took the name Catherine when she converted to Orthodoxy. She had become his mistress around 1703–4; by the time of their wedding in 1712, she had borne him several children. The wedding celebration was conducted in the spirit of the new era and featured ladies wearing low-cut gowns and elaborate French wigs sitting in the same

---

[12] The law of 1701 is translated in Cracraft, *Major Problems*, 110.

[13] Lindsey Hughes, *Russia in the Age of Peter the Great* (New Haven, Conn.: Yale University Press, 1998), 201.

[14] Olga Glagoleva, "Imaginary World: Reading in the Lives of Russian Provincial Noblewomen (1750–1825), in Wendy Rosslyn (ed.), *Women and Gender in Eighteenth Century Russia* (Aldershot, England: Ashgate Publishing, 2002), 130.

room with men garbed in naval uniforms. This elaborately staged wedding served as a kind of public spectacle, in which participants acted out the new manners, thereby instructing the public in the new ways.[15]

Peter's second marriage also represented a new understanding of private life. Peter loved his second wife Catherine passionately and deeply and made no secret of his feelings. In this, Peter departed significantly from the official morality of his time, which portrayed the goal of marriage as reproduction and social stability, rather than emotional fulfillment or sexual enjoyment. To be sure, husbands were expected to love their wives. However, such love meant mutual respect and cooperation within a framework of patriarchal discipline, not passionate personal attachment. Enjoyed for its own sake, sexual pleasure was supposedly sinful. Russian Orthodoxy regarded sexuality as a manifestation of human sinfulness after the Fall. Favoring chastity even within marriage, the church discouraged spouses from sexual activity without procreative purpose and the *Domostroi*, mirroring such views, taught regular sexual abstention. Peter's second marriage thus represented a new conjugal ideal.[16] The new, more affective ideal was disseminated in portraits of Peter, Catherine, and their children, depicted individually and as a family group.

Peter sought to transform the intimate lives of his subjects along similar lines. Peter attempted to alter the Muscovite custom, wherein marriages were contracted by the parents, or if they were dead, by close relatives of the bride and groom, who usually saw each other for the first time only after the wedding ceremony. A law of 1702 required a six-week betrothal period before the wedding, enabling the betrothed couple to meet and become acquainted with one another. Should they decide against marriage, all parties gained the right to terminate the match, the betrothed as well as their parents.[17]

Subsequently, Peter made it more difficult to dissolve a marriage. Believing celibacy preferable to married life, the church permitted spouses to dissolve their marriage in order to enter monastic life, if they had the permission of their spouse and had fulfilled their obligations to children. If a spouse continued to live in the secular world, she or he was entitled to remarry. Peter abused this tradition to rid himself of his own first wife, as did other powerful men. After 1721, however, this informal means of divorce became unavailable. Henceforward, divorce permitting a partner to enter monastic life was permissible only after the spouses had made "representation in detail concerning the divorce" to their bishop, who then forwarded the petition to

[15] Hughes, "Peter the Great's two weddings," 40.

[16] Nancy Shields Kollman, "What's Love Got to Do with It?: Changing Models of Masculinity in Muscovite and Petrine Russia," in Barbara Clements, Rebecca Friedman, and Dan Healey (eds.), *Russian Masculinities in History and Culture* (New York, Palgrave 2002), 15–32.

[17] The law was rescinded in 1775.

the Holy Synod for a decision. Divorce became a formal procedure.[18] Peter intended marital reform to affect everyone. An edict of 1722 explicitly forbade forced marriages, including those arranged for "slaves" by their masters, and obliged both bride and groom to take an oath indicating that they consented freely to their union. The requirement that elites participate in social events also threatened parents' monopoly on arranging their children's marriage by expanding personal contacts.

Although Peter recast Russia's patriarchal order, he by no means ended it. Authority remained in the hands of husbands and fathers, who exercised virtually unlimited power over other family members. Marital law required a wife to submit to her husband as head of the household and to live with him in love, respect, and unlimited obedience. Except for ladies-in-waiting, women enjoyed no independent civil status. Women of the lower orders were neither counted in censuses nor assessed for purposes of paying taxes or performing services. As was the case elsewhere in Europe, a woman's status was determined by the rank of her husband or father. The law continued to deal far more harshly with women than with men. A wife who murdered her husband was buried up to her neck in the ground and left to die; a husband who killed his wife was flogged with the knout. An adulterous woman was punished by forced labor, usually in a textile mill. "Loose" women met a similar fate.[19]

Moreover, as bearers and nurturers of future subjects, women were expected to make their primary contribution to Russian society in the family. Peter defined women's most important duties as wifehood and motherhood, thereby giving motherhood new meaning. The sixteenth century *Domostroi* had had "curiously little" to say about children and nothing whatever to say about their education, assuming that children would learn what they needed from their parents.[20] Now, mothers of future servitors held the key to Russia's future. Recognizing this, in 1713 Feodor Saltykov had proposed the establishment of girls' schools to teach reading, writing, French, German, needlework, and dancing "so that our women will be equal to those of European countries."[21] Only educated women, Saltykov argued, were capable of rearing useful servants for the Russian state. However, like many projects proposed in Peter's reign, plans to educate women went nowhere. To ensure that women became wives and especially, mothers, Peter forbade women to enter a monastery during their reproductive years. The Spiritual Regulations of 1721 barred women from taking the veil before the age of fifty, the age when, presumably, their reproductive lives had ended. Henceforward,

[18] Brenda Meehan-Waters, *Autocracy and Aristocracy: The Russian Service Elite of 1730* (New Brunswick, N.J.: Rutgers University Press, 1982), 123.

[19] Hughes, *Russia*, 200.   [20] Carolyn Johnston Pouncy, "Introduction," *The Domostroi*, 29.

[21] Quoted in Hughes, *Russia*, 195.

women would have to fulfill their reproductive duty. Should a young girl wish
to remain a virgin for the purpose of taking monastic vows, she would simply
have to bide her time. Under strict supervision, she must "remain without
orders until she is sixty, or at least fifty, years old," the Spiritual Regulations
decreed.[22] Nuns were also supposed to engage in productive activity: in 1722,
the state dispatched seamstresses to Moscow convents to instruct the nuns
in spinning.

The changes that Peter initiated put down roots only gradually. During
his reign, they affected mainly women of the imperial family and the court.
Some women reacted with distaste to fashions that required them to display
their bodies in a manner that just a few years earlier would have shamed
the woman and dishonored her family. "In my old age," complained the
31-year-old Daria Golitsyna around 1700, "I was reduced to showing my
hair, arms and uncovered bosom to all of MOSCOW . . . the only advantage
I see [in this change] is to offend modesty, the treasure that every woman
should boast."[23] Others who were prepared to alter their appearance nevertheless retained the values with which they had been raised. Peter's own sister,
Natalia Alexeevna (b. 1673) converted completely to Western dress. A 1715
portrait of her shows her in an elaborately fashionable hairstyle and low-cut
gown. But even she clung to aspects of an older way of life, owning icons as
well as paintings and a library composed mainly of religious books. A foreign
visitor was struck by the inability of Russian ladies of Peter's time to converse in an appropriate manner, the result of their "in-born bashfulness and
Awkwardness."[24]

Outside the court, change proceeded more fitfully still. Moscow lagged
behind St. Petersburg, the new capital created by the force of Peter's will.
A visitor to Moscow in 1716 observed, "Russian wives and Daughters are
extremely retired and never go abroad, unless it be to church or to see their
nearest Relations." Messages to young women about their behavior continued
to be mixed – on the one hand, they were instructed by the tsar to put on
revealing dresses and to socialize in public, while on the other, they were
raised to be good Russian Orthodox maidens. *The Honorable Mirror of Youth*,
a manual of etiquette published in 1717, offered advice to young women that
could have come straight from the *Domostroi*: "Of all the virtues which adorn
well-born ladies or maidens and are required of them, meekness is the leading
and chief virtue," the book advised. The book emphasized the importance in
women of such qualities as industriousness, bashfulness, restraint, chastity,
and taciturnity and of the knowledge and fear of God.[25]

[22] Quoted in Brenda Meehan-Waters, "Popular Piety, Local Initiative and the Founding of Women's
    Religious Communities in Russia," *St. Vladimir's Theological Quarterly*, 30, no. 2 (1986), 112.
[23] Quoted in Schlafly, "A Muscovite Boiarynia," 262.
[24] Quoted in Hughes, *Russia*, 189.   [25] Ibid., 190, 193.

Women in Public

In the post-Petrine period, the most dramatic evidence of women's new visibility was in the realm of politics. Sophia, Peter's half-sister, had laid claim to the throne as regent, and initially ruled behind the scenes. In the eighteenth century, four women sat on Russia's throne: Peter's second wife, Catherine I, reigned from his death in 1725 until her own in 1727; Anne of Courland, the daughter of Peter's half-brother Ivan, ruled from 1730–40; Peter's daughter Elizabeth reigned from 1741–61 and finally Catherine the Great, born to a petty German ruling house, sat on Russia's throne for 34 years, from 1762 until her death in 1796. The fact that the elite accepted women rulers is a measure not only of the success of Peter's efforts to bring women into public life but also of the careful crafting of the empresses' public image. In Peter's time, the image of the ruler had assumed an aggressively masculine character. By contrast with Peter, the women rulers, and Elizabeth and Catherine the Great in particular, emphasized the civilian and humanistic aspects of rule. Presented to their subjects as powerful yet disarmingly mild and loving, they proclaimed that they ruled by love rather than by force, as Peter had done. The empresses thus revived the ruler's feminine dimension, building on Muscovite precedents for women's empowerment. Yet they also represented something new. References to Classical and allegorical female figures, as well as to religious models, underpinned the authority of the empresses. Instead of helping the people to redeem their sins or ensuring their afterlife, the empresses were portrayed as showering their bounty upon their people and bringing them earthly happiness.[26] Their rule benefited elite women directly. During their reigns, women acquired greater public visibility and assumed prominent ceremonial roles. Such women also enjoyed unprecedented access to female rulers.[27]

The state first assumed responsibility for women's education in the reign of Catherine the Great. Before then, what a girl learned had depended entirely on the values and economic wherewithal of her parents or guardians. In the decades that followed Peter's death, some elite parents sought to bestow upon their daughters the fruits of Western culture. Sharing the new belief that refined society required women's participation, they hired foreign governesses and tutors to instruct their daughters at home. Remembered Princess Catherine Dashkova, born 1743, soon orphaned and raised by her uncle together with his own daughter: "My uncle spared nothing to give us the best tutors and according to the ideas of the time we received the best

---

[26] Richard Wortman, *Scenarios of Power: Myth and Ceremony in Russian Monarchy* (Princeton, N.J.: Princeton University Press, 1995), 84–8.

[27] Jehanne Gheith, "Introduction," *The Memoirs of Princess Dashkova: Russia in the Time of Catherine the Great* (Durham, N.C.: Duke University Press, 1995), 8.

education; for we had perfect knowledge of four languages, particularly French; we danced well and drew a little . . . we were attractive to look at and our manners were ladylike. Everyone had to agree that our education left nothing to be desired," she wrote, implicitly criticizing such a lady's education.[28] The practice of educating daughters accelerated after the 1760s, as increasing numbers of "new men" left secondary school, having received a humanistic education. First appearing in the reign of Elizabeth, during Catherine's reign private boarding schools proliferated. By the close of the eighteenth century, there were more than a dozen in Moscow and St. Petersburg and more in provincial cities, invariably run by foreigners. However, only a minority of nobles had sufficient means to hire tutors or governesses or to send their daughters to boarding school.

Catherine intended to address this gap; she also sought to further the Westernization of Russia's manners and morals, thus extending the "civilizing mission" begun by Peter the Great. The initiative came from Ivan Betskoi, her first chief advisor on education. An advocate of complete equality in education for boys and girls, Betskoi believed that in education lay the seed of all good and evil. By instilling proper ideas in parents who would then pass them on to their children, education would produce a "new order" of individuals. Mothers, in particular, would be the moral educators of their young. Educating women thus formed part of Catherine's far-reaching efforts to improve Russian family, social, and civic life. Two years after assuming the throne, in 1764, Catherine established Russia's first school for noble girls. Called the Society for the Training of Well-Born Girls (better known as Smolnyi Institute, after the former monastery in which it was housed), the school primarily admitted daughters of servitors from the elite as well as the middling-level ranks of military and civil service – girls who either lacked a father or whose father had insufficient funds to educate them. The Smolnyi Institute aimed to refine the "vulgar" noble family by preparing better companions for servitor husbands and more caring and competent mothers of future state servitors. To promote refinement and prevent students becoming "spoiled" by contact with Russian provincial reality or their own family's crude habits, the girls were admitted at an early age and kept separate from their families during twelve or more years of schooling. They were brought into contact with the court and high society. In addition to preparing women for motherhood, the school strove to cultivate them as *citizens*, that is, as participants in the nascent public life. Students performed in plays and enjoyed outings and amusements. On Sundays and holidays, the oldest girls presided over receptions to prepare for the role they would play in society. The school graduated 70 students its first

[28] Gheith, *Memoirs*, 32.

year and about 900 women altogether during Catherine's reign. Catherine also established schools that admitted girls from more humble social backgrounds. About twenty other institutes, organized along lines similar to Smolnyi, were opened in Russia's major cities and towns in the years after its founding.[29]

Catherine believed that society required cultivated women, and she encouraged aristocratic women to follow her lead. By the close of the eighteenth century, women's cultivation had become a distinctive characteristic of the cream of Russia's elite. Judging by the women's dress, their hairstyles, the dances that they knew, and the language that they spoke – almost invariably French – they were virtually indistinguishable from their Western European counterparts (Fig. 2). The artist Elisabeth Vigée Lebrun, who visited Russia in the 1790s, returned to Paris impressed by what she saw: "There were innumerable balls, concerts and theatrical performances and I thoroughly enjoyed these gatherings, where I found all the urbanity, all the grace of French company." She believed, in particular, that it would be impossible "to exceed Russian ladies in the urbanities of good society."[30]

Some of these cultivated women also developed independent intellectual interests and enthusiastically pursued them; the erudition of a few rivaled that of their European counterparts. Catherine the Great herself was an enormously prolific writer, founding Russia's first satirical journal and authoring works in a wide variety of genres, among them comedies and plays, pedagogical works, and children's stories. Princess Catherine Dashkova (1743–1810), née Vorontsova, who at the age of nineteen assisted her friend Catherine the Great in the coup that brought her to the throne, wrote numerous plays and articles and in 1783 became one of the first Russians to edit a journal, *The Companion of Lovers of the Russian Word*. That same year, Dashkova became one of the first women in Europe to hold public office, appointed by Catherine the Great as Director of the Academy of Sciences. The appointment was so unusual that Russian officials had no idea how to proceed: Prince Viazemskii, the Minister of Justice, asked the empress whether Dashkova should be sworn in as were other state employees. The empress responded that Dashkova should be treated like the rest: "Unquestionably [she should be sworn in] ... for I have never made a secret of Princess Dashkova's appointment to the Directorship of the Academy...," Catherine replied.[31] Dashkova proved an able administrator. She supervised the refurbishment

[29] J. L. Black, "Educating Women in Eighteenth Century Russia: Myths and Realities," *Canadian Slavonic Papers* 20, no. 1 (1978), 23–43.

[30] Quoted in Judith Vowles, "The 'Feminization' of Russian Literature: Women, Language, and Literature in Eighteenth-Century Russia," in Toby W. Clyman and Diana Greene (eds.), *Women Writers in Russian Literature* (Westport, Conn.: Greenwood Press, 1994), 42.

[31] Quoted in Gheith, "Introduction," *Memoirs*, 5.

2. Portrait of S. Iakovleva, from *The Female Portrait in Russian Art*

and expansion of the Academy's library, increased the Academy's budget, oversaw the construction of new buildings, and instituted lectures for less privileged nobles. In 1783, Dashkova also founded and became President of the Russian Academy (1783–94). The most widely known example of women's cultivation, Dashkova was hardly unique. Highly cultivated women dwelt in provincial towns as well as Moscow and St. Petersburg. In his semifictional autobiography set in the reign of Catherine the Great, the writer Sergei Aksakov presents us with such a woman, Sofia Nikolaevna Zubina, a character based upon his own mother. The daughter of a leading official in the provincial town of Ufa, Sofia Nikolaevna corresponded with the writer and journalist Nikolai Novikov in far-off Moscow. She so impressed him with her letters that Novikov regularly sent her all new and important books in Russian. "[A]ny learned or casual travelers who visited the new and ravishing District of Ufa never failed to make Sofia Nikolaevna's acquaintance, and to leave written tributes of their admiration and regard," wrote her son, citing the names of leading intellectual figures of the time, foreigners as well Russians.[32]

In their civilizing role, such women exerted influence over the development of Russian culture. In urban salons and elite intellectual circles, cultivated women became arbiters of taste. Writers now wrote for a society that had been transformed by the presence of aristocratic women, influencing both the style that writers adopted and the themes that they raised in their poetry and prose. Literary language became feminized, with women's tastes and language, untouched by Church Slavonic or chancellery idiom, the measure of cultural excellence. Sentimentalism, in vogue from the 1780s to around 1820, contributed to this feminization by encouraging a perception of women as "vessels of emotion" and models of virtue. Such influence, however, did not authorize women to step outside socially prescribed feminine roles. Granting women a central civilizing role, it left gender differences intact. Men continued to monopolize literary production, their repertoire now expanded to incorporate a feminine, emotional component.

By contrast, for women to adopt male competencies risked violating the natural order. Thus, feminization remained a "male enterprise."[33] Nowhere is the ambiguous cultural role of women clearer than when they sought to wield pens of their own. Those who took up their pens were expected to do so *as women*, by contributing to the "moral refinement of the nation," rather than by writing for pleasure or pursuing their own aims, as men were free to do.[34] Nevertheless, it was in this period that substantial numbers of women first found their way into print. They translated from foreign languages or wrote prose and most commonly, poetry of their own. To legitimize their writing, women adopted traditional roles, primarily that of moral educator of family and nation. Most women writers made their appearance in print

---

[32] Sergei Aksakov, *The Family Chronicle* (New York: Dutton, 1961), 79.

[33] Carolin Heyder and Arja Rosenholm, "Feminisation as Functionalisation: The Presentation of Femininity by the Sentimentalist Man," in Rosslyn, *Women and Gender*, 57.

[34] Ibid., 61; Wendy Rosslyn, "Making Their Way into Print: Poems of Eighteenth-Century Russian Women," *Slavonic and East European Review* 78, no. 3 (July 2000), 413.

only fleetingly, but a few, for example Princess Ekaterina Sergeevna Urusova (1747–post-1817) produced a substantial body of work. Responding to the unease elicited by women writers, in her early poems Urusova mounted a spirited defense of "the civilizing power of women and love in Russian culture" and, by implication, of the importance of women in public. Without love and without women, Urusova contended, neither civilization nor enlightenment was possible.[35]

The Backlash

Whatever the ambiguities of women's public role, that role nevertheless made some of their contemporaries uneasy. Increasingly troubled by the negative effects of Western influence, writers began to identify women's unprecedented freedom and presence in public life as one of Westernization's most objectionable consequences. Aimed at women in public, their critiques were often explicitly sexual in character. They echoed pre-Petrine concerns about women's sexual honor, its preservation now linked with preserving the honor not only of family but also of Russianness itself. In the view of Nikolai Novikov, the feminization of literary language signified its debasement. Women's language was "the coin of a Westernized society corrupted by frivolity and fashion, love affairs, and contemptuous of Russian manners and morals."[36]

To Novikov and to others, educated women ran the risk of becoming *dandies*, that is, associated with vice and corruption. Education for women was acceptable only if it prepared them for virtuous wifehood and motherhood. The conservative Prince M. M. Shcherbatov blamed women's purported sexual license for the decline in public morals. A vocal critic of late eighteenth century court culture, Shcherbatov, in *On the Corruption of Morals in Russia* (1787), professed outrage at the luxurious habits and alleged corruption of the empresses and their supposed encouragement of sexual license. "Scorning modesty and decency, which is one of women's chief virtues," elite women now violated the sanctity of marriage with impunity. According to Shcherbatov, Russia suffered from an epidemic of divorces, the result of wives deserting husbands and taking lovers.[37] Alexander Radishchev, who disagreed with Shcherbatov on a wide range of issues and is often considered the first Russian radical, nevertheless echoed Shcherbatov's anxieties in a different key. In a *Journey from St. Petersburg to Moscow* (1790), Radishchev accused noblewomen of having "yearly, monthly, weekly, or God forbid! daily

---

[35] Quoted in Vowles, "The 'Feminization' of Russian Literature," 45–7.　　[36] Ibid., 35–38.
[37] "M. M. Shcherbatov Laments Corruption at Court, 1730–1762," in Cracraft, *Major Problems*, 163–5.

lovers. Having made his acquaintance today and satisfied her desire, she does not know him tomorrow."[38]

This backlash mirrored changes occurring in France, which served as the model for Russia's intellectual elites. There, enlightenment ideals that supported woman's participation in intellectual life were giving way to views, in particular those articulated by Jean Jacques Rousseau, that emphasized woman's exclusively domestic calling. The shift could complicate a woman's own attitude about herself and her public accomplishments. Catherine Dashkova was an erudite and accomplished individual. Well-traveled, she knew many of the leading figures of her day, both male and female. Yet her memoirs, composed in the early nineteenth century when the emphasis had shifted decisively away from women's intellectual aspirations toward women's role as wife and mother, reveal an uneasy relationship with her own public role and personal choices. When Catherine the Great proposed that Dashkova direct the Academy of Sciences, Dashkova wrote, her initial reaction was to say no. "God himself, by creating me a woman, had exempted me from accepting the employment," she stated in a letter to the empress that she never sent.[39] Dashkova interspersed accounts of her own accomplishments with claims of self-abnegation, and she repeatedly asserted that she undertook many of her activities, including an extended stay in Europe, "primarily for the sake of her children and their education."[40]

Toward the end of the eighteenth century, the bonds of marriage tightened, too. Over the course of the eighteenth century, the Russian Orthodox Church had steadily increased its authority over marriage and divorce and become more adept at administering its affairs and at recordkeeping. Systematizing laws affecting marriage and marital dissolution, the church emphasized more than ever before the sacramental and indissoluble nature of marriage. The result was to make ending a marriage exceedingly difficult for the Russian Orthodox faithful, the majority of the population. Grounds for annulling a marriage narrowed and were even more narrowly applied. Divorce became possible only on the grounds of adultery (preferably, with eyewitnesses), desertion, exile to Siberia after conviction for a felony, or long-standing sexual incapacity that had arisen before marriage and could be verified by a medical examination.[41] Marital law also strictly forbade any act that might lead to the separation of spouses. It became impossible for a woman to escape an abusive or unsatisfactory marriage by obtaining a divorce and very difficult for her even to leave her husband, unless he proved willing to let her go.

[38] Alexander N. Radishchev, *A Journey from St. Petersburg to Moscow*, Leo Wiener, trans. (Cambridge, Mass.: Harvard University Press, 1966), 131.
[39] Gheith, *Memoirs*, 201.   [40] Vowles, "The 'Feminization' of Russian Literature," 44.
[41] Gregory Freeze, "Bringing Order to the Russian Family: Marriage and Divorce in Imperial Russia, 1760–1860," *The Journal of Modern History* 62, no. 4 (1990), 709–46.

The New Domesticity

The new celebration of domesticity was far more easily reconcilable with Russian tradition than was the visibility of women in political and cultural life. Books and articles promoting domesticity circulated widely among the reading public. By the middle of Catherine's reign, that public had grown large enough to provide a buyer for just about every book for which there was a market in the West. Magazines designed for girls instructed them to be pious and pure, to restrain their intellectual ambitions, and to focus on household affairs. Russians were especially interested in works that addressed childhood and childrearing. Conduct books and education manuals imported from abroad offered a new conception of motherhood. In place of the down-to-earth and practical understanding that had previously prevailed among the Russian nobility, these works celebrated motherhood's sanctity and instructed mothers to be the moral and spiritual guides of their children.[42] This literature redefined women's family roles in other ways as well. By elevating the role of mothers, it suggested greater equality between husbands and wives and parents and children, even as it emphasized the new importance of private and family life.

The increasing popularity of sentimental literature contributed to this re-definition as well. Presented by sentimentalist writers as sensitive and emo-tional, a woman could be a friend to the man whom she married. Love and friendship became almost indissolubly linked, captured in this verse by Nikolai Karamzin:

> Love is useful to us only
> When it is like dear friendship
> And friendship is lovely only
> When it equals love[43]

By the turn of the century, the ideal of the sensitive wife, as promoted by the sentimental literature of the late eighteenth century, had become widely accepted in some provincial circles.[44]

Intellectual trends emanating from the West influenced Russian Orthodox views of marriage as well. The church likewise placed new emphasis on

---

[42] Diana Greene, "Mid-Nineteenth Century Domestic Ideology in Russia," in Rosalind Marsh (ed.), *Women and Russian Culture* (New York: Berghahn Books, 1998), 84–7; Catriona Kelly, *Refining Russia: Advice Literature, Polite Culture and Gender from Catherine to Yeltsin* (New York: Oxford University Press, 2001), 28.

[43] Quoted in Gitta Hammarberg, "Flirting with Words: Domestic Albums, 1770–1840," in Helena Goscilo and Beth Holmgren (eds.), *Russia. Women. Culture* (Bloomington, Ind.: Indiana University Press, 1996), 303.

[44] Olga E. Glagoleva, "Dream and Reality of Russian Provincial Young Ladies, 1700–1850," *The Carl Beck Papers*, no. 1405, 44.

the affective ties of spouses and their reciprocal responsibilities toward one another, while downplaying – although not eradicating – the patriarchal and misogynist elements of its previous stance. According to Orthodox writers, couples were to be respectful, tolerant, and forgiving of one another. Fidelity was required of husbands as well as wives. At the same time, church teaching clearly demarcated the differing responsibilities of women and men. Men, whose role was to provide materially for and represent the family in public life, were destined for "society beyond the family circle" in addition to family life, whereas women's role was exclusively to raise the children and tend to the domestic affairs of the household.[45] The church, like the state, affirmed that woman provided the family's moral center.

The purpose of women's education was redefined accordingly. After Catherine's death in 1796, supervision of women's education passed into the hands of empress Maria Feodorovna, first as the wife Paul I and then as dowager empress and mother of Alexander I and Nicholas I. Only forty-two years old when her husband died, Maria Feodorovna remained the principle figure at the imperial court. Subscribing to a sentimental notion of family life and marital love, Maria attempted to impress those ideas upon her children and the broader public. Her vision is evident in instructions to administrators and students of the Smolnyi Institute, of which she had become guardian. In 1804, for example, she advised Smolnyi graduates to be obedient and respectful daughters; faithful, virtuous, and modest wives; solicitous mothers; and conscientious housekeepers. Emphasizing the need for religious and moral training, Maria urged Smolnyi graduates to seek comfort and pleasure only within themselves and their families.[46] Life at Smolnyi became more monastic; most student social engagements ceased.

Thus, by the early nineteenth century, a striking unanimity on the subject of woman's domestic destiny seemed to prevail among educated elites. It united those who disagreed about much else. Sergei Glinka, a conservative opponent of the French revolution and all that it represented, believed that only a life in the home could bring a woman true happiness. To mothers, he accorded the "highly important role of raising virtuous citizens for the fatherland."[47] The Decembrists, who were inspired by many of the French revolutionary ideals that Glinka sought to combat, concurred completely with his ideas about women's proper place. Deriving from elite families, the Decembrists acquired their name from the date (December 14, 1825) that they staged an

---

[45] William Wagner, *Marriage, Property and Law in Late Imperial Russia* (New York.: Clarendon Press, 1994), 76.

[46] Wortman, 250–54; Barbara Alpern Engel, *Mothers and Daughters: Women of the Intelligentsia in Nineteenth Century Russia* (Evanston, Ill.: Northwestern University Press, 2000), 24.

[47] Quoted in Alexander M. Martin, "The Family Model of Society and Russian National Identity in Sergei N. Glinka's Russian Messenger (1808–1812)," *Slavic Review* 57, no. 1 (Spring 1998), 39.

abortive insurrection against Nicholas I. The rebels aimed to establish some form of representative government and a constitutional order, from which they explicitly excluded women. "Woman not only cannot be the subject of political rights, she is even barred from attending open sessions of the legislature," reads the constitutional project of Nikita Muraviev, a member of the more moderate Northern Society.[48] Instead, women's primary role would be "the education of children in accordance with the principles of virtue and faith."[49]

In the wake of the Decembrist uprising of 1825, this vision of the family became linked with the restoration of social and political order. Blaming the Decembrist uprising in part on faulty education at the hands of foreign tutors, the new tsar, Nicholas I (1825–55) laid fresh emphasis on parental participation – which, in practice, meant women's participation – in their children's moral upbringing. Nicholas and his wife presented to his people a modified patriarchal ideal: the private life of the tsar was staged so as to portray him as a loving and devoted husband and caring father, while the empress provided a model of maternal love and tenderness – a family idyll that was disseminated in paintings and engravings to a broad audience as well as to the elite. The new imagery dramatized a "sharp division of sexual spheres" that mirrored developments in other European courts and reconfigured political authority as exclusively male.[50] Relegated to their own sphere, the private, the empresses self-consciously distanced themselves from politics. A new balance had been struck between the spheres of women and men, and it bore the imperial seal.

Conclusion

In some respects, by the early nineteenth century, the Petrine revolution appeared to have come full circle. Once again, elites praised women most when they acted as good and virtuous wives and criticized them when they enjoyed the sexual freedom men had long taken for granted or dared to enter domains that men claimed as their own. Yet much had changed for good. The Petrine revolution, especially as recast by Catherine the Great, opened doors to elite women that never again shut completely. Educational opportunities slowly but steadily expanded. Women's domestic responsibilities, now including a civilizing mission, acquired new value thanks to the influence of advice books and sentimental literature. Moreover, as seen in the next chapter, this definition of domesticity existed in tension with noblewomen's property rights and

---

[48] Quoted in Leonid Poliakov, "Zhenskaia emansipatsiia i teologiia pola v Rossii XIX v.," in M. T. Stepaniants (ed.), *Feminizm: Vostok. Zapad. Rossiia* (Moscow, 1993), 61–2.

[49] Quoted in Engel, *Mothers and Daughters*, 18.   [50] Wortman, Scenarios of Power, I, 261.

3. The Boiarynia Morozova, from *The Itinerants* (Leningrad, 1974)

responsibility for estate management, both enhanced in the eighteenth century. At the same time, older models of ideal womanhood continued to coexist
with the new and to provide sources of moral authority rooted in Russia's past.
The *boiarynia* Morozova, for example, lived on in myth and image: in 1887,
the artist V. Surikov painted her portrait, celebrating her martyrdom (Fig. 3).

The pre-Petrine ideals that she embodied, incorporating aspects of the new era, would also encourage women to expand and eventually to transcend the boundaries of their culturally assigned sphere.

Suggestions for Further Reading

Black, J. L. "Educating Women in Eighteenth Century Russia: Myths and Realities." *Canadian Slavonic Papers* 20, no. 1 (1978), 22–43.

Gheith, Jehanne, ed. *The Memoirs of Princess Dashkova: Russia in the Time of Catherine the Great.* Durham, N.C.: Duke University Press, 1995. *Autobiography of one of the most remarkable women of Catherine's period.*

Hughes, Lindsey. "Peter the Great's Two Weddings: Changing Images of Women in a Transitional Age." In Rosalind Marsh, ed., *Women in Russia and the Ukraine.* New York: Cambridge University Press, 1996, 31–44.

Hughes, Lindsey. *Sophia, Regent of Russia 1657–1704.* New Haven, Conn.: Yale University Press, 1990.

Kollman, Nancy Shields. "What's Love Got to Do With It? Changing Models of Masculinity in Muscovite and Petrine Russia." In Barbara Evans Clements, Rebecca Friedman and Dan Healey, eds. *Russian Masculinities in History and Culture.* New York: Palgrave, 2002, 15–32. *Explores the Petrine revolution in emotional life.*

Kollman, Nancy Shields. "Women's Honor in Early Modern Russia." In Barbara E. Clements, Barbara A. Engel and Christine Worobec eds. *Russia's Women: Accommodation, Resistance, Transformation.* Berkeley, Calif.: University of California Press, 1991, 60–73.

Pouncy, Carolyn, ed. and trans. *The Domostroi: Rules for Russian Households in the Time of Ivan the Terrible.* Ithaca, N.Y: Cornell University Press, 1994.

Schlafly, Daniel. "A Muscovite *Boiarynia* Faces Peter the Great's Reforms: Dar'ia Golitsyna Between Two Worlds." *Canadian-American Slavic Studies* 31, no. 3 (Fall 1997), 249–68. *The Petrine revolution as experienced by an elite woman.*

Thyret, Isolde. *Between God and Tsar: Religious Symbolism and the Royal Women of Muscovite Russia.* DeKalb, Ill.: Northern Illinois University Press, 2001. *Groundbreaking exploration of the significance of women's separate sphere in Muscovite political culture.*

Ziolkowski, Margaret, ed. *Tale of Boiarynia Morozova: A Seventeenth-Century Religious Life.* Lanham, Md.: Lexington Books, 2000. *Contains the biography of Feodosiia Morozova as well as her correspondence with others.*

2

THE PETRINE REVOLUTION

Noblewomen at Home

The Petrine revolution only slowly reached the many noblewomen who lived far from court and aristocratic circles. For every salonniere or woman poet or writer, hundreds more noblewomen dwelt in provincial obscurity, never donning a corset or low-cut dress from one year to the next. Instead of exchanging ideas, these women engaged in the mundane tasks that ensured their families' survival. Just one of five noble households owned the one hundred or more male serfs needed to live "nobly"; most of the remainder belonged to the petty nobility who owned fewer than twenty or even none whatsoever. Thus, only a small minority of noblewomen owned sufficient serfs to perform all the "woman's work" that a family's survival required. Clothing had to be sewn, cleaned, and mended; animals tended; and food grown, gathered, preserved, and prepared. "For Pulkheriia Ivanovna, house-keeping meant continually locking and unlocking the larder, salting, drying, and preserving an endless number of fruits and vegetables," wrote Nikolai Gogol in "Old World Landowners."[1] Even if the housewife did not herself engage in housekeeping, she often had to supervise closely those who toiled at those tasks, day after day, year after year.

On such women, the initial impact of Peter's reforms was almost entirely negative. Requiring noblemen to serve the state for life, primarily in the army, the Petrine revolution deprived wives of husbands and mothers of sons for months or even years on end or forced the women to follow their husbands to unfamiliar places. Fedosia Nepliueva (née Tatishcheva, b. before 1698, d. 1740) was married in 1711 to Ivan Nepliuev, who became one of Peter's first military cadets. In the first years of the marriage, Nepliuev was almost perpetually absent on various missions abroad. Subsequently, after six months' service in St. Petersburg, Nepliuev was dispatched to Turkey as

---

[1] Quoted in Darra Goldstein, "Domestic Porkbarreling in Nineteenth Century Russia, or Who Holds the Keys to the Larder," in Helena Goscilo and Beth Holmgren (eds.), *Russia. Women. Culture* (Bloomington, Ind.: Indiana University Press, 1996), 126.

ambassador. During these lengthy absences, Nepliuev left his wife to fend
for herself in the countryside and to subsist on whatever their modest estate
provided. Six years elapsed before Nepliueva saw her husband again, when
the authorities permitted her to join him in Constantinople. She remained
for five years. The couple spent only about half of the twenty-nine years of
their married life together.[2]

Even after the reduction and, in 1762, abolition of the service requirement,
most men continued to serve at least for a time. The majority of noble families
needed the income, and moreover, serving the state had become a measure
of noble status, evidence of the impact of the Petrine revolution on men. In
contrast with their husbands, noblewomen experienced the Petrine revolution
primarily through their family roles. Yet women's family roles remained
linked to public life and in the second half of the eighteenth century, assumed
new public significance.

Domesticity, Old and New

Hard as it was to transform political habits and institutions, changing elites'
private life and family values proved more difficult still. New ideals that elevated the status of wives and mothers took root only gradually. At the end of
the eighteenth century, many nobles lived much as their parents and grandparents had done; for them, the *Domostroi*, the sixteenth-century household
guide, or books with similar principles served as the primary guides to conduct, if they consulted books at all. Stepan Bagrov, the old world patriarch
of Sergei Aksakov's semiautobiographical novel, *The Family Chronicle*, is
scarcely able to read and write. In the era of Catherine the Great, Bagrov
remains largely untouched by the consequences of the Petrine revolution.
The state is merely a distant presence. Bagrov holds absolute sway over his
small domain. During outbursts of rage, he beats and drags his poor old wife
around by her hair and terrifies everyone in his household. "What's the good
of *them?*" he was prone to ask when another daughter was born. "They look
out of the house, not in; if their name is Bagrov today, it may be anything on
earth tomorrow."[3]

Older patterns remained particularly influential when it came to marriage,
still the primary goal of noblewomen's lives. By raising the age at which women
could take the veil, Peter had sought to make marriage and childrearing a
woman's only option. Society frowned upon a woman who lived alone. If a
woman failed to marry, she was fated to spend decades as a dependent in the

---

[2] Olga E. Glagoleva, "Dream and Reality of Russian Provincial Young Ladies, 1700–1850," *The Carl Beck Papers*, no. 1405, 19–20.

[3] Serge; T. Aksakov, *The Family Chronicle* (New York: Dutton 1961), 3.

4. Portrait of A. A. Olenina, from *The Female Portrait in Russian Art*

household of someone else. The prospect could evoke understandable panic: "O God, how old I am! But what can I do?" wrote Anna Olenina in her diary when, still unmarried, she reached the age of twenty (Fig. 4).[4] Women had little say in this, the most important decision of their life.

[4] Anna Olenina, *Dnevnik 'Annette'* (Moscow: I. D. Sytina, 1994), 89.

In the eighteenth century, the Russian Orthodox Church prescribed twelve as the minimum age of marriage for girls, fourteen for boys. Until the end of the century, if not later, women continued to enter marriage at a very tender age. When he married in 1764, the nobleman Andrei Bolotov wed a thirteen-year-old girl. Anna Labzina (née Iakovleva, 1758–1821) was likewise thirteen when she married Alexandr Karamyshev. Marriages contracted when the bride had little experience of life or of men ensured parental control over matchmaking and bridal virginity. "And so the matter was resolved without me," Labzina later recalled.[5] As the age of marriage rose for women, as impressionistic evidence suggests it did in the course of the eighteenth century, women became more likely to develop their own preferences. Rarely, however, were they able to act on them.

Arranged marriages remained the norm. Peter's decree requiring that both groom and bride consent to a marriage was often observed only in the most formal sense. In her study of the post-Petrine service elite, Brenda Meehan-Waters emphasized the instrumental purposes of marriage. "Marriages could augment family wealth (through a financially well-endowed daughter-in-law); cement political alliances; advance careers; and maintain or improve family status."[6] Against such considerations, the feelings of the betrothed mattered little. Meehan-Waters offered the example of Princess Ekaterina Dolgorukaia, deeply in love with the brother of the Prussian ambassador, who submitted to the will of her father and in 1729 became engaged to the fifteen-year-old emperor, Peter II, whom she never ceased to regard with distaste.

Likewise, Sofia Skalon related the story of her uncle, Nikolai Vasilievich Kapnist, his wealthy mother's eldest and most favored son. Sometime around the end of the eighteenth century (neither Skalon's memoir nor its notes offer dates), his mother ordered him to retire from state service and to marry a woman of good family "whom he did not love at all." His wife suffered bitterly for the remainder of her life.[7] Despite Peter the Great's efforts to formalize the system, patronage and clientelism continued to characterize Russian politics. In these patronage games, unmarried daughters became pawns deployed by heads of households to secure the family's interests.[8]

Men were usually the first to exercise greater choice. Even when parents were still living, they came to exert decreasing control over adult sons. Meehan-Waters noted a tendency to later marriage among the post-Petrine

---

[5] *Days of a Russian Noblewoman: The Memories of Anna Labzina, 1758–1821*, Gary Marker and Rachel May (ed. and trans.), (DeKalb, Ill.: Northern Illinois University Press, 2001), 21.

[6] Brenda Meehan-Waters, *Autocracy and Aristocracy: The Russian Service Elite of 1730* (New Brunswick, N.J.: Rutgers University Press, 1982), 111.

[7] I. I. Podol'skaia (ed.), *Russkie Memuary. Izbrannye stranitsy, xviii vek* (Moscow: Pravda, 1988), 463.

[8] John LeDonne, *Absolutism and Ruling Class: The Formation of the Russian Political Order, 1700–1825* (New York: Oxford University Press, 1991), 21.

service elite. Impressionistic memoir evidence also suggests that men married far later than did women, having already embarked upon careers. Karamyshev was twenty-eight when he wed his thirteen-year-old bride; Andrei Bolotov was twenty-six. As intellectual cultivation came increasingly to characterize noble self-definition, men seeking a bride added new expectations to old. A good dowry, a virtuous and submissive character, and competency in household management had been sufficient qualifications for a future bride in the pre-Petrine period. Prospective suitors exposed to Western ways continued to expect such qualities, but by the end of the eighteenth century, these qualities were found to be no longer sufficient. The well-educated Anna and Alexandra Panina, renowned for their knowledge and intelligence at mid-century, had no difficulty making excellent marriages.[9] Some men also embraced new affective ideas concerning marriage and the family. For them, personal fulfillment as well as material gain had become a goal of matrimony. Andrei Bolotov, for example, acquired new-fangled ideas while serving in Prussia during the Seven Years War (1756–63). After retiring from military service in 1762, he returned to his estate in Tula province and began to search for a wife. In addition to the traditional requirement of good character and substantial dowry, he sought an educated woman, someone with whom he could share his intellectual interests, to whom he could "communicate all my thoughts and cares and whose advice and comfort I could enjoy – someone who would participate fully in my life."[10]

Physical attraction and love, understood as amorous attachment, assumed new significance. Among the reasons for Bolotov to reject one prospective bride was that she was so stout that he could hardly bear to look at her.[11] Nobleman became drawn to their future brides because they were "sweet" or "attractive," or had a "charming appearance." Love lyrics of the late eighteenth century that implicitly challenged the reigning Orthodox conception of sexual love as sinful encouraged men to be more attentive to their sexual feelings. Aksakov's old-world patriarch, Stepan Bagrov, regarded amorousness as humiliating and unworthy of a man. His son Aleksei, who matured in an era when the literature of sensibility reigned, experienced passionate love for the woman he married. Other men, too, began to express romantic tenderness toward their wives in their memoirs and correspondence, and to acknowledge being "madly in love," "passionately in love," and "adoring."[12]

[9] Meehan-Waters, *Autocracy and Aristocracy*, 113.

[10] Quoted in Carol Nash, "Educating New Mothers: Women and the Enlightenment in Russia," *History of Education Quarterly* 21 (Fall 1981), 303.

[11] Andrei Bolotov, *Zhizn' i prikliucheniia Andreia Bolotova, opisannye samim i dlia svoikh potomkov* (Moscow: TERRA, 1993) 3 vols. V. 2, 251.

[12] Natalia L. Pushkareva, *Chastnaia zhizn' russkoi zhenshchiny i nevesta, zhena, liubovnitsa (xynachalo xix v.)* (Moscow: Ladomir, 1997), 174–6.

To be sure, as Natalia Pushkareva reminds us, tender feelings were rarely so overwhelming that they led a man to marry hastily or disadvantageously. Even as he selected his own bride, Andrei Bolotov regretted not having close relatives nearby with whom he might consult about such a serious matter. Men of limited means or lacking patronage connections were likely to exercise their freedom of choice in order to maximize their well-being and opportunities for advancement. When he selected his bride in the 1830s, the gendarme officer E. I. Stogov made his choice sight unseen. Her dowry of 1000 male serfs and the sterling reputation of her family were enough to convince him of his future wife's suitability.[13]

Women continued to exercise greater emotional restraint than men did and to pay closer attention to the economic and social considerations that remained uppermost in parents' or guardians' minds. In her diary, Anna Olenina anxiously contemplated a wife's responsibilities. "They require so much self-abnegation and indulgence, they bring so many tears and so much grief," she wrote at the end of the 1820s. Still, women were now supposed to feel love too. "Will I love my future husband?" Olenina asked her diary, and answered, "Yes, because I promise to love and obey him before the throne of heaven."[14] Although Stogov's bride agreed to his proposal only to please her parents, Stogov assured her that eventually she would come to love him. Once every month, he inquired as to whether she had begun to experience the desired emotion. Within the year, she acknowledged that yes, she had. Whether by *love* these women meant the traditional understanding (respect and mutual cooperation) or the new, affective ideal is left to the reader to guess.

When change did come, it was books that most often introduced it. Initially, this meant that new ideas affected only the small minority of noblewomen able to read and write. Michelle Marrese has calculated that in the mid-eighteenth century, only a small fraction (4 to 26 percent) of noblewomen dwelling in the provinces knew how to read and write; a quarter of a century later, the proportion was closer to half. Thereafter, women's literacy rates rose dramatically, to roughly 92 percent at the start of the nineteenth century.[15] For women who could read, books offered not only a pleasurable pastime but also a means to be in touch with a larger world.

New intellectual currents, which had begun to penetrate the provinces in the 1760s, became far more accessible in the 1780s, when the book trade reached there. The first journal for women began publication in 1779. Mainly devoted to fashion and light entertainment, several such journals for women

---

[13] "Zapiski Evrastii I. Stogova," *Russkaia Starina* 115 (March, 1903), 51–3.
[14] Olenina, *Dnevnik 'Annette'*, 62, 68.
[15] Michelle Lamarche Marrese, *A Woman's Kingdom: Noblewomen and the Control of Property in Russia, 1700–1861* (Ithaca, N.Y.: Cornell University Press, 2002), 213–5.

circulated by the first decades of the nineteenth century. Authors took for granted the significance of reading for noble families, even if, in reality, it remained the pastime of only a minority. "The soft heart of dear beauties finds in books the sensibility and ardent passions it vainly seeks in suitors; mothers read in order to better perform their sacred duties – and a provincial nobleman's family whiles away autumn evenings by reading a new novel," observed Nikolai Karamzin in 1802.[16] By the 1820s, far more women subscribed to books, discussed their reading in letters, and even aspired to publication, than had been the case just a few decades before. Reading encouraged literate provincial noblewomen to embrace the ideal of marriage that sentimental literature promoted. A century after the Petrine revolution, the language of submission and self-denigration had vanished from noblewomen's correspondence with their husbands, and terms of endearment often took its place. "My dear, invaluable friend," a wife wrote to her husband in 1812, signing herself "thy friend forever, Annushka." Other women of the late eighteenth and early nineteenth centuries addressed their spouses as "my dearest treasure," "my dear friend," "my joy."[17]

To be sure, neither affective relations nor family happiness originated with the literature of sentiment. Princess Daria Golitsyna, still inhabiting the *terem*, spoke affectionately of her husband, Petr, but with appropriate restraint: "It is my lot to enjoy the favor of a most gracious husband, who knows full well how to flatter me that I please him."[18] Since the seventeenth century, and likely earlier, the family had occupied a central place in provincial noble life. What sentimentalism and, subsequently, romanticism did contribute was a language that encouraged the cultivation and expression of feeling. The result was a new emphasis on the emotional importance of marriage and close and loving family relations. "Can a marriage be stable and happy, when it is not based on feelings of mutual respect and the most tender love?" rhetorically inquired the governor of Nizhnii Novgorod province in 1828. An "idealized domesticity" had become one of the foundations of provincial noble life by the end of the 1820s.[19] Natalia Grot (1825–99) captured this ideal in her retrospective picture of her provincial childhood, "full of love, peace and piety."[20]

[16] Quoted in Glagoleva, "Dream and Reality," 27.   [17] Ibid., 45.

[18] Quoted in Daniel Schlafly, "A Muscovite *Boiarynia* Faces Peter the Great's Reforms: Dar'ia Golitsyna Between Two Worlds," *Canadian-American Slavic Studies* 31, no. 3 (Fall 1997), 256.

[19] Gosudarstvennyi arkhiv Rossiiskoi Federatsii (hereafter GARF), Tret'e otdelenie sobstvennoi ego imperatorskogo velichestva kantseliarii, 1826–1880, fond 109, 2 ekspeditsiia, 1828, op. 58, ed. kh. 199, ll. 1–19; Mary Wells Cavendar, "Nests of the Gentry: Family, Estate and Local Loyalties in Provincial Tver, 1820–1860" (Ph.D. diss., University of Michigan, 1997), 29.

[20] Natalia Grot, "From a Family Chronicle: Reminiscences for Children and Grandchildren," in Toby Clyman and Judith Vowles (eds.), *Russia Through Women's Eyes* (New Haven: Yale University Press, 1996), 225.

The new emphasis on family happiness undermined the strict hierarchy of Russia's patriarchal family order and may have made family unhappiness, marital unhappiness in particular, more difficult to bear. "You must obey your husband in everything," Anna Labzina's mother informed her on her wedding day. "It is not him you'll obey but God, who gave your husband to you and made him your master." Twenty years later, in the winter of 1792–3, Petr Rimskii-Korsakov advised his daughter, the twenty-four-year-old Elizaveta, in much the same language: "Love and respect your husband and submit to him. Remember that he is the head of the household and not you, and obey him in everything."[21]

Wifebeating remained widespread among the nobility. Stepan Bagrov engaged in it whenever he lost his temper; so did other noblemen. Nikolai Vasilievich Kapnist, highly educated in Western ways but unhappily married at his mother's behest, became a great despot in his family. If his wife left the house in disorder, even if a meal was poorly prepared, he would not only scold her "in the most vile language" but also beat her with his own hands in the presence of others. Natalia Pushkareva has found hundreds of cases in the archives, dating from the late eighteenth and early nineteenth centuries, in which women appealed, unsuccessfully, for divorce on the grounds of physical abuse.[22] Accused by his wife of beating and abusing her in 1828, army major Kushev did not deny it: to beat his wife was his right, he asserted, and no one had the authority to stop him. However, the new emphasis on family and domestic felicity offered a language with which to articulate grievances. In a petition requesting that the authorities intervene, Kusheva couched her plea for better treatment in terms of the new dignity of motherhood: her husband, she implored, should be made to behave properly to "the mother of his children...."[23] Anna Kern (née Poltoratskaia) steeped in the literature of sentiment and romance, and subsequently famous as one of Alexander Pushkin's lovers, went further. Believing that deep attachment was "virtually obligatory" in marriage, "where two fates are intertwined and two hearts beat as one, so to speak," she was thoroughly miserable in her forced marriage to an aging general. The husband proved not only coarse but also "immune to the gentling influence of her beauty and intellect," in the words of the censor Aleksandr Nikitenko.[24] Unwilling to endure after eight years of marriage, she convinced her husband to grant her a separation.

[21] *Days of a Russian Noblewoman*, 21; Elizaveta Iankova, *Rasskazy Babushki. Iz vospominanii piati pokolenii zapisannye i sobrannye ee vnukom D. Blagovo* (Leningrad: Nauka, 1989), 49.

[22] I. I. Podol'skaia, *Russkie Memuary*, 474; Pushkareva, *Chastnaia zhizn'*, 243.

[23] GARF, fond 109, 1828, op. 58, ed. kh. 199, 1.

[24] Anna P. Kern, *Vospominaniia. Dnevniki. Perepiski* (Moscow: Khodozhestvennaia literatura, 1974), 204; *Diary of a Russian Censor: Aleksandr Nikitenko*, Helen Saltz Jacobson (ed. and trans.) (Amherst, Mass.: University of Massachusetts Press, 1975), 15.

An Expansive Sphere

Although the "domestic" was defined as women's proper sphere, as it was in Europe and the United States, in Russia the domestic extended well beyond the confines of home and housework. Women's subordinate status in life and law coexisted, sometimes uneasily, with their legal right to own and manage immovable property, which Russian wives, as well as single women and widows, enjoyed. Even married women could buy and sell and enter contracts, a status that was unique in Europe. During the eighteenth century, Russian women's rights to property became more, not less, secure, reversing a seventeenth century trend toward restricting women's right to inherit. To be sure, patrimonial property laws continued to privilege male heirs. Nevertheless, the law of 1731 that abolished the Petrine policy of single inheritance not only permitted nobles to bestow land on a widow or marriageable daughter but also invested women with full rights of ownership of their estates.

A decree of 1753 formalized married women's separate control of property and granted them the freedom to dispose of assets without their husband's consent. Thereafter, many noble families acted to secure their daughters' right to property in land in the form of the dowry. In such cases, she bore responsibility for collecting taxes, supplying serf recruits, and fulfilling other obligations connected with the ownership of land. In subsequent decades, women actively defended their legal prerogatives, pressing claims to inheritance and control over property during marriage. When they did, courts often found in the women's favor, suggesting widespread acceptance of women's right to property. The number of women buying and selling estates also increased dramatically after 1753, culminating in women controlling as much as a third of landed estates in private hands by the eve of emancipation.[25] Visiting Russia early in the nineteenth century, Martha Wilmot was surprised to hear young and coquettish ladies speaking amongst themselves about the sale of land and the purchase of peasant serfs. "The full and entire dominion which Russian Women have over their own fortunes gives them a very remarkable degree of liberty and a degree of independence of their Husbands unknown in England," Wilmot observed in 1806.[26]

As wives and as landowners in their own right, many noblewomen assumed full responsibility for estate management. Until 1762, when obligatory service ended, noblemen were required to serve the state for decades. Even after 1762, many nobles remained in service, leaving their wives fully responsible for managing their property. Countess Ekaterina Rumiantseva, for example,

---

[25] Marrese, *A Woman's Kingdom*, 17–43; 71–101; 145.
[26] Martha Wilmot, *The Russian Journals of Martha and Catherine Wilmot* (New York: Arno Press, 1971), 271.

looked after their estate while her husband was off in military service during the reign of Catherine the Great. Her complaining letters indicate that she found her situation burdensome. But others apparently took pleasure in the exercise of their managerial talents whether or not their husband was away from home, and they enjoyed considerable success. Natalia Grot remembered her mother as a practical and energetic housekeeper who ensured their household's solvency. "She knew my father's often extravagant generosity and propensity to forget himself and so she moderated expenditures and helped him to keep the household accounts in order."[27]

Personal narratives and testimonials from this period depict many noblewomen not only as capable housewives but also as competent and careful businesswomen who personally took charge of estate finances and knew when to buy and sell. Contemporaries apparently saw housewifery and estate management as complementary rather than contradictory roles, parts of noblewomen's sphere. Service to the state was men's sphere by contrast and barred to women (Ekaterina Dashkova's appointment to the Academy of Sciences being the exception). Women's activities as property managers brought such women into contact with local and central authorities and with the legal process. Given the lawlessness of provincial life and women's control of human chattel, estate management could require determination, even ruthlessness. The responsibilities that came with managing property often took precedence over childrearing. Despite the new views of motherhood, anecdotal evidence suggests that it was a rare noblewoman who devoted herself to raising children; instead, mothers relegated that task to peasant nurses, then to governesses and tutors.

How to reconcile married women's legal rights as property owners with their marital obligation to obey their husband unconditionally? The English visitor Martha Wilmot believed that ownership of property significantly enhanced a woman's rights in marriage: "Here a Woman's powers to dispose of her own wealth is a great check on her husband's inclination to forsake her or to Tyrannize."[28] The answer, however, is not so simple. Although her husband refused to live with her and carried on with other women, for example, Countess Ekaterina Rumiantseva continued to send him money, even as she went into debt herself. Court cases from the eighteenth and early nineteenth century provide evidence of husbands who beat or tormented their wife in order to force her to mortgage or sell her dowry, or who dissipated the woman's property without her knowledge. On the other hand, court records also show noblewomen taking action on their own behalf against husbands who dispossessed them, and in property disputes between married couples, courts

[27] Marrese, *A Woman's Kingdom*, 176–7; Quote from Grot, "From a Family Chronicle," 227.
[28] Wilmot, *The Russian Journals*, 271.

honoring the wife's claims. Women could, and did, escape abusive husbands by retiring to their own estates. Michelle Marrese argues convincingly that women's legal right to property permitted some noblewomen to circumvent the absolute obedience that marital law required of them.[29]

In other ways, too, the domestic sphere over which women presided was rarely sealed off from the larger world. What is often perceived as the private domain of the family was not particularly private in Russia. Russian hospitality was lavish and legendary. Whether resident in city or countryside, the Russian noble family was expansive. Under the roofs of well-to-do households might live dozens of impoverished relatives or neighbors, orphans, physicians, tutors, and governesses, along with a retinue of servants. When country roads were passable, visiting was the custom – to neighbors or to family members resident elsewhere. Visitors might stay for weeks. Less well-to-do households practiced similar hospitality, albeit on a much lesser scale. For the lady of the house, guests brought additional responsibilities as well as the pleasures of company: their needs had to be attended to, menus overseen, order kept in households that might hold dozens of people. Surrounded by members of the household and guests, women would have had difficulty finding time to be alone. As a consequence, concludes Olga Glagoleva, "Conjugal relations and family matters were largely exposed to public observation."[30]

Among the educated and Westernized, the expansive noble household sometimes offered sociability of a more cultivated sort. Toward the end of the eighteenth century, Russians began to hold salons in their homes. Neither as official nor as influential as its French counterpart, the Russian salon was an intimate gathering composed of "literary and other artists, relatives, family and friends," that is, likeminded individuals who gathered in private homes.[31] Women usually presided over salons and attended them as guests. The hostess selected her salon guests and exercised authority over everything that took place: how long the salon lasted, its atmosphere, its success. One of Russia's first was organized toward the end of the 1780s in the province of Tula, 200 kilometers south of Moscow. Hosted by Varvara Afanasievna Iushkova (née Bunina), well-educated, fluent in French and German, and an outstanding musician, the salon provided a magnet for local elites and intellectuals. In Iushkova's salon, visitors enjoyed musical soirees and evenings in which the latest literature was read aloud and discussed.

Salons influenced intellectual life and the development of Russia's nascent public sphere. They brought writers together and linked them with their

---

[29] Marrese, *A Woman's Kingdom*, 94–100.   [30] Glagoleva, "Dream and Reality," 13.
[31] Gitta Hammarburg, *From the idyll to the novel: Karamzin's sentimentalist prose* (Cambridge, Eng.: Cambridge University Press, 1991), 94.

audience. Poets read their works aloud and hostesses and guests critiqued them. Salons offered a place to meet and converse that stood beyond the reach of the state. Across the political spectrum, from conservatives to radicals, intellectuals nurtured their ideas in the supportive atmosphere of the salon. Varvara Iushkova's daughter, Avdotia Elagina (1789–1877), who at sixteen married the future Slavophile Ivan Kireevskii, presided over one of the most important. Her salon flourished in the aftermath of the failed Decembrist uprising, which cast a pall over intellectual life. By the late 1820s, Elagina's salon in Moscow had become *the* meeting place for those who thought critically, and it provided the setting in which Slavophile's ideas first took shape. At times, the gatherings there resembled university seminars on literary, philosophical, and moral issues. Elagina made her salon an extension of her family, presiding in a maternal fashion and befriending the young people who attended. Her salon lasted into the 1840s.[32]

Through the salon, then, women contributed to the refinement of Russian language and the evolution of Russian thought. Konstantin D. Kavelin, nineteenth century historian and philosopher, found the role of women "absolutely essential to the moral and aesthetic formation of his generation of the Russian intelligentsia."[33] By entertaining Russia's emergent intelligentsia and shaping the atmosphere in her home, the salon hostess contributed to defining the values of literature and public life.

Service of a Different Kind

Ideas and practices imported from the West never fully crowded out older ways of seeing and behaving, even among Russia's elites. Elements of the old world lived on within the new, sometimes in harmony, sometimes in opposition, most often blended with imported ways in a kind of hybrid. Far less affected than men by the secularizing trends that the Enlightenment encouraged, women found in religion, in particular, a source of meaning and value. "Christian family principles" animated the happy childhood of Natalia Grot, born in 1825, as they animated the childhood and guided the adulthood of many other women, too.[34] Religion also provided comfort in the face of death, a constant presence in the lives of elite as well as other women. Although there are no accurate figures for the late eighteenth and early nineteenth centuries, at all levels of Russian society, infant mortality was very high. The memoirs of men and women alike offer numerous accounts of infant deaths. According to the Sergei Aksakov, the demise of his mother Sofia's adored

---

[32] Lina Bernstein, "Women on the Verge of a New Language: Russian Salon Hostesses in the First Half of the Nineteenth Century," in Goscilo and Holmgren, *Russia. Women. Culture*, 209–20.
[33] Ibid., 220.   [34] Grot, "From a Family Chronicle," 230.

first-born daughter drove the mother to the depths of despair. But most nobles seem to have encountered infant death more stoically, comforted, perhaps, by religion. Religious faith surely helped women to face the considerable risk of their own death in childbirth. A study conducted in the 1860s and 1870s found that the risk was more than ten percent over the course of a woman's childbearing years. "The coffin lid does not close for a birthing mother until forty days pass," a Russian proverb warned.[35]

Through the lives of saints, Orthodoxy also offered inspiration, encouraging women to conceive their lives within a framework of active, rather than passive, sacrifice for others. The impact of hagiography on women's self-presentation and conduct can be seen in the first autobiography to be published by a woman (in 1810). Natalia Dolgorukova (1714–71) was born Sheremetieva and betrothed at the age of 15 to a confidante of Tsar Peter II, Ivan Dolgorukii. When, following the death of Peter II, Dolgorukii took part in an abortive attempt by his clan to control the succession to the throne, Dolgorukova chose to marry Dolgorukii despite the punishment that awaited him, and then to follow him into exile. She began her memoirs at the urging of her grown son in 1767, twenty-seven years after her husband's arrest and execution and nine years after she took the veil. They represent her as a devout and selfless woman, steadfast in her loyalty to her husband. Elizaveta Rubanovskaia behaved with equal selflessness. Rubanovskaia, a graduate of Smolni, was the sister-in-law of Russia's first radical, Alexander Radishchev, whom Catherine the Great banished to Siberia as punishment for writing *The Journey from St. Petersburg to Moscow*. Forbidden to marry her widowed brother-in-law because of close kinship, Rubanovskaia nevertheless chose to follow him into Siberian exile, sacrificing her own comfort and health. In Siberia, she lived with Radishchev for six years and bore three children, dying on the eve of his reprieve in 1797. "A skilled pen might compose a whole book about her virtues, her sufferings and her constancy of spirit," wrote a former schoolmate, one of the few aware of her sacrifice.[36]

Spiritual values might also inspire critiques of the post-Petrine public sphere. Such can be seen in the memoirs of Alexandra Labzina (1758–1828), who employed depictions of her own virtue to critique the values of her husband. She was married to Alexandr Karamyshev, a man who gambled, womanized and caroused, justifying it all in terms of Enlightenment philosophy. Labzina presented her life with him as a long and tormenting trial, which she bore as a "this-worldly Christian martyr." Without questioning

---

[35] David Ransel, *Village Mothers. Three Generations of Change in Russia and Tataria* (Bloomington, Ind.: Indiana University Press, 2000), 26.

[36] "Introduction," *Russia Through Women's Eyes*, 14–5; Quote from David Marshall Lang, *The First Russian Radical. Alexander Radishchev, 1749–1802* (Westport, Conn.: Greenwood Press, 1979), 211.

the patriarchal order, in her account of her marriage Labzina nevertheless emphasized her own fidelity to a loftier set of values than her husband's. While her husband devoted himself to the pleasures of the flesh, she performed God's work in the world. She dispensed charity and cared for the poor and dispossessed with her own hands, interceding with the authorities on their behalf much as had pious women in the Muscovite period. Religious faith thus offered women a source of authority that might be counterposed to, might even triumph over, the worldly authority of men.[37]

Finally, spiritual values provided women with the most acceptable avenues of activity outside the household. Monastic life, especially, remained one of women's few alternatives to family life. Women unable to enter a nunnery would join informally with other unmarried women and widows in communities (*obshchiny*). Wearing dark clothing to indicate their abdication from the world, taking shelter under a single roof, the women would pray together and labor together in the gardens that sustained them. Such informal associations multiplied after 1764, when Catherine confiscated church lands, depriving monastic communities of their source of support and forcing small monastic communities to join larger ones for the sake of economy. The number of women's monasteries dropped precipitously: of the 203 that existed in 1762, only 67 remained after the reform of 1764. *Obshchiny* emerged to replace them. One began in the town of Arzamas in 1764, on the site of a recently suppressed monastery, to shelter displaced and would-be nuns. Within a decade, 270 women were living unofficially in cells that had been ordered closed. Other communities followed a similar pattern: local women initiated them in order to meet their need for a spiritually based life and security. From the mid-eighteenth century to 1917, more than 200 such communities were formed, virtually all of them in rural areas. Self-supporting, these communities resulted from local initiative and drew on local support. Some formed around locally renowned holy men or women; widows from all social levels, from the elite to the peasantry, composed others. Noblewomen sometimes founded religious communities on their own estates, donating land, property and capital, which was theirs to dispense because of Russian women's right to property under the law. By contrast with nuns, however, women who entered these communities did not take monastic vows. Expected to be celibate while part of the community, they were free to leave if they chose. Both communities and nunneries served the community through charitable activity.[38]

[37] Gary Marker, "The Enlightenment of Anna Labzina: Gender, Faith, and Public Life in Catherinian and Alexandrian Russia," *Slavic Review* 59, no. 2 (Summer 2000), 370–1; 376; 384–6.

[38] Brenda Meehan-Waters, "Popular Piety, Local Initiative and the Founding of Women's Religious Communities in Russia," *St. Vladimir's Theological Quarterly* 30, no. 2 (1986), 117–33.

Women and Charity

The imperative to charity ran deep in Russian Orthodoxy. According to Orthodox understanding, wealth was a gift from God that brought the obligation to work for the general good. Ideally, charitable activity was direct and face-to-face, involving personal sacrifice and service to the unfortunate. The church elevated certain women to the status of heroines on the basis of the physical care and comfort they provided the poor. An exemplar of this behavior was "Blessed Ksenia," who lived in St. Petersburg in the second half of the eighteenth century. Devastated by grief after the early death of her husband, a chorister in the imperial court, she gave away to the poor all of her possessions and, dressed in a ragged skirt and blouse, wandered about the city, earning the veneration of the church and ordinary people because of her self-sacrifice and generosity toward the poor.[39]

Charity thus became part of a pious woman's mission. Virtually all nunneries and women's communities performed charitable activities. They cared for the sick, fed the poor, took in orphans, and sheltered homeless, elderly or widowed women. Pious married women likewise engaged actively in charitable endeavors. Anna Labzina's mother served the poor regularly: she distributed money and clothing that she made herself to people in prison; she offered food and clothing to beggars. A talented healer, she also treated her ailing serfs and comforted the dying. Her daughter, Anna, followed her example. During eighteen months with her husband in the town of Nerchinsk, Siberia, just north of the Chinese border, she cared for exiles and comforted the sick. "Every day God presented me with an opportunity to do good for those around me," she remembered.[40]

In the late eighteenth century, women's charitable activity began to acquire a secular dimension. Previously, the charitable actions of empresses and other female members of the imperial family had demonstrated their piety. In the reign of Catherine the Great, the state itself provided a model of enlightened charity, intended to foster human welfare on earth rather than eternal salvation. In 1764, the first foundling home was opened in Moscow, with the most liberal admissions policy in Europe. Welcoming virtually any child, this and the St. Petersburg Foundling home, opened in 1771, were intended as incubators of a new kind of individual, a future member of the educated, urban estate that Russia lacked. After Catherine's death, Maria Fedorovna, wife of Paul I, assumed charge of existing charitable institutions and initiated numerous charitable ventures of her own. Her specialty was widows, mothers,

[39] Adele Lindenmeyr, "Public Life, Private Virtues: Women in Russian Charity, 1762–1914," *Signs* 18, no. 3 (Spring 1993), 564.
[40] *Days of a Russian Noblewoman*, 93.

and children of the lower classes, on whom she bestowed the maternal concern that complemented the emperor's fatherly image. Maria set the standard
for succeeding empresses and female members of the imperial family, whose
principal public activity became patronage of charities. Henceforward, they
lent their names, as well as varying amounts of money and effort, to highly
visible charitable endeavors.[41]

The Napoleonic Revival

Awakening intense patriotic feelings, the Napoleonic invasion moved women
to serve their nation in ways both traditional and new. Penetrating deep into
Russian soil and wreaking havoc in their wake, Napoleon's troops occupied
Moscow in the fall of 1812, after 95 percent of its entire population had
fled elsewhere. Adding to the feeling of violation, rumors that Napoleon's
soldiers raped and murdered Russian women circulated among elites. Many
interpreted the invasion as a sign of God's punishment for Russia's sins
and it encouraged members of the elite to reject Western rationalism and
materialism and the French influence that had dominated elite culture since
the days of Catherine the Great. The trauma led some pious women to resume
the traditional role of intercessor with God on behalf of their threatened
nation. "We are debauched, owing to the French," wrote Maria Volkova, a
graduate of Smolnyi, to a school friend in 1812. "Imitating them, we accepted
their vices and errors. . . . They rejected faith in God and authorities and we,
slavishly imitating them, embraced their horrid rules and took pride in our
resemblance to them." In the provincial town where she and her family settled
after fleeing Moscow, she attended church regularly in order to "propitiate
God" on behalf of herself and her countrymen.[42] Anna Rimskaia-Korsakova
vowed that if God preserved the Russians from Napoleon, she would enter a
nunnery. Having accustomed herself to the rigors of the monastic life, after
the Russian victory, she fulfilled her vow.

Women also became involved in public life in new ways. In 1807, the
noblewoman Nadezhda Durova had fled her home in the Ural Mountains
determined to escape her woman's lot. Disguising herself as a boy, she joined
the Russian cavalry and served with distinction during the Napoleonic Wars.
Waiting out the war in the countryside, Maria Volkova and the women of her
family prepared bandages for the wounded, which were then dispatched to
hospitals closer to the front. Praskovia Ilinichna Manzei, already in debt and
accustomed to pinching every kopek, contributed substantial sums to the war

[41] David Ransel, *Mothers of Misery: Child Abandonment in Russia* (Princeton, N.J.: Princeton University Press, 1988), 31–41; Lindenmeyr, "Public Life," 569–71.

[42] "Pis'ma 1812 goda M. A. Volkovoi k V. A. Lanskoi," in M. I. Vostryshev (ed.), *Zapiski Ochevidtsa.
Vospominaniia. Dnevniki. Pis'ma* (Moscow: Sovremennik, 1989), 297, 314.

effort, enough to purchase ammunition to equip twenty fighting men. She also gave four sons to the war, each of whom served with distinction. For these contributions, she was awarded a bronze medal in 1814. Swept up in the national consciousness that resulted from Napoleon's invasion, Russian women felt the need to prove that their love for their fatherland was, as some put it, "no less than that of their husbands, brothers and sons."[43]

If the Napoleonic Wars were the "seed around which civil society crystallized," then women were present at the creation.[44] They founded one of the nation's earliest voluntary associations, the Women's Patriotic Society, in November 1812. "Women, too, desire to be useful to society," read its invitation to potential members.[45] Made public on November 15, the Society sought members in other cities besides St. Petersburg. Although the initiative came from elites, the Society welcomed women of other estates than the nobility; its members, who numbered 74 in 1812, included wives of wealthy merchants and bankers. Women from distant Perm, Saratov, and Astrakhan provinces sent money to support the Society's work. Initially formed for the purpose of aiding the victims of Napoleon, the Society continued to function after he was driven from Russia.[46] The members' public presence violated Maria Volkova's sense of the proper role of women: "Frankly speaking," she observed disapprovingly, "if you want to engage in worthy and charitable acts, it's best to do so without publicity. In these ladies' enterprise I see a sign of vanity, which I thoroughly dislike in women, whose role is to stay on the sidelines. . . . "[47] But many welcomed the opportunity to assume a more public role. In subsequent years, such charitable associations became almost the norm, "virtually part of the job description for the wives of high officials."[48] In this way, charitable impulses rooted in religious values were reconfigured for a more secular era, offering women an entry into public life.

Women, Gender, and the Emergence of Opposition

The failed Decembrist uprising stimulated a different kind of female heroism, which likewise drew upon a blend of older, self-sacrificial models of womanhood and new secular ideals. Condemned by the government as potential

---

[43] V. V. Gur'ianova, "Tverskaia pomeshchitsa vtoroi poloviny xviii veka Praskov'ia Il'inichna Manzei," in V. I. Uspenskaia (ed.), *Zhenshchiny v sotsial'noi istorii Rossii: Sbornik nauchnykh trudov* (Tver: Tverskoi gos. universitet, 1997), 28; Quote from Iulia Zhukova, "Pervaia zhenskaia organizatsiia v Rossii (Zhenskoe Patrioticheskoe Obshchestvo v Peterburge v period 1812–1826 gg.) in *Vse Liudi Sestry*, Peterburgskii Tsentr Gendernykh Problem, Biulleten' no. 5 (St. Petersburg, 1996), 50.

[44] Marc Raeff, *Political Ideas and Institutions in Imperial Russia* (Boulder, Colo.: Westview Press, 1994), 136.

[45] Zhukova, "Pervaia zhenskaia," 41.   [46] Ibid., 44–52.   [47] "Pis'ma 1812 goda," 318.

[48] Lindenmeyr, "Public Life," 570.

regicides on account of their attempt to seize power, five of the conspirators paid with death by hanging, hundreds more with a lifetime of penal servitude in Siberia. Among the most outraged by their punishment were "121 wives, sisters, mothers, female relatives, friends and the friends of friends of the criminals," in the words of a police informant.[49] Defying the government, which encouraged them to take advantage of their right to divorce a criminal husband, or to sever their ties with brothers, wives and sisters elected to follow the men into a lifetime of exile in Siberia. Most came from aristocratic families. Women had to leave behind their own children and to renounce all the comforts and privileges they had enjoyed as members of the elite.

Judging by their own writings, feelings of profound and self-sacrificial love led most of the women to this decisive step. "To tell the truth, I feel that I won't be able to live without you," wrote Ekaterina Trubetskaia to her "dear friend," her husband Nikita, author of a draft constitution for the Northern Society. "I am prepared to bear everything for you. I'll regret nothing when I'm together with you.... Only one thing can bring me joy: to see you, share your grief...and devote every moment of my life to you." Having lived fourteen years with her husband as the "happiest wife on earth," Maria Iushnevskaia likewise wanted to share her husband's fate. "I want to fulfill my most holy duty and share with him his grievous position," she explained in her appeal to the authorities. "I am prepared to endure all the misery and poverty the world offers, and would willingly give up my own life if it would ease his lot."[50] Maria Volkonskaia was unusual in being motivated less by deep feeling for her husband than by the desire to support demonstratively a man who had risked his life for his convictions. Having spent a mere three months with her husband before his arrest, she defied members of her own family as well as the state in order to join him in Siberia. In choosing loyalty to husband over loyalty to state, these women turned the family values of Nicholas I on their head. Rather than promoting political order, wifely devotion rewarded rebelliousness instead.

The Decembrist wives, as these women became known, won enormous sympathy (Fig. 5). During the reign of Nicholas I, it was forbidden to refer to the rebels or their wives in public, but after his death in 1855, society discovered them, and writers and publicists elevated the women to almost saintly status. Their demonstration of female heroism, combining as it did the ethos of self-sacrifice and womanly devotion, resonated deeply in elite cultural consciousness, reflecting aspects of the most exalted post-Petrine family ideals.

[49] Quoted in E. A. Pavliuchenko, *V dobrovol'nom izgnanii* (Moscow: Nauka, 1976), 15.
[50] Ibid., 19, 20.

5. Portrait of A. Muravieva Decembrist wife, from *The Female Portrait in Russian Art*

Conclusion

How well the Decembrist wives' experiences captured most noblewomen's everyday realities is, of course, more difficult to judge. As Iurii Lotman observed, the Decembrist represented a new kind of man, whose efforts to behave according to elevated ideals even in everyday life remained unusual.[51] The perspective of women who were neither married to moral paragons nor content with their customary sphere is found in the writings of Maria Zhukova and Elena Gan, both of whom began publishing in the late 1830s. Their work emphasized the plight of the educated and able woman whom society subordinated to men and denied an outlet outside the family. In her short story, "Ideal," Gan's heroine bemoans a woman's fate: "sometimes it seems to me that the world is created just for men. Men have access to the universe with all its secrets; they enjoy fame, art and knowledge; they have freedom and all the joys of life. But from the cradle, a woman is fettered by the chains of respectability . . . and if her hopes for family happiness are not realized, what does she have left?"[52] Such dissident voices went against the grain of prevailing expectations of womanhood. "To a wife are entrusted the responsibilities that are particular to her abilities and her character. Her dominion is kindness and gentleness," advised Maria Korsini in a book that appeared in 1846. "A woman is given inexhaustible patience, which helps her endure the screams of children, lack of sleep, and many minor domestic unpleasantries."[53] Although writers and intellectuals had begun to question women's proper place, in the absence of other outlets, the family remained noblewomen's destined sphere. And for most, it would seem, the world of the family, with its newly elevated roles of wife and mother and extensive responsibilities for the household economy, was world enough.

Suggestions for Further Reading

Bernstein, Lina. "Women on the Verge of a New Language: Russian Salon Hostesses in the First Half of the Nineteenth Century," in Helena Goscilo and Beth Holmgren (eds.), *Russia. Women. Culture.* Bloomington, Ind.: Indiana University Press, 1996, 209–24.

Durova, Nadezhda. *The Cavalry Maiden. Journals of a Russian Officer in the Napoleonic Wars.* Edited and translated by Mary Fleming Zirin. Bloomington, Ind.: Indiana University Press, 1988.

Glagoleva, Olga E. "Dream and Reality of Russian Provincial Young Ladies, 1700–1850," *Carl Beck Papers,* no. 1405.

Labzina, Anna. *Days of a Russian Noblewoman: The Memories of Anna Labzina, 1758–1821.* Edited and translated by Gary Marker and Rachel May. DeKalb, Ill.: Northern Illinois University Press, 2001. *A valuable memoir.*

---

[51] Iurii Lotman, "The Decembrist in Everyday Life," in Alexander D. Nakhimovsky and Alice Stone Nakhimovsky (eds.), *The Semiotics of Russian Cultural History* (Ithaca: Cornell University Press, 1985).

[52] Quoted in Barbara A. Engel, *Mothers and Daughters: Women of the Intelligentsia in Nineteenth Century Russia* (Evanston, Ill.: Northwestern University Press, 2000), 31.

[53] Robin Bisha, Jehanne M. Gheith, Christine Holden and William G. Wagner (eds.), *Russian Women, 1698–1917: Experience and Expression. An Anthology of Sources* (Bloomington, Ind.: Indiana University Press, 2002), 28.

Lindenmeyr, Adele. "Public Life, Private Virtues: Women in Russian Charity, 1762–1914," *Signs* 18, no. 3 (Spring 1993), 562–91.

Marker, Gary. "The Enlightenment of Anna Labzina: Gender, Faith, and Public Life in Catherinian and Alexandrian Russia," *Slavic Review* 59 no. 2 (Summer 2000), 369–90.

Marrese, Michelle Lamarche. *A Woman's Kingdom: Noblewomen and the Control of Property in Russia, 1700–1861.* Ithaca, N.Y.: Cornell University Press, 2002. *A pathbreaking work, based on extensive archival research, which explores the evolution of women's property rights and the ways in which those rights were exercised.*

Meehan-Waters, Brenda. "Popular Piety, Local Initiative and the Founding of Women's Religious Communities in Russia," *St. Vladimir's Theological Quarterly*, 30 no. 2 (1986), 117–33.

Rosslyn, Wendy, ed. *Women and Gender in Eighteenth Century Russia.* Aldershot, England: Ashgate Publishing, 2002. *An important collection on an understudied topic.*

3

OUTSIDE THE CIRCLE OF PRIVILEGE

I thought I saw two people, but it was only a man and his wife.
A hen is not a bird and a woman is not a human being.
A dog is wiser than a woman; he doesn't bark at his master.

Russian peasant proverbs

The Petrine revolution and its consequences brought the state more closely than ever before into the lives of Russia's people. For the peasantry, constituting over 90 percent of the population in 1719, and for townspeople, a mere 3.6 percent, Peter's innovations proved almost entirely negative, at least in the short run. They became the means for the state to satisfy its ever-increasing need for labor, soldiers, and revenue. The changes weighed most heavily on privately owned peasant serfs, whose numbers significantly increased. Approximately half of peasants belonged to noble landowners; the rest were attached to lands belonging to the crown, the state, or, until 1764, the church. The law code of 1649 had already reduced to the status of serfs those peasants who lived on the estates of noble lords. During the eighteenth century, privately owned serfs lost almost all semblance of a civil identity. Women shared the fate of their menfolk but also experienced it in ways specific to their gender.

It is difficult to capture the experience of women who lived outside the circle of privilege. Until the early twentieth century, the overwhelming majority remained unable not only to read but also to sign even their name. To tell their story, the historian must rely primarily on the words of others. Their narrative has a kind of timeless quality that reflects the fact that, despite the changes to be described in this chapter, from Peter the Great until the abolition of serfdom in 1861 and even thereafter, many of the basic patterns of peasant life continued. Women outside the circle of privilege first experienced the positive dimensions of change in cities and towns, rather than in peasant villages.

6. Portrait of a Peasant Woman in Russian costume, from *The Female Portrait in Russian Art (Leningrad, 1974)*

Peasant Women and Their Work

Peasant life was harsh. Peasants dwelt in a world over which they exercised little control. Subject to the demands of landlords or their bailiffs, to the exactions of the tsarist state, to the uncertainties of the weather, and to the requirements of the agricultural calendar, peasants arranged their lives to suit their circumstances. Their life required long periods of intense, backbreaking toil. Peasant women's labor was as necessary to survival as a man's. Women performed all the work that sustained the peasant household. Tending the kitchen garden that produced most of the household's food, women pickled the cabbage and brewed *kvas*, a lightly fermented, almost non-alcoholic beer that peasants consumed daily. Women cooked cabbage soup or borshcht. They ground the grain and baked the rye bread or prepared the grain-based porridges and gruels that remained the staple of peasant diet. In the northern forested lands, women gathered and preserved mushrooms and berries to supplement their family's diet or to sell for a little cash. Women sent the livestock to the fields and brought them back home in summer and tended them in winter. They milked the cow, and prepared butter, cottage cheese, and sour cream. During planting and harvesting, when the need for laborers was greatest, they joined men in the fields, where they harvested rye, winter wheat, and oats; tied grain into sheaves for drying; and raked the hay and loaded it onto carts. When harvesting was most intensive, from mid July until the end of August, peasant women and men essentially lived in the fields, where they slept no more than three to four hours each night. After the harvest was gathered, women gleaned the fields for leftover grain.

Women clothed their family. They made linen from the flax that they sowed in the spring and harvested in the fall. Removing the seeds, they would soak the stalks in water and then dry them to make the outer layer rot and crack. This process could take up to two weeks. Then they would soften the stems by beating them, and then comb and comb again the threads to separate them into single strands. These strands would be wrapped around a distaff, and two or three threads would be drawn out at a time to twist onto the spindle that in the winter was rarely far from a woman's side. The resulting thread was usually left in its natural color. Weaving the thread into cloth, embroidering or decorating it, then making clothing was work that also occupied women in the winter months. Transforming fleece into woolen garments involved much the same processes. The family's well-being depended on a woman's diligence and skill.

Becoming a Wife

Peasant woman's value as a labor resource shaped her life cycle. Marriage was the central event, her early life a preparation. Learning the skills that she would need as an adult while at the same time easing her mother's burdens, a girl began to prepare at a tender age. Peasant "nurses" as young as six years of age tended younger siblings or the children of a neighbor. Girls fed the chickens and fetched eggs; as they grew, they gradually mastered the various tasks that constituted the work of the adult woman. Around the age of twelve, preparations for marriage grew serious. The girl assembled her trousseau, the clothing, sheets, pillows, towels, and pillowcases, much of it her own handiwork, which would last her for most of her married life and remain her personal property. For all the preparation, a maiden was often in no hurry to wed and her parents, pleased to retain her labor power.

By comparison with the responsibilities of wifehood, maidenhood represented a carefree time in a young woman's life. It was a time when relations with boys were playful, to be enjoyed so long as they remained within limits. Marriageable girls attended round dances and gatherings where young people sang, danced, and took part in kissing games. Girls had to exercise restraint, however. Ethnographers suggest that women's sexual honor remained important in the countryside, and that men were its guardians. Through the middle of the nineteenth century, it remained widespread practice to display the blood-stained bridal shirt to demonstrate bridal virginity. Parents who had failed to guard their daughter's honor became subject to public humiliation.[1]

Marriage came more often sooner than later. Everyone except a maiden and her parents preferred early marriage. Local authorities, noble landowners, and the relatives of marriageable men seeking brides viewed women as both a demographic and an economic resource. Local administrators preferred early marriage because it not only created a new taxable unit (the *tiaglo*) but also promoted population growth, regarded by eighteenth century European rulers as a source of national strength. In pursuit of early and universal peasant marriage, administrators proved ready to exercise coercion. In 1771, for example, the governor, D. I. Chicherin, surmised that in many Western Siberian villages "large numbers of peasant males remain single and cannot find brides into their thirties, while girls remain single until the same age because their fathers keep them home for work." Assuming that the threat of exile would convince unmarried women to wed, he ordered that all "wenches" above the age of twenty-five who remained single as of January 1, 1772, be sent off to Baraba, a factory village near the Ural mountains, to be forcibly wed to male residents.[2] Noble landlords had an interest in early marriage, too: each marriage meant the formation of a *tiaglo*, a new workteam, and hence, greater productivity on the estate. Landlords encouraged and sometimes forced their peasants to wed. In 1777, Prince V. G. Orlov required that all women on his estates at Sidorovskoe marry by the age of twenty. When in 1779 his bailiff complained that widowed men were having difficulty finding new brides, Orlov ordered that brides be chosen and ordered to marry "without fail, any

[1] Christine Worobec, *Peasant Russia: Family and Community in the Post-Emancipation Period* (Princeton, N.J.: Princeton University Press, 1991), 171–2.

[2] Quoted in Nina Minenko, "'Vsepreliubeznaia nasha sozhitelnitsa . . .'" *Rodina* 7 (1994), 105.

excuses from the women notwithstanding." On the estates of Prince Usupov, unmarried girls older than fifteen were fined and so were widows younger than forty. Some landowners made peasants marry by lots and others forced peasants to move to other villages on their estates where spouses could be found, as did A. B. Golitsyn in 1772.[3]

Peasants themselves also exerted great pressure on reluctant women. Peasant men received their full allotment of land only after they married and only then did their community recognize them as adults. Peasant widowers needed a wife to care for children and to assume a woman's share of the farm work. The addition of a female laborer enhanced the well-being of a household. Consequently, although she might have her parents' support, a peasant maiden who wished to remain single gained no sympathy from her community. Viewing women as a crucial labor resource, peasants (female as well as male) joined together, if they were serfs perhaps soliciting the help of their noble owner or the bailiff, to ensure that unmarried or widowed male kin found a bride.[4] The consequence of these combined efforts was early and almost universal marriage. By the age of twenty, most peasant women had become wives.

Parents, rather than the young, had the final say in this all-important decision. To make parting with a daughter easier and to reduce the financial loss to her parents, in many locales a groom's parents presented the bride's family with a *kladka*, or brideprice, which also helped to defray the costs of the wedding. The *kladka* represented a major expenditure. Understandably, the parents of a marriageable son, eager to recoup their loss, sought a maiden who was healthy and a good worker. His parents took the initiative, dispatching a matchmaker (usually an older female relative) to view a perspective bride. If she proved satisfactory, the parents would inspect each other's households. Then, if both found the arrangement suitable, they would negotiate the content of the trousseau and the amount of brideprice and strike a deal orally, the fathers or heads of households clapping hands to make it binding. Then everyone would drink. The arrangement was primarily economic: "We've got a buyer and you've got the goods," the matchmaker would announce to the parents of a prospective bride. Celebrated with elaborate ritual, the wedding integrated the couple into the community. Ribald jokes and emblems of marital fertility figured prominently.

Early marriages were fruitful marriages. Wed young, peasant women (like other Russian women), spent far more of their fertile years as married women than did their contemporaries in the West. They lacked any knowledge of

---

[3] John Bushnell, "Did Serfowners Control Serf Marriage?" *Slavic Review* 52, no. 3 (Fall 1993), 424–6; Janet Hartley, *A Social History of the Russian Empire* (London: Addison Wesley Longman, 1999), 204–5.

[4] Bushnell, "Did Serfowners Control," 435–6.

birth control so far as the literature reveals. The state, with its own vested interest in marital fertility, punished "ferociously" women who used infanticide as a means of birth control: the women were subjected to prolonged and painful execution.[5] Fruitfulness carried risks for a mother, who faced death each time she gave birth. If she managed to survive her childbearing years, a peasant woman would give birth, on the average, to seven children. Perhaps half of those children would live to adulthood. The care of infants and small children necessarily took second or even third place to work required for a household's survival. And some child care practices were downright harmful: the ubiquitous pacifier, made from chewed bread or gruel, wrapped up in a rag and stuffed in the infant's mouth to satisfy hunger while her mother was working; swaddling; the custom of feeding an infant solid food at a very early age. "My early childhood was not accompanied by any particularly outstanding events, unless one counts the fact that I survived," wrote Semen Kanatchikov in his autobiography. "I wasn't devoured by a pig, I wasn't butted by a cow, I didn't drown in a pool, and I didn't die of some infectious disease the way thousands of peasant children perished in those days, abandoned without any care during the summer harvest season.... [M]y own mother, according to some sources, brought eighteen children into this world – according to others the number was twelve – yet only four of us survived."[6] Born in 1879, Kanatchikov grew up in a child care culture little changed from a century before. Practices such as those he described contributed to making Russia's rate of infant mortality among the highest ever known.

Women and Peasant Patriarchy

Serfdom intensified the patriarchal patterns that governed the peasant household, the basic economic unit of peasant society. Instead of interfering in peasant life themselves, most noble landlords and their bailiffs relied on the control exercised by the head of the household, known in Russian as the *bol'shak*, or "big one." In a sense, the *bol'shak* became their agent, even as he sought to protect household members from bailiff and serfowner. Allocating tasks to the ablebodied and punishing miscreants, he forced household members to conduct themselves properly and work hard, thus ensuring agricultural productivity and community stability. To this end, the *bol'shak* was invested with near absolute power over everyone else in his household, sons

---

[5] David Ransel, *Village Mothers: Three Generations of Change in Russia and Tataria* (Bloomington, Ind.: Indiana University Press, 2000), 20.

[6] David Ransel, "Infant-Care Cultures in the Russian Empire," in Barbara Evans Clements, Barbara Alpern Engel, and Christine Worobec (eds.), *Russia's Women: Accommodation, Resistance, Transformation* (Berkeley, Calif.: University of California Press, 1991), 114–19; Reginald Zelnik (ed.), *A Radical Worker in Tsarist Russia: The Autobiography of Semen Ivanovich Kanatchikov* (Stanford, Calif.: Stanford University Press, 1986), 1.

as well as daughters and daughters-in-law. For the young, marriage rarely meant the establishment of an independent household; instead, the couple joined the household of the husband's parents, bringing an additional worker (the bride) and an increased allotment of land. Serf households often consisted of three-generational multiple families. Not until well into adulthood would a married man normally form a household of his own, usually at the death of the *bol'shak*, to whose authority he remained subject until then.

Where a woman stood on the ladder of household authority depended greatly on her age, childbearing status, and relationship to the household's head. She began at the lowest rung following her marriage, which brought her into an alien household, the bride of a man she might barely know. At the beck and call of her mother-in-law and sisters-in-law, living in a hut where in winter everyone slept in a single room and privacy was nonexistent, she was expected to perform the lowliest of labor. If her husband was underage or absent, she might even become subject to the sexual advances of her father-in-law. Sexual relations between the two were considered incestuous by the Russian Orthodox Church and condemned by the peasant community. Nevertheless, such sexual relations occurred sufficiently often to be denoted by special words in the Russian language: *snokhachestvo*, derived from the word *snokha* (daughter-in-law), and meaning sexual relations between father and daughter-in-law; *snoshnik*, meaning a man who had sexual relations with his daughter-in-law.

The picture seems pretty grim. Yet when they evaluate peasant women's status, historians disagree. Some, drawing attention to the unquestionably patriarchal character of the peasant household, have emphasized a woman's subjection. Peasant custom, they note, granted a husband the right to "instruct" his wife, with his fists if necessary, and peasants exercised that right freely, often, and usually with impunity. Historians who have worked with court records from the 1870s and later have turned up occasionally horrific accounts of wifebeating; in the second half of the nineteenth century, many educated observers would describe in grisly detail the brutality with which peasant husbands treated their wives. This evidence has led them to conclude that peasant women were "slaves of slaves."[7]

Others, however, present a more complex and positive picture. Without disputing the power relations in the peasant household, they emphasize the many ameliorating factors. The community placed limits on wife abuse, they observe, and point to decisions by such communities to punish those who exceeded the norms or beat a woman "without good reason." In 1741, for example, peasants in a Siberian village unanimously condemned one of their

---

[7] Rose Glickman, *Russian Factory Women: Workplace and Society, 1861–1914* (Berkeley, Calif.: University of California Press, 1984), 28–33.

members for "living with his wife without love and beating her...prematurely and without cause." In 1782, the fellow villagers of another denounced him to the authorities for beating his wife "for no good reason." Faced with a brutal husband, some women simply fled, or they lived separately with the community's approval, even remarrying without divorcing, or so cases from Siberia indicate. Other women gave as good as they got: when Savva and Ekaterina Balashev fell to quarreling in 1741 and he slammed her with his fist, she slapped him, seized him by the hair and beat his head against the wall, scraping his face with her nails. In 1818, Domna Khvostova explained to a local court that she could not bear to live with her husband, Grigorii, despite the injunctions of the local authorities, because he always beat her. Wives sometimes resorted to magic to deal with difficult husbands, giving them the evil eye in order to force them to cease their abusive behavior or, sometimes, to do away with them altogether.[8]

But most of all, such historians draw attention to the positive dimensions of peasant marriages. Russian popular culture was very far from prudish. Bawdy songs, jokes, and sayings often referred to sexuality quite explicitly and marriage rituals were saturated with erotic symbols and references to sexual activity. Relations between peasant couples could be warm and mutually supportive, these historians contend. The few documents left by literate peasants who lived in Siberia do, indeed, provide examples of great mutual tenderness and affection. In 1797, the peasant Ivan Khudiakov, working elsewhere, implored his wife Anna to "tell me as much as you can about your health, my dearest love." Egor Tropin, likewise away at work pined so painfully for his wife that he fled back to the village to visit her. A third requested his wife, Katerina, to heat up the bathhouse so that he could toast himself "there on your lap, like a little child, or rather like a great big child."[9] These court cases and letters derive from Siberia, where serfdom was never in force and central authority relatively weak; it is hard to know whether the relations they portray prevailed elsewhere as well.

What is certain is that other satisfactions awaited a peasant woman who proved patient and hard-working and whose husband remained alive. A married woman's situation improved with time. The birth of her first child, preferably a son, established her position in her husband's household. As she continued to bear sons, her status further improved and she assumed responsibility for their early acculturation. Around the age of forty, she and her husband would set up a household of their own, usually following the death of the *bol'shak* and his wife. Now the peasant woman herself was the

---

[8] Quoted in Minenko, "'Vsepreliubeznaia,'" 108–10.
[9] Quoted in Nina A. Minenko, *Russkaia krest'ianskaia sem'ia v zapadnoi sibiri (xviii–pervoi poloviny xix v.* (Novosibirsk: Nauka, 1979), 138.

bol'shukha, the "big one's" wife, with authority over the female half of the household and greater stature in the community. Preparing food, welcoming guests, her hospitality provided a crucial ingredient in village social and religious festivities. It became her responsibility to allocate the labor of other women – to decide who would do the cooking, tend the animals, look after the children, and so forth. The rewards that came to a wife with time, however, depended on her husband's survival and continuing role in the community.

In this patriarchal culture and household-based economy, the loss of her husband altered a woman's status at once. High rates of mortality meant that the chances of widowhood were likewise high. Women's inferior status vis-à-vis men made it difficult for a widow to remain head of her own household. Although most peasant communities recognized a widow's right to a share of the household property, including an allotment of land, that plot of land was usually too small to support an independent household, especially if the widow was raising small children. Taking advantage of her vulnerability, fellow villagers might try to repossess the widow's allotment. Grown sons brought more land and security but more problems, too, because sons might challenge the mother's authority within the household. Widows' requests for support from estate authorities suggest that such women often found it hard to manage adult sons. These difficulties surely encouraged widows to consider remarriage. In any event, the authorities and fellow villagers who sought to ensure that single women married applied much the same pressures to widows. The result was that widows rarely lived independently in the village. A few left the estate altogether. Most either resided in the deceased husband's household or remarried, often to a *bol'shak*, which made them *bol'shukha* in their new husband's household.[10]

Nobles and Serfs

Peasant serfs dwelt in the shadow of their owners' arbitrariness. To some nobles, power brought a sense of paternalistic (or in the case of women, maternalistic) responsibility, or so some memoirs suggest. "When someone happened to fall ill in the village, my mother, eschewing medical assistance, treated all the illnesses herself," remembered Anna Labzina. On festive days occasionally arranged for their peasants, mother and daughter would serve the peasants with their own hands. "I'm very worried about the fate of our servants," wrote Maria Volkova in 1812. The servants had been left behind in Moscow to guard belongings when the family fled to the provinces during Napoleon's invasion. "None of us care about the financial losses, however

---

[10] Rodney Bohac, "Widows and the Russian Serf Community," in Clements, Engel and Worobec (eds.) *Russia's Women*, 95–112.

large they might be; but we won't rest easy until we learn whether our people, both in Moscow and at [our estate] in Vysokii, have remained safe from harm."[11]

Although most noble landowners refrained from interfering in the everyday life of peasants, it is indubitable that some female as well as male landlords sometimes abused their authority over their peasants in gross and destructive ways. Few were as cruel as the notorious Daria Saltykova, who inherited 600 serfs from her husband and over the course of seven years, tortured scores of them to death. Six years after the investigation was launched in 1762, Saltykova was stripped of her noble status, pilloried for an hour in Moscow and imprisoned in a convent in Arkhangel province for the remainder of her life. Less spectacular cruelty was more common, especially toward houseserfs, who far more than fieldworkers were likely to come into contact with their mistress or master. Avdotia Borisovna Alexandrova, who owned several hundred serfs, was a "holy terror" to her houseserfs. She thrashed her favorite housemaid with a rolling pin, boxed the others' ears, and flogged all her female serfs with nettles.[12] In order to ensure that her seamstresses did not doze off in the evenings, Maria Nekliudova would fasten the irritant Spanish fly to their necks and, to keep them from fleeing, would seat them in her own room and attach them to their chairs by their braids.[13] Other mistresses and masters were simply very unkind, unwilling to recognize that their serfs had feelings just like theirs. Advertisements for serfs reflect this vividly: "For sale, a 35-year-old village *baba* [married peasant woman] of good behavior" or "for sale 27-year-old *baba* with her ten year old son."[14] Varvara Turgeneva, mother of the novelist Ivan Turgenev, sometimes ordered the marriages of her female houseserfs. When an infant was born he was sent away from the house, so that Turgeneva could enjoy his mother's undivided attention. Although women owners as a group were no more prone to cruelty than men, there is little evidence that the womanhood that mistress and woman serf shared offered the latter either protection or a common bond.

Their sexuality made serf women uniquely vulnerable to their masters. Sexual relations between noblemen and female peasants appears almost to have been commonplace. There was a lively trade in young serf women;

[11] Gary Marker and Rachel May (ed. and trans.), *Days of a Russian Noblewoman: The Memories of Anna Labzina, 1758–1821* (DeKalb, Ill.: Northern Illinois University Press, 2001), 6; "Pis'ma 1812 goda M. A. Volkovoi k V. A. Lanskoi, in *Zapiski ochevidtsa: Vospominaniia, Dnevniki, pis'ma* (Moscow: Sovremennik, 1989), 296–7.

[12] Jerome Blum, *Lord and Peasant in Russia from the Ninth to the Nineteenth Century* (Princeton, N.J.: Princeton University Press, 1961), 426–7, 437; Aleksandr Nikitenko, *Up from Serfdom: My Childhood and Youth in Russia, 1804–1824*, Peter Kolchin (ed.), Helen Saltz Jacobson (trans.) (New Haven, Conn.: Yale University Press, 2001), 22–3.

[13] Elizaveta Iankova, *Rasskazy Babushki. Iz vospominaniii piati pokolenii zapisannye i sobrannye ee vnukom D. Blagovo* (Leningrad: Nauka, 1989), 219.

[14] Hartley, *A Social History*, 69.

attractive ones brought good prices at the marketplace. At the turn of the nine-teenth century, a young man about town might spend as much as 500 rubles for a woman who caught his fancy, while ordinary housemaids sold for no more than 50. Even the writer Ivan Turgenev, an opponent of serfdom, proved unable to resist the temptation. In 1852, after being exiled to his estate for his writings about the injustice of serfdom, Turgenev entertained himself with a young chambermaid whom he had reportedly purchased for 700 rubles. A few men pressed their authority further, creating entire peasant harems for themselves. One example is the wealthy A. P. Koshkarev, who divided his house into male and female halves, and kept a harem of twelve to fifteen female serfs. The young women were outfitted in European clothing, pre-sented with a dowry, salaried, and educated. In addition to sexual services, their position required them to read to their master and play cards with him. Although their status left them subject to slaps and whippings for al-leged misdemeanors, most apparently preferred it to the heavy toil that was a peasant woman's usual lot. Another example is Alexandr Iakovlev, Alexander Herzen's uncle, who "created a whole harem of country girls," and was nearly murdered by his serfs for his "interference" with their daughters.[15]

For peasant men, whose sense of honor rested in part on their ability to uphold the chastity of their wife and daughters, the inability to protect their women from an owner's depredations must surely have intensified feelings of helplessness and rage. In 1828, peasants owned by the landowner Iosif Chesnovskii unanimously denounced him for "committing forcible fornica-tion with their wives and for corrupting the virginity of their young daughters of ten years of age and younger," in a case brought by a priest before the Synod, which ordered that Chesnovskii be deprived of the management of his peas-ants.[16] Few peasants found such powerful protectors. Decisions such as the Synod's were difficult to enforce.

Between Elite and Peasant

In many ways, the lives of women who resided in cities or towns differed little from those of the peasantry. Like everyone else, they were assigned to estates – mainly artisans, townspeople (*meshchane*), and merchants following Catherine the Great's Charter to the Towns of 1775. Constituting somewhat over one-third of urban dwellers through the end of the eighteenth century according to Boris Mironov's calculations (the remainder belonged to the

---

[15] Alexander Herzen, *Childhood, Youth and Exile* (New York: Oxford University Press, 1994), 15.

[16] Robin Bisha, Jehanne M. Gheith, Christine Holden, and William Wagner (eds.), *Russian Women, 1698–1917: Experience and Expression, An Anthology of Sources* (Bloomington, Ind.: Indiana Uni-versity Press, 2002), 125.

nobility, the peasantry, and other estates), townspeople often tilled the soil just as peasants did, whereas merchants usually originated as either peasants or townspeople, intermarried with these groups, and maintained their family ties.[17] One difference between peasants and urban dwellers was that nuclear families, consisting of just a husband, wife, and children, were more common in the towns, representing anywhere from fifty to ninety percent of households, judging by surviving records. However, large households also existed. In the early eighteenth century, the household of the wealthy Kitaev family of Ustiuzhna contained seventeen members, including uncles, aunts, nephews, and nieces. Larger households tended to be wealthier.[18]

Urban family life was self-consciously patriarchal and conservative. The father commanded and everyone obeyed. Initially, and despite Peter's laws mandating German clothes, most members of the urban estates remained little affected by Western ways. In the early nineteenth century, an English observer noted the elaborate clothing donned by merchant women at Easter: "Headdresses of pearls and veils of muslin embroid'd with gold and with silver, or silk embroider'd with ditto, their pelises of gold silk lined with the most expensive furs, their faces painted red and white altogether gave them a very shewy and handsome appearance."[19] In the town of Riazan in the 1830s, merchant wives still went about in sarafans (a sleeveless dress, worn also by peasant women) and long mantles. Merchant families were insular. Success in preserving the merchant way of life depended on raising children at home, "sealing them off from the outside world in the tightly knit, isolated life of the family," and preserving the highly stylized etiquette that made it difficult to socialize with anyone outside the immediate circle of relations.[20] Women's lives were confined to the household. Married women mostly devoted themselves to tending the home, sewing, and preserving food. If they had idle hours, women passed them doing needlework. Daughters rarely left the house except to go to church on Sundays and to visit girlfriends of an evening, "where they would pass their time playing various peasant games."[21] Iulia, the daughter of a well-to-do Moscow merchant, complained to her diary in 1831, "We spend all our time at home or if they do let us go somewhere, it's only to visit relatives living nearby."[22]

Parents arranged marriages, often with advantageous connections uppermost in their minds. "On January 6 [1773] with the approbation and

---

[17] Boris Mironov, *Russkii gorod v 1740–1860 gody* (Leningrad: Nauka, 1990), 82.

[18] Hartley, *A Social History*, 201–2.   [19] Quoted in Hartley, *A Social History*, 181.

[20] Alfred Rieber, *Merchants and Entrepreneurs in Imperial Russia* (Chapel Hill, N.C.: University of North Carolina Press, 1982), 24.

[21] Irina G. Kusova, *Riazanskoe kupechestvo. Ocherki istorii xvi–nachala xx veka* (Riazan: Mart, 1996), 112.

[22] G. T. Polilov-Severtsov, *Nashi dedy-kuptsy* (St. Petersburg, 1907), 109.

inducement of my father, I decided to marry," wrote the merchant Ivan Tolchenov in his diary. "On the 9th, we rode to Moscow on that matter. The 14th, I viewed the young woman, the daughter of the merchant Aleksei Ivanovich Osorgin in Kozhevniki, who was destined by heavenly fate to be my spouse. The 17th the agreement [between the father of the bride and the father of the groom] was negotiated."[23] In Moscow, elaborate "showings" of eligible merchant daughters took place regularly, the girls with their mothers proceeding slowly down a lane in the park, permitting eligible bachelors and matchmakers to survey them at their leisure.

Even if they lived in some respects as the *Domostroi* had instructed centuries before, merchant and townswomen nevertheless might play a role in business. Businesses were almost invariably family affairs. Wives and daughters sometimes helped behind the scenes, providing advice or keeping accounts, as Iulia did at her father's behest. Or they took their turn behind the counter or at a desk, especially when family enterprises were small and new, very much as did their counterparts in France or Great Britain in the early phases of industrial development. Aided by the unusually high level of literacy in their communities and by their community's support, some Old Believer women took part in entrepreneurial activities and ran family enterprises. One example is the Vikula Morozov and Sons Manufacturing Company, founded by Savva Morozov while he was still a serf. In 1837, Savva's son, Elisei, established a dyeworks of his own. A devout Old Believer who devoted most of his time to religious activities, Elisei Morozov left the management of the business to his wife.[24]

Other women traded independently. It has been estimated that there were some 9,000 female hawkers and traders in Moscow in 1805 (as compared with 14,000 men).[25] One such independent trader was Katrya Nikitenko, the wife of a serf. Married to a man unable to support her, she earned a pittance by buying and selling second-hand goods in the town of Ostrogozhsk. Women who ran more lucrative businesses on their own were usually widows, such as Evgeniia Rastorgueva. Married to a man who traded in gold, silver, and diamonds, after her husband's death in 1848, Rastorgueva managed the business for nine years until she married her own head clerk and transferred the responsibilities to him. Most women who traded independently owned

[23] Quoted in David Ransel, "An Eighteenth Century Russian Merchant Family in Prosperity and Decline," in Jane Burbank and David Ransel (eds.), *Imperial Russia: New Histories for the Empire* (Bloomington, Ind.: Indiana University Press, 1998), 264.

[24] Muriel Joffe and Adele Lindenmeyr, "Daughters, Wives and Partners," in James L. West and Iurii Petrov (eds.), *Merchant Moscow: Images of Russia's Vanished Bourgeoisie* (Princeton, N.J.: Princeton University Press, 1998), 102.

[25] Catriona Kelly, "Teacups and coffins: the culture of merchant women, 1850–1917," in Rosalind Marsh (ed.), *Women in Russia and Ukraine* (New York: Cambridge University Press, 1996), 74, fn. 25.

only a small business or a string of small businesses: they made and sold an enormous variety of goods, from bricks to fish, from tobacco to steel buckets. They ran haulage and cab firms and owned grain-importing businesses and hotels. Most of the women traders probably lacked a husband because until 1863 married women faced substantial obstacles to registering as independent tradeswomen.[26]

The State Intervenes

In 1701, a peasant woman had her tongue cut out for spreading the rumor that Peter the Great was the son of a German, swapped at birth for a daughter. The belief that Peter was the Anti-Christ was widespread, especially among Old Believers. How else to explain the new burdens that Peter imposed on his people? The changes introduced by Peter and his successors affected women of Russia's taxpaying population, townspeople as well as peasants, in a number of enduring ways. The most profound derived from the military draft that Peter introduced. From the time of his reign until the reform of the military in 1874, recruitment into the army removed millions of able-bodied men from their families. The draft created a new social category, the soldier's wife (*soldatka*). In times of warfare, recruitment could remove a substantial number of young men from their villages. On one large estate in Tambov province, for example, the war of 1812 took the husbands of over a quarter of the women aged twenty-five to twenty-nine. Initially, service was for life; in 1793, the term was reduced to twenty-five years and in 1834, to twenty. The impact on the woman left behind could be devastating. "What sort of tsar is it who destroys the peasants' homes, takes our husbands for soldiers and leaves us orphaned with our children and forces us to weep for an age?" a woman complained about Peter the Great.[27]

If she derived from the peasantry, the *soldatka* often found herself in the most marginal position. Because conscription legally emancipated the serfs from the authority of the landlord, his wife and children, too, became legally "free." As free persons, they often lost their husbands' share of the communal land and all other benefits from the estate. Some were reduced to begging for alms in the village; others continued to live as dependents with their husband's family or with relatives. However, because each represented an extra mouth to feed and a potential threat to the other women of the household and community, *soldatki* might be driven from the village. Such women became highly vulnerable. They might even be unlawfully re-enserfed, as was

---

[26] Ibid., 65–6; Michelle Lamarche Marrese, *A Woman's Kingdom: Noblewomen and the Control of Property in Russia, 1700–1861* (Ithaca, N.Y.: Cornell University Press, 2002), 130–1.

[27] Quoted in Lindsey Hughes, *Russia in the Age of Peter the Great* (New Haven: Yale University Press, 1998), 196.

one soldier's wife who worked for a state official and bore him several illegitimate children. Claiming that she was the wife of one of his household serfs, he eventually sold her to another noble. She was freed after her original owners verified that she was a soldier's wife, but her children, having been raised and fed by her employer, remained serfs.

The cities to which such women migrated offered them little in the way of respectable employment, and large numbers of men who were prepared to pay for sexual companionship. Some women took up petty trade, many more hired out as domestic servants. A few became minor success stories, owning small workshops or commercial establishments. Others entered a bigamous marriage, as did Evdokia Ivanova doch', who married the state peasant Mikhei Dorofeev in 1739, ten days before he began his military service. Having heard no news from him for six years, in 1745 she married another man.[28] However, enough women turned to prostitution as a temporary or permanent expedient that soldiers' wives acquired an unsavory reputation. In 1800, when Tsar Paul I ordered prostitutes to be rounded up and sent off to work in factories in the Far East, half the women who were arrested in Moscow turned out to be *soldatki*. Soldiers' wives also figured prominently among the mothers of illegitimate children. In the course of the eighteenth century, illegitimacy and infanticide became much more visible than they had been in the earlier period and perhaps more commonplace as well.

The social problems engendered by the Petrine revolution moved the state to action. Concern to increase the population prompted initial attempts to preserve the lives of illegitimate children. In 1712, and again in 1714 and 1715, Peter the Great ordered the establishment of hospitals in which mothers were permitted to deposit their illegitimate children in secret. After Peter's death, however, the shelters were dismantled. When, in the reign of Catherine the Great, the state again took steps to deal with illegitimate children, it adopted a substantially different approach. Prompted by Ivan Betskoi, Catherine the Great established foundling homes in Moscow in 1764 and St. Petersburg in 1771. Catherine intended the homes to preserve the lives of illegitimate children, and equally important, to create an entirely new kind of individual, an industrious citizen imbued with enlightened morality, who would promote the welfare of the country. The homes, which raised no barriers to admission, became magnets not only for illegitimate children but also for the legitimately born offspring of mothers and fathers unable or unwilling to care for them, who abandoned their children to the homes in the hope of retrieving them later, when the children reached working age. Despite

---

[28] Robin Bisha, "Marriage, Church, and Community in Eighteenth-Century St. Petersburg," in Wendy Rosslyn (ed.), *Women and Gender in Eighteenth Century Russia* (Aldershot, England: Ashgate Publishing, 2002), 236.

problems with extraordinarily high infant mortality rates and the continuing abuse of the system by parents seeking to free themselves from the burdens of childrearing, the Russian government proved reluctant to adopt measures to limit open admissions. The foundling homes represented one of the very few state-sponsored charitable institutions in Russia. They served as a sign of imperial good works and of rulers' maternal or paternal care for their most vulnerable and unfortunate subjects.[29]

The state extended no such care to their mothers, however, should the women be known to engage in "vice." Instead, the state showed its strictest and most controlling face, incorporating into public policy the misogynistic and repressive aspects of popular and religious culture. Slavic ecclesiastical literature, which regarded all nonprocreative sex as sinful, drew little distinction between a woman who had sex in exchange for money and a woman who slept with a man other than her husband without financial gain. In both cases, she was called a *Bludnitsa*, a "loose woman," who offended morality and public decency. The view of women as sexually insatiable creatures who deliberately enticed men to sin was reflected in eighteenth century *lubki* (popular prints), which show women being beaten for having lovers. But the popular prints also suggest a "rough-and-ready equality and openness" about the relations between the sexes that resembled what we know of peasant culture. They depict men and women enjoying one another, singing, dancing, sledding on ice hills, drinking. In these prints, seduction is a game, deception is part of it and the relations between men and women are playful.[30]

As the state intensified its control over Russian society, the more repressive and misogynist view of sexuality became reflected in some aspects of law and public policy. Sexual relations became matters of political concern. The law code of 1649 ordered anyone who arranged "lecherous relations" between men and women to be beaten with a knout. Embraced by Peter the Great, the idea of the well-ordered police state (*Polizeistaat*), which promoted well-being through active social intervention, intensified state concern with individual sexual conduct. In 1716, Peter the Great ordered that "loose women" be kept away from the regiments. If women violated his order, they risked being driven away naked. Two years later, Peter instructed the police chief of the recently founded city of St. Petersburg to close all "obscene establishments" in the city, such as taverns and gambling parlors. For the crime of adultery, women were sentenced to forced labor, usually in spinning mills. A decree of July 26, 1721, stated that women and girls convicted of "loose behavior" were

---

[29] David Ransel, *Mothers of Misery: Child Abandonment in Russia* (Princeton, N.J.: Princeton University Press, 1988), 31–83; 154–8.

[30] Dianne Ecklund Farrell, "Medieval Popular Humor in Russian Eighteenth Century *Lubki*," *Slavic Review* 50, no. 3 (Fall 1991), 559.

to be handed over to the College of Mines and Manufactures and given as workers to industrialists or sent to Moscow. In 1736, Empress Anna ordered all "debauched" women to be beaten with a cat-of-nine-tails and thrown out of their homes.[31]

Even as she permitted unwed mothers to abandon infants anonymously, Catherine the Great laid the foundation for police supervision of women's public behavior and the regulation of their morality. In 1762 she designated a hospital in St. Petersburg for the confinement of women of "debauched behavior." The intensified effort to control illicit sexual behavior resulted from growing fears about the spread of venereal disease. Women identified by soldiers as the source of their venereal infection were to be confined and, after treatment, sent to labor in the mines of Siberia if they lacked a means of support. In 1800, Emperor Paul I sentenced to forced labor in Siberian factories all women who "have turned to drunkenness, indecency and a dissolute life."[32] Laws also enjoined the police to pick up "vagrant maids" of dubious character who belonged to "the poorest and most disreputable classes" if they might be harboring venereal disease.[33]

Beginning in 1843, the government adopted a different approach to the problem of "loose women." Following the example of the French, the Russians moved to regulate prostitution with the aim of controlling venereal disease. Illicit sexual behavior would henceforward be tolerated, but only within the boundaries set by the state. In a number of major cities, the police organized a system of licensed brothels, where physicians conducted regular examinations to ensure the venereal health of the prostitutes. Women who "traded in vice" on their own were likewise required to register as prostitutes, to carry a ticket attesting to the state of their health, and to undergo weekly medical examinations. If they sold their sexual favors without this official stamp, women risked prosecution for "secret debauchery."

The policy clearly targeted lower-class women who lived outside the boundaries of the patriarchal family. The women identified as responsible for spreading syphilis were soldier's wives living apart from their husbands, domestic servants, peddlers, factory workers, and vagrants. To ensure the health of the population, the police conducted periodic roundups near barracks and factories, in taverns and flophouses, and in places where members of the lower classes dwelled and disported themselves. Police forced women found to be diseased to register as prostitutes. Prostitution thus became

---

[31] Laurie Bernstein, *Sonia's Daughters: Prostitutes and Their Regulation in Imperial Russia* (Berkeley, Calif.: University of California Press, 1995), 13–4.

[32] Ibid., 15.

[33] Quoted in Laura Engelstein, "Gender and the Juridical Subject: Prostitution and Rape in Nineteenth Century Criminal Codes," *Journal of Modern History* 60 (September 1988), 485.

tolerated, although not strictly legal. And "loose women," now patrolled by the police, had been transformed into "public women."

Across the Divide of Culture

By making education and culture as well as birth a measure of elite status, the changes introduced in the eighteenth century both intensified social distinctions and provided new ways to overcome them. Nonelite women gained access to education for the first time. In the 1750s, midwifery courses for women were first introduced; obstetrical institutes opened in St. Petersburg in 1785 and in Moscow in 1801. Attached to Smolnyi Institute was a school that admitted daughters of townsmen, although by 1791 nobles so inundated it that they outnumbered commoners. In 1786, Catherine also established state primary and high schools that admitted girls and educated them for free. Alexander I extended her work, establishing parish schools at the base of the educational system. Some nonelite parents were prepared to spend money to educate daughters in private schools. "During my childhood," recalled the clergyman Dmitrii Rostislavov, born in 1809, "many clergymen, townspeople, and even rich peasants saw a need to teach reading . . . to their daughters."[34] In Anna Virt's private school in Moscow, daughters of townsmen and a priest studied together with the offspring of officials, military officers, and foreigners in 1818–20. The numbers remained small. Altogether, there were 1178 female pupils in Russia by 1792, and 2007 by 1802 (of 24,064 total pupils). In 1824, it was calculated that there were 338 girls in district schools and 3,420 in private schools. Most female students undoubtedly derived from the elite.[35]

Education remained inaccessible to the overwhelming majority of women who were not of genteel birth. Literacy rates for Russia's population were very low: in 1834, only 1 of 208 Russians could read and write; in 1856, 1 of 143, the vast majority of them male. And the opportunities for education that did exist aimed primarily at preparing women for family life. At Smolnyi, townswomen were taught to be "accomplished seamstresses and weavers, stocking knitters and cooks," and once married, to divide their time among the nursery and the kitchen, the barn, the courtyard and the kitchen garden.[36] The private schools to which townsmen and merchants sometimes

---

[34] Dmitrii Ivanovich Rostislavov, *Provincial Russia in the Age of Enlightenment. The Memoir of a Priest's Son,* Alexander Martin (ed. and trans.) (DeKalb, Ill.: Northern Illinois University Press, 2002), 40.

[35] Hartley, *A Social History,* 142.

[36] Quoted in Natalia L. Pushkareva, *Chastnaia zhizn' russkoi zhenshchiny: nevesta, zhena, liubovnitsa (x–nachalo xix v.)* (Moscow: Ladomir, 1997), 209–10.

sent their daughters set themselves much the same goals. So did education for daughters of the clerical estate, whose women lived much as did their peasant neighbors. In 1843, in response to clerical concerns about lagging behind educated society and complaints about uneducated wives, the Russian Orthodox Church opened a special school for daughters of the clergy, with the goal of preparing them for marriage: "to provide pleasant company for their husbands, to help them keep church buildings in good order, to prepare medicine for the ill, to be occupied with the rearing of their children, and to maintain the household in good order."[37] The family remained women's destined sphere.

Conclusion

In some ways, the impact of the Petrine revolution on women of Russia's nonelite population was barely perceptible. Peasant women continued to conduct themselves much as they had for centuries, the struggle for survival shaping their choices, their own culture shaping their worldview, and village institutions governing their daily lives. The lives of townswomen and merchant women, too, differed little from those of their pre-Petrine forebears. To be sure, an upper crust came to share aspects of the new elite worldview. In the late eighteenth century, the wealthy Dmitrov merchant Ivan Tolchenov and his wife entertained dignitaries in their home and socialized frequently with the privileged. In 1812, the wives of bankers and wealthy merchants, like some noblewomen, joined the Women's Patriotic Society, seeking to be "useful to society." But the majority lived far more traditional lives, passing their days within the realm of the family, preparing for marriage, and thereafter, bearing and raising their children and tending their household. At least until the mid-nineteenth century, and arguably, even later, the Westernizing trends that Peter initiated made barely a dent on most women's lives.

When the state did touch women's lives, the impact was primarily negative. Serfdom intensified the patriarchal character of peasant household and community life. The extension of serfdom left peasant women vulnerable to sexual as well as economic exploitation. The state took the husbands of peasants and townswomen for soldiers; it burdened the lower orders with new demands for taxes and other services. Those women who wished – or were forced – to seek a life outside the family might become subject to police surveillance and punishment and after 1843, they risked being labeled as *public women* by officials and police. Policing women's sexual morality had become a state concern.

---

[37] Quoted in Gregory Freeze, *The Parish Clergy in Nineteenth Century Russia* (Princeton, N.J.: Princeton University Press, 1983), 178.

Suggestions for Further Reading

Bisha, Robin. "Marriage, Church and Community in Eighteenth-Century St. Petersburg," in Wendy Rosslyn (ed.), *Women and Gender in Eighteenth Century Russia*, 227–43. Aldershot, England: Ashgate Publishing, 2002. *Sheds light on little-known aspects of female commoners' lives.*

Bohac, Rodney. "Widows and the Russian Serf Community," in Barbara Evans Clements, Barbara Alpern Engel and Christine Worobec (eds.), *Russia's Women: Accommodation, Resistance, Transformation.* Berkeley, Calif.: University of California Press, 1991, 95–112.

Czap, Peter. "The Perennial Multiple Family Household, Mishino, Russia, 1782–1858," *Journal of Family History* 7, no. 1(Spring 1982), 5–26.

Kusova, Irina G. *Riazanskoe kupechestvo. Ocherki istorii xvi-nachala xx veka.* Riazan: Marta, 1996. *Provides insight into the family and domestic practices of provincial merchants.*

Minenko, N. A. *Russkaia krest'ianskaia sem'ia v zapadnoi Sibiri (xviii-pervoi poloviny xix v.)* Novosibirsk: Nauka, 1979. *A pioneering ethnographic study of family life and women in the eighteenth and early nineteenth century, drawing upon archival materials.*

Ransel, David. *Mothers of Misery: Child Abandonment in Russia.* Princeton, N.J.: Princeton University Press, 1988. *A groundbreaking history of the foundling system and of the women who used it.*

Rostislavov, Dmitrii Ivanovich. *Provincial Russia in the Age of Enlightenment.* Edited and translated by Alexander Martin. DeKalb, Ill.: Northern Illinois University Press, 2002. *Chapter 10 contains a useful discussion of the daily labors of clerical wives and daughters.*

Vasilieva, M. E. "Notes of a Serf Woman," *Slavery and Abolition* 21, no. 1(April 2000) 146–58.

4

$=====$ • $=====$

REFORMERS AND REBELS

> Whatever noble family you asked about in those days, you heard one and the same
> thing: the children had fought with the parents.... "Their beliefs are different" –
> and that was enough. An epidemic seized girls in particular – an epidemic of flight
> from their parents' home. You would hear that a daughter had fled the household
> of one or the other noble family.[1]

The death of Tsar Nicholas I in 1855 and the ascension of his son, Alexander
II (1855–81) introduced far-reaching changes into the lives of Russia's women
and men. Censorship eased and the parameters of public discourse widened.
The emancipation of the serfs was proclaimed in 1861; other reforms followed. In 1864, the government initiated a new judicial system, modeled on
systems in the West, and a new, elective organ of local self-government, the
zemstvo. These new public institutions, the first to exist relatively independently of the autocracy, fostered the development of a class of professionals
whose role was to serve the public, rather than the state. An effort to overcome Russia's political, economic and social backwardness, the reforms led
to the emergence of a more vital, diverse, and assertive civil society. They
also unleashed new challenges to the traditional gender and family order,
increasingly from women themselves.

The Woman Question

Educated society experienced a sense of hope in the early years of
Alexander II's reign. As controls were lifted, social forces long held in check
burst forth in luxuriant profusion. Public opinion of a recognizable sort began
to emerge, nourished by the proliferation of journals; at informal gatherings
in private homes, heated discussions of contemporary issues might last far

---

[1] Quoted in Barbara Engel, "Women as Revolutionaries: The Case of the Russian Populists," in
Renate Bridenthal and Claudia Koonz (eds.), *Becoming Visible: Women in European History*, 1st ed.
(Boston: Houghton-Mifflin, 1977), 350.

into the night. People of diverse views and backgrounds debated and some eventually joined forces to work for the betterment of society during those early, optimistic years. Seeking curtailment of arbitrary political authority and enhancement of individual rights, among other changes, socially conscious Russians subjected every traditional institution to reevaluation, the patriarchal family included. Authoritarian family relations, some believed, reproduced and reinforced the social and political hierarchy; to foster the democratization of society, family relations would have to be democratized, too.

Social critics hoped that women would play a vital role in creating a new social order. They saw women as victims: of an educational system that retarded intellectual inquiry and individual development, of a patriarchal family order that distorted the human personality. At the same time, they believed that women possessed qualities that made their participation in social change essential, in particular, a capacity for moral action that seemed so lacking in public life and so crucial for social regeneration. Critics disagreed, however, about the character of women's contributions. Was women's primary role to devote themselves to the family and to appropriate mothering of future citizens? Or did the broader society need women's energies, too? As substantial numbers of women and men sought to answer these questions for themselves and others, the "woman question" emerged as one of the central issues of the day.

The debate unfolded in 1856, when Nikolai Pirogov (1810–81), the surgeon and educator, published an essay entitled "Questions of Life" that posed explicitly the question of women's social role. Pirogov had just returned from the Crimean War (1854–6), where he had supervised some 160 women who had volunteered as nurses. Moved by patriotism and the desire to sacrifice themselves for the fatherland, the women had served without pay and working right at the front, faced many of the same dangers and hardships as soldiers. To Pirogov, the women's exemplary work demonstrated that "up to now, we have completely ignored the marvelous gifts of our women."[2] To his mind, those gifts were mainly applicable at home. "Woman is already emancipated, perhaps even more than man," Pirogov asserted in his essay. "Though she cannot, according to our laws, become a soldier, a bureaucrat, a minister. But can a man really nurse, raise and nurture children younger than eight years old? Can he really be society's bond, its flower and ornament? And so, let women understand their high purpose . . . that they, by attending to the cradle of man, setting up the games of his childhood, teaching his lips to babble their first words and first prayers, are the main architects of society."[3]

---

[2] Quoted in John S. Curtiss, "Russian Sisters of Mercy in the Crimea, 1854–55," *Slavic Review* 25, no. 1 (March 1966), 106.

[3] Quoted in Adele Lindenmeyr, "Public Life, Private Virtues: Women in Russian Charity, 1762–1914," *Signs* 18, no. 3 (Spring 1993), 574.

For the sake of these responsibilities, Pirogov advocated improvements in women's education. Educated women would be better mothers to future male citizens and truer companions to their husbands, thus able to share more fully in men's concerns and struggles. "Let the thought of educating herself for this goal, to live for the inevitable struggle and sacrifice, permeate the moral fiber of women," Pirogov proclaimed.[4] Pirogov set a goal that the tsar also could embrace. In 1858, Alexander II approved a proposal for secondary schools for girls. The purpose: to improve the quality of public life by providing that "religious, moral and mental education which is required of every woman, and especially, of future mothers."[5] The new schools, called *gimnazia*, were to be day schools, open to girls of all estates. Modeled on secondary schools for boys, they offered a six-year course of study that included Russian language, religion, arithmetic, and a smattering of science. *Progimnazia* were opened the same year, offering a three-year course of training and a similar curriculum, exclusive of the science. The government offered the schools only a small subsidy; to cover the remaining costs, the schools depended on student fees and the contributions of public organizations. That support was forthcoming, but only slowly. By 1865 there were 29 *gimnazia* and 75 *progimnaziia* in all of Russia; by 1883, there were 100 and 185 of each respectively, with an enrollment of roughly 50,000 students. In 1876 a supplementary year of pedagogical training became available to *gimnazia* students. It qualified graduates for employment as a domestic teacher or tutor and as teachers in elementary schools and the first four classes of girls' secondary schools.

Some social critics adopted a more radical stance. For the critic Nikolai Dobroliubov, writing in 1856, the family was a "Realm of Darkness," in which "despotism" bore most heavily on women. Although his essay by that title focused on the merchant milieu as depicted by the playwright Alexander Ostrovskii, in Dobroliubov's view family despotism was more widespread. Almost everywhere, he contended, "women have about as much value as parasites." Degradation of women is so pervasive that even the men who allow their wives some say in the household would never think that "a woman is also a person like themselves, with her own rights. Indeed, women themselves don't believe it."[6] A new concern with women's rights in the family prompted critiques of imperial family law, which endowed the head of the household with virtually unlimited authority over its members. There can be no true Christian love or hatred of vice and despotism in a family where despotism,

---

[4] Quoted in Barbara Alpern Engel, *Mothers and Daughters: Women of the Intelligentsia in Nineteenth Century Russia* (Evanston, Ill.: Northwestern University Press, 2000), 52.
[5] Ibid., 50.   [6] Quoted in Engel, "Women as Revolutionaries," 349.

arbitrariness, and coercion reign and "wives are given over in slavery to their husband," declared the liberal jurist Mikhail Filippov in 1861.[7]

The forthcoming emancipation of the serfs added an economic dimension to the woman question. The loss of serf labor would deprive many nobles of an easy living and force their daughters, who by custom had remained at home until marriage, to seek their own livelihood. Equally important, progressive young people of this era, in renouncing serfdom as an immoral institution, rejected the elite culture that they associated with it – a life of idleness and luxury, supported by the toil of others. For some, even dependence on a husband became unacceptable. The more radical were convinced that whether married or single, a woman must never "hang on the neck of a man."[8]

Women's Rights, Women's Opportunities

Discussion of the "woman question" took place in university hallways, in student apartments and the salons of the elite, and on the pages of the "thick journals" to which educated society subscribed. These journals had an immense impact, even in the provinces, where reading provided the primary contact with a larger world. The ideas prompted some readers to alter the way that they lived. Shortly after reading about "the woman question," in journals provided by a clergyman's son, Anna Korvin-Krukovskaia, the daughter of a well-to-do provincial noble family, put aside her fancy clothes and began to dress simply. She lost interest in parties, instead spending her time with her nose in her books. Anna's aunt criticized her unconventional niece in a letter to her own daughter: "Anna appears only at dinner," she complained. "The rest of the time she spends in her room, studying. She never keeps anyone company, never does needlework, never takes walks."[9]

Encouraged by the attention of the press, elite women began to seek each other and to develop a sense of shared interests and identity as women. In 1859, noblewomen in the province of Vologda established separate meetings at gatherings of the provincial nobility. To minimize distinctions of wealth, they required participants to wear simple dress. Speaking in 1860, in the provincial town of Perm, a young teacher, E. A. Slovtsova-Kamskaia, emphasized the primacy of women's shared identity. "The morally developed woman of our time suffers for every injustice borne by another woman. Feelings of envy, ambition, coquetry, a slavish desire to please men at the expense of her sisters, should be alien to her. . . . Each act of kindness she performs for her sisters, she

---

[7] Quoted in William Wagner, *Marriage, Property and Law in Late Imperial Russia* (New York: Clarendon Press, 1994), 106.
[8] Engel, *Mothers and Daughters*, 80.   [9] Ibid., 66.

performs for herself."[10] In 1859, Russia's first association aimed specifically at women emerged, the Society for Inexpensive Lodgings. Three well-educated women from elite backgrounds took the lead. They were Anna Filosofova (1837–1912), the wife of a high-ranking bureaucrat; Nadezhda Stasova (1822-?), the daughter of a court architect and godchild of Alexander I; and Maria Trubnikova (1835–97), the daughter of an exiled Decembrist (Vasilii Ivashev), who had been raised by an aristocratic aunt and was married to the founder of the *Stock Market News*. With the goal of providing decent housing and otherwise assisting needy women, the Society resembled the philanthropic endeavors with which elite women had long been engaged. But it also went further. The Society established a sewing workshop to provide employment for the residents of their housing, and to free them from domestic chores, it provided day care for small children and a communal kitchen to prepare meals. To traditional philanthropy, the women had brought the democratic spirit of the new era.

Other women took action on their own behalf. In 1859 women began to audit university lectures, which had just been reopened to the public. The first to attend was Natalia Korsini, half Russian, half Italian, daughter of an architect. Simply dressed, her hair cut short, Korsini was introduced to the roomful of men by the rector of St. Petersburg University. Other women followed. Within a year, women's presence during university lectures had become almost commonplace. Most of the women sought only to supplement their superficial educations, but a few studied systematically and attempted to earn a degree. In 1861, several scientists at the St. Petersburg Medical Surgery Academy opened their laboratories to women. Among those who began to audit medical lectures were Maria Bokova and Nadezhda Suslova, the daughter of a serf. Suslova went on to complete her medical studies in Zurich, where she earned the degree of Doctor of Medicine in 1867, the first woman to receive such a degree from a European university. Her success inspired hundreds of other women to follow her example.

Women's aspirations for education and independence enjoyed the support of many men. By and large, professors and students welcomed women into lecture halls and laboratories and treated them respectfully. Asked for their opinion in 1861, university authorities in St. Petersburg, Kharkov, Kazan, and Kiev endorsed the presence of women in university halls. Some professors even advocated awarding women degrees on an equal basis with men. Progressive young men sometimes contracted "fictitious marriages" with young women whose parents forbade them to pursue their goals. In these supposedly unconsummated unions, a man would wed a woman solely in order to liberate her from her parents. Not infrequently, a "fictitious marriage" became a real

---

[10] Quoted in Engel, "Women as Revolutionaries," 350.

7. Photograph of Sofia Perovskaia, from *Katorga i Ssylka*, no. 17, 1925

one. Such was the case with Peter Bokov, a medical student, who contracted a "fictitious marriage" to enable his wife Maria to pursue her medical studies. However, when Maria Bokova fell in love with the noted physiologist, Ivan Sechenev, her husband made no fuss.[11] "New people" rejected the ownership of human beings and with it, sexual jealousy. The three settled down in a ménage à trois, one of two that are known about in the early 1860s.

This was a period when some women openly flouted conventional gender expectations. They cropped their hair, dispensed with crinolines, and simplified their dress; they smoked in public, went about the streets without an escort, and wore blue-tinted glasses. A few even donned the clothing of men in order to enjoy greater freedom (Fig. 7). Young rebels became known to their critics as nihilists (*nigilistki* is the female version in Russian) because of their rejection of "the stagnant past and all tradition." Their aspirations sometimes brought them into conflict with their parents. "How can you express ideas without my permission?" queried a mother of her newly assertive

---

[11] Richard Stites, *The Women's Liberation Movement in Russia: Feminism, Nihilism and Bolshevism, 1860–1930* (Princeton, N.J.: Princeton University Press, 1990), 91.

eighteen-year-old daughter. "What sort of disrespect is this?" rhetorically inquired another. "Remember, you are in the presence of your elders."[12]

A few went still further. Viewing family life as constricting for women, they sought to reject it altogether. Their views can be heard in the credo of Lelenka, the heroine of Nadezhda Khvoshchinskaia's novella *The Boarding School Girl*, published in 1860. Lelenka proclaims "I will never fall in love, never. It's stupid . . . I swear that I will never again grant someone power over me. . . . On the contrary, I say to everyone, do as I have done. Liberate yourselves, all you people with hands and a strong will! Live alone. Work, knowledge, freedom – that's what life is all about." Similarly dismissive of the pleasures of personal and family life, Nadezhda Suslova confided to a friend in 1861, "The thought of locking oneself up in the tiny world of the family, where a person acts as the knight of one's own private interests strikes me as vile."[13]

Nikolai Chernyshevskii's enormously influential novel, *What Is to Be Done?* (1863), offered an answer to the "woman question." Drawing upon his contemporaries' efforts to create new ways of living, loving, and working, Chernyshevskii created a model for women and men to follow. The heroine is Vera Pavlovna, the daughter of humble parents. Oppressed by her greedy and materialistic mother, who tries to force her into marriage with a nobleman, she escapes with the help of her brother's tutor, who marries Vera to free her. They achieve near-perfect equality. Vera enjoys a room of her own, respect from her husband, and meaningful, socially useful work. She organizes a sewing workshop according to collective principles, sharing the profits with the women workers, who soon realize it is best to live collectively, too. Personal possessiveness has no place in the lives of these "new people," as Chernyshevskii entitled them. When Vera Pavlovna falls in love with another man, her husband gracefully bows out of the picture, leaving her to marry the other. Toward the end of the novel, Chernyshevskii introduced the issue of higher education for women. Vera Pavlovna trains as a physician and begins to practice medicine; she also becomes a mother, although it is never quite clear who cares for the children while she is at work. A satisfying and egalitarian family life, organization of labor and life according to collective principles, work for the social good – here was Chernyshevskii's formula for women's liberation, inspired by the writings of the French utopian socialists and the actions of his own contemporaries. By depicting the personal and productive relations that would constitute the socialist future, Chernyshevskii's novel linked women's liberation with the more sweeping goals of social

---

[12] Quoted in Engel, *Mothers and Daughters*, 67.

[13] Ibid., 69; Peter Posevsky, "Love, Science and Politics in the Fiction of Shestidesiatnitsy N. P. Suslova and S. V. Kovalevskaia," *Russian Review* 58, no. 3 (July 1999), 368.

transformation and revolution. His book became a key work in shaping the outlook of this and subsequent generations.

Women and the Radical Movement

In their own fashion, conservative officials shared Chernyshevskii's belief in the radical implications of women's liberation. Almost from the first, they associated women's efforts to forge new lives with threats to the political order. The outbreak of student unrest in the early 1860s brought women's presence in university classrooms to an end, although women had played only a minimal role in the disorders. In July 1863, the Ministry of Education issued a directive to university councils banning women from the university; that winter, women were expelled from university lecture halls. A year later, the Medical Surgery Academy expelled women, too. "The question of the introduction of female physicians is, in my opinion, the first step in accomplishing the so-called emancipation of women, which has its origin and foundation in the communistic theories of St. Simon and others," explained P. A. Dubovitskii, the president of the Academy.[14] Varvara Kashevarova-Rudneva, an orphan of Jewish background, succeeded in remaining at the academy by promising to treat Bashkir women of Orenburg province, who refused treatment by male physicians on account of their religion. One of the physicians who sponsored her cautioned her to avoid student meetings at any cost. Recognizing that "the smallest slip would be grounds for expulsion," Kashevarova-Rudneva followed his advice "to the letter."[15]

Women such as Kashevarova-Rudneva, pursuing studies in fields that had previously been restricted to men, threatened to transgress the boundaries that separated women's work from men's. In response, the government reconfigured those boundaries by explicitly excluding women from state service for the first time and defining fields it considered appropriate for women. An imperial decree of January 14, 1871, encouraged women to train for work as midwives and elementary school teachers, but sought to limit women's employment in other occupations, among them clerical work, stenography, and telegraph operation. From some occupations, women were to be excluded altogether. The decree ordered government and public (*obshchestvennyi*) institutions to fire any woman who was currently employed in a position other than those the decree defined as appropriate. Over the next sixteen months, agents of the political police sought out hundreds of "persons of the female

[14] Quoted in Christine Johanson, *Women's Struggle for Higher Education in Russia, 1855–1900* (Montreal: McGill-Queens University Press, 1987), 25.
[15] Varvara Kashevarova-Rudneva, M. D., "An Autobiography," in Toby W. Clyman and Judith Vowles (eds.), *Russia Through Women's Eyes* (New Haven, Conn.: Yale University Press, 1996), 173–4.

sex," as police reports invariably phrased it, who were employed, for example, as cashiers and ticket sellers in railroad stations, as librarians in public
libraries, and as clerks in government offices and pressured their superiors
to dismiss them.[16] The decree became law. Although in the years to follow,
public and semipublic institutions increasingly hired women to fill clerical
and similar positions, and the law was both revised and flouted, civil service
positions remained permanently closed to women. When, in the early 1880s,
Kashevarova-Rudneva sought to fulfill the obligation she had incurred to the
Orenburg officials who had supported her education as a physician, this law
prevented her from doing so. The only position the local military administration could offer her was in the military hospital. Part of the state system, the
position would have granted her all the privileges enjoyed by male servitors.
Consequently, in the eyes of the authorities, it would have created a dangerous
precedent. So, recalled Kashevarova-Rudneva, "they decided not to give me
a position, despite the money they had spent on my education!!"[17]

It is a measure of the determination and skill of women's movement leaders
that they accomplished so much in the face of such anxieties. By the late 1860s,
they aimed to establish advanced education for women. Dmitrii Tolstoy, the
conservative Minister of Education from 1866 to 1880, adamantly opposed it.
To admit women into universities, Tolstoy believed, "threatened to disturb
the seriousness of university teaching and to lower the intellectual and moral
level of these higher educational institutions."[18] Women's personal connections and political skills helped to overcome his resistance. Anna Filosofova
took to lobbying Tolstoy at the society functions and balls to which she accompanied her well-placed husband. Although Filosofova's behavior earned
her the reputation of being a "red" in high government circles, she, like her
colleagues, self-consciously adopted moderate tactics and avoided the violent confrontations that increasingly characterized the student and radical
movements. Instead, the women sought to attain their goals through personal appeals and petitioning. They gathered signatures in favor of advanced
education for women from hundreds of women, including members of high
society, from liberal members of the government, and many male professors.
These tactics worked. Thanks to them, women gained access to advanced
secondary courses (the Alarchinskii courses, 1869), university preparatory
courses (the Liubianskii courses, 1869), and courses that prepared women
for secondary school teaching (the Guerrier courses, 1872).

Government fears concerning female radicalism actually assisted the campaign for women's higher education, at least in the short run. Frustrated by

---

[16] Gosudarstvennyi Arkhiv Rossiiskoi Federatsii, fond 109, Third Section, 2 ekspeditsiia, 1870, delo
685.
[17] Kashevarova-Rudneva, "An Autobiography," 184.
[18] Quoted in Johanson, *Women's Struggle*, 33.

their inability to earn a university or medical degree at home, and inspired by the example of Nadezhda Suslova, women sought professional training abroad. Most went to Zurich, Switzerland, where the university admitted women: by 1873, 104 women had enrolled. But the Swiss canton of Zurich also harbored the largest and most active Russian émigré colony in Western Europe. The government grew concerned that in foreign lands, women students would imbibe dangerous ideas. To provide educational opportunities in the relative security of the homeland, as well as to satisfy Russia's pressing need for trained medical personnel, in 1872 the government established four-year-long Courses for Learned Midwives in St. Petersburg. The following year, a government decree ordered women studying abroad to return to Russia, threatening that those who resisted would be barred from licensing examinations in Russia. In 1876, an additional year was added to the Courses for Learned Midwives and the courses renamed Women's Medical Courses. Graduates became qualified to work as physicians. That same year, the government sanctioned the opening of "higher courses" for women, essentially, women's universities that awarded no degree. Kazan University became the first to take advantage of the opportunity; in 1878, Kiev and St. Petersburg followed. The St. Petersburg courses, known as the Bestuzhev courses, became the most well-known and long-lasting. Within a decade, the advanced educational opportunities that Russia offered women had surpassed those of every other nation in Europe.

The Quest for Knowledge

Many women eagerly grasped new educational opportunities. When Elizaveta Kovalskaia organized free courses for women seeking higher education in Kharkov in the mid 1860s, so many women wanted to audit that she had trouble squeezing them all into her house. The first year that the Lubianskii courses opened, they admitted 190 students; the Alarchinskii courses admitted more than 100. The numbers grew rapidly. By 1878–9, some 1300 students attended higher courses during the academic year.[19] Although the majority of these students derived from elite backgrounds, there were women of more humble origins among them. Praskovia Ivanovskaia, the daughter of a village priest in Tula province, had long dreamed of enrolling in the Alarchinskii courses. After graduating from the local parish school, she set off for St. Petersburg together with her sister. The courses, she discovered, were set up "strictly on democratic principles. . . . Everyone who was fresh and alive passed through its laboratory, as water passes through sand."[20] Alongside

[19] Ibid., 42, 45–7, 65.
[20] Barbara Alpern Engel and Clifford Rosenthal (eds.), *Five Sisters: Women Against the Tsar* (New York: Knopf 1975), 101.

daughters of nobles and bureaucrats, merchants, clergy, and professionals sat the daughters of lower officials, townsmen, craftsmen, soldiers, and peasants. And although anti-Semitism was rife in Russian society, it appears to have been entirely absent in the hallways of the Women's Medical Courses, where Jewish women comprised close to one-third of students at the end of the 1870s. The social distinctions that continued by law to divide tsarist subjects seemed to dissolve in the hallways of women's educational institutions.

To gain access to those institutions, women often had to pay a hefty price, financial and, sometimes, personal. To be sure, some parents proved supportive. The three Subbotina sisters, for example, noblewomen by birth, were fortunate in their widowed mother, Sofia. In addition to subsidizing the studies of her daughters in Zurich, Sofia Subbotina also paid for the education of their friend, Anna Toporkova, the daughter of a silversmith. The father of Alexandra Kornilova, a merchant who oversaw a flourishing trade in porcelain, regarded benignly the behavior of his four daughters and their friends. To an aunt who was appalled by their "nihilist" appearance and the fact that the girls attended the Alarchinskii courses and returned home late and unescorted in the evenings, the father responded laughingly, "I can't hire four governesses for them."[21] But other parents regarded their daughter's aspirations with suspicion. Faced with her father's adamant refusal to permit her to pursue advanced studies in mathematics, Sofia Kovalevskaia contracted a fictious marriage in 1868. She went off to study at Heidelburg, and became Europe's first woman doctorate in mathematics and the first woman to hold a university chair (in Stockholm). Closely guarded by her father, who hated "superfluous" learning, Anna Evreinova, the daughter of the high-ranking commandant of Pavlovsk, crossed the frontier illegally in order to pursue her studies at the University of Leipzig.[22] Some women students bore the scars of the bitter struggle they had had to wage on behalf of their right to study. According to those who knew her, that struggle left Teofilia Poliak, a student at the Women's Medical Courses and the daughter of a Jewish townsman, sarcastic, distrustful, and pessimistic.

Students also endured material deprivations for the sake of their education. It cost an annual fee of fifty rubles per year to attend the higher courses, severely reducing the presence of women of the lower social orders. Daughters of the nobility, unlike sons, were ineligible for government stipends. On their own, women students lived in damp and crowded quarters, three or four of them to a room, often sleeping in the same bed by turns, eating meals in cheap cookshops and subsisting on sausage, black bread, and tea. To earn a few

---

[21] Quoted in Engel, *Mothers and Daughters*, 112.
[22] Stites, *The Women's Liberation Movement*, 106.

kopeks, they stayed up all night copying documents.[23] Some failed to survive: at least three of the auditors of women's higher courses died of starvation; of the eighty-nine students who enrolled in the Courses for Learned Midwives in 1872, twelve were dead before their graduation in 1876. One, the daughter of a rank-and-file soldier who had gained entry to medical school entirely through her own efforts, died during the final examination itself. In subsequent years, better funding increased the survival rate of women medical students. Even so, by 1880, death had claimed fifteen more of them.

Nevertheless, many found this an exciting time. In the classroom and student quarters of cities, students discovered others like themselves, young women with whom they could share ideas and experiences, often for the first time. The experience was electrifying, especially for those women who had grown up in provincial isolation or in sheltered households. Circles and discussion groups proliferated. In St. Petersburg, meetings of women's circles became so common that women barely had time to go from one meeting to the next. In smoke-filled rooms, fortified by endless cups of tea, young women in simple clothing – the uniform of the *nigilistka* – discussed "the woman question" and exchanged their views on marriage and the family, on women's position in society, and on their purpose in life. Some adopted extreme positions, seeking "to liberate themselves from the stagnant past and all tradition, from the family and from the marital authority that had enslaved them," as did Alexandra Kornilova and her closest companions.[24] Social themes also drew women's attention, partly under the influence of Chernyshevskii. In addition to their regular coursework, women read and discussed books that dealt with social problems and their solution. They read Chernyshevskii, John Stuart Mill, even Karl Marx, following the translation of *Das Kapital* into Russian in 1872.

After completing schoolwork, most former students sought employment as midwives, medical assistants (*fel'dshery*), pharmacists, physicians, journalists, and most commonly of all, teachers. Of the 796 women who enrolled in the Women's Medical courses, 698 graduated, giving Russia a far larger number of practicing female physicians than other European nations. Most graduates of the Bestuzhev courses became teachers. The profession of teaching became increasingly feminized: in rural areas, women constituted 20 percent of rural teachers in 1880, and close to 40 percent by 1894. In addition to being a means to earn a living, many women viewed their work in broader terms as well. For some, it offered a means to improve women's status: "in the name of advancing our movement forward . . . I would not only walk through the mud

---

[23] Johanson, *Women's Struggle*, 64.   [24] Quoted in Engel, *Mothers and Daughters*, 113.

but wallow in it," declared Varvara Nekrasova, a graduate of the Women's Medical Courses who served at the front during the Russo–Turkish war of 1877–8. In 1885, after becoming the first woman to be appointed to the staff of a hospital, A. F. Zhegina confided to a friend: "If I do nothing else worthwhile in my life, this will provide a bit of comfort in my old age. I have cast at least one more stone amidst the countless stones that have begun to fill the immense chasm that separates one half of humanity from the other."[25] Others acted on religious and philanthropic imperatives that their mothers and grandmothers had fulfilled in more traditional ways. In their diaries, for example, women teachers commonly depicted themselves as having sacrificed lives of comfort and forsaken friends and family in order to teach the children of the peasantry.[26]

These women professionals rarely lead easy lives. The demand for positions, especially as teachers, often exceeded the supply. Paid less than their male counterparts and often hired in less prestigious positions, many toiled in remote villages or in the most impoverished sections of the city. Ekaterina Slanskaia, who worked as a physician in the slums of St. Petersburg, received patients in the tiny apartment that was all that she could afford. Some patients waited in the entryway, some in her kitchen, some on the stairs. On the days she made house calls, she worked from 8:00 A.M. until late into the night. As women, they faced prejudice from their superiors and in the countryside, from those whom they sought to serve. Considering the woman teacher a *baryshnia*, that is, a lady, peasant villagers regarded her as incapable of disciplining their children. They distrusted her knowledge and believed she should be paid less than a male teacher. In some cases, peasants even tried to drive women teachers from the village by making life thoroughly miserable for them.[27] Persevering in the face of such obstacles, these professional women devoted their lives to serving the people.

Service of Another Sort

Others chose to serve in a different fashion. Precisely as government officials had feared, educational opportunities eventually led a minority of women students to oppose the social and political order. Vera Figner was one of them. Born in 1852, the oldest of six children in a well-to-do noble family, she spent her childhood in the backwoods of provincial Kazan, her adolescence in the Smolnyi Institute. After her graduation, a liberal uncle drew her

---

[25] Ibid., 169, 170.

[26] Christine Ruane, *Gender, Class, and the Professionalization of Russian City Teachers, 1860–1914* (Pittsburgh, Pa.: University of Pittsburgh Press, 1994), 33, 71.

[27] Ben Eklof, *Russian Peasant Schools: Officialdom, Village Culture, and Popular Pedagogy, 1861–1914* (Berkeley, Calif.: University of California Press, 1986), 188–9.

attention to the disparity between her own privileged status as a noble and the destitution of the peasantry, and she resolved to devote her life to working for their benefit. The example of Nadezhda Suslova convinced her to become a physician. Because it was impossible to study medicine in Russia at the time, she resolved to go to Zurich. When her father refused his permission, she accepted a marriage proposal from Aleksei Filippov, a young candidate in law, and convinced her smitten husband to accompany her abroad. She embarked on her studies in the spring of 1872, at the age of 19. In Zurich, discussions with women like herself eventually convinced her that her own privileged position rested upon the exploitation of "the people," that is, Russia's peasantry and that however dedicated, professionals of every stripe nevertheless "lived at the people's expense."[28] The only way to draw close to "the people" was to abandon one's privileged position and live among them. A semester short of earning her degree, Figner quit medical school, returned to Russia, and became involved in the radical movement that her schoolmates had already joined.

Hundreds of young women followed a similar path. Abandoning or neglecting their studies, they joined forces with men to serve the greater good. Convinced that the Russian peasantry was inherently socialist by virtue of its communal landownership and administration, these radicals (called populists, or *narodniki*, in Russian) aspired to devote themselves to "the people." These populists wanted to repay the debt that they believed they owed "the people." Some wished, sooner or later, to help foment a peasant-based socialist revolution. Very few were themselves peasants. Instead, the majority of women activists came from noble or bureaucratic or other privileged backgrounds; virtually all of them had received some advanced education. Most took up the cause of the Russian peasantry at a very early age (under twenty). They joined a movement that was self-consciously egalitarian and based on principles of honesty and mutual respect among comrades.

In 1874, women went to "the people" as men did, in an effort to overcome the vast social chasm that separated them from the peasantry. Some disguised themselves as peasants or factory workers. Praskovia Ivanovskaia reaped and bound hay alongside peasant women, ate the same watery gruel for breakfast and slept with her co-workers under an open sky after a workday that lasted from sunup to sundown. Beta Kaminskaia, the only child of a well-to-do Jewish merchant, labored in a rope factory. She, too, lived just like her co-workers, in an airless, filthy, and vermin-ridden dormitory, beginning work at 4:00 A.M., and ending it at 8:00 P.M., and working while sitting on a damp and filthy floor. Others took positions in the countryside that were somewhat less demanding – that is, they worked as teachers, midwives, and medical

[28] Engel, *Mothers and Daughters*, 138.

aides. Vera Figner became one of these, finding a position as a paramedical worker for a *zemstvo*.

Everywhere, these young idealists met frustration. Co-workers, exhausted after a long day, proved deaf to attempts to promote socialist ideas, which bounced off them "like peas off a wall." Two or three months working in a rope factory was more than enough for Praskovia Ivanovskaia, who found the conditions difficult and depressing. Women encountered suspicion, too. Very quickly, Vera Figner found that a whole league of local officials had organized against her. "They spread all sorts of false rumors: that I had no identity card, that my diploma was false, and so forth. . . . People began to be afraid of me: peasants made detours through back yards when they visited my house."[29] When they tried to spread socialist propaganda, few of the women exercised the necessary care; they spoke openly, carried leaflets on their person, rarely attempted to conceal their ideas and goals. Yet discussing socialism, or even hinting at injustice in the existing order, was cause for arrest. By the end of the 1870s, hundreds of populist women sat in prison.

A woman initiated the next phase of the radical movement. In January 1878, Vera Zasulich, a member of a revolutionary circle from the south of Russia, shot General Trepov, the governor general of St. Petersburg, before a room full of witnesses. A daughter of impoverished nobility, Zasulich had already suffered four years of prison and exile for her involvement in the notorious Nechaev affair of the late 1860s. At her trial for the shooting of Trepov, she explained that she had acted because Trepov had ordered a political prisoner beaten for his refusal to remove his cap in the governor's presence. "I waited for some response," she declared. "There was nothing to stop Trepov, or someone just as powerful as he, from repeating the same violence over and over. I resolved at that point, even if it cost my life, to prove that no one who abused a human being that way could be sure of getting away with it."[30] The jury that considered her case acquitted Zasulich, ending the government's willingness to bring political cases before the new courts.

The revolutionary movement divided over the use of violence for political purposes. Some (including Zasulich herself) held to the peaceful populist program and rejected the use of terror. Others embraced terrorism, with bloody consequences. Their rationale was both personal and political. They wanted to avenge themselves for their comrades' sufferings in prison; they hoped to force the government to concede civil liberties such as freedom of speech, press, and assembly. Many had grown impatient for change. "My past experience had convinced me that the only way to change the existing order was by force," Vera Figner explained at her trial. The target was the

[29] *Five Sisters*, 41.   [30] Ibid., 78.

tsar himself and prominent government officials. Five abortive attempts to assassinate the tsar preceded the successful assault of March 1, 1881. Each attempt cost the lives of innocent people. A woman, Sofia Perovskaia, led the successful attack on Tsar Alexander II. She became the first Russian woman to be executed for a political crime. Perovskaia claimed to have no regrets about what she had done: "I have lived according to my convictions; I could not have acted otherwise, and so I await the future with a clear conscience," she told her mother on the eve of her execution by hanging.[31]

To the modern eye as well as to their own contemporaries, these women appeared as strikingly self-denying. They brought an exaltation and intensity to their radical activity that often distinguished them from their male comrades. In order to act upon their commitment to "the people," women neglected or denied their conventional social roles. They refused to be dutiful daughters or submissive wives. Instead, they entered fictitious marriages to elude parents who sought to limit their freedom, and left husbands whose views did not coincide with their own, as Figner eventually did. To avoid pregnancy or emotional entanglement, some sought to avoid sexual relations altogether. This was the course adopted by the women's circle that Figner joined in Zurich. When the women negotiated their union with a group of men in preparation for activity back in Russia, the women pressed for the inclusion of celibacy in their organization's regulations. The men over-ruled them.

Sofia Perovskaia, who began an affair with her comrade Andrei Zheliabov in the final year of terrorist struggle, had insisted to her brother only a year before that she would never become involved with a man so long as the struggle continued. "That sort of personal happiness would be absolutely impossible for me, because however much I loved a man, every moment of attraction would be poisoned by the awareness that my beloved friends were perishing [in prison]...and that 'the people' still suffered under the yoke of despotism."[32] Neither she nor Zheliabov allowed the relationship to interfere with their revolutionary work. Women who did become sexually involved with men and bore children usually left the children in the care of others and returned to the revolutionary movement. Olga Liubatovich, a former member of Figner's Zurich circle, posed the problem dramatically: "Yes, it's a sin for revolutionaries to start a family. Men and women both must stand alone, like soldiers under a hail of bullets. But in your youth, you sometimes forget that revolutionaries' lives are measured not in years, but in days and hours."[33] At times, women's self-denying asceticism risked becoming

[31] Ibid., 43; Engel, *Mothers and Daughters*, 199.

[32] Vasilii I. Perovskii, *Vospominaniia o sestre* (Moscow: Gosudarstvennoe Izd-vo, 1927), 50.

[33] *Five Sisters*, 196.

absurd, as for example, when Sofia Bardina, also a member of Figner's circle, confessed to loving strawberries and cream and thereafter, was considered a *bourgeois* by other members of her group. But for the most part, others found women's self-denial compelling and not ridiculous.

Radical women's asceticism had deep roots in Russia's culture. Although most of them were atheists, in explaining themselves, women sometimes invoked principles rooted in the Russian Orthodox religious faith that remained a powerful element in their culture. Vera Zasulich serves as one example. After fleeing abroad following her acquittal in the Trepov affair, she became one of the founders of Russian Marxism. Later, reflecting on her own life, she attributed her first moral lesson to the Gospels, and wrote that it was her quest "for a crown of thorns" that attracted her to the revolutionary movement. Vera Figner, too, claimed the Gospels influenced her and her classmates. "It was the most authoritative source we knew, not only because we had grown used to seeing it as a holy book in childhood, but because of its inner spiritual beauty." From the Gospels, she and her friends drew the lesson that "self-sacrifice is the most supreme act of which man is capable."[34]

Radical women's selflessness and readiness for self-sacrifice greatly endeared them to their comrades, who regarded them as moral exemplars and inspirations. "She seemed to us the embodiment of everything elevated, excellent, altruistic and ideal. She was self-sacrificing in matters large and small," reads a typical description.[35] Such behavior also won them the sympathy of the educated public. "They are Saints!" declared the spectators at one political trial, the Trial of the Fifty (1877), which included many women who had abandoned lives of privilege to work in factories. These exemplary attributes were gender-neutral, in the sense that men, too, could embody them. But judging by the accounts of the people who knew them, men felt far less impelled than women to become exemplars.

Conclusion

The reform era offered far-reaching challenges to Russia's elite gender order. The subordination of women to men and the family became subject to biting critiques; progressive opinion encouraged women to contribute their special energies to the regeneration of society as a whole. Advanced education became available to women for the first time. New employment opportunities opened, especially in the fields of medicine and teaching. For the first time, thousands of educated women attained economic independence and a greater freedom to shape their own lives. Hundreds more joined radical movements that sought

---

[34] Quoted in Engel, *Mothers and Daughters*, 141.   [35] Ibid., 180.

to overturn Russia's social and political order. Social boundaries dissolved when the daughters of townsmen, clergy, peasants, soldiers, and merchants joined the daughters of nobles and bureaucratic elites in lecture halls and prison cells.

Yet for all these changes, some things remained the same. When they rebelled against the confining aspects of the traditional female role, women often drew upon ideals of altruism and self-sacrifice that were rooted in religious tradition – just as the Decembrist wives had done half a century before. "We aspired to a pure life and to personal sanctity," recalled Vera Figner.[36] These ideals offered a compelling alternative to the ideology of domesticity that some elites had embraced and they allowed women to insert themselves into the public events of their time. Despite the radical women's more visible role, their moral aspirations and rationale for activism resembled those of their law-abiding sisters. Like radicals, women teachers often sought to serve "the people" and they too, renounced their own sexuality to pursue their pedagogical mission. By caring for young children, teachers believed that they fulfilled their religious and family roles – but not within the family.

Self-denial and altruism – service of another sort – provided women with access to a life outside the home. It also set a standard of behavior that people of subsequent generations would expect from women in public life and that women themselves would often strive to emulate.

Suggestions for Further Reading

Chernyshevskii, Nikolai. *What Is to Be Done?* Translated by Michael Katz and introduced by William Wagner. Ithaca, N.Y.: Cornell University Press, 1989. *An outstanding translation of Chernyshevkii's influential novel.*

Curtiss, John S. "Russian Sisters of Mercy in the Crimea, 1854–55," *Slavic Review* 25, no. 1 (March 1966), 84–100.

Engel, Barbara Alpern. *Mothers and Daughters: Women of the Intelligentsia in Nineteenth Century Russia.* Evanston, Ill.: Northwestern University Press, 2000.

Engel, Barbara Alpern and Clifford Rosenthal (eds.). *Five Sisters: Women Against the Tsar.* New York: Routledge, 1992. *The memoirs of five revolutionary women of the 1870s.*

Johanson, Christine. *Women's Struggle for Higher Education in Russia, 1855–1900.* Montreal: McGill University Press, 1987. *An important study of the campaign for women's education.*

Khvoshchinskaia, Nadezhda. *The Boarding School Girl.* Translated, annotated, and introduced by Karen Rosneck. Evanston, Ill.: Northwestern University Press, 2000. *A woman's perspective on the changes wrought by the 1860s.*

[36] Ibid., 200–1.

Koblitz, Ann Hibner. *A Convergence of Lives. Sofia Kovalevskaia: Scientist, Writer, Revolutionary*. Boston: Birkhauser, 1983. *A biography of Europe's first doctorate in mathematics.*

Stites, Richard. *The Women's Liberation Movement in Russia: Feminism, Nihilism, and Bolshevism, 1860–1930*. Princeton, N.J.: Princeton University Press, 1990. *A pioneering study.*

Tishkin, Grigorii A. *Zhenskii vopros v Rossii v 50–60gg. xix v.* Leningrad: Leningrad University, 1984. *The first full-length study of the "woman question" to appear in Russia.*

5

PEASANTS AND PROLETARIANS

"I come from a peasant family with a home in the village of Mozhaevo, Kisemskii *uezd*, Vesegonsk district, Tver, where my family spends the summer; winters, they live in the town of Krasnoi Kholm. I had not yet reached the age of sixteen [the legal age of marriage] or become a woman when my parents, having overcome my resistance, married me off to the nineteen-year-old peasant Dmitrii Kulikov. . .who had already become corrupted. . ."[1]

Thus began the petition, five type-written pages in length, that Evdokia Ivanovna Kulikova addressed to the tsar on June 11, 1897. In it, Kulikova claimed to have endured virtually every abuse that a peasant household could inflict on a woman: an unwanted marriage to a drunken and abusive husband who "tyrannized" and mistreated her and fooled around with other women, a widowed father-in-law who seemed bent on seducing her while her husband was absent for military service. Having fled the village, Kulikova earned her living as a seamstress in the city of St. Petersburg. At the close of her petition, she requested the right to separate formally from her husband. Tens of thousands of peasant women deluged state and local authorities with similar requests toward the end of the nineteenth century, encouraged by new economic and cultural opportunities to sever their ties with their former way of life. Yet although these numbers are substantial, they represent but a tiny fraction of the more than 80 million peasants (about 86 percent of the population, according to the census of 1897) who lived scattered over the vast expanse of European Russia. Peasant women's petitions for marital separation signified both how much and how little had changed in their lives.

The Post-Emancipation Village

When it finally began in 1861, the emancipation of the serfs made remarkably little difference to the lives of most peasant women. Neither the terms of

---

[1] Russian State Historical Archive (hereafter RGIA), fond 1412, opis 221, ed. kh. 204 (Kulikova, 1897), 1.

the emancipation nor its immediate consequences disturbed long-standing patriarchal patterns of village life. Indeed, in some respects, the emancipation intensified them by shifting to peasant institutions the powers that noble masters had once enjoyed. Peasant life remained a struggle for survival, requiring unremitting toil and offering to most peasants little more than subsistence. In this struggle, the collective "we" took precedence over the individual "I." Although in the decades following the emancipation, far-reaching economic and cultural changes sweeping Russia began to impinge on village life, villagers accepted innovation selectively and only when the advantages were obvious and threats to the peasant way of life minimal or non-existent. Neither the emancipation nor subsequent changes upset the gendered hierarchy.

Peasant men, collectively, determined the community's common good. As a result of the emancipation, the assembly of male heads of household (the *skhod*) acquired the responsibility to maintain peace and order and the authority that went with it. The *skhod* was also responsible for land, which was the property of the community rather than of individuals. Allocating land as well as tax and redemption obligations to each household, the *skhod* became the primary arbiter of village life. Ordinarily, the *skhod* allocated land according to the number of adult males. Thus, land and formal authority in the community remained "male attributes"[2] except under unusual circumstances.

Women's authority, by contrast, was informal. As did men, women gained authority with age. The *bol'shukha*, wife of the household's head, supervised the women beneath her in the household hierarchy, assigning work, overseeing its performance, and punishing those who failed to do their share. Older women's words carried weight in the community, where reputation remained key to honor, which women's talk might make or break. Older women with the requisite skills served as healers or as the granny midwives (*babki*) who delivered virtually all village children. By contrast with male peasants who practiced a trade in the village and were paid in cash (blacksmiths and carpenters, for example), healers and midwives were usually compensated in kind: a loaf of bread, a few eggs, a length of fabric. *Babki* nevertheless enjoyed an honored place in village society.[3]

That women's position in the community could empower them is evident in instances where women defended their community's well-being against threats from outsiders. Take, for example, the behavior of the women of Arkhangelskaia, a village in Viatka province. In October 1890, the entire

---

[2] Rose Glickman, *Russian Factory Women: Workplace and Society, 1880–1914* (Berkeley, Calif.: University of California Press, 1984), 27.

[3] Rose Glickman, "The Peasant Woman as Healer," in Barbara Evans Clements, Barbara Alpern Engel, and Christine Worobec (eds.), *Russia's Women: Accommodation, Resistance, Transformation* (Berkeley, Calif.: University of California Press, 1991), 156–7.

village mobilized to prevent the police from inventorying and confiscating the moveable property of villagers in arrears on their tax payments. The women figured among the more aggressive. One threw mud at a policeman and threatened another with her stick; another woman struck a policeman. Two more women pushed a policeman in the chest, while a third tore the scarf from yet another policeman's neck as the crowd of peasants surrounded the intruders, calling them thieves and brigands. The police were forced to beat a hasty, if temporary, retreat. Brandishing hoes and pitchforks, women attacked policemen who sought to confiscate village property. Women figured prominently in other cases, too. They used their bodies to block efforts to survey disputed land. Axe-wielding women joined peasant men cutting trees in noblemen's forests. In the decades following the emancipation, women often played a visible role in defense of household and community.[4]

Most women found it more difficult to defend or assert themselves as individuals, however, and as far as can be determined, few tried. The necessities of collective survival determined women's choices and shaped their lives and life cycles. As long as the household formed the basic unit of production, marriage (and remarriage) remained an economic necessity as well as the expected mode of life. The young enjoyed somewhat more freedom to select their spouse than they had in the days of serfdom, engaging in lively courtship games and even, in some villages, pairing off and spending the night together in a version of the "bundling" practices that were widespread in colonial America. The final decision, nevertheless, belonged to the parents, who kept the interests of their household uppermost in their mind. Take the case of Evdokia Kulikova, whose impoverished peasant parents arranged for their daughter's marriage to Dmitrii, the son of a wealthy household, in order to ensure her economic well-being and perhaps, their own. Dmitrii's marital choices were limited by the bad reputation he had already acquired in the village. In marrying him off to a respectable and hardworking young woman, his parents hoped to settle him down as well as to add a woman worker to their household. Near-universal, early, and patrilocal marriage continued to be the norm. Most women wed by the age of twenty-two; by age fifty, only 4 percent of peasant women had not yet married.[5] Some of these spinsters had declined to marry for religious reasons, one of the few reasons that villagers honored. Commonly known as *chernichki* (literally, black wearers because of the dark clothing they habitually wore), these women lived alone in a hut on the outskirts of the village. Practicing celibacy and living a life of prayer, they

---

[4] Barbara Alpern Engel, "Men, Women and the Languages of Russian Peasant Resistance," in Stephen Frank and Mark Steinberg (eds.), *Cultures in Flux: Lower Class Values, Practices and Resistance in Late Imperial Russia* (Princeton, N.J.: Princeton University Press, 1994), 41–5.

[5] Christine Worobec, *Peasant Russia: Family and Community in the Post-Emancipation Period* (Princeton, N.J.: Princeton University Press, 1991), 124–8.

earned a meager income from spinning, weaving, or hiring out by the day or from preparing the dead for burial and reading the Psalter for them. They, and widowed female heads of households, were unique in their freedom from male authority.

But most women spent their lives directly subject to male authority. Regarding women as potentially unruly and disruptive, peasants believed that a woman required a man's control. Custom granted a husband the right to "instruct" a wife, by force if necessary, when the woman erred or was disobedient. "The more you beat your wife, the tastier the cabbage soup," as the saying went. Women's unchaste or adulterous behavior could sully a household's honor; contentious or discontented wives might damage its economic well-being. When complex households divided prematurely, peasants usually attributed the division to women's quarrels or to young wives' eagerness to escape their in-laws' authority. When a household's well-being and a woman's interests conflicted, village authorities almost invariably sided with the household.

This order of priorities is clear from the decisions of cantonal (*volost'*) courts, introduced by the government in 1864 to adjudicate disputes between peasants on the basis of customary law. Unlike the courts instituted by the judicial reforms of 1864, over which educated men presided, in the cantonal courts peasants themselves acted as judges. In respect to women's rights in marriage, peasant courts and regular courts usually rendered very different decisions. Historians have found that in the decades after their establishment, post-reform courts often rendered decisions that enhanced the rights of women. To Jewish women, the courts offered a means to defend rights to alimony and property that had hitherto been denied them, making divorce more expensive and difficult for men. The reformed courts defended the rights of peasant women, too. Toward the end of the nineteenth century, the State Senate, Russia's equivalent of a supreme court, rendered decisions that served to extend the grounds upon which peasant women might leave an abusive or neglectful husband, thereby increasing the ability of both regular courts and peasant officials to respond to such women's pleas.[6]

Such trends offer a contrast to the deliberations of the cantonal courts, to which peasant women most frequently appealed. To be sure, peasant women enjoyed considerable success when they sought to protect their property rights against the incursions of others. They were far less successful, however, when they sought relief from a husband's physical abuse. Many of the wifebeating cases that came before cantonal courts involved truly horrific

---

[6] ChaeRan Y. Freeze, *Jewish Marriage and Divorce in Imperial Russia* (Hanover, N.H.: University Press of New England, 2002), 205–10; William Wagner, *Marriage, Property and Law in Late Imperial Russia* (Oxford, England: Clarendon Press, 1994), 216–23.

treatment: a husband hitching his wife to a cart along with the horses, then flogging her and making her run all the way back to his village; a husband mercilessly beating his wife with an iron implement, and suchlike. However, even when a woman could provide evidence of chilling brutality by supplying the requisite witnesses, the court most often punished the husband by sentencing him to time in the "cooler," or to a fine or beating. The court then ordered the wife to return to his household and admonished her husband to treat her properly in the future. In rare cases, a cantonal court or village elder might accede to a woman's request to live separately; when that happened, they usually required her to pay a sum of money (known as *obrok*, or quitrent in popular parlance), to enable her husband's household to hire a replacement worker.[7] A household's viability remained the community's highest priority.

Even the welfare of infants took second place. Thus, Russian peasants had an unusually high rate of infant mortality, even by comparison with their Muslim Tatar neighbors, in part because Russian mothers, unlike Tatar mothers, were not spared from fieldwork even when their infants were nursing. In summer when they worked in the fields, Russian women usually left their infants at home, in the care of the elderly or young children, to be fed when hungry with the *soska* (a rag covering chewed bread or grain), which quickly putrefied in hot weather. The resulting stomach ailments carried off "astounding numbers" of village children.[8] Between 1887 and 1896, childhood mortality in European Russia was recorded as 432 per 1,000 live births. When physicians sought to ameliorate these conditions in the late nineteenth century, however, they encountered the resistance of peasant women. With the aid of scientific pamphlets aimed at a peasant audience, physicians campaigned against the widespread use of the *soska* and birthing with the aid of a "backward" village midwife, among other practices. Their campaign foundered, however, in the face of peasant women's interdependence and mutual support, which somehow coexisted with the tensions that occasionally tore a household apart. A young woman giving birth ordinarily relied on older women of her household for assistance and advice. When the advice of medical experts came into conflict with the methods of female kin, mothers rejected the experts. As a result, physicians who tried to reform ingrained practices waged a losing battle.[9]

---

[7] But see: Beatrice Farnsworth, "The Litigious Daughter-in-Law: Family Relations in Rural Russia in the Second Half of the Nineteenth Century," *Slavic Review* 45, no. 1 (Spring 1986), 49–64.

[8] David Ransel, "Infant-Care Cultures in the Russian Empire," in Clements, Engel, and Worobec, *Russia's Women*, 115–19.

[9] Nancy M. Frieden, "Child Care: Medical Reform in a Traditionalist Culture," in David Ransel (ed.) *The Family in Imperial Russia: New Lines of Historical Research* (Urbana, Ill.: University of Illinois Press, 1978), 249–51.

The Outside World Intrudes

Nevertheless, in the decades following the emancipation, the insularity of peasant life slowly began to give way. Efforts to increase popular literacy brought outside cultural influences to the village; the growing cash economy affected peasant consumption and patterns of work. Peasants adapted to these changes cautiously and selectively, however, and the changes were far more likely to affect men than women.

Education offers a good example. Following the emancipation of the serfs, the number of schools in the countryside expanded steadily. Between 1856 and 1896, the number of primary schools grew from 8,227 to 87,080 and the number of pupils from roughly 450,000 to roughly 3.8 million, the equivalent of 3.02 percent of the population. However, although the proportion of girl pupils grew from 8.2 to 21.3 percent, girls remained a distinct minority. Recognizing literacy as necessary for a son's future, most peasant parents regarded educating a daughter as frivolous. "Why should I teach a girl to read and write?" inquired one peasant. "She won't be a soldier, she won't be a shop assistant, and a peasant woman has no time to busy herself with reading books the way the lords do." "If you send her to school, she costs money; if you keep her at home, she makes money," declared another. Peasants regarded traditional skills such as a weaving and knitting as sufficient for girls. The results are reflected in rates of literacy. At the close of the nineteenth century, under 10 percent of peasant women could read and write according to the minimal standards of tsarist census-takers, by comparison with over a quarter of peasant men. Yet even this low rate represented an advance over earlier times, and rates were rising among the younger age groups. Peasant reluctance to send daughters to school eased only slowly. By 1911, when the number of primary school students reached more than 6.6 million (4.04 percent of the population), the proportion of girls stood at just under one-third.[10]

The expansion of the cash economy in the aftermath of emancipation likewise affected the sexes differently. For women, it meant most of all a change in consumption patterns: the wearing of colorful wool or silk dresses, expensive shawls, belts and leather shoes, even hats on special occasions. Manufactured clothing and urban-style fashion increasingly became a mark of prestige in the countryside. Marriageable young women sometimes took up seasonal summer work to afford them. But initially, men rather than women were the more likely to participate in the marketplace regularly and as individuals. To pay taxes and redeem their land, as well as to purchase consumer goods such

---

[10] Quoted in Jeffrey Brooks, *When Russia Learned to Read: Literacy and Popular Literature, 1861–1917* (Princeton, N.J.: Princeton University Press, 1985), 13; Ben Eklof, *Russian Peasant Schools: Officialdom, Village Culture and Popular Pedagogy, 1861–1914* (Berkeley, Calif.: University of California Press, 1986), 279, 310–13.

as kerosene, nails, tea, and sugar, or clothing for their daughters, peasants experienced a growing need for rubles. Increasing numbers took up other trades in addition to or instead of farming, especially in the area around Moscow known as the Central Industrial Region. Some men worked at home in their cottages, but ever more departed, leaving the wife to tend the land. The husband would visit on major holidays or during the slow season and send a portion of his earnings home. Because wives of absent husbands had to deal with local authorities and correspond with their men about domestic matters, literacy gained importance. In areas that had substantial male outmigration, women's literacy rates were noticeably above the average. But such women interacted with the marketplace mainly through men. "My dear husband, bring tea with you. . . . If there were money, we could have shoes made; in fact, one of the leather boots is falling apart and we need fur coats," wrote a wife to her migrant husband in the 1880s.[11]

In some respects, men's absence made women's lives more difficult. If the wife remained in the household of her in-laws, tensions could escalate, as they had in the Kulikov household. If the wife lived separately, the burden of farm work and household responsibilities fell squarely on her shoulders. In addition to her customary work in the fields and at home, she had to perform her husband's labor, too, including plowing, which is physically very demanding. But in other ways, women's lives might improve. In villages with a high proportion of absent men, wife beating became less frequent and was judged more harshly by fellow villagers. As was the case in Cossack villages of the Don Region, where men's absence to perform military duties left women in charge of farming, peasant men's dependence on women's labor afforded women an unusual degree of independence. Some even gained authority over village affairs. In villages where substantial numbers of male heads of households worked elsewhere, their wives might participate in the decisions of the *skhod*, ordinarily an exclusively male institution. As one village correspondent put it, "Women's vote is necessary, because men are absent, and it is just, because women do all the work."[12] If a household also needed women's income, they initially sought it close to home.

Many of the trades women practiced in their cottages, such as producing homespun flax and hemp for the market, or wet nursing and raising children from foundling homes in Moscow or St. Petersburg, were extensions of the work they had always performed. Laboring within the peasant household for the market added a new dimension to peasant women's work. The decades that followed the emancipation saw a rapid expansion of the number of women

[11] Quoted in Barbara Alpern Engel, *Between the Fields and the City: Women, Work and Family in Russia, 1861–1914* (New York: Cambridge University Press, 1994), 42.

[12] On Cossacks, see Shane O'Rourke, *Warriors and Peasants* (New York: St. Martin's Press, 2000), 161; Quote from Engel, *Between the Fields*, 54.

and girls thus employed, some as young as six. Stuck in the countryside, peasant women offered a limitless reserve of cheap labor. Working in their cottages, they wound cotton thread on bobbins for a factory or sewed kid gloves or rolled hollow tubes for cigarettes from materials distributed by an entrepreneur, who paid them for their work and sold the finished product. Even independent craftswomen such as lace makers and stocking knitters often depended on middlemen to market their goods.

In many respects, these women had the worst of both worlds. Their intermediary position between household and market left them vulnerable to exploitation by middlemen and, much more rarely, middlewomen (often widows), who took advantage of the other women's inability to leave home to seek better terms. Nor did their modest financial contributions noticeably enhance women's status at home.[13] Connected to the market by virtue of their income-producing activities, they nevertheless worked within the traditional patriarchal household. This was often the case even for the tens of thousands of peasant women who earned wages in nearby factories. Almost two-thirds of Russian industry, most of it producing textiles, was located in or near peasant villages. In the Vladimir-Kostroma textile region northeast of Moscow, women came to constitute over 40 percent of the rural-based industrial labor force by the end of the nineteenth century. However, household need continued to govern the rhythms of most peasant women's labor. Women labored at the factory while they were young and single, and they quit when they married or had children, unless there were older women in the household to raise the children for them. They regularly handed over a portion of their wages to the household head. As long as women remained in or near the village, patriarchal patterns continued to govern their lives. The vast majority of peasant women never ventured far from home.

Nevertheless, a growing minority of peasant women did leave to seek their fortune elsewhere. Many of them really needed the money, either for themselves or more likely, to help out the folks back home. Over time, it grew harder to earn money in the village. Factories began producing more cheaply the goods that women had once made by hand, reducing what women could earn from them to a bare pittance. Unmarried older women and widows found it relatively easy to depart, because they were the village's most marginal members. The obstacles were far greater for a marriageable girl or a married woman. Women's chastity remained important for a household's honor. Away from the patriarchal controls of village life and the scrutiny of fellow villagers, a woman might succumb to sexual temptation, might fall "despite herself."[14] Married women needed their husband's permission to leave and if they had children, usually left them in the care of others.

[13] Glickman, *Russian Factory Women*, 34–52.   [14] Engel, *Between the Fields*, 65.

Most women who departed did not go alone. Women from the same village or district might form *artels* (work collectives) and travel together to labor in other people's fields, cut peat in the swamps around Moscow, make bricks, harvest tobacco, or perform a variety of other poorly paid and backbreaking tasks. Women who worked year-round most often became domestic servants, as Evdokia Kulikova did when she first left her husband. Like most female migrants, Kulikova initially went to a place where she knew someone, in her case the town of Krasnoi Kholm. Kulikova eventually made her way to a larger city, another common pattern. By the early twentieth century, women constituted a significant minority of the migrant peasant population of both St. Petersburg and Moscow. Unlike Kulikova, however, most women migrants, having spent a few years in the city and scraped together a dowry, returned to the village to wed and settle down.

In the City

The move from village to city dramatically altered some migrant women's lives, although very few had sought the change for its own sake. Historians disagree about the impact of migration and waged labor on women. Peasant women usually left home in order to feed themselves, earn a dowry, and, if possible, contribute to their family economy. Economic necessity drove the women whom Praskovia Ivanovskaia encountered at an Odessa rope factory in the late 1870s; they had nowhere else to go "but the streets." They were "driven to the rope factory by the most pressing need, by the cruellist misfortune," Ivanovskaia concluded.[15] Peasant women who earned wages, Kulikova among them, sent a portion to parents or in-laws.

Most women who worked experienced demoralizing working and living conditions. Women's proportion in the burgeoning factory labor force grew from about one in every five workers in 1885 to about one in every three by 1914. Before 1897, when factory legislation mandated a workday of eleven and one half hours, women workers often labored fourteen or more hours a day, six days a week. They lived in factory dormitories, where dozens crowded together in a single large room, or they rented a corner just big enough for their bed in an apartment. Factory women may have dreamed of a room of their own, but on their meager earnings, it was an unattainable luxury. The working and living conditions of the domestic servant were even more austere. In overcrowded urban apartments, many domestic servants lacked even the modest refuge available to their servant sisters in the West. Instead, they spent the night behind a screen in the passageway, or in the kitchen, or

---

[15] Barbara Alpern Engel and Clifford Rosenthal (eds.), *Five Sisters: Women Against the Tsar* (New York: Knopf 1975), 104.

even by the bed of their employer. The servant's wage was low, her position often insecure, the work never-ending. Many enjoyed hardly any life outside the workplace. Did industrial labor leave the woman worker isolated and oppressed, so poorly paid that she was barred from the entertainments that her male counterparts enjoyed, as Rose Glickman has contended?[16] Were domestic servants merely "white slaves," performing the most degrading and undesirable of women's work, existing as easy prey for sexual exploitation? Or did migration offer women a new kind of independence and freedom from patriarchal control?

There is evidence to support both sides of the argument. Particularly in the early post-emancipation years, the lives of laboring women were grim indeed, as radical women who attempted to organize women factory workers learned to their dismay. The women who labored beside Praskovia Ivanovskaia spent every break in their workday asleep, curled up on the filthy ropes on which they worked, breathing air thick with resin and soap. Of her co-workers' misery and desperation, Ivanovskaia observed: "Only women in this situation would put up with the ubiquitous rudeness, the men's disrespectful treatment of them, the pinches and searches as they entered or left the factory."[17] Women workers had lower rates of literacy than men and received a fraction of men's wages. Earning barely enough for subsistence, they seemed to have survived on a diet of bread and cucumbers. And their gender barred them from many of the opportunities to socialize and exchange ideas enjoyed by men. Male sociability based on drinking took place in taverns, inns, and alehouses, which were all-male spaces. A woman who turned up there risked being labeled a prostitute. The domestic servant was even more isolated and vulnerable than the worker. Perhaps as a result, domestic servants were disproportionately represented among women who abandoned their illegitimate children to foundling homes.

Migrant women also encountered male misogyny in some ways reminiscent of village life but perhaps even more intense on account of the women's relative freedom from patriarchal control and the change in migrant men's status. Now living and working separately from women, men no longer derived their sense of masculinity from their patriarchal role in the family. Instead, struggling to compensate for their helplessness in the capitalist workplace, they forged an intensely masculinized culture at work. Swearing, telling dirty jokes, and boasting about sexual conquests were ways of letting off steam and of demonstrating that a worker was "one of the lads."[18] When work was slow, printworkers would gather around the shop window, rating the legs of

---

[16] Glickman, *Russian Factory Women*, 80–1, 105–32.   [17] Engel and Rosenthal, *Five Sisters*, 104.

[18] Steve A. Smith, "Masculinity in Transition: Peasant Migrants to Late-Imperial St. Petersburg," in Barbara Clements, Rebecca Friedman, and Dan Healey (eds.), *Russian Masculinities in History and Culture* (New York, Palgrave: 2002), 99.

the women passing by. In tales of sexual adventures with women, "All was spoken openly, shamelessly, down to the last detail."[19] Excluding women constituted an important component of this workplace culture, making sharing the shop floor unpleasant, even dangerous, for women workers. Working men sometimes sexually harassed their female co-workers or treated them as if they were prostitutes. "All the time one hears from them [nothing but] insults and obscene propositions," a woman worker complained.[20] Men who had become politically and socially "conscious" eschewed this kind of behavior, forming instead a community of brothers. Still, for some, misogyny acquired a new dimension: the woman worker was "backward," a "creature of a lower order," an extension of the peasant milieu and an obstacle to men's development. Men who embraced the cause of revolution often viewed a negative attitude toward the family, marriage, even women in general as "a necessity."[21]

Even so, cities offered peasant women opportunities. With a wage of their own in hand, women could extend their horizons and alter their fates in ways that were unthinkable in the village. Evdokia Kulikova was one beneficiary, aided by her ability to read and write. After a few years as a domestic, she enrolled in tailoring courses, where she mastered the craft of sewing women's clothing and men's and women's underclothes, and began working as a skilled seamstress. Other women, too, felt "the ground of independence" beneath their feet, in the words of the weaver Taisia Slovachevskaia. Aspiring to emulate the appearance of their social betters, women workers spent their wages on urban-style fashions, skimping on food in order to afford a pair of boots or an attractive dress, which they paid a seamstress to copy from a shop window or a magazine (Fig. 8). Or like Kulikova, they made their clothing themselves. When, sporting a gold watch and fashionable dress, she returned to her husband's village to renew her passport, to the villagers Kulikova looked "just like a lady."[22] In their free time, women workers sought to enjoy themselves. Urban fairs and pleasure gardens offered them inexpensive entertainments. Women eagerly participated in the amateur workers' theaters that proliferated after the turn of the century, which cost them nothing. A few women workers attended the theater, too, purchasing the inexpensive tickets offered by the People's House, an organization designed to provide edifying culture to the masses. Many more were likely to go to the movies, which became more accessible in the years before the outbreak of World War I. By inviting women to dress and amuse themselves in ways that women of other classes did, city life could erode social boundaries and make social distinctions seem less relevant.

[19] Quoted in Mark Steinberg, *Moral Communities: The Culture of Class Relations in the Russian Printing Industry, 1867–1907* (Berkeley, Calif.: University of California Press, 1992), 78.
[20] Quoted in Glickman, *Russian Factory Women*, 205.   [21] Engel, *Between the Fields*, 137.
[22] Engel, *Between the Fields*, 152; RGIA, fond 1412, opis 221, ed. kh. 204 (Kulikova, 1897), 20.

8. The Vorobieva sisters, courtesy of Iurii Bogorodskii

The experience of urban life could also leave women dissatisfied with circumstances that they had once taken for granted. Young village women, sent off to provincial towns for training as skilled midwives, refused to return to the countryside once their education ended. Instead, they took examinations to qualify them for urban practice and quickly moved to the city. Some migrant women lost the habit of fieldwork and developed a taste for urban amenities. City life could make social difference seem more burdensome and unjust. Proximity to the more well-to-do, the sense of new possibilities in life, raised laboring women's expectations without providing the women with the economic wherewithal to satisfy them or altering workplace practices that humiliated and demeaned women. Rising expectations would contribute to women's militancy.

Working women who had acquired a sense of their own dignity became more likely to resist abuses. Although women played a minor role in underground worker circles or in the strikes and labor organizations that remained illegal until 1905, in the 1890s a few working-class women sought to organize women such as themselves. One was Vera Karelina, born in 1870 and abandoned to a foundling home shortly after her birth. Following the death of her peasant foster mother, Karelina became a hospital worker and then a worker at a cotton spinning mill. In a workers' study circle, Karelina read radical literature at the end of a fourteen to sixteen hour workday and on Sundays. Another activist was Anna Boldyreva, a peasant from Tver province. Born the same year as Karelina, Boldyreva began her working life at the age of nine. A weaver at the Paul cotton weaving plant in St. Petersburg, she attended a Sunday school for workers in the mid-1880s and was drawn into an underground workers' study circle. In the early 1890s, the two women collaborated in organizing a small circle of women workers who read and discussed socialist literature together. They conducted themselves in the tradition of intelligentsia radicals of the 1870s. Living communally with working-class men, they shared wages, cooking, and housework. Equality and comradeship replaced traditional sex roles: "Among us there were no stupid jokes or coquetry. There was only purity of relations," remembered Karelina.[23]

Whatever the experience of an individual woman, and whatever the nature of her relations with men, it was women's freedom rather than its limitations that most struck many of their male contemporaries, tsarist officials among them. The growth of prostitution served as the most visible and troubling symbol of women's license. Suspecting all lower-class women on their own of "trading in vice," the state attempted to substitute for absent husbands and fathers its own patriarchal power. Women of the lower classes who thronged to Russia's cities in the latter part of the century felt the weight of laws governing prostitution, which were augmented following the emancipation of the serfs. The vague definition of the prostitute as a woman who "traded in vice" meant that women who plied the trade casually and intermittently – or perhaps not at all – risked encountering the police and becoming registered as a "professional" prostitute. A registered prostitute had to surrender her internal passport in exchange for a "yellow ticket" that clearly

---

[23] Quoted in Glickman, *Russian Factory Women*, 173–80.

identified her trade and subjected her to police surveillance and weekly medical examinations to check for syphilitic infection.

The regulation system seriously reduced lower-class women's autonomy and freedom of movement. To ensure that women did not ply the trade secretly, special police agents encouraged yardmen (*dvorniki*) and landladies to keep an eye on unattached women suspected of prostitution. Ordinary citizens wrote letters to the medical police, anonymously denouncing women as prostitutes. "Such women spread disease and they should be given a ticket so that doctors will know who they are," reads one such anonymous letter, like most deriving from a lower-class male who had had sex with the woman he denounced.[24] Unattached women who were temporarily without a job were the most vulnerable to enforced registration. Once registered as a prostitute, women found it difficult to leave the profession because the process was lengthy and cumbersome. Establishing a relationship with a man offered one of the easiest ways to escape, thus encouraging women's dependence on men.

Courtship and Family Life

Women migrants brought many peasant expectations with them to the city, including the expectation of marrying. Economics added a practical dimension. A talented seamstress, Kulikova, for example, earned about twenty-five to thirty rubles a month, which was roughly twice as much as the average for women in the tailoring trades. Most women barely scraped by. In every trade, men earned much more than women. Having a claim on a man's wage could bring greater comfort and a higher level of material well-being than most women could attain on their own, in addition, perhaps, to emotional satisfaction. Marriage also provided social security in a society with no systematic provision for sickness or old age. Some women nurtured romantic aspirations, perhaps because they encountered images of romantic love in many of the new urban entertainments. "I wanted to marry for love," remembered a woman worker.[25] Others simply sought a refuge from the hardships of the world. But courtship, highly ritualized in rural areas, could prove problematic in an urban setting.

Urban life itself was not welcoming to families. In terms of housing costs, Moscow and St. Petersburg were among the most expensive cities in Europe. Most men simply could not earn enough to support a wife, let alone raise their children in a big city. Men's attitudes sometimes made matters worse. Conceiving of women as inferior to themselves, some tended to view relations with them as a contest from which a man should take what he could get. In the words of Maxim Gorky, "For the real-life working man, women were only a

---

[24] Engel, *Between the Fields*, 190.   [25] Ibid., 137.

source of amusement – but a dangerous one: with women one always had to be cunning, or else they would get the upper hand and ruin one's life."[26] Because in the city, migrant women often lacked the family or community backing that could ensure a man's honorable intentions, in the relations between the sexes men often held the upper hand. Just as successful courtships are reflected in rates of marriage, failed courtships can be quantified, if crudely, by looking at urban illegitimacy rates. In working-class sections of Moscow and St. Petersburg in the late nineteenth and early twentieth century, women bearing illegitimate children usually outnumbered women who wed.

Most men who migrated to Moscow and St. Petersburg married a village woman and left her back home with their family. That way, their hearts were "more inclined toward the village," as peasant parents preferred. At the close of the nineteenth century, roughly 95 percent of married male workers in those cities did not live with their wives and children. Although the wages men earned elsewhere helped to make the peasant economy viable and provided men with a home to return to in difficult times, lengthy separations were hard on both partners. They could fray the emotional ties between a village wife and a migrant husband.

Urban Family Life

Married life in the city often represented little improvement. Lower-class families became somewhat more common in Russia's major cities as the nineteenth century drew to a close. Almost invariably, a married woman continued to earn an income herself: the cost of living was too high and most men's wages too low for any other arrangement. Besides, peasants expected women to labor and to contribute to the family economy – why else marry in the first place? But a married woman who continued to labor might find it difficult to cohabit with her husband. Some women worked as domestic servants, as did Olga Mitrofanova, who together with her husband Pavel left their village in Novgorod province in 1901 because they could no longer make a living there. Pavel found a job as a watchman in one part of the city; Olga worked for a family in another. The two saw each other on her day off. Cohabitation might be no less difficult for factory women. Domna Maksimova, a peasant from Riazan, had been employed for six years when, in 1887, at age twenty-one, she married a worker at another factory in the city of Moscow. After the marriage as before, the couple lived apart, until the Easter holiday when they took off for his village to spend some time together. Even couples who worked in the same factory might have to wait to obtain a place for themselves. Until then, the woman would sleep in the

[26] Maxim Gorky, *My Apprenticeship* (Harmondsworth, England: Penguin, 1974), 315.

woman's quarters, her husband in the men's, and their "conjugal life" would consist of the occasional stolen night together beneath his cot, with a curtain drawn to secure a bit of privacy.[27] The high cost of housing, the lack of affordable and accessible transport, and employment in different locations made cohabitation unusually difficult in Russia's major cities. For many, family and private life seemed an inaccessible luxury.

As a result, a sense of entitlement to the comforts of married life came to constitute part of working men's self-assertiveness by the early twentieth century. "I didn't marry for the village, but for myself," one peasant worker declared to his father as they struggled over whether the wife should stay in the village or move to Moscow, where her husband had a job.[28] The Stolypin reforms, which made it easier for peasants to sever their ties with the village, intensified the tendency of married men to bring wives to the city: in St. Petersburg, around 71 percent of married workers lived with their families by 1918.[29] Marriage provided men with domestic services, such as laundering, cleaning, and cooking that most single men either had to pay for or do without. Women who worked outside the home rose earlier than husbands to do some of the housework before they left; at the midday break, if women factory workers lived nearby, they would race home, prepare food, serve it, clear up and then race back to the factory and work until closing. More chores awaited them when women returned at night. A woman worker with a family had not a second of free time and rarely enough sleep.

Pregnancy and childbirth added to a married woman's burdens. Until 1912, no woman enjoyed maternity leave; thereafter, leave became available on a limited basis. Most women workers stayed on the job until the very last moment. The extended family that might share responsibility for child care in villages and factory settlements was rarely available in the city. Some women sent their babies back to the village to be raised during the early years. Other women left infants and toddlers to nurses of twelve, thirteen, or fourteen years of age, to landladies, to aged women, or to themselves, simply locking them in rooms. Such practices, combined with overcrowding, lack of sanitation, and poor food resulted in infant mortality rates that were even higher than in the villages. Working women and men who sought to improve their children's quality of life attempted to control their fertility. Judging by birthrates, the methods they employed rarely proved effective.

Family life in the city could bring a conflict between work and home that women in the village rarely experienced. As the number of children increased, their demands might stretch a woman's time to the breaking point. Yet few men earned enough to support a wife and children. The solution most women

---

[27] Engel, *Between the Fields*, 203–4.   [28] Ibid., 206.
[29] Smith, "Masculinity in Transition," 103.

9. Shared kitchen, courtesy of Gosudarstvennyi Muzei Istorii Leningrada

adopted resembled that of working-class women elsewhere in Europe: they substituted occasional wage-earning at home for regular, better-paid work outside of it. Olga Onufrieva, mother of four and wife of a metalworker in the Baltic Shipyards in St. Petersburg, contributed to the household income by taking in laundry and scrubbing the floors of well-to-do families.

Mrs. Aleksandrov, wife of a Putilov metalworker and mother of seven children, rented rooms in their three-room apartment to boarders, reserving the kitchen and dark storeroom for the family. Like many other landladies, Mrs. Aleksandrov maintained the apartment, fetched wood and water, heated the cook stove, and looked after her boarders.

In urban families, relations between the sexes remained much as they had been in the village. Working-class men assumed the prerogatives of their peasant fathers and brothers, running the affairs of their own household and managing financial and other transactions with outsiders. "My father was master of the house," remembered the son of one Moscow worker.[30] Although women often established personal ties and developed friendships in their neighborhoods and in the marketplace, married women did not exercise the same informal power in the city that they did in the village. Nor could they look forward to enhanced household authority in the future, given the fact that the urban family was most often a nuclear one. A married woman's horizons tended to be more limited than her husband's; she was almost twice as likely to be illiterate, thus unable even to decipher a street sign or read an advertisement or scratch her name on a piece of paper. Straitened circumstances and multiple responsibilities limited her opportunities for amusement and leisure.

Their different experiences might also set women at odds with their husbands, and husbands with their wives. Men worked hard, too, but they could, and did, take refuge from overcrowded apartments, wailing infants, and dulling routine in taverns and pubs, which remained important sites of male sociability and self-definition. Alcohol, usually vodka, constituted an essential element in many workplace rituals. Few men, married or single, abstained entirely. Convinced that they enjoyed the right to dispose of what they earned, male workers often found themselves defending their wages against wives who sought to claim a share for the family before the money disappeared at the tavern. Every payday wives waited for husbands and "expropriated" their wages, remembered a Moscow metalworker. "This involved considerable struggle, and sometimes the couple wound up in a brawl, with male comrades standing on the sidelines, cheering on the 'oppressed' husband."[31] Print workers called such wives "tugboats." In the Russian working-class community, where men forged bonds on the basis of gender as well as workplace and craft, women represented the obligations of home and family, and became "figures against whom this male worker community defined itself."[32] A countervailing tendency, toward more companionate marriages, did emerge, however, among the "conscious" minority of workers, who adopted a more respectful, although not necessarily egalitarian, attitude toward their wives.

---

[30] Engel, *Between the Fields*, 227.   [31] Ibid., 234.   [32] Steinberg, *Moral Communities*, 79.

Conclusion

It was in the cities and factory settlements, rather than in peasant villages, that women became most likely to experience the changes that swept Russia in the final decades of the century. In villages, the patriarchal household remained the primary unit of production. Outside it, urbanization and the burgeoning market economy expanded women's menu of choices by providing opportunities to earn an independent income and to refashion and perhaps even indulge the self. Spending time in the city could increase a woman's concern for her own needs and well-being and arouse her dissatisfaction with traditional gender, social, even political hierarchies.

Yet the degree of freedom should not be exaggerated. Only a minority of women ever left home, and their mobility always depended on the willingness of household and village authorities to release them. Women's apparent freedom from patriarchal controls aroused anxiety in men across the social spectrum. Lower-class misogyny intensified and took new forms. Women who engaged in "disreputable" behavior or disported themselves in "inappropriate" places risked attracting the attention of their yardman or worse, of agents of the medical police. Most women who migrated to a city worked either as domestic servants or industrial workers, where long hours, low wages, and demoralizing conditions took a serious toll.

Nor did women invariably abandon their traditional aspirations in response to new circumstances. Marriage and the family remained the goal of most migrant peasant women's lives. Urban life raised formidable obstacles for those who sought to marry and remain in the city. The vast majority of women stayed away from home only long enough to acquire a trousseau and help the folks back in the village and then returned home to wed. As a result, although the city tempted some women to forge new lives for themselves, others with migrant experience continued to live much as had their mothers and grandmothers before them. Nevertheless, few women remained entirely unaffected by the transformations that took place in the second half of the century. The upheavals of the early twentieth century would provide evidence for both the continuities and the changes in their lives.

Suggested for Further Reading

Bernstein, Laurie. *Sonia's Daughters: Prostitutes and Their Regulation in Imperial Russia.* Berkeley, Calif.: University of California Press, 1995.

Engel, Barbara Alpern. *Between the Fields and the City: Women, Work and Family in Russia, 1861–1914.* New York: Cambridge University Press, 1994.

Frieden, Nancy M. "Child Care: Medical Reform in a Traditionalist Culture," in David Ransel, ed. *The Family in Imperial Russia: New Lines of Historical Research.* Urbana,

Ill.: University of Illinois Press, 1978, 236–59. *A study of the conflict between medical and peasant childcare cultures.*

Glickman, Rose. *Russian Factory Women: Workplace and Society, 1880–1914.* Berkeley, Calif.: University of California Press, 1984. *A pioneering study of peasant women and their work.*

Meehan-Waters, Brenda. "To Save Oneself: Russian Peasant Women and the Development of Women's Religious Communities in Prerevolutionary Russia," in Beatrice Farnsworth and Lynn Viola, eds. *Russian Peasant Women*, 121–144. New York: Oxford University Press, 1992. *An exploration of peasant women's spirituality.*

Pallot, Judith. "Women's Domestic Industries in Moscow Province, 1880–1900," in Barbara Clements, Barbara Alpern Engel, and Christine Worobec, eds. *Russia's Women: Accommodation, Resistance, Transformation.* Berkeley, Calif.: University of California Press, 1991, 163–84.

Ransel, David. "Abandonment and Fosterage of Unwanted Children: The Women of the Foundling System," in David Ransel, ed. *The Family in Imperial Russia; New Lines of Historical Research.* Urbana, Ill.: University of Illinois Press, 1978, 189–217.

Smith, S. A. "Masculinity in Transition: Peasant Migrants to Late-Imperial St. Petersburg," in Barbara Clements, Rebecca Friedman, and Dan Healey, ed. *Russian Masculinities in History and Culture.* New York: Palgrave, 2002, 92–113. *A pioneering exploration of changing masculinities.*

Worobec, Christine. *Peasant Russia: Family and Community in the Post-Emancipation Period.* Princeton, N.J.: Princeton University Press, 1991. *A major study of the peasant way of life, rich in information on peasant women's lives.*

6

A WIDENING SPHERE

"It is better to endure this domestic prison for three years and thereafter to be free, than [to marry] in a moment of despair and pay with the rest of my life," the eighteen-year-old Elizaveta Diakonova confided to her diary in 1890.[1] Rejecting marriage as a means to escape her provincial merchant milieu, Diakonova sought a broader sphere. Diakonova's world, the world of the middling strata of Russia's cities and towns, had remained largely untouched by the cultural upheavals of the 1860s and 1870s. Her prospects scarcely differed from her mother's: an early marriage, most likely arranged, then motherhood and housekeeping. To Diakonova, as to countless other young women with similar prospects, higher education appeared to offer more: opportunity for intellectual development, greater freedom, a means to participate in public life. Such aspirations contributed to women's prominence in Russia's emergent civil society, both as individuals and as symbols, despite government policies that aimed to curtail their presence.

The death of Tsar Alexander II at the hands of populist terrorists and the ascension to the throne of his son, Alexander III (1881–94), brought far-reaching efforts to restore the prereform political, social, and gender order. The counterreforms eroded the already limited authority of the *zemstva* (plural of *zemstvo*) and circumscribed that of the new judicial system. The government endeavored to restrict lower class access both to education beyond the primary level and to literature that might encourage critical thinking. It also attempted to remove women from public life and return them to their traditional place by ending their access to higher education and fortifying the patriarchal family. Regarding his own family as a "sacred personal sphere" and himself as the "guardian of the sanctity and steadfastness of the family

---

[1] *Dnevnik Elizavety D'iakonovoi, Literaturnye etiudy-stat'i*, v. 1 (St. Petersburg: Kushnerov, 1905), 81, 91.

principle," Tsar Alexander III strove to secure the inviolability of the marital bond.[2]

Yet what the government attempted to accomplish with one hand, it undermined with the other. The industrialization drive gained substantial momentum in the final years of Alexander III's reign and continued into the reign of his son, Nicholas II (1894–1917). Industrialization uprooted hundreds of thousands of peasant women and men and brought them into contact with different modes of life. Industrialization, urbanization, and the growth of a market economy increased the demand for education and encouraged the expansion of schooling. The new market economy also engendered a consumer culture that blurred the social boundaries that autocracy sought to preserve and encouraged the pursuit of pleasure in a population long accustomed to subordinating individual needs to family and community. People grew more assertive, both on their own behalf and on behalf of others. Although the counterreforms severely restricted the emergent civil society, they failed to suppress it altogether. Instead, those who aspired to play a role in public life lowered their profile and found other ways to articulate and realize their aspirations.

Defining Woman's Proper Place

In the reactionary years of Alexander III's reign, the "woman question" assumed new meanings. For conservative officials, chief among them Konstantine Pobedonostsev, Chief Procurator of the Holy Synod, the tsar's former tutor and his most trusted advisor, women's exclusively domestic role served as an article of faith. Like other conservatives who now enjoyed unrestricted access to the ear of the tsar, Pobedonostsev believed that the patriarchal family constituted the foundation of Russia's social order. Fostering hierarchical relations and discipline and respect for authority, firmly subordinating women to men, the patriarchal family served as a kind of dike that might hold back the flood of change that threatened to engulf Russia's ruling elites. It was the responsibility of the state to shore up that dike to the best of its ability.

Restricting women's access to higher education offered a primary means to that end. Blaming higher education for women's political radicalism, conservative officials attempted to render it off limits. In 1882 the Women's Medical Courses ceased to accept new students and, in 1887, ceased operation. Admissions to all other women's courses ended in 1886, while the government

[2] Quoted in Richard Wortman, *Scenarios of Power: Myth and Ceremony in Russian Monarchy*, v. 2 (Princeton, N.J.: Princeton University Press, 2000), 176; S. N. Pisarev, *Uchrezhdenie po priniatiiu i napravleniiu proshenii i zhalob, prinosimykh na Vysochaishee imia, 1810–1910 gg. Istoricheskii ocherk* (SPb: T-vo Golike; A. Vil borg, 1909), 163.

considered its next moves. Only the Bestuzhev courses were permitted to continue. They survived mainly because Elena Likhacheva, president of the courses' funding society, adroitly addressed the political fears of the tsar. Women's courses in Russia, she claimed, would deter women from studying at foreign universities, which spawned "ideals and an orientation that are incommensurate with our way of life." Likhacheva also linked women's education with conservative values: according to her, the truly educated woman "is the truest conservator of religiosity, morality, and order in the family and society."[3] Although Likhacheva succeeded in preserving the Bestuzhev courses from conservative assault, the courses did not emerge unscathed. The Ministry of Education now appointed all personnel and had to approve the hiring of academic staff. Curriculum was restricted to exclude the teaching of human and animal physiology and natural history. Non-Christians (meaning Jews) became subject to a 3 percent quota; admission grew more difficult for lower-class women. Enrollment was capped at 400 students. Auditors now required parents' or husbands' written permission. You are not preparing yourself for professional activity, but for life, "mainly family life," the new director V. P. Kulin admonished incoming students in his speech celebrating the reopening of the courses in 1889.[4]

Officials also attempted to shore up the patriarchal family against continuing challenges. In the early 1880s, progressive jurists undertook efforts to reform the family order by revising the laws governing marriage. The revisions that they proposed would have facilitated legal separation and expanded the grounds for divorce to include spousal abuse. Proclaiming their desire to protect women from the arbitrary authority of husbands, progressive jurists also pursued other, more ambitious goals; to reconfigure the family along more egalitarian and democratic lines, to enhance the rights of individual family members, and to limit the exercise of arbitrary authority. In so doing, progressives hoped to reshape society and politics, too. Conservatives resisted successfully. Efforts to revise marital law repeatedly foundered on the rock of opposition from the Russian Orthodox Church, led by Pobedonostsev.[5] Although in 1914 internal passport law was modified to allow married women a passport of their own, until the fall of the autocracy in 1917, marital law continued to forbid the separation of spouses, to restrict access to divorce, and to grant virtually unlimited authority to husbands and fathers.

3 Robin Bisha, Jehanne M. Gheith, Christine Holden, and William Wagner (eds.), *Russian Women, 1698–1917: Experience and Expression, An Anthology of Sources* (Bloomington, Ind.: Indiana University Press, 2002), 319–20.

4 Christine Johanson, *Women's Struggle for Higher Education in Russia, 1855–1900* (Montreal, Canada: McGill-Queens University Press, 1987), 95–101.

5 William Wagner, *Marriage, Property and Law in Late Imperial Russia* (Oxford, England: Clarendon Press, 1994), 101–205.

Nevertheless, reactionaries proved unable to turn back the clock, especially in the realm of education. Public demand for women's education was substantial. During the reign of Alexander III, girls' *gymnaziia*, secondary schools dependent on donations and charging high tuition, almost doubled in number. During the height of the reaction, hundreds of Russian women traveled abroad to attend Swiss universities. Women continued to press for more opportunities, and after the death of Alexander III, officials became more receptive to their appeals. In 1894, so many applicants to the Bestuzhev courses qualified for admission that the ceiling was lifted; six years later, enrollment had expanded to almost 1,000. In 1895, the tsar approved the St. Petersburg Women's Medical Institute. The Moscow Higher Women's courses (the Guerrier courses) reopened in 1900–01. In 1903, a special pedagogical institute for women opened in Odessa, enrolling 600 students in the first two years. Over time, the social background of students grew increasingly diverse. For example, in the mid-1880s, close to a third of 851 Bestuzhev students derived from the families of merchants or artisans, with daughters of nobles and officials comprising most of the rest. Twenty years later, when the number of students had quintupled, the proportion of elite women had dropped below 45 percent, and daughters of townspeople and peasants constituted over a third of students.[6] In lecture halls and reading rooms, young women from clerical, merchant and artisan, even peasant backgrounds took their places beside the daughters of privileged elites.

Nonelite students sometimes had to surmount formidable obstacles to obtain an education. When Elena Andreeva, daughter of a prominent Moscow merchant family, expressed a desire to attend the Bestuzhev courses, her mother initially opposed her, fearful that the impressionable Elena might come under the influence of "those short-haired nihilist women who deny God and morality."[7] The mother granted permission only after she was assured that the days of nihilism had ended and students now derived from good families and studied seriously. Long after merchant elites had accepted the idea of women's higher education, those further down the social ladder and those who resided outside a major city remained decidedly ambivalent about education beyond the basics. "Why is it that the slightest desire to study is encouraged and praised in a man and distrusted, ridiculed and rejected in a woman?" Elizaveta Diakonova complained to her diary in 1890.[8] Diakonova

---

[6] Johanson, *Women's Struggle*, 74–5, 99–101; *Sankt-Peterburgskie vysshie zhenskie kursy. Slushatel'nitsy kursov. Po dannym perepisi (ankety), vypolnennoi statisticheskim seminarom v noiabre 1909 g.* (SPb, 1912), 4; Susan Morrissey, *Heralds of Revolution: Russian Students and the Mythologies of Radicalism* (Berkeley, Calif.: University of California Press, 1998), 161. Many of the more impoverished students failed to graduate.

[7] Ekaternia A. Andreeva-Balmont, *Vospominaniia* (Moscow: Sabashnikovykh, 1997), 229.

[8] *Dnevnik*, 81.

10. Bestuzhev students, from *Sankt-Peterburgskie Vysshie zhenskie (Bestuzhevskie) Kursy*, 1978–1918 (Leningrad, 1973), n.p.

managed to enroll in the Bestuzhev courses only after she reached the age of majority, that is, twenty-one, and only after convincing the Ministry of Education to set aside the requirement of parental permission. Students who came from humble backgrounds continued to suffer pressing need, sharing rooms in cold, dark, roach-infested apartments and struggling to support themselves while attending school. The back pages of newspapers were peppered with ads from such women students, seeking employment as private tutors, translators, companions, copyists, part-time private secretaries, and the like. The growing proportion of women students from nonelite backgrounds thus serves as evidence not only of a greater acceptance of women's higher education but also of the strength of women's aspirations to break "a window to the world."⁹

The late nineteenth and early twentieth century saw a dramatic expansion of women's employment in positions requiring education. Roughly 750 women practiced medicine in Russia in 1906, many of them employed by the public sector as *zemstvo* physicians or employees of urban councils. The number of women teaching in rural schools grew from 4,878 in 1880 to 64,851 in 1911, and their social backgrounds became increasingly diverse. By 1911, over 20 percent of the teachers were townswomen, another 21.6 percent were peasants, almost surpassing the number of clergymen's and noblemen's daughters, who had dominated the profession in the earlier years. Some

⁹ Morrissey, *Heralds*, 177.

60 percent of the teachers had received a secondary education.[10] As were their counterparts elsewhere in Europe and the United States, women increasingly filled positions as clerks, secretaries, and typists in private and even government offices. The government steadily retreated from the law of 1871 that forbade women to occupy government positions. Although still barred from posts that awarded rank, in the 1880s and 1890s, women worked for the State Senate and the Chancellery of the Council of State, in the state bank, as cashiers and stationmasters for the railroad, and as secretaries to local officials. Women also took up their pens becoming novelists, poets, critics, playwrights and journalists, even editors and publishers of journals. Rhonda Clark has counted at least fifty-three female editors and publishers in Moscow and St. Petersburg during the 1880s.[11] Women's writing really came into its own in the late nineteenth century, aided by the willingness of female publishers, most notably Liubov Gurevich, editor of the *Northern Herald* (*Severnyi Vestnik*) to open their publications to unknown women writers. Less extensive and costly training as nurses, midwives, and medical aides provided employment to thousands of other women, many of humble origin. In the late 1870s, more than twenty schools training midwives operated in the provinces; by 1905, there were more than fifty such schools, with an enrollment of nearly 4,000 and at least 10,000 midwives already practicing their profession.

Education could broaden horizons and raise expectations. To the fictitious Sasha, daughter of a cook in Olga Shapir's short story "Avdotia's Daughters" (1898), the career of a midwife offered a "free and rational existence," as well as escape from domestic slavery.[12] A midwife's career provided the basis for economic independence for the real-life Maria Bolshikh, a townswoman. In 1887, two years after leaving a miserable marriage, Bolshikh completed the course at the Midwifery Institute attached to the Moscow Foundling home and began to practice. With another midwife, she operated a small maternity shelter in their apartment, in addition to assisting the staff midwife at the Foundling home and occasionally accompanying on his rounds a physician who performed venereal examinations on women factory workers.[13] Able to support themselves, other women likewise grew less willing to endure marital mistreatment. In the final decades of the nineteenth century, tens of thousands of women requested the right to separate from their husband, despite marital,

---

[10] Ben Eklof, *Russian Peasant Schools: Officialdom, Village Culture and Popular Pedagogy, 1861–1914* (Berkeley, Calif.: University of California Press, 1986), 189, 195.

[11] Adele Lindenmeyr, "Anna Volkova: From Merchant Wife to Feminist Journalist," in Barbara T. Norton and Jehanne Gheith (eds.), *An Improper Profession: Women, Gender and Journalism in Late Imperial Russia* (Durham, N.C.: Duke University Press, 2001), 126.

[12] Olga A. Shapir, "Avdot'iny Dochki," in V. Uchenova (ed.), *Tol'ko chas. Proza russkikh pisatel'nits kontsa xix-nachala xx veka* (Moscow: Sovremennik, 1988), 25.

[13] Rossiiskii Gosudarstvennyi Istoricheskii Arkhiv, fond 1412, op. 213, ed. kh. 98 Maria Bolshikh, 1886, 19.

laws that strictly forbade such separation. Petitioning local officials, the, courts and finally the tsar himself in the hope of relief, women from all social strata declared their unwillingness to continue living with drunken, adulterous, and abusive men and their desire to "earn their own crust of bread," as so many of them put it. By enabling women to earn their own living, the economic changes of the late nineteenth century eroded institutions that reactionaries sought to preserve, the patriarchal family in particular.

The burgeoning marketplace had much the same effect. A by-product of Russia's industrialization drive, the market encouraged the desire for individual pleasure and gratification and fostered patterns of consumption that cut across social divides. The advertising industry enticed women to consume the fashionable clothing and other items displayed in department store windows and on the pages of popular magazines and to employ makeup, hair coloring, and other beauty aides to decorate the self. Advice books proliferated, aiming to instruct the newly wealthy on how to dress, how to furnish and keep the home, and how to behave with refinement. New pastimes such as bicycling enhanced women's mobility and personal independence. Stringent censorship did not prevent popular magazines from spreading the word of women's abilities and attainments. Aiming mainly to entertain literate urban women of moderate means, the widely read *Messenger of Fashion* (*Vestnik Mody*) offered its readers a popularized version of the "woman question," questioning notions of women's inferiority and extolling women's achievements in fields such as medicine. *Niva* (*The Cornfield*), with a circulation of 100,000 the most popular magazine in Russia, likewise celebrated women who stepped outside their customary sphere. Among the women featured in 1890 were the singer Alexandra D. Kochetova, who had to overcome the suspicion of her family to make a career in music and for thirteen years was a professor at the Moscow Conservatory of Music; and the Americans Miss Nelly Bly and Miss Elizabeth Wayland, both of whom succeeded in circling the globe in 72 days, "faster than Phineas Fogg."[14] It is hard to avoid the impression that much of educated society, if not conservative officials, had come to accept women's presence in public life.

Most women who contributed to public life did so in more modest ways. Charity remained the main avenue for women's public action. In the decade following the ascension of Alexander III, it became far more difficult to form new charitable organizations, which were viewed as potential fronts for radical endeavors. But women could still act as individuals. The historian Galina Ul'ianova has identified 79 female philanthropists from among the Moscow merchantry, who in the years before the outbreak of World War II

---

[14] Carolyn Marks, "'Providing Amusement for the Ladies': The Rise of the Russian Women's Magazine in the 1880s," in *An Improper Profession*, 110–12; *Niva*, 1890, n. 6 and 7.

donated millions of rubles to charitable endeavors and municipal organizations that contributed to the public welfare. Among them was Agrippina Abrikosova (1833–1901), married to the head of the famous Abrikosov and Sons confectionary factories and mother of twenty-two children, seventeen of whom survived. In 1889, Abrikosova established a free maternity shelter and gynecological clinic in Moscow, bequeathing 100,000 rubles to the city for a second maternity shelter when she died in 1902. More well-known, but by no means the most lavish in her generosity was the merchant Varvara Morozova, after her husband's death in 1883 until 1892 the director of the family firm, the Tver Cotton Goods Manufacturing Company. Between 1883 and 1914, Morozova donated almost 280,000 rubles to the city of Moscow to fund, among other endeavors, a reading room, a primary school for girls, and, after the revolution of 1905, a people's university.[15] Taking advantage of Russian laws that endowed even married women with the right to dispose of their property independently, and in accordance with Orthodox religious traditions that endorsed sharing one's wealth with the poor, such women established and supported a range of charitable endeavors. Women's religious communities likewise provided charity to the poor, education to the young, and care to the sick, particularly in rural areas where such organized activities remained relatively free of government interference during the worst of the reaction. The numbers of such communities expanded dramatically toward the end of the century, part of a broader religious revival.[16]

As restrictions eased in the early 1890s, unprecedented opportunities became available for women to contribute to and define the public welfare. Women began pressing harder for the reopening of women's courses. New charitable organizations emerged in record numbers. City governments began to assume far more extensive responsibility for the untutored rural masses that had begun to inundate urban areas. In 1894, Municipal Guardianships for the Poor, a form of welfare organization, were established in all major cities. Private charitable organizations proliferated, offering a broad range of services. Women became involved at almost all levels. They directed charitable organizations, served on governing and advisory boards, and worked for charitable establishments either as volunteers or as salaried employees, influencing the goals and orientations of their organizations. Many such endeavors served the needs of mothers and children. Interestingly, most eschewed the maternalist discourse that dominated such charitable endeavors to the West,

[15] Galina N. Ul'ianova, *Blagotvoritel'nost' moskovskikh predprinimatelei, 1860–1914* (Moscow: Mosgorarkhiv, 1999), 281–2, 406–8.

[16] Adele Lindenmeyr, "Public Life, Private Virtues: Women in Russian Charity, 1762–1914," *Signs* 18, no. 3 (Spring 1993), 574–8; Brenda Meehan-Waters, "From Contemplative Practice to Charitable Activity: Russian Women's Religious Communities and the Development of Charitable Work, 1861–1917," in Kathleen McCarthy (ed.), *Lady Bountiful Revisited: Women, Philanthropy and Power* (New Brunswick, N.J.: Rutgers University Press, 1990), 142–56.

emphasizing instead the importance of child care institutions such as nurseries and asylums and the role of women as workers. The Elizabeth Society, named for a sister of the Empress, even developed day nurseries for middle-class working women, long before such institutions were developed in the West.[17]

In addition, by writing about their encounters with the lower classes, educated women helped to shape the way that society perceived both themselves and the "others" whom they described. The results of Mina Gorbunova's massive research on Moscow peasant women and their crafts appeared in 1882, under the auspices of the Moscow Statistical Bureau; Alexandra Efimenko's ethnographic study "Explorations of Popular Life" was published in 1884. In 1894, the physician Ekaterina Slanskaia's "House Calls: A Day in the Practice of a Duma Woman Doctor in St. Petersburg" appeared in the popular *Messenger of Europe*; four years later, the physician Maria Pokrovskaia published a similar account, "My Duma Practice," in another "thick" journal. Russian women journalists viewed journalism itself as "a venue for social action" and a means to transform society, by contrast, for example, with their British counterparts.[18] In describing the situation of the lower classes, many of these women writers focused in particular on the experiences and needs of lower-class women and children. Speaking on behalf of those less fortunate than themselves, educated women sought to influence the concerns and perceptions of the emergent civil society.

A New Woman?

By the 1890s, thanks in part to the impact of the marketplace, a new concern for the self increasingly vied with impulses to help "the other." The publication in 1892 of Maria Bashkirtseva's diary both reflected and contributed to these trends. The diary, kept by Bashkirtseva from the age of thirteen until her premature death in 1884, had an enormous impact on some female readers. Initially preoccupied with her own personal appearance and erotic experiences, Bashkirtseva eventually turned to art as a means to express herself and to attain the fame she sought. Her willingness to sacrifice everything for her art and her struggles for self-perfection offered a new model of female behavior. Liubov Gurevich, the child of a liberal and cultivated St. Petersburg family, was a schoolgirl when she first read Bashkirtseva. The diary, she was convinced, enabled her to reject the dominant cultural expectations of her as a woman and live more "fully and intensely" than

---

[17] Adele Lindenmeyr, "Maternalism and Child Welfare in Late Imperial Russia," *Journal of Women's History* 5 (Fall 1993), 119–20.

[18] Jehanne Gheith, "Introduction," *An Improper Profession*, 7.

she otherwise would have.[19] The diary had an equally profound impact on Elizaveta Andreeva, the daughter of a well-to-do merchant family. Twenty years of age at the time she read it, Andreeva knew she wanted to be independent and to "do something," but she had little idea what to do. She found feminism, as embodied in the previous generation of feminists, unappealing: they were "old and unattractive, with their hair cut short, wearing loose gray overalls, with cigarettes constantly in their mouths." Bashkirtseva's "bold self-assertion" provided a more attractive model. Andreeva elaborated a program for herself: first she had to overcome her own timidity and lack of confidence; thereafter, she would learn to ignore established authorities and the prejudices of her own merchant milieu. Her goal? "To be utterly true to myself."[20]

Images that circulated in the popular media reinforced more individualistic trends. In the mass circulation press of the early twentieth century, personalities became important, including those of popular women writers, such as Anastasia Verbitskaia and Lydia Charskaia, beloved of teenage girls. Using their own images to market their works to a broader female public, women writers gained new visibility and popularity. Although many adopted conventionally feminine poses, none embraced the image of happy wife and homemaker, the "rigorously domesticated" womanhood still prevalent in Western societies.[21] Consumer culture tended to promote individual indulgence over family values. Anastasia Vialtseva vividly personified the new trend. Born a peasant in 1871, the daughter of a woodcutter and his laundress wife, at the turn of the century Vialtseva became a celebrity who sang bittersweet romances about sexual desire, and she earned fabulous sums of money, which she spent lavishly and conspicuously on herself. With her blend of female charm and effective self-promotion, Vialtseva attracted hordes of worshipping fans. Her popularity, like the marketing of women writers, reflected a new acceptance of women in public spaces.[22]

The new individualism coexisted with long-standing restrictions on women and hostility to women professionals. Practicing in village or city, women physicians encountered prejudice from the authorities and their fellow physicians, and earned less than men in comparable positions. Women who graduated from women's higher courses received only a certificate of completion, not an academic degree, for which a person was required to pass

---

[19] Stanley J. Rabinowitz, "No Room of Her Own: The Early Life and Career of Liubov' Gurevich," *Russian Review* 57, no. 2 (April 1998), 240–1.

[20] Andreeva-Bal'mont, *Vospominaniia*, 227.

[21] Beth Holmgren, "Gendering the Icon: Marketing Women Writers in Fin-de-Siecle Russia," in Helena Goscilo and Beth Holmgren (eds.), *Russia. Women. Culture* (Bloomington, Ind.: Indiana University Press, 1996), 334–41.

[22] Louise McReynolds, "The 'Incomparable' Vial'steva and the Culture of Personality," in *Russia. Women. Culture*, 273–91.

a state examination. These examinations, like state service and the Table of Ranks, were reserved for men. Women were barred from careers in civil service and law, offering women who graduated from higher courses few career options apart from teaching. Yet women teachers labored under disabilities from which their male colleagues remained free. Authorities expected women to be pure sexually as well as politically, and subjected woman's personal lives to greater scrutiny than men's: in at least one school district, women teachers actually had to submit proof of virginity. In a decree of 1897, the St. Petersburg city government forbade women teachers to marry, forcing them to choose between marriage and a career.[23] Women who married were likewise dismissed from the classroom in the provinces of Arkhangelsk and Tobolsk.

But if women's circumstances had changed very little, women were less willing to endure them. Ideas about the rights of the individual person, which circulated widely in the literature of this period, reverberate in the language of women seeking to improve their condition. Responding to condescending treatment by university officials and male students, at the turn of the century women students increasingly framed their demands for change "in terms of the individual right to self-expression and self-determination."[24] The marriage ban limited the personal freedom of women teachers, argued Nadezhda Rumiantseva at a conference of teachers.[25] Women professionals used their pens to enhance their professional standing. Writing of their experiences in the thick journals that circulated among the educated, they stressed their own competence and ability to overcome obstacles and presented themselves as performing as well as men or better.

Women's new visibility in public life revitalized the "woman question" or perhaps more properly, "woman questions," at the close of the nineteenth century. In addition to long-standing concerns with education, work, and the relations between the sexes, the "woman question" now embraced issues of sexual desire and power. In response to the increasing numbers of women who penetrated into public and previously male space, women's bodies became part of the terrain over which educated society struggled for power. The restrictions on women, however, reduced their ability to shape their own fate. Marginalized by their exclusion from government bodies, women were rarely in a position to influence decisions that affected their lives. Thus, male jurists revising laws treating sexual crime and prostitution, by emphasizing female dependence and vulnerability, denied women's capacity for independent action and ensured that individual autonomy remained a male preserve. When they opposed state regulation of prostitution, male physicians rarely argued

---

[23] Christine Ruane, *Gender, Class and the Professionalization of Russian City Teachers, 1860–1914* (Pittsburgh: University of Pittsburgh Press, 1994), 73, 76–81.

[24] Morrissey, *Heralds*, 84.   [25] Ruane, *Gender*, 115.

for complete abolition of the system of surveillance and regulation; instead, they wanted the system reformed, and for medical authority over women to replace the authority of the police.[26] Although women spoke forcefully about these issues, too, as long as they remained excluded from the domains where policy was forged, they could affect public policy only by influencing men.

Revolution of 1905

The revolution of 1905 raised hopes for changing this situation. That year, long-suppressed discontents finally exploded. Industrial workers, students, professionals, even nobles and industrialists became caught up in the wave of resistance that swept Russia in the wake of Bloody Sunday (January 9, 1905), when tsarist troops fired upon a peaceful demonstration of working-class women and men, killing more than 100 people and wounding many more. In the ensuing upheaval, women across the social spectrum mobilized in enormous numbers, joining with men to demand an expansion of political rights and greater social justice. Women industrial workers, clerical workers, pharmacists, professionals, even domestic servants, joined unions and walked off their jobs to attend mass meetings and demonstrations that called for an end to autocracy and a representative form of government. The intense politicization and pervasive use of a language of rights stimulated women to speak on their own behalf and to claim their place in the expanding public sphere.

Working-class women were among the first to raise their voices. At the end of January 1905, they objected in print when the government called for the convening of the Shidlovskii commission to study the reasons for worker discontent, and permitted women to vote for representatives to the commission but only male workers to be elected to it. Only women, they claimed, could properly represent themselves. They protested the loss of an opportunity to "loudly proclaim . . . the oppression and humiliation that no male worker can possibly understand."[27] Working-class women also took to the streets on an issue closer to home, initiating a boycott of taverns and alcohol stores in St. Petersburg and, in November, mounting an enormous demonstration to demand the closure of taverns serving liquor to workers. During 1905, violence against drinking establishments in St. Petersburg province cost the state more than 30,000 rubles.[28]

---

[26] Laura Engelstein, *The Keys to Happiness: Sex and the Search for Modernity in Fin-de-Siecle Russia* (Ithaca, N.Y.: Cornell University Press, 1992), 28–95.

[27] Rose Glickman, *Russian Factory Women: Workplace and Society, 1880–1914* (Berkeley, Calif.: University of California Press, 1984), 190.

[28] Laura L. Phillips, "In Defense of Their Families: Working-Class Women, Alcohol, and Politics in Revolutionary Russia," *Journal of Women's History*, 11, no. 1 (Spring 1999), 108–9.

Women also took active part in the increasingly political strike movement that became the primary medium through which workers expressed their discontent and aspirations. In factories where women predominated, the textile industry in particular, strike demands clearly reflected their presence. Factory after factory demanded day care, maternity leave, nursing breaks, and protection of women workers, reflecting not only the preponderance of women but also the influence of the Marxist Social Democratic Labor Party (SDLP) and liberals, both of which had long supported maternity-related benefits. Even as they claimed for women significant rights in the workplace, however, such demands also reinforced gender differences and a gender division of labor: virtually all the demands that applied to women touched on their role as mother, not on their actual working conditions, and only in a few known instances did workers claim that a woman should be paid the same as a man for performing identical work. Most commonly, existing wage differentials and women's unequal status were reinscribed in strike demands that called for raises that would have maintained women's earnings at a fraction of men's. In a few cases, in an effort to assert a solidarity based on gender, male workers went even further and sought to exclude women workers altogether from "men's" trades.[29] Nevertheless, vast numbers of working-class women embraced the working-class movement as their own. This became clear in December 1905, during a last, desperate confrontation with the authorities, when working-class women and men took to the barricades. Alongside men, women labored tirelessly, chopping wood, breaking up telegraph poles, and disassembling tram cars to construct barricades against government troops, who nevertheless crushed the working-class movement.

During the revolution of 1905, women of the educated classes took political action of a different sort. Feminist movements reemerged on a much more substantial scale than before and embraced far larger numbers. The primary goal was women's suffrage, which became an issue as soon as men claimed a political voice. The largest and most visible feminist group and the only one to play a significant role in 1905 was the All-Russian Union for Women's Equality, a national women's political organization established by thirty women liberals a month after Bloody Sunday. Their first public meeting on April 10 was also the first political meeting for women in Russia, and it attracted 1,000 people. By the time of their first Congress, held in Moscow, May 7–10, 1905, twenty-six chapters had formed. Feminist activists derived primarily from the middle classes; however, independent professional women such as journalists, physicians, and teachers appear far more numerous than historians have found them to be in other contemporary feminist organizations.

---

[29] Glickman, *Russian Factory Women*, 190–94

From the first, the Union for Women's Equality cast its lot with the broader liberation movement, embracing the idea that women's liberation was inseparable from the liberation of society as a whole. The Union's platform, adopted in May 1905, repeated the demands of the liberation movement in addition to its call for specifically women's rights such as equality of the sexes before the law, equal rights to the land for peasant women, laws to protect women workers, and coeducation at all levels of schooling. Their common ground of opposition to autocracy led the women of the Union for Women's Equality to collaborate with liberal and leftist men far more extensively than feminists did elsewhere. They participated in radical demonstrations and openly supported workers, raising money to help those on strike and the unemployed. In petitions and demonstrations, they demanded amnesty for political prisoners and abolition of the death penalty, as well as rights for women.

In addition, reflecting the social sympathies that had long characterized educated women, the Union worked to forge alliances across the social divide that continued to separate privileged Russians from the laboring classes and to encourage lower-class women to speak for themselves. In St. Petersburg, they assisted women workers to formulate their protest against exclusion from the Shidlovskii Commission. At its very first conference, the Union invited "women of the toiling classes" to formulate their own demands and pledged to support them, in an effort to avoid the distrust that lower-class women "inevitably feel" for demands formulated for them by others.[30] Feminist demands included laws providing for the welfare, protection, and insurance of women workers. Abolition of the regulation of prostitution became a feminist demand in 1905. Feminists also tried to reach out to peasant women who, like men, had become far more militant and aggressive in 1905–7, although as earlier, mainly on behalf of family and community. Feminists joined the Peasant Union and convinced it to adopt the plank of women's suffrage.[31]

Feminist efforts to expand their social base bore some fruit. Women domestic servants in Moscow and St. Petersburg joined feminist-organized unions; they attended feminist-sponsored clubs. Women workers added their signatures to petitions favoring women's suffrage. A number of peasant women's groups were formed and some petitions signed by peasant men took up the demand for women's suffrage. In 1906, peasant women in Tver and Voronezh provinces sent petitions to the newly elected legislature, the Duma, laying independent claim to the political voice so recently granted their men, and denying the prevailing stereotype of peasant women as backward and mute.

---

[30] Gosudarstvennyi Istoricheskii Arkhiv gorod Moskvy [hereafter GIAgM], fond 516, op. 1, ed. kh. 5, ll. 45–50.

[31] Linda Harriet Edmondson, *Feminism in Russia, 1900–1917* (Stanford, Calif.: Stanford University Press, 1984), 38–47.

Protesting the assertion of a peasant Duma deputy that peasant women had no interest in the vote, fifty-five Voronezh women signed a letter stating: "There are no women deputies in the Duma who could represent all peasant women, so how does he know? He is wrong to say that the peasant woman doesn't want rights. Did he ask us? We, the peasant women of Voronezh province, understand perfectly well that we need rights and land just as men do."[32]

Nevertheless, 1905 brought the feminists very little in the way of measurable political gains. To be sure, the granting of civil liberties, however limited, allowed more scope for organizing. In 1904, the physician Maria Pokrovskaia began publishing a feminist newspaper, *The Women's Herald* (*Zhenskii vestnik*), which, during 1905, maintained a barrage of propaganda on behalf of women's rights and continued in print until 1917. Other, more short-lived feminist newspapers emerged. The revolution also marked a watershed in the history of women's education. The curriculum of women's higher courses expanded and between 1906 and 1910 new women's courses opened in many provincial cities. In addition, a number of private coeducational universities were established, offering new curricula and electives. The enrollment of women students increased exponentially: in 1900–01, there were 2,588 women students enrolled in higher education in Russia; by 1915–6, the number was 44,017. However, the status of women's education remained insecure and career options limited, leaving an enormous gap between education and employment opportunities.[33]

Moreover, feminist support for the liberation movement, so generously given, was rather less generously returned. The October manifesto enfranchised only men, leaving women dependent on the loyalty of their former male allies. The liberal Kadet party, which dominated the first Duma, divided over the issue of women's suffrage; parties to the left, although staunch advocates of women's rights, because of their working-class orientation were with one notable exception suspicious of and reluctant to support "bourgeois feminism." Further, the evidence suggests that working-class and peasant women felt more affinity with the men of their class than they did with middle-class feminists, however much lower-class women might have hankered after fancy clothing or admired lavishly spending women artists. Even when feminists succeeded in organizing women workers, they had trouble retaining their loyalty. As one feminist lamented, it was relatively easy to establish circles among laboring women, but as soon as their political consciousness was raised, they wanted to work with the men of their class. "They quickly join the ranks of one of the [socialist] parties and become party workers. In

[32] GIAgM, fond 516, op. 1, ed. kh. 4, l. 42.   [33] Morrissey, *Heralds*, 161.

a number of cities, the Union [for Women's Equality] has acted as a kind of preparation for party work."[34] Thus, the social divisions that weakened opposition to autocracy divided the women's movement as well.

But more decisive than male ambivalence or social divisions was the fact that the revolution had ended and the tsar was regaining control. When the first Duma was dissolved after three months, its members were preparing to consider the fruit of feminist lobbying, a draft law on women's equality. The erosion of civil liberties and the "coup" of June 3, 1907, which gave still greater electoral weight to the propertied sectors of society, brought political demoralization: membership in the women's movement sharply declined, as it did in radical political parties in general. Despite the lack of concrete feminist achievements, women's experience of 1905 and, in particular, participation in acts of protest and the use of a language of rights left an ineradicable trace on the consciousness of thousands at all levels of society, from the most privileged to the most deprived. Nowhere is this clearer than in an unusual letter, signed by prostitutes in the provincial town of Vologda and published in the newsletter of the Union for Women's Equality in June–July 1907. Observing that everyone was now "gaining their rights," the signatories claimed rights of their own, including the right to leave a brothel when they chose, the subjection of their male customers to venereal examinations, and the limitation of their customers to no more than five a night. Most of all, however, the women wanted an end to state regulation of prostitution, which greatly limited the ability of lower-class women to control their own lives. If regulation were abolished, in the words of the letter, "Then a girl could sell herself only when she pleased and when she pleased, she could stop."[35]

The Aftermath

Following the failure of 1905, new concerns eclipsed traditional feminist issues. Between June 1907 and the outbreak of World War I, the demoralized women's movement lost membership and momentum. Women remained divided along ideological lines. While liberals sought to expand women's rights in the public sphere, radicals, the Marxist parties foremost among them, believed that nothing short of a thoroughgoing revolution could achieve women's equality. The movement's most significant achievement, an All-Russian Women's Congress, held December 10–6, 1908, divided along these fault lines. In addition, other issues, especially "the sexual question," now absorbed the public's attention. Relatively free of censorship, newspapers and magazines provided the means for personal and commercial communication.

---

[34] GIAgM, fond 516, op. 1, ed. kh. 5, p. 73. Report of the Third Congress, May 22, 1906.
[35] Ibid., ed. kh. 6, p. 311–12.

They listed the services of divorce lawyers and midwives who would deliver babies with "complete discretion" and enumerated the requirements of men and women seeking mates. Advertisements encouraged women to develop more beautiful busts; they offered cures for sexual troubles; they touted contraceptives. On the back pages of newspapers, "models" boasting "attractive bodies" offered to pose for a fee.[36] Women were as likely as men to advertise for partners in newspapers with titles such as *The Amour Post* or the *Moscow Marriage Gazette*, which assisted the lonely to meet and mate. The educated public had come to accept the presence of women on the streets unescorted, without the male protection that was so central to the Western liberal vision. In 1910, the popular middlebrow *Niva* featured a lesson in female self-defense, complete with photographs demonstrating appropriate postures. (Fig. 11). By learning jiu-jitsu, the author explained, "Women can face the dangers of the city streets without needing the protection of a man."[37]

The "new woman" symbolized the new era. Freed from the constraints of conventional morality, she dominated the imagination of the reading public. The immensely popular boulevard novel, Anastasia Verbitskaia's *The Keys to Happiness* (published 1908–13) was one of the best-selling works of the time. In six volumes and 1,400 pages, the author explored the life of a sexually self-assertive modern heroine, Mania, a beautiful dancer, who takes several lovers and struggles to retain her independence and artistic ambitions in the face of intense passion. The novel addressed women of all classes who felt stifled by societal and professional restraints and emphasized their right to sexual adventure and professional achievement.[38] Nonreaders might encounter the "new woman" on the silver screen. With tickets priced low enough for working-class patrons, film gained great popularity in the postrevolutionary years. The cinematic version of *The Keys to Happiness* became a box office sensation in 1913, setting the standard by which all other films were measured. The "new woman" likewise figured in the films of director Evgenii Bauer, whose heroines were more often rewarded than punished for their desires.[39] The prominence of the "new woman" prompted the feminist-oriented Marxist, Alexandra Kollontai, to revise Marxist theory in a 1913 essay, appropriately entitled "The New Woman." Exploring women's psychology and treating sexuality and sexual relations as proper topics for political discussion, Kollontai emphasized the historical significance of the single woman who earned her own living and found the meaning of life in independence and

---

[36] Engelstein, *The Keys to Happiness*, 360.   [37] *Niva*, 1910, no. 32, 568.

[38] Anastasya Verbitskaya, *Keys to Happiness*, edited and translated by Beth Holmgren and Helena Goscilo (Bloomington, Ind.: Indiana University Press, 1999), xiii.

[39] Louise McReynolds, "The Silent Movie Melodrama: Evgenii Bauer Fashions the Heroine's Self," in Laura Engelstein and Stephanie Sandler (eds.), *Self and Story in Russian History* (Ithaca, N.Y.: Cornell University Press, 2000), 139.

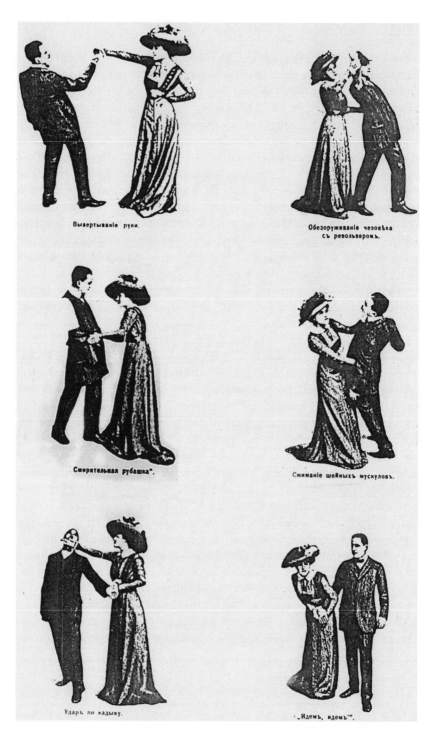

Вы
вертываніе руки.

Обезоруживаніе человѣка
съ револьверомъ.

Смирительная рубашка".

Сжиманіе шейныхъ мускуловъ.

Ударъ по кадыку.

„Идемъ, идемъ".

11. A lesson in self-defense, from *Niva*, no. 32, 1910

work. Unconstrained by "bourgeois morality" and its double standard, according to Kollontai, the new woman followed her sexual inclinations where they led her and claimed new rights in the public world, "walking the streets with a businesslike, masculine tread."[40]

Yet more restrictive ways of regarding women by no means disappeared and drew new life from the fears that revolution evoked. Thus, the debate over abortion acquired new intensity, as progressive physicians sought, unsuccessfully, to decriminalize abortion, which Russian law treated as a form of murder. Supposedly, its incidence had escalated dramatically following the revolution of 1905. At professional meetings, women physicians spoke vociferously on behalf of reproductive freedom. Among the most vocal was the feminist physician Maria Pokrovskaia, who denounced Russia's punitive abortion laws as unwarranted restrictions on female autonomy. Invoking the concept of voluntary motherhood, she called for full decriminalization of abortion, claiming that only women were in a position to know their own needs. For her as for other proponents of decriminalization, abortion symbolized women's autonomy. For others, however, abortion symbolized women's sexual license and underscored the dangerous aspects of women's liberation. Women's freedom from legal and career restraints was one thing, sexual liberation quite another. The physician Dmitrii Zhbankov, a proponent of women's rights and women's education, nevertheless regarded the upper-class woman who wanted to abort as corrupt and self-indulgent. If women wanted to achieve equal rights, they would have to reject their culture's emphasis on nonreproductive sexual gratification and return to their "natural" function of motherhood, he insisted.[41] This period, too, saw new welfare initiatives that aimed to strengthen the family by supporting women as mothers.

Women themselves spoke with many voices. When questioned in 1909, women Bestuzhev students claimed to reject the new "pornographic" literature in favor of classical works. Despite Verbitskaia's claim that her most loyal readers were women students, only 5 percent of the students queried acknowledged Verbitskaia as one of their "favorites" and then with reservations. Students were equally unenthusiastic about feminism. Most professed traditional intelligentsia values, including the goal of serving society and "the people."[42] Most feminists, too, promoted a view of female sexuality more conservative than that embodied in the "new woman." While endorsing women's sexual choice, they nevertheless regarded women more as sexual victims than sexual agents. Maria Pokrovskaia, advocate of decriminalizing abortion, promoted "sexual purity" rather than sexual freedom and encouraged men to

---

[40] Engelstein, *Keys*, 398–99.   [41] Ibid., 341–4.
[42] *Sankt-Peterburgskie vysshie zhenskie kursy*, 124; Morrissey, 171–2.

embrace chastity, too. The Russian Society for the Protection of Women offered a still more extreme version of sexual puritanism. Formed in 1900 as part of the struggle against "white slavery" and composed of women from the social elite, the Society sought to save working-class girls not only from "falling," but also from sex itself.[43]

Conclusion

Despite the efforts of reactionary officials and concerns of conservative critics, by the outbreak of World War I, it appeared as if the "new woman" had come to stay. She was very much a product of the changes that had swept Russia, beginning in the reign of Alexander III. The expansion of women's education, the growth of the market economy, and the new emphasis on the self and its gratification contributed more to undermining the patriarchal family than did the radical critiques of the 1860s and 1870s, although those critiques continued to resonate. While they might disagree about where the "new woman" should direct her energies and how she should use her body, only the most conservative of her contemporaries questioned her right to occupy public space. Significantly, wifehood and motherhood played a minimal role in the woman-related discourse of the early twentieth century, although those themes did become more prominent following 1905. In the 1920s, after revolution had utterly transformed the political but not yet the cultural context, the new government would struggle hard to harness the "new woman" to its own ends and to stuff the genie of sexuality back into its bottle.

Suggestions for Further Reading

Edmondson, Linda Harriet. *Feminism in Russia, 1900–1917*. Stanford, Calif.: Stanford University Press, 1984. *A careful study of the re-emergence and politics of the women's movement.*

Engelstein, Laura. *The Keys to Happiness: Sex and the Search for Modernity in Fin-de-Siecle Russia*. Ithaca, N.Y.: Cornell University Press, 1992. *A brilliant study of the role of sex and gender in the evolution of Russian thought.*

Glickman, Rose. *Russian Factory Women: Workplace and Society, 1880–1914*. Berkeley, Calif.: University of California Press, 1984. *The most complete treatment of working-class women's activism in 1905 and after.*

Holmgren, Beth. "Gendering the Icon: Marketing Women Writers in Fin-de-Siecle Russia," in Helena Goscilo and Beth Holmgren (eds.), *Russia. Women. Culture.* Bloomington, Ind.: Indiana University Press, 1996, 321–346.

---

[43] Laurie Bernstein, *Sonia's Daughters: Prostitutes and Their Regulation in Imperial Russia* (Berkeley, Calif.: University of California Press, 1995), 203.

Lindenmeyr, Adele. "Maternalism and Child Welfare in Late Imperial Russia," *Journal of Women's History* 5 (Fall 1993), 114–126.

Lindenmeyr, Adele. "Public Life, Private Virtues: Women in Russian Charity, 1762–1914," *Signs* 18:3 (Spring 1993), 562–91. *On women's charitable endeavors during this period.*

McReynolds, Louise. "The 'Incomparable' Vial'steva and the Culture of Personality," in *Russia. Women. Culture*, 273–294. *A study of the popular singer, her cult, and its significance.*

Rabinowitz, Stanley J. "No Room of Her Own: The Early Life and Career of Liubov' Gurevich," *Russian Review* 57, no. 2 (April 1998), 236–252. *A revealing portrait of a pioneering woman publisher.*

Ruane, Christine. "Clothes Shopping in Imperial Russia: The Development of a Consumer Culture," *Journal of Social History* 28 (1995), 765–82.

Slanskaia, Ekaterina. "House Calls: A Day in the Practice of a Duma Woman Doctor in St. Petersburg," in Toby W. Clyman and Judith Vowles (eds.), *Russia Through Women's Eyes: Autobiographies from Tsarist Russia*. New Haven, Conn.: Yale University Press, 1996, 186–216. *A woman physician describes her practice among the urban poor.*

Verbitskaia, Anastasia. *Keys to Happiness: A Novel*. Edited and translated by Helena Goscilo and Beth Holmgren. Bloomington, Ind.: Indiana University Press, 1999. *Verbitskaia's blockbuster, reduced to manageable size.*

7

———————— • ————————

WAR AND REVOLUTION

The outbreak of World War I in August 1914 set the stage for revolution and the profound transformations that the Bolsheviks would undertake after 1917. Millions of men left for the front. By the end of 1916, the number called into service had reached the staggering figure of 14,600,000, including young men who had been solely supporting their families. Just under half (47.8 percent) of the able-bodied rural male population had been called to war; about a third of all peasant farms had lost all their male laborers. By claiming the lives of millions of men, World War I transformed the lives of women. It upset gendered hierarchies and drew out to work thousands, perhaps millions of women for the first time. Women's vastly expanded roles in the public arena enhanced their claims for equal citizenship. Yet to the majority of Russia's women, the war and its revolutionary aftermath brought hardship, not opportunity.

World War I and Women

If ever Russia's educated elites felt part of a "nation," they did at the outbreak of World War I. Most middle- and upper-class women became swept up in the burst of patriotic fervor. Among them were feminists who had once identified themselves as pacifists. The moderate feminist journal, *Women's Cause* (*Zhenskoe Delo*), for one, adopted a tone of elevated patriotism from the first.

> The days of endurance impose on every one of us a great duty – to devote our strength to the defense of the fatherland. . . . At a time when it sends our fathers, husbands, sons and brothers into the line of battle it entrusts us, women, with sacred duties. If the loss of a dear person strikes us, too, we must not forget that it is a holy sacrifice for our sins, laid on the altar of the fatherland for its future well-being."[1]

---

[1] Quoted in Linda Edmondson, *Feminism in Russia, 1900–1917* (Stanford, Calif.: Stanford University Press, 1984), 160.

Thousands sought to do their part as nurses, some drawn by the promise of adventure as well as duty to the fatherland. "In virtually every educated family where the daughters did not have to work for a living, the girls volunteered in the hospitals," remembered Nadezhda Iakusheva, resident in the town of Chernigov.[2] In the early months of war, so many women volunteered that substantial numbers had to be turned away. Even women of the imperial family donned nurses' uniforms. The Empress Alexandra and her daughters became nurses in the Tsarskoe Selo Court Hospital, attending operations and bandaging the wounded. "For the Princess, neither day nor night exists," a newspaper enthused, discussing the grand duchess Olga Alexandrova, sister-in-law to the empress, who served as an ordinary sister of mercy at a hospital in the town of Rovno, safely away from battle.[3]

Women's wartime service could blur gender boundaries. Women who served at the front often had to display qualities, such as courage and toughness, that their contemporaries considered masculine. In preparation for her departure for the front, Lidia Zakharova, an upper-class woman, acquired a pair of sturdy peasant boots and a man's leather jacket. "With God's help," she wrote, "my transformation went well, the feminine in me decreased more and more, and I did not know whether to be sad or glad about this."[4] At the front, Russian nurses faced all the hardships that soldiers did. They served in regimental aid stations and as litter bearers, sometimes even entering no-man's-land to retrieve casualties. Their proximity to war and soldiers and, perhaps, the sexual adventures of some, gave nurses who worked at the front a reputation as sexually promiscuous. "Did you know that the general run of Sisters at the Front had a bad name?" a new nursing recruit was asked.[5] However, the press rarely portrayed them taking the risks that many faced on a daily basis, nor did it purvey sexual innuendos. Instead, the wartime press upheld gender distinctions, portraying nurses as caring mothers, handholding lovers, and untouchable beauties. Nurses became gendered symbols of patriotic virtue, the feminine counterpart of the masculine soldier.

Women who took up arms were not so easily categorized. Initially, most disguised themselves as men: they cut their hair, tried to acquire a masculine demeanor, donned a uniform, and attempted to enlist in an army unit. Although most were rejected, a few managed to win the consent of a company or regimental commander and succeeded in joining a fighting unit. They derived from every level of Russian society. A Princess A. M. Shakhovskaia,

---

[2] Nadezhda Iakusheva, "1914 god. Provintsiia," *Moskovskii Zhurnal*, 5 (1993), 55.

[3] *Petrogradskaia gazeta*, 272 (Oct. 4, 1914).

[4] Quoted in Alfred Meyer, "The Impact of World War I on Russian Women's Lives," in Barbara Clements, Barbara Engel, and Christine Worobec (eds.), *Russia's Women: Accommodation, Resistance, Transformation* (Berkeley, Calif.: University of California Press, 1991), 209.

[5] Florence Farmborough, *With the Armies of the Tsar* (New York: Stein and Day, 1975), 151.

who held a pilot's license, served as a military pilot. Another wealthy woman donated her automobiles to the army and drove one of them in reconnaissance missions along the front lines. After the fall of the tsar in February 1917, women soldiers would become more common. The most famous was Maria Bochkareva, daughter of a former peasant serf from Novgorod province, who found the very idea of battle enticing: "My heart yearned to be there in the seething cauldron of war, to be baptized in its fire and scorched in its lava," she later recalled in her characteristically overheated language.[6] Decorated for bravery several times, Bochkareva made a specialty of rescuing wounded soldiers from under fire. Some women found her actions inspiring. Learning of Bochkareva's exploits, "we sisters [nurses at the front] were of course thrilled to the core."[7]

But most women contributed to the war effort in more conventionally feminine ways. Instead of attending parties, women of the elites gathered to knit scarves for the wounded while sharing news of the front. "How could we enjoy ourselves when blood was being spilled?" wondered Irina Elenevskaia, daughter of an official at the Ministry of Foreign Affairs. The wife of the Minister of Foreign Affairs called on the wives of all senior officials in her husband's ministry, requesting them to appear at her home twice a week to sew bandages for the wounded.[8] In provincial Chernigov, young women unable to serve as nurses instead rolled bandages on a special machine. The Winter Palace, too, was turned into a gigantic workshop where women prepared linens and bandages for the war. Other women made clothing and assembled food packages for the troops. They also staffed tearooms and soup kitchens for soldiers in transit and assisted the wounded and disabled in a variety of ways.

Women's mobilization to assist refugees added a new dimension to their public role. The German invasion of Russia's western borderlands forced millions from their homes. Comprised mostly of women and children, refugees encountered enormous difficulty finding housing and work and re-creating some semblance of normal life. All over Russia, "ladies committees" and "ladies circles" sprang up to assist them. The ladies collected money to support refugees, set up kitchens and canteens to feed them, found them housing, and created sewing circles to provide the women refugees with work. In keeping with middle-class women's self-appointed role as moral guardians of the less fortunate, the ladies assumed responsibility for the moral well-being of their charges, too. Concerned to "protect" refugee women from the dangers of rape and prostitution, their benefactors monitored their sexual behavior,

---

[6] Quoted in Jane McDermid and Anna Hillyar, *Women and Work in Russia, 1880–1930. A Study of Continuity Through Change* (New York: Longman, 1998), 141.

[7] Farmborough, *With the Armies*, 300.

[8] Irina Elenevskaia, *Vospominaniia* (Stockholm: n.p., 1968), 57–63.

endeavoring to keep them "straight and out of temptation."[9] Women's assumption of responsibility for the welfare of refugees, even more than their participation in war work, expanded their role in the public sphere.

War offered new opportunities to women in other spheres as well. New jobs opened up in factories that men abandoned for the front: from 26.6 percent of the workforce in 1914, the proportion of women in Russian industry as a whole rose to 43.2 percent by 1917. Over a quarter of a million women workers joined the industrial workforce in those years, raising the number of women workers to over a million. Although, as before, the majority of women remained concentrated in trades such as domestic service and laundry, which required little skill and paid low wages, unprecedented numbers gained access to well-paying positions in male-dominated trades, in the chemical and metalworking industries in particular. In Petrograd (formerly St. Petersburg), the heart of Russia's elite metalworking industry, women constituted 20 percent of metalworkers by the end of 1916. Women broke into other occupations hitherto closed to them, such as the postal service and transport, and their numbers expanded in white collar positions, such as accountancy, office work, and telegraph operation.[10] Women teachers finally gained the right to teach in secondary schools. Under the pressures of war, official efforts to limit women's participation in the workforce to spheres associated with their gender collapsed almost completely.

These changes raised feminist hopes for the future. In an effort to impress upon others the magnitude of women's role, feminist newspapers celebrated the new responsibilities that women assumed:

> Now in the epoch of the great war, it becomes clear that, in spite of her present lack of civil rights, woman is strong. . . . According to the obsolete male philosophy, sorry and helpless tears should have been the destiny of the women left behind. But at this historical moment for Russia, women are proving that they have no time to cry. Merchants' wives are running vast trading businesses, peasant women are responsible for the cultivation of the land, and we now have female tram conductors, points-women, cab-women, female porters and street-cleaners, dray-women and even female soldiers. . . . All we have to do is prove ourselves in our new jobs so that in the future, after the war, we shall remain in our present, newly gained positions.[11]

Women's wartime activities served to strengthen the feminist argument on behalf of women's rights. At the same time, anticipated gains in the postwar future helped to sustain feminist enthusiasm for the war effort long after the hope for quick victory had been lost.

---

[9] Peter Gattrell, *A Whole Empire Walking: Refugees in Russia During World War I* (Bloomington, Ind.: Indiana University Press, 1999), 115–26.

[10] Meyer, "The Impact," 213–4.

[11] Quoted in Jane McDermid and Anna Hillyar, *Midwives of the Revolution: Female Bolsheviks and Women Workers in 1917* (Athens, Ohio: Ohio University Press, 1999), 119.

Far less is known about the initial reaction of lower-class women to the outbreak of war. There is evidence that some of them, like their upper class sisters, longed to be part of the "nation," and a few even joined the army, as did Maria Bochkareva. But far more expressed indifference or hostility to the war. During the induction of breadwinner husbands, peasant wives would sometimes riot in protest. And subsequently, as desertion mounted, peasant women concealed husbands, sons, and brothers who fled the fighting. Whatever their feelings, the war unavoidably involved millions of village women in national politics. Peasant women participated in record numbers in adult education courses, seeking to obtain the literacy necessary to correspond with soldier husbands and to stay abreast of the news. With men dead or at war, all the responsibility for heavy fieldwork descended onto the shoulders of women, children, and the elderly, sometimes assisted by political prisoners. In men's absence, women gained greater rights in the village assembly, the *skhod*.

Their experience of war both raised and frustrated the expectations of soldiers' wives (*soldatki*). In 1912, the government had assumed responsibility for caring for the families of men called to active duty, establishing an obligatory state allowance to be distributed to wives and children. On August 11, 1914, the Supreme Council for the Care of Soldiers' Families and of the Families of the Wounded and the Dead was formed under the presidency of the Empress Alexandra. But the government, lacking both the necessary personnel and adequate finances, proved unable to fulfill its promises. Despite the failure, public acknowledgment that soldiers' wives had particular needs and their husbands certain rights gave the women a new sense of entitlement to public resources. During the war, *soldatki* mobilized to an unprecedented degree. As individuals, they bombarded officials with letters and petitions setting forth their economic circumstances and demanding that the state fulfill its promises. Dozens, sometimes hundreds of *soldatki* also staged riots in the small towns and district centers to which village women sometimes traveled to complain about officials' neglect or to receive their stipend.

Whatever their initial reaction to the outbreak of war, most lower-class women soon ceased to support it. Severe economic dislocations markedly increased political discontent among the urban lower classes. Consumer prices rose sharply; items of prime necessity like bread and sugar grew scarce. When it became evident that the war would require enormous sacrifices from workers but bring few benefits, the strike movement resumed and quickly acquired an antiwar flavor. Thousands of workers went on strike daily; the strike movement cost roughly $4\frac{1}{2}$ million lost working days between the fall of 1915 and the fall of 1916, with skilled trades such as metalworking taking the lead. Women remained less militant than men. Trades in which women predominated, such as textiles, tobacco, and food processing, which had been inundated with new and very youthful workers (many aged twelve to fourteen), played a relatively minor part in war-time protests. Nevertheless, in metal-working and other war-related industries, women and men went on strike together. As the strike movement became politicized, some of these women workers, more educated and skilled than their sisters in other trades, began to speak in a distinctively female voice. Hundreds called for equalizing men's and women's wages at two different meetings held in late February 1916, indicating a growing self-assertiveness among a sector of women workers.

Lower-class women became more assertive in their domestic roles as well. In the cities, scarce goods and rising prices made it increasingly difficult for women to sustain their families. In the spring of 1915, women began to protest the hardships, sometimes by themselves, sometimes accompanied by men or youths. Subsistence revolts rocked Russia's cities and towns. Women work-ers, soldiers' wives, and working-class housewives, outraged by the escalating cost of essential goods, took the lead. With an aggressiveness born of des-peration, they attacked the shops of merchants suspected of speculation and appropriated goods for themselves at prices they believed to be just. Women defied the efforts of police and Cossack detachments to stop them, sometimes defending themselves by tossing stones and bricks. Women's anger at mer-chants and tradesmen for allegedly robbing the people reflected the growing alienation of Russia's lower classes, and their anger at the "well-to-do" who supposedly enjoyed privileged access to short supplies exacerbated growing social polarization.[12]

Popular dissatisfaction took a political direction. When women demanded that civil authorities satisfy their demand for affordable goods, the authorities failed to respond. Consequently, as the food situation deteriorated, popular attitudes became fiercely antiwar and antigovernment. According to police reports, among themselves in the marketplace, women complained bitterly: "They are slaughtering our husbands and our sons in the war, and at home, they want to starve us to death."[13] Equally unnerving for the authorities, women's protests in the marketplace frequently spilled over onto the factory floor. In the wake of subsistence riots, thousands of male and female workers sometimes walked off the job, demanding higher wages, lower prices, and an end to war.

The February Revolution

The situation reached a critical point on International Women's Day, February 23 (March 8), 1917. Over the winter, the numbers of both strikes and

---

[12] Barbara Alpern Engel, "Not by Bread Alone: Subsistence Riots in Russia During World War I," *Journal of Modern History* 69 (December 1997), 696–717.

[13] Quoted in Ibid., 717.

strikers had increased dramatically, and the numbers of women who joined the strikes were growing. The tone of strikes was often explicitly political. In Petrograd, angry working-class women, both housewives and factory workers, staged an enormous demonstration on February 23rd, calling for bread and peace. Stopping at factories that were still in operation, they demanded that others join them. Recalled a worker at the Nobel Engineering Works in the heavily working-class Vyborg district of St. Petersburg:

> We could hear women's voices in the lane overlooked by the windows of our department: "Down with high prices!" "Down with hunger!" "Bread for the Workers!" I and several comrades rushed at once to the windows. . . . The gates of No. 1 Bol'shaia Sampsonievskaia mill were flung open. Masses of women workers in a militant frame of mind filled the lane. Those who caught sight of us began to wave their arms, shouting: "Come out!" "Stop work!" Snowballs flew through the windows. We decided to join the demonstration.[14]

Over the next few days, hundreds of thousands of other workers followed suit. The critical moment came when tsarist troops refused orders to fire on the demonstrators, transforming the women's protest into full-scale revolution. On March 2, 1917 (Old Style), Tsar Nicholas II agreed to abdicate the throne. A provisional government stepped into the vacuum of authority.

From the first, women claimed citizenship rights in the new political order. Feminist leaders, jubilant at the fall of the tsar, launched a successful campaign for the vote. When the provisional government failed to include sexual equality in its original political program, feminists mobilized. They held conferences and meetings that sometimes proved so popular that people had to be turned away. On March 20, 1917, they mounted a huge procession numbering up to 40,000 people, who marched from the Petrograd city Duma to the Tauride palace where the provisional government was in session, to lobby it on behalf of women's suffrage. A female militia mounted on horseback accompanied the procession and marchers carried streamers reading: "The Woman's Place – Is in the Constituent Assembly."

The procession was led by Vera Figner, released from prison following the revolution of 1905, and Poliksena Shishkina-Iavein, a physician and since 1910, head of the Russian League of Equal Rights for Women. Addressing the nation's new leaders, Shishkina-Iavein declared: "We have come here to remind you that women were your faithful comrades in the gigantic struggle for the freedom of the Russian people; that they also have been filling up the prisons and boldly marched to the gallows." She demanded that women be recognized as citizens: "We declare that the Constituent Assembly in which

---

[14] Quoted in Steve Smith, "Petrograd in 1917: The View from Below," in Daniel Kaiser (ed.), *The Workers Revolution in Russia, 1917: The View from Below* (New York: Cambridge University Press, 1987), 61.

only one half of the population is represented can in no wise be regarded as expressing the will of the whole people, but only half of it."[15]

The provisional government eventually acquiesced. In June 1917, women lawyers finally gained the right to serve as attorneys and represent clients in court. Women also obtained equal rights with men in the civil service – especially important for teachers. On July 20, all adults over the age of twenty, women and men alike, gained the right to vote for the forthcoming Constituent Assembly. The provisional government's willingness to accede to feminist demands won it the cautious support of feminists, including support for Russia's continued participation in the war.

The war itself, now viewed as truly national (as opposed to tsarist-imperial), elicited new enthusiasm in some quarters. The Ministry of War began receiving requests to form all-female military units. In the hope that women soldiers would shame male recruits, now refusing to fight and deserting in record numbers, at the end of May 1917 the Minister gave Maria Bochkareva the go-ahead to recruit for the 1st Petrograd Women's Battalion of Death; a second Moscow Women's Battalion of Death was also formed. Thousands of women volunteered. Others formed independent women's military units. A woman soldier "was no unusual sight" in the Russian army, a frontline nurse observed in the summer of 1917. In order to gain control of these units as well as to satisfy women's demand for expanded military opportunities, the government was forced to increase the number of women's military formations. The number of women involved in combat and combat-related activities grew so large that in August 1917, a Women's Military Congress was held in Petrograd to coordinate their work.[16] By the end of the war, some 6,000 Russian women had engaged in combat, a record unique for World War I (Fig. 12).

Although lower-class women shared in the general postrevolutionary euphoria, their needs and aspirations often differed from those of liberal feminists. When one of the feminists approached a crowd of women lined up at a bakery after the suffrage victory and declared: "I congratulate you, citizenesses, we Russian women are going to receive [our] rights," she was met with indifference and incomprehension.[17] When, in the aftermath of the February Revolution, lower-class women grew more assertive, they rarely pursued women's political rights as such or the right to take up arms. Take

[15] Quoted in Edmondson, *Feminism in Russia*, 166. Author's Note: I have slightly altered her translation.

[16] Farmborough, *With the Armies*, 300; Laurie Stoff, "They Fought for Russia: Female Soldiers of the First World War," in Gerard J. DeGroot and Corinna Peniston–Bird (eds.), *A Soldier and a Woman: Sexual Integration in the Military* (Essex, England: Pearson Education, 2000), 69–78.

[17] Quoted in Richard Stites, *The Women's Liberation Movement in Russia: Feminism, Nihilism and Bolshevism* (Princeton, N. J.: Princeton University Press, 1990), 294.

12. Women's naval crew, courtesy of the New York Public Library

the example of soldiers' wives (*soldatki*), among the most forceful in the aftermath of the February Revolution. Disrupting a meeting of women in the harbor region of Petrograd and demanding an increase in their allotment in mid–March 1917, the *soldatki* asserted the primacy of their needs. "Everyone speaks of the women workers, the domestic servants and the laundry workers,

13. March of soldiers' wives, courtesy of the New York Public Library

but about soldiers' wives not a word."[18] The *soldatki* subsided only after the meeting passed a resolution addressing the allotment issue. On April 11, 1917, about 15,000 soldiers' wives took their cause to the streets in a massive demonstration along Nevskii Prospekt. "Increase the allotments to families of soldiers defending freedom and the people's peace" and "Feed the children of the defenders of the motherland" their handmade placards declared. In June, the women formed the Union of Soldiers' Wives; soldiers' wives also organized in the city of Tula. Linking their demands with the interests of the nation, *soldatki* sought economic rather than political rights and identified themselves as wives and mothers, rather than as autonomous citizens (Fig. 13).

Among workers, the language of class rather than gender exerted the greatest rhetorical force in 1917. "We, a group of Russian women and mothers, are joining the protest of the working people against the war," reads the proclamation of the Smolensk Initiative Group of Women and Mothers, published in an independent socialist newspaper in May 1917. "Enough of this horrible bloodshed, which is utterly pointless for the working people. Enough of sacrificing our sons to the capitalists' inflamed greed."[19] Emboldened by the new freedom to organize, women workers in trades hitherto quiescent

[18] Quoted in Rex Wade, *The Russian Revolution, 1917* (New York: Cambridge University Press, 2000), 121–2.

[19] Mark D. Steinberg (ed.), *Voices of Revolution, 1917* (New Haven: Yale University Press, 2001), 98.

demonstrated unprecedented readiness to defend their interests. In May, over 3000 laundresses walked out in a strike led by their new union. To their demands for an eight-hour day and a minimum wage of 4 rubles a day, employers responded with threats to lock them out and evict them from their dwellings. Some of the picketers were attacked physically, others were arrested. The owners organized a rival union; strike-breaking became widespread. However, the laundresses persisted and, after a month, won a modest victory.

Another strike of mainly female dye workers lasted from May 13 to September 1917. Led by the new chemical workers union, the strike was widely supported by labor organizations; it nevertheless ended in failure. Most women workers proved more reluctant to strike, however, and when they did strike, their actions were most often defensive. Recognizing the odds against victory, women feared that plants would be closed, depriving them of the ability to support themselves and their children. Their fears were only heightened by the fact that male workers, when threatened with layoffs, sometimes suggested that women be laid off first.

Economic anxieties intensified instead of diminishing as 1917 proceeded; inflation outpaced raises and food disappeared from the cities. It was women whose bodies reflected the strain. "Everyone's gone gray, worn down with care, their faces long," a Petrograd woman confided to her diary in early October. "The faces of simple women are especially striking... care is inscribed on their worn faces."[20] The streets had emptied, except for the endless lines in front of food shops. Food-related disorders erupted again in late summer and early fall, with women's active participation.

Recognizing women's new visibility, during 1917 all the socialist parties, and the Bolsheviks in particular, intensified their efforts to garner support from women. Pressured by women activists, in March the Bolsheviks abandoned their initial reluctance and approved a Bureau of Women Workers to agitate among women and shortly thereafter revived publication of the *Working Woman* (*Rabotnitsa*), which had appeared briefly in 1914. Its editorial board soon became the unacknowledged center for Bolshevik work among women: organizing meetings, setting up a school for agitators, attempting to popularize Bolshevik positions, and trying to raise women's consciousness. Activists sought to convince lower-class women that their interests lay with their fellow workers, rather than with "bourgeois" feminists and the provisional government, and that only socialist revolution could bring genuine liberation. Bolshevik press carried reports of women's strike actions and street protests and accounts of women's particular grievances. At meetings and demonstrations that attracted thousands of women workers as well as on the pages of

---

[20] " 'Nu polno, mne zagadyvat' o khode istorii . . .' (Iz dnevnika materi-khoziaiki v gody revoliutsii v Rossii," *Otechestvennaia Istoriia*, 3 (1997), 83.

Rabotnitsa, organizers pointed out the reasons for the continued suffering of lower-class women – the war and high prices – and promised to end them when the Bolsheviks came to power. The Bolsheviks enthusiastically supported the strike of the laundresses and the demands of *soldatki* for higher wages.[21] The Mensheviks, the Bolsheviks' more moderate Marxist rivals, who also published a magazine aimed at working women, were less active than the Bolsheviks; the Socialist Revolutionary party was less active still, despite the prominence of a woman, Maria Spiridonova, in the left wing of the party.

Nevertheless, it is difficult to know where lower-class women's political sympathies lay. Lower-class women were rarely in the forefront of organized political action. Contemporary sources such as newspapers tended to ignore women, except when their activities, such as charitable work and care of refugees, fell within women's traditional sphere or when they engaged in strikes and protests, as *soldatki* frequently did. Consequently, in the records of the eight months between the February and October Revolutions, a time of widespread popular activism and intense political struggle, it is surprisingly difficult to detect lower-class women's voices or to discern their aspirations. When women's voices do become audible, it is often because they attended meetings inspired or organized by one of the socialist parties, the Bolsheviks in particular, or wrote to a Bolshevik newspaper. By working together hand in hand, women workers could "make this life more beautiful, pure and bright for ourselves, for our children and for the whole working class," a woman worker wrote in *Rabotnitsa*.[22] A document collection published in the Soviet Union revealed that on March 17, a meeting of women workers in Petrograd passed a resolution demanding full equality for women, laws to protect the labor of women and children, and the abolition of night work, as well as a democratic republic, the eight-hour day, and land for the peasantry. Later that month, women workers in the city endorsed a similar resolution in which they also expressed solidarity with the workers movement and distinguished themselves from "women of the bourgeois movement."[23] However, it is hard to know how representative such statements were.

What can be said with certainty is this: Lower-class women took enthusiastic advantage of new political opportunities, but the greater the responsibility or commitment required, the fewer the women involved. Record numbers of women participated in meetings and demonstrations. In the city of Moscow, so many women turned out to vote in municipal elections that they surprised observers. Yet only a few of the factories where women

[21] Moira Donald, "Bolshevik Activity Amongst the Working Women of Petrograd in 1917," *International Review of Social History*, 27, pt. 2 (1982), 142–8.

[22] Steinberg, *Voices*, 106.

[23] *Revoliutsionnoe dvizhenie v Rossii posle sverzheniia samoderzhaviia. Dokumenty i materialy* (Moscow: Izd-vo Akademii Nauk SSSR, 1957), 470, 578.

predominated formulated the resolutions on pressing economic and political issues that became ubiquitous in 1917. Women were poorly represented in the trade unions and factory committees that spoke on behalf of workers' interests. Despite the high proportion of women in the factory labor force, at the First Conference of Factory Committees, held in Petrograd in late May, only 4 percent of the delegates representing particular factories were women. Few women offered themselves as candidates or were chosen to run in elections to local *soviets* (councils), and fewer still were elected, even where women numbered over half of the labor force.

Women's low political profile was surely the result of their lack of political experience and long-standing habits of deference. It also followed from the gendered nature of working class self-identification. At factory meetings, men often stopped women from speaking or did not listen to women when they spoke. Members of the working class perceived themselves as a brotherhood, not a sisterhood, even when the members themselves were female. "Let us, Russian women and mothers, be proud knowing that we were the first to extend our brotherly [sic] hand to all the mothers the world over," reads the proclamation of the Smolensk Initiative Group.[24] Long-standing distinctions between male and female workers based on skill, attachment to the village, and cultural practices grew in symbolic significance. Women rarely figured even as symbols of the socialist movement and when they did, it was never as a female factory worker. On the other hand, images of male workers were ubiquitous, "either as the brother of the male peasant and/or the soldier . . . or else as the liberator of the world, breaking chains and crowns." The masculine identity of the worker, forged in the prerevolutionary workplace and essential to the development of the revolutionary movement, reinforced the assumption among lower-class women as well as men that active political participation remained a male prerogative.[25] In consequence, with the exception of feminists, men far outnumbered women in the organizations that struggled for political power and control over everyday life during the eight months that followed the fall of the tsar.

Engendering Revolution

The Bolshevik seizure of power never displaced this gendered hierarchy, codifying it instead. On October 24–6, 1917 (Old Style), the Petrograd Bolsheviks overthrew the provisional government in the name of a government of Soviets but in fact reserving power for themselves. After several

[24] Steinberg, *Voices*, 98.
[25] Orlando Figes and Boris Kolonitskii, *Interpreting the Russian Revolution: The Language and Symbols of 1917* (New Haven, Conn.: Yale University Press, 1999), 110.

weeks, the Bolsheviks assumed control of Moscow and other cities of Central and Northern Russia. Although in actuality a coup d'etat, the Bolshevik action nevertheless enjoyed substantial support from the working class in whose name they acted, as their garnering of about a quarter of the votes in elections to the Constituent Assembly held in November demonstrated. Nevertheless, by excluding liberals and other leftist parties and redefining citizenship as arising from class rather than nation, the Bolshevik leadership substantially narrowed its appeal and created enemies where it might have found friends. From the outset, the new government faced massive opposition, supported by Russia's former wartime allies with money and troops. In spring of 1918, a civil war erupted in earnest.

The extent of female participation in that war effort suggests a substantial reservoir of support for Bolshevik rule. Unlike laboring men, all of whom became subject to military conscription, women's participation in military operations was voluntary. By fall of 1920, between 50,000 and 70,000 women had joined the Red Army, constituting about 2 percent of the armed forces. Many engaged directly in combat, serving as riflewomen, commanders of armored trains, even machine gunners. Some women actually assumed command of men; others worked as political officers, carrying out agitation and propaganda among Red Army soldiers. But most were assigned to clerical work or to medical units as nurses, a role that women had also played during World War I. About 20,000 women provided medical support at the front.[26] By taking part in the struggle to defend the revolution, these women staked claim to a place in the new social and political order.

In the grim circumstances of Civil War, the Bolsheviks first attempted to carry out a vision of social transformation that included the emancipation of women. Prerevolutionary feminism, condemned as bourgeois, disappeared as an independent political and intellectual current. However, drawing on Marxist thought, a Bolshevik variety of feminism became part of the political discourse. The Bolsheviks proposed to equalize the relations between the sexes by socializing housework – that is, entrusting household tasks to paid workers, thus enabling women to become full and equal participants in waged labor, which Marxists viewed as the key to their liberation. The party leader, Vladimir I. Lenin, was particularly emphatic about the need to relieve women of household chores so that they could participate in "socially useful" production. "Petty housework crushes, strangles, stultifies and degrades" a woman, he wrote, chaining her to the kitchen and to the nursery and wasting her labor.[27] Some Bolshevik feminists went further: they called for the

[26] Elizabeth Wood, *The Baba and the Comrade: Gender and Politics in Revolutionary Russia* (Bloomington, Ind.: Indiana University Press, 1997), 56.

[27] Vladimir I. Lenin, *Women and Society* (New York, 1938), 13–5.

emancipation of women from all social constraints, the family included, except for those that women chose for themselves. Both agreed that once free
of the need to exchange their domestic and sexual services for men's financial
support, women would encounter men as equals. Eventually, the family itself
would wither away and women and men would unite their lives solely for
love. Historians disagree about motivation. Some take the Bolsheviks at their
word, pointing to new initiatives undertaken and the many doors that opened
to women; others, however, question the sincerity of the Bolshevik commitment to women's emancipation, emphasizing its instrumental nature and the
persistence of gender stereotypes. The record offers evidence to support both
positions.

Almost immediately, the new government took steps to democratize the
family. In 1918, the government produced a family code that fulfilled some
of the long-standing aspirations of progressive jurists. The code equalized
women's status with men's, removed marriage from the hands of the church,
allowed a marrying couple to choose either the husband's or the wife's sur-
name, and granted illegitimate children the same legal rights as legitimate
ones. Divorce, exceedingly difficult in the tsarist period, became easily ob-
tainable at the request of either spouse. Laboring women gained eight weeks
of paid maternity leave, before and after childbirth. In 1920, abortion became legal if performed by a physician. Whenever possible, new decrees used
language that was deliberately gender-neutral. "Spouses" could retain their
nationality upon marriage. A "spouse" unable to work could request support
from the other. A decree on wages stated that "women who do equal work
with men in quantity and in quality" should receive equal pay.[28] Coeducation
became the rule.

The revolution also opened new doors to lower-class women and sought
to eliminate the political, social, and gender hierarchies that relegated them
to the lowest status. Workers, formerly at the bottom of society socially and
politically, now supposedly stood at the top, a new "ruling class." Gender
and sexual relations became open to redefinition and renegotiation. In small
meetings and large, the party encouraged women to imagine a better future,
even as it sought to harness women's dreams to the revolution's political purposes. Kristina Suvorova, a housewife in a far northern town, remembered
the sense of inclusion she felt during weekly meetings between soldier's wives
like herself and the local Bolshevik party secretary: "We talked about freedom
and the equality of women, about warm sinks for rinsing clothes; we dreamed
about running water in the apartment. . . . [The local party committee] workers treated us with sincere attention, respectfully listened to us, delicately

---

[28] Wood, *The Baba*, 50.

pointed out our errors, little by little taught us wisdom and reason. We felt like we were one happy family."[29]

In November 1918, the first All-Russian Conference of Working Women took place, organized by Alexandra Kollontai and Inessa Armand, leading proponents of Bolshevik feminism. The conference attracted 1,147 women, far more than the 300 that organizers expected. Women's emancipation was a crucial component of socialism, the organizers reiterated; women should create a new life for themselves. Armand lectured about the need to establish state-sponsored nurseries, laundries, and kitchens in order to free women to participate in public life. In August 1919, the Central Committee of the Communist Party, as the Bolsheviks had renamed themselves, granted permission for the formation of a Women's Bureau (*Zhenotdel*) to coordinate the party's work among women. Armand, less militant than Kollontai, was designated its first director. The party conceived of the *Zhenotdel* as an agency to mobilize women to support its objectives and to inform women of their new rights. It was to be a transmission belt for party policy, from the leadership downward.[30] However, because *Zhenotdel* leaders had their own vision, it quickly became far more. Despite a perpetual shortage of funds, the *Zhenotdel* did its best to establish a basis for women's liberation by setting up child care centers, communal dining halls, and other services.

The *Zhenotdel* also mobilized factory women to become advocates on their own behalf. Selected as delegates to the *Zhenotdel*, factory women temporarily left the workplace to gain the political experience that would enable them to become more active in their local soviets, trade unions, and party organizations. Delegates attended literacy classes and meetings where they heard reports on political issues and learned how to organize facilities for working women, such as factory daycare centers. After three to six months, the delegate would return to full-time factory work, report on her experiences to her female co-workers, and be replaced by a new delegate.[31] In this way, the *Zhenotdel* broadened the horizons of millions of women and encouraged them to take active part in public life. Thousands of women joined the party. By 1922, the number of female members exceeded 30,000, although they still remained a minority, about 8 percent of party membership.

However, the material conditions that followed the revolution were not propitious for anyone's emancipation. The civil war brought hardship and misery. About a million men perished in the civil war, in addition to the $2\frac{1}{2}$ million

[29] Quoted in Barbara Evans Clements, *Bolshevik Women* (New York: Cambridge University Press, 1997), 169.

[30] Ralph C. Elwood, *Inessa Armand: Revolutionary and Feminist* (New York: Cambridge University Press, 1992), 236–9, 242–4.

[31] Stites, *The Women's Liberation Movement*, 336–8.

lost on the battlefields of World War I. The economy disintegrated almost completely. When the food situation, critical at the time of the Bolshevik takeover, became catastrophic for urban dwellers, the Bolsheviks assumed control of the economy. They abolished trade and shut down privately owned services. Returning to Russia in 1919 to assist her imprisoned husband, the aristocratic Sofia Volkonskaia discovered to her dismay that "hostels did not exist, there were no apartments or rooms to let; all restaurants had been closed, all shops abolished. You were not allowed to buy either a piece of bread or a pair of stockings – not even a button."[32] Those who could escaped the city: by the end of the civil war, Moscow had lost half of its population, Petrograd had lost two thirds. The majority of those remaining were women left to fend for themselves in desperate circumstances. Women deriving from the formerly privileged classes, formally excluded from government rations, were in the worst position, forced to sell clothing and other goods merely to put food on the table. Lower-class women, however, were scarcely better off. Their men dead or fighting in the civil war, women worked for wages all day, then scrounged for food and fuel at night. Wrapped up in the "most peculiar ways," they stood freezing in lines in front of grocery stores, "waiting for the pathetic pittance of another ration."[33] People starved to death or froze. Epidemic diseases killed millions; typhus alone took the lives of 1.5 million people between 1918 and 1919. Millions of homeless children wandered the streets, their parents dead or unable to care for them.

State-sponsored efforts to assume domestic functions were crippled by the terrible material scarcity of those years as well as by their ad hoc nature. To feed the urban population, the government forcibly requisitioned grain from the peasantry and opened public dining rooms and canteens. The regime established shelters and children's homes to care for homeless children. But instead of serving as shining examples of the socialist future, these depressing and underfunded institutions made a negative impression on those who used them. If this was socialized housework, then who needed it? In the short run at least, the revolution and civil war worsened most women and children's lives. The deaths of millions of men deprived wives of husbands and children of fathers and destroyed fragile family economies.[34]

Moreover, waves of change encountered an undertow of gendered resistance from the first. The strain of years of warfare left its mark on people's

[32] Sheila Fitzpatrick and Yuri Slezkine (eds.), *In the Shadow of Revolution: Life Stories of Russian Women from 1917 to the Second World War* (Princeton, N.J.: Princeton University Press, 2000), 150.

[33] Fitzpatrick and Slezkine, *In the shadow*, 107.

[34] Wendy Goldman, *Women, the State and Revolution: Soviet Family Policy and Social Life, 1917–1936* (New York: Cambridge University Press, 1993), 60–7.

psyches. Although images of domesticity had played little role in World War I propaganda, the war intensified nostalgia for hearth and home, a nostalgia that became embodied in idealized images of family and village that, in the eyes of ordinary soldiers, had come to represent the nation. But the new leadership was also responsible for the reassertion of gender differences. During the civil war, the Red Army became the crucible of citizenship and the building block of the new state order. However, as a result of the authorities' decision against obligatory military service for women, the army became identified as a male domain. Even the oath taken by new recruits adopted the male voice: "I, a son of the laboring people, citizen of the Soviet Republic, take on the calling of warrior in the Worker and Peasants Army."[35]

In addition, the brutalizing circumstances of civil warfare seemed to necessitate traditionally masculine qualities. A willingness to be hard and tough was required not only of people who participated in combat but also of those who occupied responsible administrative positions because, frequently, they succeeded in enforcing decisions only at the point of a pistol. Plenty of women were prepared to be tough, but many more could not, or would not, embrace the necessary hardness. And women's attempts at toughness evoked an ambivalence that men's did not. Red Army soldiers complained about the women in their midst and harassed them verbally and physically. The leadership itself sent women a mixed message, emphasizing the uniquely feminine contribution that women could make even as it tried to efface distinctions of gender. Civilian women were encouraged to take presents to wounded soldiers, to sew linens for them, and to help them to read and write letters. A labor conscription decree of October 30, 1920, actually required that all townswomen between ages sixteen and forty-five sew undergarments and linen for the Red Army. Slogans reinforced the notion that it was women's responsibility to care for fighting men and men's to protect women and children: "Proletarka! The Red Army soldier is defending you and your children. Ease his life. Organize care for him."[36] Women themselves often accepted a gendered definition of their appropriate role. Anna Andzhievskaia, a party member who went as a medic to the front, volunteered to organize a communist sewing shop for the fighters, in which women communists and Communist wives sewed the fighters' uniforms and linen.[37] The highly militarized atmosphere that prevailed during the civil war tended to reinforce rather than undermine traditional gender stereotypes.

---

[35] Quoted in Wood, *Baba and Comrade*, 53.   [36] Ibid., 58–9.
[37] Fitzpatrick and Slezkine, *In the Shadow*, 77.

Conclusion

The period of upheaval that began in February 1917 came to a close with the Bolshevik victory in the civil war. As political struggle assumed more institutionalized forms, the women who had occupied center stage in February receded into the background, their places assumed by men. Nevertheless, although women's visibility diminished, it did so only relative to their earlier prominence during the revolution and civil war. Never before had so many of Russia's women felt such a stake in politics; equally unprecedented was the need felt by political leaders to secure women's support. Even after liberal advocates of women's rights had been silenced, Bolshevik feminists continued to press for women's emancipation within the framework of Marxist discourse. If traditional gender stereotypes had resurfaced, they nevertheless coexisted with other messages that empowered and encouraged women to reshape their lives according to their own desires.

Yet, instead of the bread and peace for which they had fought in 1917, what lower-class women obtained during the civil war was years of hunger and the loss of family members. "You have deceived us," women workers complained to the leadership. "You told us that there would be plenty but the opposite is true. Life is growing more difficult."[38] When in February 1921, angry urban crowds consisting mainly of women and youths turned yet again on government soldiers to demand an increase in the supply of bread, it appeared that in some respects, remarkably little had changed.

Suggestions for Further Reading

Clements, Barbara Evans. *Bolshevik Feminist: The Life of Alexandra Kollontai.* Bloomington, Ind.: Indiana University Press, 1979. *A biography of a pioneering Marxist feminist.*

Clements, Barbara Evans. *Bolshevik Women.* New York: Cambridge University Press, 1997. *A collective portrait of the female members of the Bolshevik party.*

Donald, M. "Bolshevik Activity Amongst the Working Women of Petrograd in 1917," *International Journal of Social History* 27, pt. 2 (1982), 131–160.

Elwood, R. C. *Inessa Armand: Revolutionary and Feminist.* New York: Cambridge University Press, 1992. *A study of an important, and neglected, revolutionary figure.*

Engel, Barbara Alpern. "Not by Bread Alone: Subsistence Riots in Russia During World War I," *Journal of Modern History* 69 (December 1997), 696–717.

Fitzpatrick, Sheila and Yuri Slezkine, eds. *In the Shadow of Revolution: Life Stories of Russian Women from 1917 to the Second World War.* Princeton, N.J.: Princeton University Press, 2000. *Part one contains the reminiscences of 1917 penned by women across the social spectrum.*

[38] Quoted in Wood, *Baba and Comrade*, 43.

Meyer, Alfred. "The Impact of World War I on Russian Women's Lives," in Barbara Clements, Barbara Engel and Christine Worobec, eds. *Russia's Women: Accommodation, Resistance, Transformation*. Berkeley, Calif.: University of California Press, 1991, 208–224.

Smith, Steve. "Class and Gender: Women's Strikes in St. Petersburg, 1895–1917 and in Shanghai, 1895–1927." *Social History* 19, no. 2 (May 1994), 143–168. *Traces the evolution of women's labor activism through 1917.*

Stoff, Laurie. "They Fought for Russia: Female Soldiers of the First World War." In Gerard J. DeGroot and Corinna Peniston-Bird, eds. *A Soldier and a Woman: Sexual Integration in the Military*. Essex, England: Pearson Education, 2000, 69–78.

Wood, Elizabeth. *The Baba and the Comrade: Gender and Politics in Revolutionary Russia*. Bloomington, Ind.: Indiana University Press, 1997. *Explores how gender structured early Bolshevik language and policy.*

8

CREATING THE "NEW SOVIET WOMAN"

In 1922, Sofia Pavlova joined the Communist party. Born in 1904 and raised in a family of railroad workers, several of whom became Bolsheviks while the party was still underground, Pavlova supported the revolution from the start. She fought in the civil war: "I had a Mauser, and we would go out to hunt down [rebel] bands – there were lots of them." When the war ended, her local party organization sent her and a girlfriend to study in a *Rabfak*, a school for workers, in Tomsk, Siberia, the nearest city. The two were among the very few women in their class, composed mainly of male civil war veterans. Pavlova performed well in school, and as a party member she engaged in a range of extracurricular, primarily political, activities. Part of this work involved mobilizing women. "I was also the organizer and leader of meetings for women delegates in the city," Pavlova recalled. "We assembled women, we told them what Communist power was, what it did. If some concrete task stood before us, such as collecting dried bread, we called upon them to do that."[1]

In 1924, the party dispatched Pavlova to Moscow, where for four years she attended the Krupskaia Academy of Communist Education. Named after Lenin's wife, Nadezhda Krupskaia, the academy prepared Communist cadres. After graduating, Pavlova became a teacher, then gradually advanced up the communist hierarchy to the International Division of the Central Committee of the Communist Party of the Soviet Union, where she worked for twenty-three years. One of tens of thousands of women to benefit from the revolution, yet no advocate of women's emancipation, Pavlova both exemplified and helped to perpetuate the revolution's ambivalent attitude toward women.

---

[1] Barbara Alpern Engel and Anastasia-Posadskaya-Vanderbeck (eds.), *A Revolution of Their Own: Voices of Women in Soviet History* (Boulder, Colo.: Westview Press, 1998), 58, 63.

The New Economic Policy

Late in 1920, the civil war drew to a close, ending seven years of warfare. The victorious communists were left with a devastated economy, producing at a fraction of its prewar level. The working class, in whose name the Bolsheviks had seized power, had almost vanished, dead on the battlefields of the civil war or reintegrated into the peasantry from which it had once derived. That peasantry was up in arms over forcible requisition of grain. In the city of Petrograd, cradle of the revolution, a temporary cut in the bread ration in February 1921 produced the most serious disturbances in years. Crowds of women and youths threw snowballs and swore at soldiers who were sent to control them. "Who are you aiming your rifle at sailor?" asked a woman aged about fifty, her coat flapping in an icy wind. "You should be helping us to go to Smolnyi [Bolshevik headquarters] and ask for bread."[2]

To resolve the economic crisis and quell widespread discontent, the new regime took steps that inadvertently undermined its ability to fulfill promises made to women. In March 1921, Lenin introduced the first of a series of measures that became known as the New Economic Policy (NEP) and that aimed at repairing relations with the peasantry. NEP replaced grain requisitioning with a tax in kind on peasant production, restored freedom of private trade, and ended the state monopoly on small and medium level manufacturing and on retail trade. While retaining ownership of the "commanding heights" of the economy, the regime permitted capitalist economic relations to prevail below and required managers of state enterprises to account for their costs. The retreat was only partial. Communists retained their monopoly of the organs of political power. Although during this period the media operated more freely and the public discussion of economic, cultural, and sometimes political matters was far more wide-ranging and diverse than would be the case for decades, the goal of building communism remained as important as ever, dominating public discourse. The questions were, at what pace would communism be built, how, and by whom?

During the 1920s, as debates raged over the answer to these questions both within and outside of the party, gender and everyday life (*byt*) acquired new significance. Gender was central to many of the key issues of the decade: Who would enjoy the fruits of socialist victory, and what form would that enjoyment take? What were the characteristics of the "new Soviet person"? How should she lead her life and where should she devote her energies? Who

---

[2] Quoted in Mary McAuley, "Bread Without the Bourgeoisie," in Diane P. Koenker, William G. Rosenberg, and Ronald Grigor Suny (eds.), *Party, State and Society in the Russian Civil War* (Bloomington, Ind.: Indiana University Press, 1989), 159.

held the authority to resolve such questions? Women's place in the new order depended on the answers.

Yet in the struggles to shape the new Soviet order, women were disadvantaged from the first. They occupied the margins, not the center, of a civic order in which the "new Soviet person" was construed as generically male and the public privileged over the private. The symbolic "brotherhood" of workers, first forged on the prerevolutionary shop floor, had been tempered in the fires of revolution and civil war, or so postrevolutionary imagery suggested. Revolutionary iconography consistently portrayed the heroic worker as male. Anyone who has ridden the Moscow subway has seen representations of him: young, muscular, often bearing arms, he stands triumphant in his victory over capitalism. He reflects the communist ideal of "conscious" worker: skilled, literate, sober, committed to revolution and to constructing the communist future. His antecedents emerged in propaganda posters during the decade following the revolution. Glorifying the working class, such posters conveyed new ideals to an illiterate or semiliterate audience. They portrayed men at the center of action, battling the opponents of revolution or refashioning the world. When women were depicted, it was sometimes as "backward," providing a foil that emphasized the ideal worker's superiority as well as reflecting assumptions commonplace among the leadership (female as well as male) about the character of lower-class women's consciousness and the danger they posed to revolution. In posters as in life, women fulfilled at best the supporting roles to which the revolution relegated them. The sole exception to women's marginal status was in posters and propaganda designed specifically for a female audience, such as those exhorting women to support the revolution or describing the benefits that the revolution had bestowed on them. Even in this case, however, women most often figured as passive beneficiaries of change, rather than its creators. Thus, proletarian domination was connected rhetorically and visually to male domination, confirming a gendered hierarchy[3] (Fig. 14). Despite claims that the sexes enjoyed equal status, men remained the measure of worth.

This symbolic hierarchy had significant practical consequences for women seeking to take advantage of the revolution's promises. For one thing, it encouraged women's exclusion from skilled trades. The revolution and its imagery empowered male workers to defend their interests. Seeking to protect their superior status in the workplace and preserve their monopoly on skilled "male" trades, male workers routinely sabotaged women's efforts to acquire advanced skills and upgrade their work status. In trades such as printing, which men had dominated before the revolution, shop floor culture remained

---

[3] Victoria Bonnell, *Iconography of Power: Soviet Political Posters Under Lenin and Stalin* (Berkeley, Calif.: University of California Press, 1997), 72–77.

14. "We defeated the enemy," courtesy of Victoria Bonnell

overtly and aggressively masculine. Men subjected women who ventured onto the shop floor to verbal, physical, and sexual harassment, making it hard for women to stay on the job.[4] For another, the tendency of leaders to dismiss women's capacity, even as they sought to "raise women's consciousness" served to undermine women's self-confidence and to deprive them of the power to define their future. Most important of all, women's marginality in the new civic order and the central importance accorded work and public life tainted everything associated with women, home, and family. Gendered expectations thus acted as a kind of undertow, restricting and undermining the regime's declared commitment to the emancipation of women. They made it difficult for women to find their place among the proletariat for whom the revolution purportedly was made.

Promises Betrayed?

The economic circumstances of the NEP era undermined the commitment to women's emancipation, too. Intense competition for jobs followed the end of the civil war. Roughly four million demobilized soldiers returned home and sought to regain their previous positions. As the economy began to recover and wages to rise, male workers also returned to the city from the villages to which they had fled, likewise seeking their former jobs. Managers often preferred to hire them. Men tended to have higher levels of skill than women. Managers worried about the additional expense of hiring a woman, who might require costly maternity leave and daycare – both gains of the revolution. Required to account for their costs in the new NEP economy, factory and plant managers sought to avoid such extra expenses, which the state lacked the funds to support. Consequently, despite decrees that forbade it, managers discriminated against women workers and dismissed pregnant and nursing women on leave. They used laws banning night work for women as an excuse to lay off women workers. They discriminated against married women, whom they assumed their husbands supported. Cutting back the number of daycare centers and other institutions for children, the state's efforts to reduce its own costs also hurt women. As a result, working mothers had no place to leave their children and the largely female staffs found themselves without employment.[5]

Thousands of women lost their jobs. Women's share of the labor force dropped from 45 percent in 1918 to under 30 percent, where it remained

---

[4] Diane Koenker, "Men Against Women on the Shop Floor in Early Soviet Russia," *American Historical Review* 100, no. 5 (December 1995), 1438–64.

[5] Wendy Goldman, *Women, the State and Revolution, 1917–1936* (New York: Cambridge University Press, 1993), 109–18; 126–31.

throughout the twenties, even as the number of workers slowly grew. By the end of 1928, women constituted 28.6 percent of the large-scale industrial workforce, a proportion scarcely higher than it had been in 1913. Women's job losses were greatest in the traditionally male, highly skilled and well-paid industries that they had entered during wartime: coal, iron ore, metalworking. The only industries in which women continued to predominate were those in which they had always worked, such as textiles and food processing, where skill levels and wages remained low. Women in low-paid trades were fortunate to hold jobs at all. Tens of thousands more women sought employment without success. Women constituted from one third to one half of the hundreds of thousands of workers who registered as unemployed during the twenties, their proportion growing as the decade drew to a close. And the actual number of unemployed women was no doubt much higher than their proportion suggests. Official unemployment figures underestimated the number of women because they included only people who had once held jobs and were registered on the labor exchanges.[6] Established in 1922, labor exchanges monopolized access to employment.

Here the definition of who was and who was not a "proletarian" became crucial. For purposes of registration on the labor exchange, a proletarian was a waged worker and not that worker's wife. A woman with no previous record of employment, for example a worker's wife who had been left by the husband who supported her, found it virtually impossible to obtain registration on the labor exchange. Without registration as officially "unemployed," she was ineligible for the stipend that the exchanges provided and lacked access to available work, which labor exchanges controlled. Trade unions, whose role it was to defend the interests of workers, were reluctant to come to women's defense because they were eager to support their "proletarian" constituency and preserve men's right to jobs in a period of high unemployment. Thus, although the Commissariat of Labor required that women be given equal access to work in conformity with the regime's ideals concerning women's equality, the institutions charged with realizing this ideal in practice discriminated in favor of men.

For women, the result was often sheer desperation. How else can one explain women's efforts to gain entry to the "labor clinics" set up to reform prostitutes? Established to cure prostitutes infected with venereal disease while re-educating them politically and culturally and offering them a vocation, labor clinics guaranteed a factory job to women who completed the program. When a facility in Leningrad opened in 1928, 700 women applied for its 100 available spaces. Many of the applicants pretended to be

---

[6] Ibid., 109–15.

prostitutes in order to gain access to work.[7] Desperation is also evident in the decision of the thousands of other women with no other recourse who turned to prostitution for real, in order to support themselves and their children.

Family instability compounded women's economic problems. In the period after the revolution, millions of Russians took advantage of the new right to divorce easily: 14 percent of Soviet marriages ended in divorce in the early 1920s, an enormous figure for those times. The divorce rate was twice as high as that of Germany and almost three times as high as that of France, which had the next highest levels. When a couple with children divorced, it was left to the courts to determine the amount of child support. Courts became swamped with alimony suits, many of them initiated by unmarried women who had borne children in unregistered unions. Even when courts ruled in the woman's favor – as they did in a substantial number of cases brought by women – it often proved difficult to collect the money. And what kind of settlement could a court award when a man was seeking to end his fourth or fifth marriage? Reports circulated of men marrying and divorcing as many as fifteen times, leaving ex-wives and their children to fend for themselves. Many working-class women found it hard to re-create the relative securities of their mother's lives, let alone to seize the opportunities that the revolution offered them.[8]

Women's family life was more stable in the village, where divorce rates remained comparatively low. However, peasant women who sought to carve out a new life encountered far greater obstacles than did urban women. To be sure, the Land Code that the Bolsheviks introduced in 1922 promised much on paper. It equalized women's legal position in the peasant household, entitled women to an equal right to land and other property, entitled women to participate in village self-government, provided protection for pregnant women, and introduced maternity leave for agricultural laborers. The press waged campaigns designed to educate village women and mobilize them to act on their own behalf: to join clubs, to set up nurseries for their children, to abandon the "backward" mothering practices that they had learned from older women, whom the press depicted as witches. But most of these initiatives went nowhere. In the countryside even more than in the city, the regime lacked the means to pursue them or to back up its promises with the material resources that might bring real change to women's lives. Moreover, the way of life of the peasants, substantially unchanged from the prerevolutionary period, proved profoundly inhospitable to the egalitarian and individualistic elements of Bolshevik policy. The peasant household, rather than the

---

[7] Frances Bernstein, "Prostitutes and Proletarians: The Soviet Labor Clinic as Revolutionary Laboratory," in William Husband (ed.), *The Human Tradition in Modern Russia* (Wilmington, Del.: Scholarly Resources, 2000), 117.

[8] Goldman, *Women, the State and Revolution*, 103–9; 133–43.

individual peasant, continued to be the holder of land and other property. Taking advantage of ambiguities in the law, peasant men successfully kept women who left the household from gaining access to the household's property. The absence of economic alternatives to the patriarchal family made it difficult for a peasant woman to live independently in the village. When a marriage broke down, the resulting conundrums were enough to drive judges in the new "people's courts" to despair. How could a peasant household provide child support to the divorced wife of one of its members, when household property was collective and consisted mainly of land and a cow or a horse?[9] To the many women more victimized than liberated by social change in both city and village, promises of sexual equality often rang hollow.

Promises Fulfilled?

Yet some women made gains, even in these early years. The regime launched campaigns to combat illiteracy and promote education. Women, three times as likely as men to be unable to read and write, had particular need of such efforts. The voluntary work of the literate played a major role in these campaigns, which drew upon post-revolutionary idealism. In the early twenties, Sofia Pavlova and a girlfriend gave up their free time to go on foot to nearby villages, where they taught the adults to read and write. In return, the peasants would give them milk and bread, on which the two would subsist while away from home. Working-class women such as Pavlova were encouraged to attend school and to upgrade their skills, and to assume elected and administrative positions. If the women demonstrated loyalty to the regime and its ideals, they were invited to join the Communist party.

The Women's Bureau (*Zhenotdel*), approved by the party in 1919, worked particularly hard to ensure that the promises of the revolution stayed on the agenda. Between 1920 and 1922, Alexandra Kollontai (née Domontovich, 1872–1952), the party's most outspoken advocate of women's rights, led the organization. Well-born and gently reared, Kollontai was already married to an engineer and the mother of a son when, at the age of twenty-four, she awakened to the situation of Russia's laboring masses and became drawn to Marxist ideas. To pursue her new interests, Kollontai left Russia to study at the University of Zurich, leaving her son and his nurse in her parents' home. She never went back to her husband. Instead, she plunged into politics and from 1905 onward spent much of her time trying to organize a proletarian women's movement and to win for it the support of the socialist movement. Kollontai was also a prolific writer and original thinker who added a feminist dimension to Marxist thought by exploring women's psychology

---

[9] Ibid., 152–63; 171–82.

and by raising sexuality and sexual relations as proper topics for political discussion.

According to Kollontai's vision, only under socialism would human beings learn how to love as equals. Kollontai also insisted on her own right to follow her sexual yearnings even as she fought for social revolution, thereby challenging a radical political culture that for decades had celebrated women's capacity for self-sacrifice and self-abnegation. As head of the *Zhenotdel*, Kollontai flung caution to the winds, rhapsodizing about "the coming world in which everyone would live in communes, women would be free to choose whatever sorts of romantic relationships met their needs, and dedication to the 'great laboring family' of the collective would be more important than 'ties to relatives.'"[10] Kollontai's efforts to incorporate intimate aspects of women's experience into the Marxist worldview appealed to younger women but won few converts among her seasoned comrades. Her aggressive advocacy on behalf of women's emancipation set other party members' teeth on edge. Kollontai was removed as head of the *Zhenotdel* in 1922, following her participation in the abortive Workers' Opposition. The more docile Sofia Smidovich, like Kollontai the daughter of elites, replaced her. In 1924, Klavdia Nikolaeva, a former print worker and long-time activist among women, replaced Smidovich; in 1925, Alexandra Artiukhina took over from Nikolaeva and led the organization until its abolition in 1930. A worker who had begun her laboring life sewing collars on shirts, Artiukhina had a long history of activism and proved an able leader. Highly determined but also politically astute, she pursued women's interests without arousing men's fears.

Under this varied leadership, *Zhenotdel* organizers did their best to adapt the Marxist vision to what they understood to be women's needs. Its activists played a leading role in combating female illiteracy. They tried to attract peasant women to literacy classes and provided child care to free the women to learn; they set up circles so that literate peasant women could share their skills with others. They continued to train delegates in political organizing: in 1926–7, some 620,000 women attended such *Zhenotdel*-sponsored delegate conferences. *Zhenotdel* activists took seriously their role of advancing women. They drew attention to economic and cultural policies that disadvantaged women as workers. They criticized discrimination against women on the job, unequal wages for equal work, sexual harassment, and massive female unemployment. They assailed NEP policies that curtailed state-sponsored institutions such as child care centers and canteens, leaving the burden on women's shoulders. In order to ensure that domestic responsibilities did not deter women from realizing their potential, activists fought to keep the transformation of daily life, or *byt*, from individual to collective, at the

[10] Barbara Evans Clements, *Bolshevik Women* (New York: Cambridge University Press, 1997), 227.

forefront of revolutionary change. In the late 1920s, as plans were proposed for constructing socialism, Alexandra Artiukhina, head of the *Zhenotdel* from 1925, demanded that among the criteria for judging the plans should be their consequences for women's emancipation.[11]

The *Zhenotdel* message reached hundreds of thousands of lower-class women through the journals *Krestianka* (*The Peasant Woman*) and *Rabotnitsa* (*Working Woman*), which by 1930 appeared bimonthly in runs of 265,000 copies. In the mid-1920s, *Rabotnitsa* celebrated the revolution's success stories, presenting its readers with models of working-class women who had learned to read and write, acquired new skills, then found well-paying positions. Writers of fiction depicted feisty heroines who fought for their rights and resisted the harassment of managers or male coworkers. Such images, crafted to instill in the magazine's working-class female readers greater confidence in their own potentials, offered models for the "New Soviet Woman" meant to compete with the "New Soviet Man."[12]

But *Zhenotdel* activists fought an uphill battle. Outside their ranks, *Zhenotdel*-style feminism had little support. Most party leaders would have preferred the *Zhenotdel* simply to transmit orders from above and implement policy. Others, including long-time female members of the party, actively opposed separate organizations for women. *Zhenotdel* members themselves disagreed over tactics and goals; some even became reluctant to work "only" on women's issues and defected to other organizations. In regional and local organizations, prejudice against the *Zhenotdel* and its work was endemic. Party members often behaved no better than nonparty members: Many party cadres resisted women's emancipation and barely concealed their contempt for the *Zhenotdel*, nicknaming it *Tsentro-baba* or "the broad's section." Trade union leaders, too, often disliked cooperating with the *Zhenotdel* or providing facilities for its meetings. Even when they were female, paid trade union organizers tended to regard the mass of women workers as hopelessly backward, "a stagnant swamp, impossible to budge."[13] In the course of the twenties, funding for the *Zhenotdel* decreased; the organization operated on a shoestring; many of its activists were simply volunteers. The fact that the *Zhenotdel* concentrated on women's issues made the organization easier to marginalize.[14] Pressures to abolish it altogether intensified as the twenties drew to a close.

[11] Wendy Goldman, "Industrial Politics, Peasant Rebellion and the Death of the Proletarian Women's Movement," *Slavic Review* 55, no. 1 (Spring 1996), 52–60, 65.

[12] Nancy Vavra, "Rabotnitsa: Constructing the Bolshevik Ideal, Women and the New Soviet State," Ph.D. diss., University of Colorado, 2002, chapter 5.

[13] Quoted in Koenker, "Men Against Women," 1443.

[14] Elizabeth Wood, *The Baba and the Comrade: Gender and Politics in Revolutionary Russia* (Bloomington, Ind.: Indiana University Press, 1997), 127–39, 181–93.

New Women, Old Men

During the 1920s, the meaning of women's emancipation itself became a subject of contention. This was a period of experimentation, of utopian visions, when ordinary people felt free to define revolution for themselves. For the young and unencumbered, giving shape to the communist future often meant acting on their own desires, flouting traditional authorities, experimenting with new living arrangements. People dashed naked through streetcars. They formed communes. In frosty Siberia, Sofia Pavlova and a girlfriend would attend the theatre with bared heads and their feet bright red. "During the intermission we proudly walked around barefoot. Everybody turned to look at us. . . . "[15] Other young working women adopted the flapper fashions of the "bourgeois" West. Their lips bright red, shod in pointy-toed, high-heeled shoes, with raised hems and bobbed hair, some daughters of the working class took their models from the latest fashion magazines. For them, emancipation meant dancing to American jazz, not sitting through dull meetings and lectures.

To the leadership, such women came to symbolize the dangers of women's emancipation, much as the "new woman" had symbolized that danger before the revolution. The leadership condemned their preferences as "bourgeois," demonstrating excessive attention to the individual rather than to the new socialist collective. Instead of dressing up, the good young Communist was supposed to devote herself to "healthy" pastimes: the Communist youth club, lectures on political issues, participation in antireligious activities. Women who refused to make the correct choices were seen as rejecting the socialist agenda and, thus, the revolution. In their campaign against "bourgeois" preferences, officials often identified women as the chief source of danger. Overly fashion-conscious youths were depicted as female, as if femininity itself bred "decadence."[16] Tellingly, *Rabotnitsa*, the magazine aimed at working-class women, toed the party line on this issue. Warning its readers that the interests of society were more important than dressing fashionably, writers asserted that healthy working women needed no cosmetics or elaborate fashions to enhance their appearance, unlike women of the bourgeoisie.

Tellingly, too, the *Zhenotdel* leadership and *Rabotnitsa* shared the leadership's emphasis on the public and the collective. Dreams of personal or family happiness had no place in the 1920s, not only because material conditions remained so inhospitable but also because private life itself had come under attack. Many male and female party members shared the contempt of their radical forebears for the personal and the domestic and incorporated that

---

[15] Engel and Vanderbeck, *A Revolution of Their Own*, 62.

[16] Anne Gorsuch, "Moscow Chic: Silk Stockings and Soviet Youth," in Husband, *The Human Tradition*, 66–75.

contempt into ideology. The promise to transform *byt* or everyday life in order to emancipate women all too often shaded off into an attack on everyday life as the repository of "petty bourgeois" values, and on the family as a threat to the revolution. "There is no personal life because all time and strength are given to the general cause," mourned Inessa Armand, a leading proponent of Bolshevik feminism, on the eve of her death in 1920. "Bolshevism has abolished private life," wrote the critic Walter Benjamin after a visit to Moscow in 1927.[17] More provocation than truth, Benjamin's observation nevertheless reflects an important theme in twenties culture. Privileging public life, the collective, and the point of production, the new culture downgraded private life and the family.

These downgraded spheres were invariably identified with women. Theorists of the *Proletkult*, a mass organization that claimed to represent the new-working-class culture, viewed the family as a negative force that threatened collectivism. In order to undercut the family's power, the organization sought to draw women into its membership and to transform their way of thinking: "Don't shut yourself off as you once did in your rooms, corners and basements," read one *Proletkult* appeal to women. "Come bravely to your *Proletkult*." Holding similar views about the family, members of the League of Young Communists (the *Komsomol*) were far less inviting to women. Although its declared goal was to liberate women, the *Komsomol* proved actively hostile to women's issues. Idealizing exuberant, unencumbered, and communal forms of behavior best befitting an adolescent male, the *Komsomol* considered all women backward and dangerous because of their association with the private sphere. Neither the *Proletkult* nor the *Komsomol* had much to offer women, especially women encumbered by family responsibilities. In the *Komsomol* environment, "all that it took to marginalize young women was their very sex, which was constructed by male *Komsomoltsy* to mean everything other than what these young men wanted to be."[18]

Such views placed women at a disadvantage in every realm, including the realm of sexual relations. In the twenties, the Soviet Union experienced a relaxing of sexual mores very similar to that taking place elsewhere in postwar Europe; however, in Soviet society, like virtually everything else, sexual relations assumed ideological significance. For young people, sex represented a way to express iconoclasm and contempt for bourgeois ways. Some representatives of "advanced" youth rejected love altogether as redolent of bourgeois

[17] Quoted in Clements, *Bolshevik Women*, 221; Svetlana Boym, *Common Places: Mythologies of Everyday Life in Russia* (Cambridge, Mass.: Harvard University Press, 1994), 73.

[18] Quoted in Lynn Mally, *Culture of Future: The Proletkult Movement in Revolutionary Russia* (Berkeley, Calif.: University of California Press, 1990), 179; Anne Gorsuch, "A Woman Is Not a Man": The Culture of Gender and Generation in Soviet Russia, 1921–1928," *Slavic Review* 55, no. 3 (Fall 1996), 660.

sentimentality: "With us there is no love," asserts the heroine of Panteleimon Romanov's controversial novel, *Without Cherry Blossom*, published in 1926. "With us there are only sexual relations, because love for us has a suspicious relation to the sphere of 'psychology' and to our way of thinking only physiology has the right to exist." In response to a questionnaire of 1927 that asked university students: "Does love exist?" about 50 percent of male respondents and 39 percent of female answered no, whereas a third of students ignored the question altogether, presumably finding it beneath contempt.[19] Considering sex merely a matter of physiological satisfaction, some changed partners freely. Many more, although rejecting such bourgeois hypocrisies as the sanctity of marriage, nevertheless preferred more stable unions, unsanctioned by law. "Free unions" proliferated. Some women found this liberating. "At that time, people paid no attention to that sort of thing," that is, to registering a sexual relationship as a marriage, remembered Sofia Pavlova, who in 1927 set up housekeeping with her "husband," then, exercising her right to leave when attraction ceased, abandoning him for another man several years later.[20] The breakdown of traditional morality, however, rendered other women more vulnerable. Women who refused sexual relations risked being labeled bourgeois by their rejected suitors. "There's no place for bourgeois morality in the party. The party has thrown it out the window," proclaimed a district party secretary as he tried to force his sexual attentions on a reluctant *Komsomol* member.[21]

To complicate matters further, the controversy surrounding sexuality bore a distinctly gendered dimension. During the twenties, scientific and professional experts expressed distaste for sexuality for its own pleasurable sake and identified sexuality with women. Health posters, for example, that aimed at stamping out venereal disease and warned against casual sex represented men as the victim of venereal infection and women as its source. Such posters portrayed women who stepped outside their proper place as diseased and threatening to men. Most "Old Bolsheviks" believed that sexual experimentation distracted from the serious business of revolution. Lenin himself took a conservative stance. In an interview with the German Communist Clara Zetkin that was widely publicized after his death in 1924, Lenin supposedly proclaimed, "The revolution demands concentration. It cannot tolerate orgiastic conditions." Women "who confuse their personal romances

---

[19] Quoted in Sheila Fitzpatrick, *The Cultural Front: Power and Culture in Revolutionary Russia* (Ithaca, N.Y.: Cornell University Press, 1992), 70, 87.

[20] Engel and Vanderbeck, *A Revolution of Their Own*, 65.

[21] Sheila Fitzpatrick and Yuri Slezkine (eds.), *In the Shadow of Revolution: Life Stories of Russian Women from 1917 to the Second World War* (Princeton, N.J.: Princeton University Press, 2000), 214.

with politics," could not be trusted to carry out the struggle.[22] Alexandra Kollontai, marginalized politically because of her affiliation with the Workers' Opposition, came to symbolize the dangers of sexual libertinism. Kollontai made no secret of her own romances. Her novella "Love of Three Generations," published in 1923, depicted a young woman who satisfied her sexual desire much as she would satisfy any physical need. According to her critics, Kollontai taught that having sex was like drinking a glass of water to satisfy one's thirst. This "glass of water" theory, a parody of Kollontai's thought, remained identified with her ideas and served to discredit them.

Workers with Wombs?

Whatever its commitment to women's emancipation, the leadership nevertheless required women's services to reproduce the working class and to replenish a society that had been decimated by war and revolution. Pronatalism, that is policies aimed at convincing women to bear children, was therefore prominent among the many, often conflicting messages conveyed to women in the decade following the revolution. Pronatalism was even a subtext of the decree that in 1920 made the Soviet Union the first nation in the world to legalize abortion. Couched in terms of protecting women's health by enabling them to obtain an abortion in the hygienic circumstances of a hospital or clinic, the decree nevertheless condemned the procedure as a serious "evil," necessitated by the "moral survivals" of the past and by difficult economic conditions. Until such time as maternity and infancy had become secure enough to render abortion unnecessary, the new government had the responsibility to combat that "evil" by means of propaganda against it.[23] Posters intended for urban women represented healthy female sexuality as linked to reproduction and offered viewers images of women as mothers surrounded by healthy children. Medical advice to peasants emphasized that conception was the fundamental purpose of sexual intercourse. Peasant women who wrote to local newspapers asking for advice about contraception might be told: "A woman should remember that her calling is to bear children" and warned that a "series of illnesses" could be the price of failing to do so, especially if she used abortion as her method.[24] In any case, peasants regarded abortion as a sin and were reluctant to seek one. In the absence of

---

[22] Quoted in Greg Carleton, "Writing-Reading the Sexual Revolution in the Early Soviet Union," *Journal of the History of Sexuality* 8, no. 2 (1997), 235.

[23] Rex Wade (ed.), *Documents of Soviet History. V. 2. Triumph and Retreat, 1920–1922* (Gulf Breeze, Fla.: Academic International Press, 1991), 145.

[24] Quoted in Steven P. Frank, "'Ask the Doctor!': Peasants and Medical-Sexual Advice in Riazan Province, 1925–1928," in Husband, *The Human Tradition*, 102.

birth control, they bore babies regularly, as their mothers had done before them, turning to peasant midwives for help despite the regime's attempts to demonize such women. They also continued to lose about a third of their infants before they reached the age of one.

Urban women were more inclined to resist pronatalist pressures. In their difficult economic circumstances and in the absence of adequate state provision for childcare and childrearing, many viewed maternity as a burden to be avoided rather than welcomed. Despite the scarcity of contraceptive devices, women tried to control their fertility by whatever means they could. They requested birth control advice from experts and, with their husband's cooperation, practiced coitus interruptus. But most of all, they resorted to abortion. As the number of abortions rose, the birthrate fell. By the late 1920s, abortions had become so commonplace that in some cities, they considerably outnumbered births. Physicians and other experts expressed profound concern about the widespread usage of abortion, which they saw as a threat to population growth. Referring to the "antisocial" nature of abortion and its "epidemic" dimensions, they emphasized the state's need for children, not women's need to control their fertility.[25]

Women Respond

In the cacophony of voices that debated the family, sexuality, and women's emancipation throughout the 1920s, the voices of the lower classes, lower-class women in particular, are scarcely audible. In 1925 and 1926, however, the leadership invited them to express their opinion about the New Family Code that had been drafted and circulated to the public for commentary. In an effort to reduce the coercive role of the state while responding to the needs of women in unregistered unions, the code proposed to permit divorce at the request of either of the partners, even if the other opposed it, and to offer women in unregistered unions the same legal protections as women in registered marriages, including the possibility of child support. The working-class and peasant women whose words have been recorded opposed these provisions. Expressing conservative opinions about sexual issues, they advocated the strengthening, not the weakening, of marriage in order to ease women's lot. Women, they believed, "needed to be liberated from the social effects of the new sexual freedom of men."[26] If advocates of sexual freedom were to be found among them, such women either dared not raise their voice or their voices were ignored.

Most of the working-class and peasant women who expressed their opinions offered a trenchant critique of the cost of family instability and male

[25] Goldman, *Women, the State and Revolution*, 257–95.   [26] Ibid., 224.

irresponsibility. It was women who bore the burden of child care and child-rearing and often the economic burden of child support as well. Recognizing that, at least at present, women with children were in no position to enjoy sexual freedom, these women speakers demanded stricter rather than more lenient divorce laws. In the words of one working-class woman, "Women, in the majority of cases, are more backward, less skilled and therefore less independent than men. . . . To marry, bear children and to be enslaved by the kitchen and then to be thrown aside by your husband – this is very painful for women. This is why I am against easy divorce." Women pointed out how the benefits working men enjoyed might actually harm their wives. Often men who took advantage of new opportunities began to regard their wives as backward. A woman factory worker put it this way: "When you are working in a factory, you note a very unpleasant picture. As long as a guy doesn't participate in political work, he works and respects his wife as he should. But just a little promotion and already something stands between them. He begins to stay away from his family and his wife, already she doesn't please him." Another woman agreed: "I can't forgive a man who lives with a woman twenty years, has five kids, and then decides his wife no longer pleases him. Why did she please him before, but now she doesn't? Shame on you, comrade men!" She castigated men who betrayed their wives and claimed they were in love with someone else. "This isn't love," she declared, "this is swinishness!"[27]

The women argued for a more responsible approach to sexuality and a much more restrictive approach to marriage. Rather than ensuring women's sexual freedom, they wanted to reduce the freedom of men. Here, their views seem directly to contradict those of Alexandra Kollontai, Bolshevism's foremost feminist theorist. Having read an article by Kollontai in her local newspaper, a *Zhenotdel* worker from a rural area took issue with her. "It seems to me that her view is directed toward the destruction of the family. She proposes 'free love' and 'free union.' Her opinion is that the spiritual life of a person, insofar as it is vast and complex, cannot be satisfied by union with one, but that a person needs several 'partners'. . . . In our opinion in the countryside, this is simply called debauchery."[28] Regarding alimony or dependence on a man as demeaning for women, Kollontai had developed a plan to ensure them other means of support. She proposed creating a general fund by levying a tax of two rubles, which would be used to support single mothers and to set up nurseries and children's homes. The plan, which would have weighed most heavily on the conservative peasantry, attracted few adherents. A more straightforward solution was to put the responsibility for their sexual behavior squarely on the men involved. As one woman put it succinctly: "If you like tobogganing, you have to drag your sled uphill."

---

[27] Ibid., 242–4.   [28] Ibid., 245.

These exchanges occurred shortly after Lenin's death in January 1924. A few years later, Joseph Stalin sealed his triumph over his rivals for political power. In some ways, the views articulated by these working-class women resemble the ideas of party conservatives, who viewed the sexual question as marginal and emphasized disciplined and responsible family sex. In the words of the physician Aron Zalkind, a leading proponent of the view that sexual energy was limited and should be harnessed to serve society, "I am very much afraid that with the cult of 'winged eros' [a reference to Kollontai's ideas] we will build aeroplanes very badly."[29] Under Stalin's leadership, such conservative views would triumph.

Evaluating the Twenties

For all the problems of the early years, and the gender bias both implicit and explicit, the revolution nevertheless offered unprecedented opportunities to lower-class women. They were most readily accessible to the young and urban, especially if they were single and unencumbered by responsibility for children. If such women embraced the new values and could negotiate or ignore the hurdles of gender prejudice, a new world opened before them. The consequences are measurable: from 1 percent of village soviet members in 1922, the proportion of women in village soviets had risen to 11.8 by 1927. From 30,547 female members, close to 8 percent of party membership in 1922, female membership in the Communist Party had grown to 13.7 percent by 1929, in a party that had almost tripled in size. These women became the vanguard of the new Soviet female labor force. They worked as administrators, teachers, doctors, lawyers, judges, professors, editors, librarians, engineers. Sofia Pavlova was but one of thousands of such beneficiaries of the Bolshevik revolution. "Nowhere else in the European world were there so many female lawyers, professors, scientists and artists, as well as judges and party secretaries, as there were in the Soviet Union by 1930," wrote Barbara Clements.[30] In light of such gains, does it matter whether the real motive was instrumental, designed to break down resistance and garner support for the regime, as many have argued? Or that when pressed, the regime chose to place its limited resources elsewhere? Or that the positions women occupied were mostly at entry level and women exercised genuine authority nowhere in Soviet society of the late 1920s? Or that postrevolutionary culture marginalized women?

How historians evaluate the twenties depends a lot on where they look for evidence and what they choose to emphasize. The twenties were a time

---

[29] Quoted in Alix Holt (ed.), *Selected Writings of Alexandra Kollontai* (New York: W. W. Norton, 1977), 204–5.
[30] Clements, *Bolshevik Women*, 250.

of enormous fluidity and flux. The state did not yet pursue a clear-cut line on gender or on many other issues, for that matter. The feminist elements of the Marxist vision authorized some to push for genuine change on women's behalf. Especially in the early 1920s, people who embraced the revolution felt empowered to express themselves as never before. Among them were not only the young but also artists, writers, critics, professionals, and scientists who sought to influence government policy concerning matters over which they claimed expertise. Many of the mixed messages of the period – and they were legion – arose from the resulting competitions for influence and authority. How the messages affected real-life women varied according to the women's character, social position, age, and marital status. In the end, what most distinguishes this period from those that followed is the fact that women had a voice in the debates and an organization, the *Zhenotdel*, committed to their inclusion in the revolutionary process, and that the very polyphony gave women room for maneuver. The difference would become clear in the thirties, when the polyphony, the room for maneuver, and the *Zhenotdel* would all disappear.

Suggestions for Further Reading

Bernstein, Frances. "Envisioning Health in Revolutionary Russia, 1921–28." *Russian Review* 55, no. 3 (Fall 1996), 191–217. *Explores the ways that gender shaped efforts to stamp out venereal and other diseases.*

Bonnell, Victoria. "The Representation of Women in Early Soviet Political Art." *Russian Review* 50, no. 3 (1991), 267–88.

Farnsworth, Beatrice. "The Rural Batrachka (Hired Agricultural Laborer) and the Soviet Campaign to Unionize Her." *Journal of Women's History* 14, no. 1 (2002), 64–91. *Analyzes the limitations of Bolshevik policies as applied to the most impoverished rural women.*

Goldman, Wendy. *Women, the State and Revolution: Soviet Family Policy and Social Life, 1917–1936.* New York: Cambridge University Press, 1993. *An important study of the efforts to carry out emancipatory policies in the circumstances of the 1920s.*

Gorsuch, Anne. "A Woman Is Not a Man": The Culture of Gender and Generation in Soviet Russia, 1921–1928." *Slavic Review* 55, no. 3 (Fall 1996), 636–660.

Gorsuch, Anne. "Moscow Chic: Silk Stockings and Soviet Youth," in William Husband, ed. The *Human Tradition in Modern Russia.* Wilmington, Del.: Scholarly Resources, 2000.

Holt, Alix, ed. *Selected Writings of Alexandra Kollontai.* New York: W. W. Norton, 1977. *Provides an introduction to this original thinker.*

Koenker, Diane. "Men Against Women on the Shop Floor in Early Soviet Russia." *American Historical Review* 100, no. 5 (December 1995), 1438–64. *A study of male resistance at the workplace.*

Tirado Isabel. "The Komsomol and the Krest'ianka: The Political Mobilization of Young Women in the Russian Village, 1921–1927." *Russian History* 23, no. 1–4 (Spring-Summer-Fall-Winter 1996), 345–66.

9

THE SECOND REVOLUTION

The wave of change that broke over the Soviet Union in the late 1920s left virtually no woman's life untouched. New factories, mines, and construction projects that provided work for millions ended the burden of unemployment that women had borne disproportionately. Propaganda encouraged working-class and peasant women to join the waged labor force, as did a wage policy that set most wages so low that families required at least two wage earners to survive. Scores of working-class and peasant women entered traditionally male industries or became the first in their families to receive professional training. By transforming ordinary women into "heroines of labor," this second revolution claimed to have fulfilled the Bolsheviks' promises to emancipate Russia's women. But this claim was belied by everyday hardships, restoration of a more conservative gender and family order, and a patriarchal political culture identified with the cult of Stalin. Those holding alternative views of women's emancipation were silenced. Periodic outbreaks of terror tore apart millions of families, leaving wives without husbands and children without parents. Nevertheless, many women appeared to herald the new order with unfeigned enthusiasm.

Collectivization

The economic crisis of the late 1920s served as the prelude to upheavals to come. In 1927, the state procured far less grain than anticipated, leading to critical food shortages in the cities. Once again, exhausted, malnourished, and increasingly angry women stood in breadlines around the clock. "There is no butter. Not long ago, there was flour. There is no kerosene. They have deceived us," declared a leaflet intercepted by the secret police that December.[1] To deal with the crisis, the regime took steps that soon brought

---

[1] Quoted in Roberta T. Manning, "The Rise and Fall of 'the Extraordinary Measures,' January–June, 1928: Towards a Reexamination of the Onset of the Stalin Revolution," *Carl Beck Papers*, no. 1504, 7.

NEP to an end. The *kulak* (supposedly wealthy peasant) became the target of attack, allegedly because he was withholding grain in an effort to sabotage the regime. Introducing more coercive tactics toward the peasantry, however, only worsened the problem and in February 1929 bread and, subsequently, sugar, meat, butter, and tea became subject to rationing. To end the procurement problem once and for all, in the fall of 1929, the government launched a campaign to collectivize agriculture and then to "liquidate the kulaks as a class." At the same time, having adopted the first Five Year Plan in spring 1929, the government undertook a massive effort to industrialize and modernize the economy – literally, to raise the nation by its own economic bootstraps – within a few short years. These campaigns reconfigured gender roles once again and profoundly altered the material conditions of almost everyone's lives.

The collectivization campaign destroyed peasants' traditional way of life. Confiscating the property of alleged *kulak* families and driving them from their houses, activists recruited from the cities brought terror to the countryside. Millions of *kulak* families were exiled to Siberia or the far North to begin farming again without implements or resources, forced to build their own homes in the dead of winter. Living in horrific conditions, without sufficient food and without any sanitary measures or health care, the children, in particular, sickened and perished by the tens of thousands. Other *kulaks* became forced laborers at new industrial sites. Most of the remaining peasants were forced to join collectives, sometimes at gunpoint, their animals and implements appropriated for collective use. Peasants who became collective farmers no longer exercised control over the product of their labor. Instead, they worked for the collective and were supposedly paid in labor days – that is, according to the amount of work that they contributed to collective production and the level of skill it involved. But in fact such pay was rare. An antireligious campaign accompanied collectivization. Activists closed down churches, arrested the officiating priests, and forced peasants to surrender their icons. "They threw out the icons, burned them, and jeered at people who had them: Silly old women, what have you got hanging up there?" remembered Anna Dubova, whose family suffered de-kulakization.[2] The leadership forbid the celebration of religious holidays and the practice of religious rituals, including baptism, without which a person could not enter heaven, according to Russian Orthodox belief.

The collectivization campaign invaded women's sphere and overturned the household and domestic order. When activists confiscated the property of alleged *kulaks*, they often took clothing, pots and pans, even food from the table before they drove people from their homes. They seized as collective

[2] Barbara Alpern Engel and Anastasia Posadskaya-Vanderbeck (eds.), *A Revolution of Their Own: Voices of Women in Soviet History* (Boulder, Colo.: Westview Press, 1998), 41.

property the hens and other livestock that women customarily tended, and most painful of all, the cow that provided milk for the children. "They took the animals, they took the horses, they took the cow – we had one cow – they took everything," recalled Irina Kniazeva, dispossessed together with her family in the early 1930s. Collectivizers arrested her father, who spent several years in prison, and drove everyone else from their house. Kniazeva, her mother, grandmother, and three children lived in a shed until someone left the village and the family moved into her tiny hut. Her grandmother, constantly weeping, went blind from grief.[3] Collectivization broke up families and dispersed their members, eroding although not sundering the links between generations of women, the foundation of women's shared culture. In addition, by depriving male household heads of their control of household property and labor, collectivization undermined the peasantry's patriarchal order.

Women activists regarded the change as a positive one, another step in the building of communism. A small minority of the tens of thousands of *Komsomol* activists, party members and workers who implemented collectivization, women activists, like men, saw collectivization as progress and the *kulak* as the enemy. The anti-kulak campaign was presented as class warfare. "Kulaks lived better than the others, they lived very well. They had cows and sheep and pigs and horses and good, strong log houses. And they ate better," claimed Elena Ponomarenko, herself of impoverished peasant background. Ponomarenko, who became a journalist after only seven years of schooling, published articles identifying supposed kulaks for arrest and persecution.[4] Antonina Solovieva, a worker at the Voevodin Factory in Sverdlovsk, responded to her party's exhortations to go to the countryside to agitate on behalf of collectivization and against kulak sabotage. She was convinced that once the kulaks had been dispossessed and their possessions transformed into collective property, formerly poor peasants who worked hard would at last live well. In addition to advancing the state's goals, the collectivization campaign offered women the prospect of adventure, similar to what an earlier generation had experienced during the civil war. Despite the condescension of some of their male comrades, Solovieva and her women friends dressed just like the men, in camouflage fatigues, to underscore their determination.[5]

Most peasant women bitterly opposed collectivization. According to rumors that circulated in peasant villages, collectivization signified that the Antichrist had arrived and the Apocalypse was at hand. To the leadership, peasant women's resistance to collectivization signified their greater

3 Ibid., 122.   4 Ibid., 151.
5 Sheila Fitzpatrick and Yuri Slezkine (eds.), *In the Shadow of Revolution: Life Stories of Russian Women from 1917 to the Second World War* (Princeton, N.J.: Princeton University Press, 2000), 236.

backwardness, which left them susceptible to manipulation by supposed kulaks. "In their agitation against collectives, the kulaks first and foremost employ women, the most backward sector of the village," reads a typical official report.[6] Taking advantage of such perceptions, enormous numbers of women engaged in acts of collective resistance, the so-called *bab'i bunty* (women's riots). Women would stand at the forefront of hostile crowds resisting collectivization; they would shriek at the top of their voices and block the path of activists who attempted to confiscate livestock. Sometimes, women set fire to collective stables, barns and haystacks; they destroyed tractors and attacked local officials. "You're thieves, show us the paper from the central authorities allowing you to steal our cattle. There are no kulaks here!" fifty women shrieked at an official overseeing collectivization in one Siberian town. When the official refused to leave the house in which he had taken refuge, the women threatened to remove him by force or pour kerosene over the house and set it alight.[7] Women often arrived at protests armed with pitchforks, staves, knives, and other farm implements, which they were quite prepared to employ. They would even defend alleged kulaks, blocking the huts of peasants slated for deportation and demanding the release of those already arrested. Women also demonstrated against the closing of churches and continued to baptize their children despite prohibitions against the practice. Baptism became a "conspicuous site of resistance" to official values, if largely a hidden one.[8] Peasant resistance proved instrumental in modifying some party policies. It brought a temporary halt to forced collectivization, permanently ended the socialization of domestic livestock, and gained peasants the right to maintain a private plot. But it halted neither collectivization nor the assault on religion.

The state also mobilized its propaganda and personnel to overcome women's resistance. In 1929, the government instructed the *Zhenotdel* to work with this "backward layer" and assume a more active role in organizing peasant women in support of collectivization. The magazine *The Peasant Woman* (*Krest'ianka*) parroted the party line, dismissing women who resisted collectivization as naive and backward, manipulated by kulaks and priests. It portrayed women as collectivization's ardent supporters. Posters and films trumpeted the advantages that collectivization brought to women.

[6] Viktor Danilov, Roberta Manning, and Lynn Viola (eds.), *Tragediia Sovetskoi Derevni. Kollektivizatsiia i raskulachivanie. Dokumenty i materialy. 1927–1939*. t. 2. Noiabr' 1929-Dekabr' 1930 (Moscow: Rossiiskaia Polit. entsiklopediia, 2000), 187.

[7] Viktor Danilov, Roberta Manning, and Lynn Viola (eds.), *Tragediia Sovetskoi Derevni*, t. 1 Mai 1927-Noiabr' 1929 (Moscow: Rossiiskaia Polit. entsiklopediia, 1999), 619; Lynn Viola, "Bab'i Bunty and Peasant Women's Protest During Collectivization," *Russian Review* 45 (1986), 23–42.

[8] David Ransel, *Village Mothers: Three Generations of Change in Russia and Tataria* (Bloomington, Ind.: Indiana University Press, 2000), 164.

15. "To collective work," courtesy of Victoria Bonnell

Propaganda designed for an illiterate audience recast the image of the peasant woman, presenting her as a *kolkhoznitsa*, a collective farm woman, the antithesis of the backward *baba* who opposed collectivization. Smiling and cheerful, she invited her fellow peasants to join a collective farm, or she sat self-confidently behind the wheel of a tractor, demonstrating the new opportunities that socialism offered (Fig. 15). Her figure sometimes assumed heroic proportions, towering over her class enemies, the *kulak* and the priest, and dwarfing the landscape around her. Young and slim, the *kolkhoznitsa* had nothing in common with the buxom, maternal figure that had previously represented peasant women.[9] She was, instead, a new woman, the rural counterpart of her newly liberated urban sisters. Enthusiastic about constructing socialism, earning her own income, and prizing her independence, she was fully committed to the goals of the regime.

Those peasant women who embraced official values received lots of publicity. "Now our female *kolkhozniks* [collective farmers] have become free," proclaimed a female brigade leader, a "Heroine of Socialist Labor." "Now they sometimes make more money than their husbands. How can your husband exploit you when you make more money than he does? That usually shuts him up."[10] Village women who overfulfilled their production quotas, known

---

[9] Victoria E. Bonnell, *Iconography of Power: Soviet Political Posters Under Lenin and Stalin* (Berkeley, Calif.: University of California Press, 1997), 100–23.

[10] Fitzpatrick and Slezkine, *In the Shadow of Revolution*, 336.

as shockworkers and after 1935 as *Stakhanovites*, often emphasized their freedom from the traditional constraints on women and from subordination to men. "Now I am a noted milkmaid, a *Stakhanovite* . . . I have become a human being. I stand on my own feet, raising my children and keeping house. I am twice as happy as any man," declared the milkmaid Natalia Tereshkova in an article that appeared in 1935.[11] Encountering doubts that women could drive a tractor, Pasha Angelina, who created the first all-female tractor brigade and became the most celebrated female labor hero in Soviet history, resolved to organize other women. "We'll all become shock workers and then we'll see if they dare say that a woman doesn't belong on a tractor."[12]

The state rewarded the women in more practical ways, too. In addition to meeting important functionaries and having their pictures displayed on posters and in newspapers, such women became eligible for goods in short supply such as quality housing and furniture, sewing machines, chintz dresses, decent footwear, and all-expenses-paid holidays in special health resorts. "In 1934 I passed the technology test and became a Class One milkmaid. I work well and live well. I have my own apartment with electric lighting, a gramophone, and a radio set," proclaimed M. K. Razina.[13] Whether in predominantly male occupations such as tractor driver or, far more commonly, in predominantly female ones such as milkmaid, exemplary workers such as Angelina and Razina became poster-children for the new era in the countryside, highly visible symbols of the success of the Stalinist revolution and of its commitment to promoting women.

The vast majority of rural women, however, enjoyed neither decent housing nor quality furniture or chintz dresses. Rural dwellers lacked access to even the most basic consumer goods, like soap or shoes. Most barely scraped by. By the late 1930s, women constituted the majority of peasants who worked on collective farms, millions of men having fled to the cities seeking better opportunity. Instead of modernization, collective farmers mainly experienced exploitation. The regime appropriated the grain that farmers grew, paying them the merest pittance, if at all, and leaving little or nothing for the farmers' own subsistence. During the years 1932–3, when a man-made famine swept parts of Russia, millions died of hunger or hunger-related diseases. Farm labor remained largely unmechanized and disproportionately performed by women. Comprising roughly 58 percent of collective farm workers, women supplied two-thirds of the backbreaking labor on collective farms. A rigid sexual division of labor prevailed. Local authorities resisted the access of women

[11] Quoted in Lewis Siegelbaum, " 'Dear Comrade, You Ask What We Need': Socialist Paternalism and Soviet Rural 'Notables' in the Mid-1930s," *Slavic Review* 57, no. 1 (Spring 1998), 129.
[12] Fitzpatrick and Slezkine, *In the Shadow of Revolution*, 312.   [13] Ibid., 339.

to nontraditional labor; their fellow peasants resented and sometimes harassed women who became shock-workers or *Stakhanovites*.[14]

During the thirties, the state failed to deliver on its promises of improved access to health and maternity care and to services designed to free peasant women from their burden of housework, although it did take steps in that direction. By 1939, there were only 7,000 hospitals, 7,503 maternity homes, 14,300 clinics, and 26,000 medical assistants in the entire Union of Soviet Socialist Republics, serving a rural population of more than 114,400,000.[15] A genuine advance over the previous decade, these facilities nevertheless remained a drop in the bucket. Especially in smaller and more remote villages, traditional healers and folk remedies remained the only medical care available. The network of rural daycare centers that were supposed to liberate women from child care fell far short of the goals set by the Five Year Plan. As always, it was women who shouldered the burden of housework, and in the absence of the most basic amenities such as running water, indoor plumbing, and electricity. Women also assumed primary responsibility for maintaining the private plot with which most fed their families. Consequently, women's workdays lasted far longer than men's. Women's work was valued less than men's, however, because most of it was considered unskilled and because a smaller fraction of it was devoted to collective production. In any case, despite the celebration of the newly independent collective farm woman with her own individual wage, collective farm wages, when they were paid at all, customarily went to the household and not the individual.

Initially, only a small minority of rural women took advantage of opportunities to improve their skills or rise into management positions. Opportunities certainly existed. During the thirties, the authorities actively sought to increase the representation of rural women in administrative posts and in nontraditional occupations. As a result, the number of women in professional positions that required some specialized training, such as bookkeepers, accountants, and agronomists, grew considerably. Nevertheless, by the end of the thirties, only a tiny fraction of women occupied administrative positions in collective farms or chaired rural soviets. Many factors prevented rural women from advancing: their burden of work, the opposition of family members, perhaps even their own reluctance to adopt a different lifestyle. A woman who did occupy a position of authority in the thirties, such as chair of a collective farm or rural soviet, had to be unusually tough. She faced the hostility of fellow villagers, who might circulate malicious rumors concerning her sex life or the favors she supposedly granted male relatives. Freer

---

[14] Roberta T. Manning, "Women in the Soviet Countryside on the Eve of World War II," in Beatrice Farnsworth and Lynn Viola (eds.), *Russian Peasant Women* (New York: Oxford University Press, 1992), 214–25.

[15] Ibid., 208.

from the burdens of family, and perhaps from traditional expectations, the next generation of women proved more ready to make a change: in the mid- to late 1930s, rural women constituted over 30 percent of students enrolled in higher agricultural education.[16] Many would seize the first opportunity to leave the village for good, supported by parents who had lost hope for a decent future in the countryside.

Industrialization, Women, and Gender

The industrialization drive had a similarly ambiguous impact on women. During the first Five Year Plan, the leadership fully abandoned its commit- ment to women's emancipation as a goal in itself. In December 1928, the government eliminated all women's organizers within trade unions, thereby halting efforts to train, promote, and defend women workers on the shop floor. On January 5, 1930, the *Zhenotdel* itself was abolished, ending advocacy within party circles on behalf of women and women's issues. Women in other official organs tried but failed to take up the slack. The absence of persistent advocacy on behalf of women left the leadership free to deploy the female labor force as it chose and at the lowest possible cost to itself.

Slowly at first, and then at breakneck speed, the industrialization drive encouraged women to take up new trades and opened the gates of the in- dustrial labor force to the women who had been barred from the shop floor in the 1920s. Wives and daughters of workers proved especially attractive as recruits to industry. Because they already lived in a city or factory center, their hire would require no additional expenditures for housing or expansion of urban services, which would be needed for peasant newcomers. In the words of two economists, "It is true that the use of women always involves more expenditure on daycare, etc., but these expenses are significantly offset by economizing on housing. The use of women creates the conditions for a permanent work force in the factories."[17] Such instrumental language – note the repeated "use of women" – had nothing in common with the stated goal of women's emancipation. Neither did the motivation of many women who joined the workforce for the first time in the thirties. Instead, they sought work for the most basic of reasons: inflationary pressures on food costs meant that their husband's or father's or brother's wage was simply inadequate to put food on the table.

Despite claims to the contrary, industrialization failed to provide women with equal opportunity. During the First Five Year Plan, women's share of

[16] Ibid., 224–5.
[17] Quoted in Wendy Goldman, *Women at the Gates: Gender and Industry in Stalin's Russia* (New York: Cambridge University Press, 2002), 143–79, 244.

every branch of industry increased, including those branches, such as chemicals, metallurgy, and mining, that traditionally had been dominated by men. Once machinery had been introduced, women's lack of skill and education proved less of an obstacle to hiring them, thus enabling the state to replace men with women and to transfer men where it needed them. Old lines of gender segregation gave way. However, new ones took their place, as planners designated industries and sectors of the economy they considered to be best suited for women's labor, thus resegregating the labor force from above. Entire sectors of the economy became designated as "female," including cotton, linen, wool, and sewing; and the lower and middle ranks of white collar and service professions. Some positions such as stenographers, secretaries, hairdressers, cooks, laundresses, and pharmacists, among others, were reserved exclusively for women.[18]

Hostility to women on the shop floor continued. To the extent that women replaced men, the reorganization of the labor force actually exacerbated it. Managers resisted training women or placing them in positions that men had previously occupied; they hired women, but then made it impossible for the women to do their work. They refused to promote women even in industries such as textiles, where women predominated. Male workers remained hostile, too. Defending their privileges as workers and as men, they fought fiercely against the efforts to break their power over the labor process by replacing them with women. Skilled male workers refused to train women. They resisted the notion that women should earn as much as, let alone more than, a man. Because male workers refused to work alongside them, women in some Moscow factories were forced to create special female brigades. Men used sexual harassment and obscene language to render the workplace inhospitable to women. In Red Putilovets, a metalworking plant, two male workers physically molested every woman who came into their shop and showered them with obscenities. When women made requests of foremen, the men sometimes responded with sexual propositions. Such treatment made it difficult for women to claim the places on the shop floor that had been designated "female," thus leaving "male" trades largely intact.[19]

Despite the highly acclaimed breakthroughs of a few, the majority of women workers continued to fill the lowest paid and most physically arduous positions. Concentrated in light industries, such as food processing, textiles, and other consumer goods, women were left behind by investment policies that favored heavy industry and neglected consumption. Some experienced a worsening of working conditions and living standards so severe that they staged protests. In 1932, some 16,000 workers, most of them female,

[18] Ibid., 149–56, 169–76.   [19] Ibid., 207–31.

went on an unsuccessful strike in the Ivanovo industrial region, protesting a cutback in rations and demanding that they be restored to their previous level. "Bread . . . give us bread and then we'll work!" they shouted to party and union officials who opposed their protest. "Down with the big-mouthed jabberer!"[20]

Nevertheless, for those with proper "working-class" credentials, the changes of the thirties provided opportunities for unprecedented social mobility. The proportion of women in institutions of higher education grew from 31 percent in 1926 to 43 percent in 1937. Women's progress was particularly marked in fields such as economics and law, industry, construction, and transport, where the proportion of women students had hitherto been quite low.[21] Most of the women who benefited from the new opportunities derived from lower-class backgrounds. One of the beneficiaries was Vera Malakhova, born to a working-class Siberian family in 1919. Supported by the state while she attended a *rabfak* (school for workers), she entered medical school in 1936, becoming one of tens of thousands of young people, mostly female, who studied medicine under an expanded medical education system. Her parents were thrilled: "In general, ordinary families like my family – after all, my father was a worker – really looked up to teachers and doctors. And then I had the chance to become a doctor!"[22] Female role models encouraged others to choose new paths. In September 1938, Valentina Griazodubova, Marina Raskova, and Polina Osipenko set a world's record for nonstop flight by women. During their flight, the radio broadcast hourly bulletins about their progress and the entire nation listened. A "call" went out: "Girls, take the wheel! Girls, go into aviation!"[23] The three inspired thousands of women to follow in their footsteps.

Daily Life

During the thirties, everyday hardships became routine. Despite ambitious goals for socializing the traditional "women's work" of cooking, cleaning, laundry, and child care, in both the First and Second Five Year Plans, progress was only modest. Investments were redirected to heavy industry; managers commandeered for other purposes buildings designated for child care. According to official figures, the number of children in child care centers in 1936 numbered 1,048,309, a tenfold increase from 1928, but still far short of the

[20] Quoted in Jeffrey Rossman, "The Teikovo Cotton Workers Strike of April 1932: Class, Gender and Identity Politics in Stalin's Russia," *Russian Review* 56, no. 1 (January 1997), 48–9.

[21] Gail Warshofsky Lapidus, *Women in Soviet Society: Equality, Development and Social Change* (Berkeley, Calif.: University of California Press, 1978), 148–9.

[22] Engel and Posadskaya-Vanderbeck, *A Revolution of Their Own*, 186.   [23] Ibid., 37.

goals. Waiting lists for places in daycare centers grew lengthy.[24] Housekeeping became more difficult. Collectivization of agriculture severely disrupted food production. Moreover, having abolished private trade with the onset of the Five Year Plan, the state experienced major problems distributing goods.

The result was shortages of everything necessary to maintain a household, food included. Bread shortages became severe in the winter of 1931, reached famine proportions in 1932–3, and became a problem again in 1936–7 and again in 1939–40. Sometimes for days on end, women stood in long lines in front of bakeries. "We stand in line for bread from 12 o'clock at night and they only give one kilogram, even if you're dying of hunger," a collective farm woman in Iaroslavl wrote to her husband in the winter of 1936–7. Wrote a housewife from the Volga region to Stalin in 1939–40, "For bread, you have to go at two o'clock at night and stand until six in the morning to get two kilograms of rye bread."[25] Other basic foodstuffs such as meat, milk, butter, and vegetables were in similarly short supply. It became almost impossible to find clothing, shoes, or basic household items. The only available appliances were electric irons. Distribution in urban areas improved after 1935, when rationing ceased. However, the quality of goods remained notoriously low. Sleeves might be missing from a shirt or a dress; matches refused to strike, the handles would fall off a pot. Goods failed to fulfill their function. Tall and wide, with uneven bottoms, for example, cups purchased at a manufactured goods warehouse in the mid 1930s teetered back and forth like little rocking horses, spilling their contents and burning the hands of those who tried to use them. To compensate for these inadequacies, they were decorated with symbols of the First Five Year Plan: tractors, cranes, cogwheels, and wrenches.[26]

Housing was almost as neglected as consumer goods. The millions of peasants who flooded into the cities created terrible overcrowding. People lived in barracks and dormitories; workers' families squeezed into corridors, corners, or rooms in communal apartments, one family to a room, sharing bathrooms and cooking facilities with other tenants. Even a tiny room could seem a luxury. Anna Dubova, the daughter of an alleged *kulak* and a skilled confectionary worker in Moscow, had no place to live at all in the early thirties, and she would spend the night with girlfriends. Marriage to a member of the *Komsomol* enabled her not only to conceal her *kulak* origins but also to obtain a room of her own. "When I went to bed, I would think to myself, Dear Lord, I'm in my very own bed. I experienced such happiness; it was like being in seventh heaven, I was that happy."[27]

[24] Goldman, *Women at the Gates*, 274.
[25] Quoted in Sheila Fitzpatrick, *Everyday Stalinism. Everyday Life in Extraordinary Times: Soviet Russia in the 1930s* (New York: Oxford University Press, 1999), 43.
[26] Fitzpatrick and Slezkine, *In the Shadow of Revolution*, 296.
[27] Engel and Posadskaya-Vanderbeck, *A Revolution of Their Own*, 32.

Women experienced enormous difficulty in meeting the conflicting demands on them to participate in the labor force and look after husband, children, and home. For help, some turned to their own mothers or to domestic workers (the word *servant* was frowned upon). Domestic workers were women too old or girls too young to take advantage of new work opportunities or peasant women in desperate flight from the village. The 1930s witnessed the continuation of the prerevolutionary pattern of young peasant girls migrating to the city to become workers in people's homes. In 1929, some 527,000 Soviet women worked as domestics, 15.9 percent of the total female workforce. In the early thirties, 50,000 of them were registered in Moscow according to an urban census that undoubtedly underestimated their numbers. Even workers' families might employ them in the 1930s and 1940s. Usually, domestics slept on a folding cot in the kitchen or foyer. However, in the end, most married women themselves had to compensate for the shortfall in consumer products and social services. They rushed from work to stand in line at food shops, pick up their children at daycare centers, and go home to cook, clean house, scrub floors, and wash and mend clothes until late into the night, only to begin all over again the next day.[28] In 1936, such women spent on housework almost five times as many of their leisure hours as their husbands, a total of one hundred and forty seven hours during that year, as compared with thirty spent by husbands. Women spent almost as many hours on housework as they spent on the job.

The New Socialist Family

The mid thirties introduced yet another shift in family policy and in official attitudes toward women's family roles. In the early thirties, the multiple demands, the overcrowded conditions, and the lack of social support led women to limit their number of children. Most resorted to abortion. The birthrate declined steadily between 1927 and 1935, dropping from 45 births per 1,000 people in 1927 to 30.1 in 1934 and 1935. The working-class family declined in size. Officials found the change alarming. Like other European states that adopted population policies in the interwar era, the Soviet state sought to increase the size of its population in order to meet the demands of industry and modern warfare. Bearing and raising children entirely ceased to be a private matter; it became woman's responsibility to society and the state. In the words of Joseph Stalin, "The Soviet woman has the same rights as the man, but that does not free her from a great and honorable duty which nature has given her: she is a mother, she gives life. This is certainly not a

---

[28] Mary Leder, *My Life in Stalinist Russia. An American Woman Looks Back* (Bloomington, Ind.: Indiana University Press, 2001), 44.

private affair, but one of great social significance."[29] Media began portraying having children as a natural part of women's lives and stressing the happiness and fulfillment that children brought them. For a woman to seek to avoid motherhood became "abnormal."

Using legislation and propaganda similar to that of other European nations, the state attempted to strengthen the family. The head of the *Komsomol* declared: "The stronger and more harmonious the family is, the better it serves the common cause. . . . We are for serious, stable marriages and large families. In short, we need a new generation that is healthy both physically and morally."[30] In 1934, homosexual acts between consenting males became a criminal offense; the state did not outlaw female homosexuality, which was less publicly visible and did not attract police attention. In 1936, the government circulated the draft of a new family law, under which only registered marriages would be recognized; divorce would become more complicated and progressively more expensive; and abortion would be prohibited except when a pregnancy threatened the mother's life or health. The draft also included incentives, similar to those offered by Catholic countries and by Nazi Germany, to encourage women to bear children. Women who bore more than six children would receive a 2,000 ruble annual bonus for each additional child and a 5,000 ruble bonus for each child over ten children. The same law raised both the level of child support and the penalties for men who failed to pay it.

The month-long public discussion that followed the circulation of the draft law elicited widely varying responses, judging by published letters as well as those preserved in Soviet-era archives. Many peasant women supported the ban. They regarded abortion as a sin and enjoyed limited access in any case. "For an abortion a woman should get three months in prison, for abortions have now become very common and the strangulation of the newborn is continuing," insisted a letter sent by women of Dnepropetrovsk Oblast.[31] For better educated rural women, however, enforced childbearing meant the loss of new opportunities. "When I read the law, I wondered if I will be able in the future to work this way if abortion is prohibited," wrote N. I. Ivleva, a zoo technician. "I love children and have a daughter whose birth interrupted my studies. I fully understand the harm of abortion. But I am against prohibiting it, because such a law will require me to change my work or risk my health."[32] Urban women echoed Ivleva's concerns, referring to lost

[29] Quoted in Choi Chatterjee, "Soviet Heroines and Public Identity, 1930–1939," *The Carl Beck Papers*, no. 1402, 13.

[30] Quoted in David Hoffman, "Mothers in the Motherland: Pronatalism in its Pan-European Context," *Journal of Social History* (Fall 2000), 45.

[31] Lewis Siegelbaum and Andrei Sokolov (eds.), *Stalinism as a Way of Life* (New Haven, Conn.: Yale University Press, 2000), 199.

[32] Manning, "Women in the Soviet Countryside," 208.

opportunities and material circumstances that prevented them from having the children that as women, they "naturally" loved and desired. Adopting pronatalist language even as they opposed the ban, no woman protested, or at least not in public, Stalin's contention that the gap between personal and collective life had disappeared.

On the other hand, many women appear to have welcomed the prospect of restrictions on divorce and more severe punishment for men who avoided paying child support. They also applauded the return to a more traditional family order. In 1934, there were some 200,000 child support cases filed in the courts of the Russian republic against "fugitive fathers" who had simply disappeared, making it virtually impossible to collect support payments from them. Thus, women cheered provisions that seemed to them aimed against sexually licentious or irresponsible men, as had women workers debating the family code of 1926. In the words of one *Stakhanovite* woman worker, abandoned by her husband five years earlier, "The new law will force such fathers to take care of their children."[33]

Pressures on men to shoulder their "family responsibilities" indeed intensified, even as it became more difficult for women to avoid childbearing. The draft became law in 1936, the language prohibiting abortion unchanged. In 1936, a secret directive from the Commissariat of Health ordered contraceptive devices, legalized in 1923, to be withdrawn from sale. After 1936, men became subject to criticism for failing to treat their wives with respect or to fulfill their husbandly responsibilities. The *Komsomol* might be faulted for assuming that a husband's infidelity was a private matter and for refraining from criticizing the erring husband as it should.[34] In *Pravda*, the Communist party newspaper, photographs of fathers with young children actually appeared more frequently than photographs of mothers in 1936. "My dream?" half-seriously responded Valery Chkalov, the most famous Soviet aviator, who "loved children with all his heart": "To have a pile of kids. Best have six. Not less."[35] The model was Stalin himself. Often depicted in propaganda posters surrounded by beaming and grateful children, Stalin was the biggest and best father of all. Thus the state sought to appropriate the "personal" or the "private" for purposes of its own.

The state's pronatalist efforts enjoyed only short-lived success, however. The birthrate grew from 30.1 births per 1,000 in 1935 to 39.7 in 1937, but after that it declined, so that the rate in 1940 was below that of 1936, partly because of mobilization for war. Illegal abortion was primarily responsible

33 Quoted in Fitzpatrick, *Everyday Stalinism*, 154.
34 Hoffman, "Mothers in the Motherland," 39, 45.
35 James von Geldern and Richard Stites (eds.), *Mass Culture in Soviet Russia: Tales, Poems, Songs, Movies, Plays and Folklore, 1917–1953* (Bloomington, Ind.: Indiana University Press, 1995), 262.

for the declining birthrate. Usually, it was painful and dangerous. Despite the "sin" attached to it, rural women resorted to it frequently, learning to do abortions on themselves or resorting to the local abortionist. Urban dwellers did the same. Anna Dubova, who endured several abortions, remembered with particular horror an underground abortion that almost cost her life, performed by a nurse who worked at a daycare center. "She pulled out a pile of dirty linen from under the bed and told me to lie down on it. And then there was a filthy sink where people washed their hands, and on it crude household soap. And she grated the soap and sprayed it up my uterus."[36] Dubova contracted blood poisoning and had to be hospitalized. She was one of hundreds of thousands of women hospitalized for incomplete illegal abortions after 1936. Women's use of illegal abortion constituted a form of resistance to the demand that they produce and reproduce, without any support from the state. At a terrible physical and, in the case of peasant women, moral price, women took control of their fertility as best they could.[37]

The New Culture

Yet for many – how many cannot be known – the very real hardship and suffering coexisted with genuine commitment to creating a new order. One component of that construction was psychological, the recasting of the very self to embody Stalinist-style modernization and to exclude inappropriate thoughts. "Only by means of persistent struggle and lengthy work on the self can a person reach the heights of science," reads the dedication on the back of Antonina Berezhnaia's photograph, taken in 1932.[38] "Human beings of a new kind were being formed," wrote Alla Kiparenko, a member of the *Komsomol* who helped to build the city Komsomolsk in the Far East. "This was true spiritual growth, a real aspiration to be better and to attain a genuine culture in everything, from attitudes towards work to personal relationships."[39] "Genuine culture" (*kul'turnost*, or culturedness) assumed enormous significance as a goal toward which the Soviet people strove. It meant behavior appropriate to a communist, such as sobriety, cleanliness, good manners – everything that the "dark" and "backward" peasants then inundating cities lacked. The expression *ne kul'turno* ("not cultured") conveyed strong disapproval. Mary Leder, U. S. born, stranded in Moscow in the mid thirties and living as a Soviet citizen, would forget herself and start whistling, only to be told it was "not cultured." "Whistling indoors was bad manners for males as well as females.

---

[36] Engel and Posadskaya-Vanderbeck, *A Revolution of Their Own*, 34.
[37] Ransel, *Village Mothers*, 115.
[38] Engel and Posadskaya-Vanderbeck, *A Revolution of Their Own*, 107.
[39] Fitzpatrick and Slezkine, *In the Shadow of Revolution*, 279.

("You're not in the middle of a field!").[40] During the thirties culturedness also came to include concerns about possessions and status, "the means and manners of a lifestyle appropriate to the new masters of the Soviet state."[41]

Gender inflected both the creation and representation of the new culture. Women's physical attractiveness and good grooming became one of its dimensions. "Soviet woman, while engaged in multi-faceted social activity, must learn to preserve her feminine countenance and to look after herself . . . she should pay attention to her appearance," *Rabotnitsa* informed its working-class female audience in 1939.[42] The female *Stakhanovites* who received attention from the press were disproportionately young and attractive; the women workers depicted in paintings tended to be attractive physically, too. The new female ideal had become softer and more feminine than that of the twenties. Women were supposed to be "modest" and "sweet" if they were single, maternal and faithful to husbands if married. Their "womanly values" would contribute to the creation of a more cultured public life, where tidiness reigned and men behaved like gentlemen. Constructing the city of Komsomolsk, women laborers demanded the inclusion of slogans such as "Keep your workplace and your work clothes clean!" and "No cursing at work or at home – especially in the presence of women!" The men grumbled but the women insisted: "Don't worry, you'll get used to it. You'll even thank us for it later."[43] Women became agents of the state's new, civilizing mission.

The home itself, such as it was, and women's role within it assumed an unequivocally positive dimension for the first time since the revolution. For married working-class and, especially, educated women, although not for collective farm women, an important goal became devoting oneself to one's man. When honoring a Soviet hero, the press would also lavish praise on his wife. Explaining how she created a supportive and "cultured" environment for her *Stakhanovite* husband, A. V. Vlasovskaia observed proudly that she had everything prepared when her husband returned from work and no longer depended on him for assistance. "Before, he used to help me around the house – bring the firewood and things like that. But now it's all ready for him. . . . My husband doesn't have to worry or get upset about household chores – his work is the only thing he knows."[44] Vlasovskaia was that rare creature, a full-time housewife. However, even when a woman earned an independent wage, her husband's role as worker took priority. In 1939, for example, in response to a campaign to recruit women to labor in the mines, a

---

[40] Leder, *My Life*, 47.

[41] Sheila Fitzpatrick, *The Cultural Front: Power and Culture in Revolutionary Russia* (Ithaca, N.Y.: Cornell University Press, 1992), 218.

[42] Quoted in Susan Reid, "All Stalin's Women: Gender and Power in Soviet Art of the 1930s," *Slavic Review* 57, no. 1 (Spring 1998), 152.

[43] Fitzpatrick and Slezkine, *In the Shadow of Revolution*, 279.   [44] Ibid., 361.

woman miner in the Donbass reported that "two months have passed since housewives . . . responded to L. M. Kaganovich's summons to women miners *to help their husbands in the fight for coal*" (emphasis added).[45] The only women released from such loyalty were those whose husbands obstructed their social contributions. Such husbands deserved only condemnation. Thus, home and family became harnessed to the production goals of the state.

The celebration of socially conscious wifehood reached its peak in the movement of wife-activists (*obshchestvennitsy*), which began in 1936. The movement invited full-time housewives to contribute their unpaid labor to the creation of a new society. First promoted by Stalin's lieutenant, the Commissar of Heavy Industry Sergo Ordzhonikidze, at its height in 1936–7, the movement mobilized tens of thousands of housewives for social, cultural, and educational work. *Obshchestvennitsy* were expected to make husbands and children their first priority. As Lazar Kaganovich reminded a group of them, women's first thoughts must always be for their husbands. Galina Shtange, married to a successful engineer, recorded his words: "The work our husbands are doing is difficult and crucial, and we must make our homes into a place where they can truly rest from their labors, we must create peace, comfort and joy for our families."[46] But *obshchestvennitsy* also contributed to the larger society. They organized kindergartens, nurseries, and camps for children; they furnished workers' dormitories and barracks, supervised factory cafeterias, planted trees and flowers, and set up discussion circles. The movement provided women with a rewarding outlet for their energies and skills, a way to contribute to the new order, to place their life, "small as it may be" on "the alter of our fatherland." "I found my element and felt wonderful," wrote Galina Shtange after she "boldly" joined the women's movement.[47] The movement served the Stalinist state most of all. Dominated by the wives of industrial managers and engineers, it bore considerable resemblance to the philanthropic endeavors of prerevolutionary "ladies." The movement extended women's domestic responsibilities into the public sphere and provided social services neglected by the economic planners. At the same time, the invariably neatly groomed and fashionably dressed *obshchestvennitsy* both promoted and served as exemplars of the "cultured" society of the future. State policy encouraged such women to develop refined tastes. In 1936, the first Soviet House of Fashion opened its doors, and French fashion magazines began publication in the U.S.S.R. Advice books taught women how to prepare elegant dishes and set a pleasing table. Working-class women often

---

[45] Reid, "All Stalin's Women,"141.
[46] Veronique Garros, Natalia Korenevskaia, and Thomas Lahusen (Eds.), *Intimacy and Terror: Soviet Diaries of the 1930s* (New York: The New Press, 1995), 172, 186.
[47] Ibid., 172.

resented *obshchestvennitsy*, whose celebration signified increased acceptance of class distinctions.

By the mid 1930s, domestic virtues were celebrated in the Soviet Union as never before in Soviet, or perhaps even Russian, history. In some ways, the new emphasis represented a compromise with the "bourgeois" yearnings of the new Soviet elite. Domestic virtues, however, had also become inextricably linked to the broader project of building socialism. By contrast with the "bourgeois" domesticity with which the new ideals otherwise shared so much, the ultimate purpose was neither to promote domestic felicity for its own sake nor to cultivate autonomous individuals. Instead, the goal remained to promote the public good and serve the needs of the state. Nowhere is this clearer than in the celebration of mothers who denounced their children for inappropriate behavior, such as the housewife Parfenova, who informed the authorities that her son had gone to work drunk and disturbed production.[48] Like the celebrated Pavlik Morozov, who was supposedly murdered for betraying his *kulak* father to the authorities, such women were perfectly conscious of where their final loyalties should lie.

Starting in the mid thirties, marriage became a measure of women's disloyalty as well as loyalty to the state. The second half of the thirties were a time of terror, which touched the lives of hundreds of thousands, perhaps millions, of people, the vast majority of them male. Barbara Clements calculated that women made up 11 percent of those formally prosecuted by the legal system in the late thirties and 8 percent of the prison population in 1940.[49] The relative absence of women had nothing to do with chivalry and everything to do with the under representation of women in the upper echelons of party membership, professional and intellectual life, and industrial management, spheres most hard hit by the terror. But women endured their own form of suffering, as mothers, daughters, sisters, and most commonly of all, wives of an "enemy of the people." Olga Adamova Sliozberg, arrested in 1936 and held in the Lubianka prison in Moscow, observed that the overwhelming majority of the women prisoners were party members or members' wives. So many wives of arrested old Bolsheviks were themselves arrested in 1937 that special camps had to be created to hold them. The very motherhood that the regime now celebrated intensified the sufferings of women prisoners. Their children were frequently sent away to children's homes, their names changed, their pasts effaced. In the communal prison cells described by Evgenia Ginsburg and Olga Adamova-Sliozberg, women who had remained stalwart under brutal interrogation and in punishment cells

---

[48] Rebecca Balmas Neary, "Mothering Socialist Society: The Wife-Activists Movement and the Soviet Culture of Daily Life," *Russian Review* 58, no. 3 (July 1999), 396–412.

[49] Barbara Evans Clements, *Bolshevik Women* (New York: Cambridge University Press, 1997), 280.

would succumb to hysterical weeping when they permitted themselves to think of their children. But wives of "enemies" who escaped arrest suffered, too. They lost their jobs. They and their children became subject to enormous pressure to renounce the "guilty" party. People avoided them, fearing guilt by association. According to Viacheslav Molotov, Stalin's lieutenant, the wives of purged men had to be isolated so that they would not spread complaints and discontent.[50] (When, in the late forties, Molotov's own wife was arrested, he remained at liberty, continuing to serve at Stalin's side.) Such women numbered in the tens of thousands. Even for those who escaped prison, the camps, or execution, terror often served as a corrosive that ate away at relationships.

Conclusion

Punctuated by terrible suffering as well as extraordinary achievements, contradictory in many respects, the Stalinist revolution was inflected by gender throughout. It reinforced gender differences at every level: in the workforce, which was intentionally segregated by sex; in imagery, which now emphasized the "feminine" features even of heroines of labor; in public life, which women had a uniquely feminine mission to beautify and render cultured, and in the family, where women fulfilled a special wifely and motherly mission. But most of all, gender saturated the very structure of political culture. Soviet society was supposedly "one big family." This was, however, not the egalitarian family of radical aspirations, not the brotherhood of worker dreams, not the reformed family envisioned by liberals, not even the loving domestic idyll of late tsarist propaganda. The ubiquitous images of Stalin, in which Stalin's wife Nadezhda Allilueva never appeared even before she killed herself in 1932, suggested another type of family altogether, with roots in both religious and peasant culture. A celibate secular saint, Stalin was also the *bol'shak*, but lacking the female helpmate no peasant household could do without. He presided over the peasant family writ large, a stern but benevolent father figure for whom everyone labored, who everyone obeyed, and who promised to care and provide for everyone – everyone at least, who retained his favor.

Suggestions for Further Reading

Bonnell, Victoria. "The Peasant Woman in Stalinist Political Art of the 1930s." *American Historical Review* 98, no. 1 (February 1993), 55–82.
Ginzburg, Eugenia. *Journey Into the Whirlwind.* New York, Harcourt Brace Jovanovich, 1967. *Vividly told story of one woman's journey through prison and the camps.*

[50] Ibid., 284.

Goldman, Wendy. *Women at the Gates: Gender and Industry in Stalin's Russia.* New York: Cambridge University Press, 2002. *An important exploration of the gendering of the Soviet industrialization drive.*

Hoffman, David. "Mothers in the Motherland: Pronatalism in its Pan-European Context." *Journal of Social History* (Fall 2000), 35–53. *Sets Stalinist family policies in the broader context of interwar European population policy.*

Ilic, Melanie, ed. *Women in the Stalin Era.* New York: Palgrave, 2001.

Manning, Roberta. "Women in the Soviet Countryside on the Eve of World War II." In Beatrice Farnsworth and Lynn Viola, eds. *Russian Peasant Women.* New York, Oxford University Press, 1992 206–35. *Examines the position of rural women in the aftermath of the collectivization drive.*

Neary, Rebecca Balmas. "Mothering Socialist Society: The Wife-Activists Movement and the Soviet Culture of Daily Life." *Russian Review* 58, no. 3 (July 1999), 396–412. *An assessment of the obshchestvennitsa movement, highlighting the contradictory messages sent to women.*

Reid, Susan. "All Stalin's Women: Gender and Power in Soviet Art of the 1930s." *Slavic Review* 57, no. 1 (Spring 1998), 133–73. *Explores the role of gender in shaping thirties culture.*

Viola, Lynn. "*Bab'i Bunty* and Peasant Women's Protest During Collectivization." *Russian Review* 45, no. 1 (1986), 189–205.

10

·

ENGENDERING EMPIRE

Well into the 1920s, Russia's imperial project was almost exclusively a male venture. Catherine the Great's territorial annexations represent a rare exception. Aggressively pursuing imperial expansion, Catherine presided over the partition of Poland and the conquest of vast tracts of land in the south, including the Crimean Peninsula and the northern shore of the Black Sea. Hundreds of thousands of Jews and Latvians, and millions of Ukrainians, Belorussians, and Poles were incorporated into the empire, reducing the proportion of ethnic Russians in the population to slightly under half.[1] But Catherine was unique. Before and after her reign, it was men who imagined, explored, conquered, and administered the domains that came to be "Russian." Women became involved as imperial agents only in the 1920s, when gender assumed central importance in the transformation of peoples to the north, south, and east.

The tsar, "Emperor of all-Russias," ruled over a hundred different peoples by the late nineteenth century. In addition to Russians, they included Germans, Jews, Poles, Armenians, Georgians, Azerbaijanis, Tatars, Kazaks, Kyrgyz, Uzbeks, Turkmen, Finns, and the various "small peoples" of the North, among others. If Ukrainians and White Russians (Belorussians), whose language and culture are related to Russian, are counted among the non-Russians, then ethnically non-Russian people comprised a majority of the empire at the turn of the twentieth century. The economies, cultures, and ways of life of the empire's peoples varied enormously, encompassing the industrialized cities of the Baltic states, the peasants of Ukraine, the nomadic and seminomadic peoples of the Central Asian steppes, and the reindeer herders of northern Siberia. The history of the Russian state's interactions with its subject peoples is equally complex. It is the gendered aspect of the imperial mission that provides the focus of this chapter.

[1] Estimates from V. M. Kabuzan, *Narody Rossii v XVIII veke. Chislennost' i etnicheskii sostav* (Moscow: Nauka, 1990), 230.

A Gendered Empire

In the nineteenth century, imperial domination itself revealed a gendered dimension. It was men, not women, who went forth to discover and map new lands to the South, North, and East and to conquer the native "other." Capturing the public imagination, tales of men's exploits in exotic areas celebrated the masculinity of the conqueror and rendered him inherently superior to the conquered. In the early nineteenth century, readers devoured sensational stories of love between Muslim women and Russian men that were set in the exotic Caucasus mountains where Russians waged a war of conquest. The Russian colonizer was a chivalrous and valiant man, an agent of progress, and the "good" native was a nurturing, sexually available, and ardent woman. By contrast with the Russian, the native men were savages, fanatical, and lustful brutes, who bought and sold their women or even murdered them for loving a Russian man. It was the Russian's task to rescue the abused woman from her male compatriots. The ardent union between the superior Russian conqueror and nurturing native woman offered a paradigm for the relationship between colonizer and colonized. Thus, gendered imagery served to underwrite and naturalize Russia's imperial mission.[2]

The tendency to represent the colonial realm as female or feminized served the same purpose. Writers of the 1830s and 1840s helped to popularize conquest by casting the relationship between conqueror and conquered in explicitly gendered terms. They would depict lands to the South and East as a kind of feminized "other," sexy and beguiling but backward and potentially dangerous, very much in need of Russia's guidance and control. Thus, as portrayed in the work of A. A. Bestuzhev-Marlinsky, Georgia was a luscious and enticing but untouched wilderness, spreading herself before the assaulting Russian conqueror: "Oh my darling! How enchanting you are now!.... I am ready to fling myself from the saddle onto your breast, to embrace you and cover you with kisses," declares Bestuzhev-Marlinsky's fictional military traveler to Georgia. The writings of the explorer, naturalist, and writer Nikolai Przhevalskii perpetuated this gendered representation of conquest. Przhevalskii gained enormous popular appeal in the second half of the nineteenth century. Aggressively virile, an exponent of "conquistador imperialism," he took pride in Russian superiority, regarding the peoples of the East as passive and helpless, desirous of Russia's hegemony and protection. Thus was the imperial mission defined as inherently masculine.[3]

When women participated, they did so in far less dashing ways. They took part in the civilizing mission that followed imperial conquest, and even

---

[2] Susan Layton, *Russian Literature and Empire* (New York: Cambridge University Press, 1994), 166–72.

[3] Quoted in Ibid., 182. See also 179–211.

in that capacity they often faced obstacles unknown to men. Thus, for example, Varvara Kashevarova-Rudneva had gained entry to medical school, her stipend paid by the Orenburg authorities, because of her willingness to practice among the Bashkir women of Orenburg province, forbidden by their Muslim faith to consult male physicians. Yet when she finally earned her degree, she was prevented from fulfilling her mission. After fruitlessly inquiring about a post in Orenburg, she traveled there herself to receive an official response to her queries. She received it. Women could not enter the service, she was told, particularly in her case, because the diploma she held entitled the holder to a rank in government service, from which women were barred. The local military command had no idea what to do with her. The only position available was in a military hospital, which was tied to government service and brought privileges enjoyed exclusively by men. "So they decided not to give me a position, despite the money they had spent on my education!!"[4] In the final decades of the nineteenth century, a few women became Russian Orthodox missionary-teachers in schools in the Volga-Urals region and Siberia. But even in this capacity, women's presence evoked ambivalence from men. At a congress of missionaries in 1910, it was proposed to involve more women in missionary work and to invite women delegates to the next congress; however, despite voices that spoke favorably, the proposal met defeat.

However, fiction could tell a different story. Her heroines' adventures on the Caucasian and Siberian frontiers earned the writer Lydia Charskaia (1875–1937) the adoration of Russian girls. Among the most popular of the more than eighty books that Charskaia published between 1901 and 1918 were those that featured the adventures of a Princess Nina (eventually, there were two Ninas). The first Nina was the only child of a Georgian prince who assisted the Russians in conquering the Moslem peoples of the Caucasus, and of a Tatar maiden who converted to Christianity and died when Nina was nine. Raised as a Christian and indulged by her adoring father, patterning her own behavior according to a military model, Nina engaged in the kind of adventures about which ordinary girls could only dream. She traversed the mountains on her favorite horse, followed bandits to their hideouts, even protected a male cousin frailer than she. As Beth Holmgren observed, "By positioning her heroines in the Caucasus, the most exotic and culturally exoticized frontier for Russian readers, [Charskaia] releases them from the strictures of urban European society in Moscow and St. Petersburg and explicitly links them with the Romantic tradition of daring Caucasian *heroes*

[4] Toby Clyman and Judith Vowles (eds.), *Russia Through Women's Eyes: Autobiographies from Tsarist Russia* (New Haven: Yale University Press, Conn., 1996), 184.

[emphasis in original]."[5] But Charskaia goes further. The Ukrainian Liuda, another Charskaia heroine, strives to spread the Christian faith among the Moslem Tatars, risking death at the hands of Moslem "fanatics." Charskaia's heroines not only challenge the prevailing stereotype of the native woman as passive and victimized but also portray women as venturesome agents of the imperial mission.

Encountering the Female "Other"

Most of the existing scholarship on non-Russian peoples offers only scattered references to real-life women, as distinct from women as objects of imperial policy or as emblems of an emergent nationalism. Historians are just beginning to explore women's family and work lives.[6] Best known are the educated and articulate women whose special status enabled them to speak and act on behalf of themselves and other women.

The Gender of Backwardness

In regions that Russians deemed to be backward, women's purportedly inferior status sometimes provided a key rationale for state intervention in native affairs. Presenting the imperial drive to the South, North, and East as a civilizing mission, Russian officialdom conceived of culture in terms of levels of development and stages, rather than in terms of difference. According to this view, "advanced" cultures, such as the Russian, had a responsibility to assist the more "backward" to catch up. One important criteria of backwardness was the status of native women. Tsarist policies toward Muslim peoples of the Volga and Central Asia in the second half of the nineteenth century provide a revealing case in point.

In the eyes of imperial officials, women in these regions (women of nomadic peoples such as Turkmen sometimes excepted) were oppressed by comparison with Russian women,[7] victims of the despotism of *shar'ia*, Islamic customary law that imperial policy sanctioned. Russian reformers of the late nineteenth century sought to end a range of customs, in particular the betrothal of widows to male in-laws, the payment of *kalym* or brideprice, and the marriage of female children and adolescents, which in the Russians'

---

[5] Beth Holmgren, "Why Russian Girls Loved Charskaia," *Russian Review* 54, no. 1 (January 1995), 98.

[6] See ChaeRan Y. Freeze, *Jewish Marriage and Divorce in Imperial Russia* (Hanover, N.H.: University Press of New England, 2002).

[7] Officials and some professionals tended to regard Russian peasant women as oppressed as well and to adopt toward them a comparable, if more muted, civilizing mission.

view infringed on the human rights of women. Especially among the Tatars who lived along the Volga River, evidence existed to complicate this one-dimensional representation of women's victimization. Resisting the efforts of Russian Orthodox missionaries, Tatar women of the middle Volga region played an important role in the struggle against religious assimilation and, in some cases, actively proselytized for their Muslim faith. In this region, almost as many girls attended religious schools as boys, in preparation for transmitting the faith to their children.[8]

Tatar and other Muslim women were also quite capable of defending themselves against family abuses. In the Muslim regions of the Volga and in Turkestan, the area of imperial administration that encompassed most of Central Asia, marital affairs remained within the bounds of Islamic customary law. Taking advantage of the legal venues available to them after the reform of 1864, as did Jewish and Russian women, Muslim women appealed successfully to Islamic law courts to curb a husband's abuses, to defend their own honor, and even to initiate divorce. According to Islamic law, a husband's "cruel treatment" gave the wife the right to seek divorce – a right that Russian Orthodox women lacked. Despite practices that contradicted stereotypes of Muslim women's victimization, by the end of the nineteenth century Russian officials had concluded that in order to raise up Muslim women it was time for a "civilized state" like Russia to rid Muslim territories of customary law, which took the "crudest and most inhumane form" and violated women's "human rights."[9] Only the fear that rapid introduction of Russian laws might arouse the opposition of natives prevented officials from proceeding with their plans. Reformers' views of native customs nevertheless influenced the aspirations of both Muslim nationalists and the reformers' Soviet successors.

Gender and Nation

The quest for greater national autonomy among the constituent peoples of Russia's empire often displayed a gendered dimension. For one thing, as elsewhere, the national community was imagined as a brotherhood. For another, even as they sought to distance themselves from Russian hegemony, non-Russian men sometimes adopted the Russian role of "progressive" in relation to their own women. Mirroring the developmental hierarchies of their Russian colonizers, peoples whom the Russians deemed "backward"

---

[8] Agnes Kefeli, "The Role of Tatar and Kriashen Women in the Transmission of Islamic Knowledge, 1800–1870," in Robert P. Geraci and Michael Khodarkovsky (eds.), *Of Religion and Empire: Missions, Conversion and Tolerance in Tsarist Russia* (Ithaca, N.Y.: Cornell University Press, 2001), 252–3, 263–5, 272–3.

[9] Quoted in Robert Crews, "Allied in God's Command: Muslim Communities and the State in Imperial Russia" (Ph.D. diss., Princeton University, 1999), 433, 435.

thus incorporated women's advancement into the nationalist agenda. Where "backwardness" did not draw attention to women's place, as in areas to the West, women themselves inadvertently contributed to the gendering process. To demonstrate the necessity of their inclusion in the fraternal polity, they employed rhetoric concerning the need for "mother-educators" to serve the nation, thereby creating a place for themselves and their issues within emergent nationalist movements. The link between gender and nation would sometimes prove a mixed blessing, however. Even as nationalism provided new opportunities for educated women to speak, it could limit what women felt able to say.

Among Muslims of the Caucasus, Volga region and Crimean peninsula, women's status came to occupy an important place in the national agenda. Nationalist movements emerged in more urbanized areas toward the end of the nineteenth century, a consequence of the same modernizing forces that had produced unrest among Russians. Jadidist reformers took the lead. Measuring progress by the criteria of the Western European "enlightenment," reformers of the Jadid movement aimed to set their nations on the road to modernity by reforming Islam itself. Male movement leaders, mainly Volga Tatar and Azeri intellectuals, not only included "the woman question" on their agendas but also accorded it key importance. Wrote the Tatar reformer Ismail Bey Gasprali (rendered as Gasprinskii in some sources) in 1913: "Whoever loves his own people and wishes it a [bright] future must concern himself with the enlightenment and education of women, restore to them [their] freedom and independence and give wide scope to the development of their minds and capabilities."[10] Reformers in the city of Baku identified the major women's issues as illiteracy, seclusion, the veil, and polygamy. Support for overcoming them became a measure of progressive politics. When Muslim parents petitioned the Baku City Council to open schools for their daughters, the Azeri representatives vigorously supported their request and used the occasion to open debate on women's place in society and to espouse an end to the veil and women's segregation. One of the representatives made a rousing "down with the veil" speech concerning the need for education to make women good citizens and good mothers, the two roles clearly inseparable in his mind.[11] The influential and popular Azeri journal *Molla Nasreddin* (1906–30), edited by Mirza-Jalil Mammed-Qulizadah (1866–1932) and his wife Hamideh Javanshir (1873–1955), also addressed a range of women's issues. Through

[10] Quoted in Azade-Ayşe Rorlich, "Intersecting Discourses in the Press of Muslims of Crimea, Middle Volga and the Caucasus: The Woman Question and the Nation," in Feride Acar and Ayşe Günes-Ayata (eds.), *Gender and Identity Construction: Women of Central Asia, the Caucasus and Turkey* (Boston: Brill, 2000), 147.

[11] Audrey L. Altstadt, *The Azerbaijani Turks: Power and Identity Under Russian Rule* (Stanford: Hoover Institute Press, Calif., 1992), 56.

satire and cartoons, the journal condemned compulsory veiling and seclusion, polygyny, wife battering, and violence against women.[12] Viewing the emancipation of women as "elevating" them to the level of their European sisters in education and enlightenment, Jadidists envisioned women's emancipation as a necessary precondition for the revival of Muslim civilization and the formation of a modern state.

The emphasis on women's emancipation encouraged women to speak for themselves. At first objects of reform by enlightened Muslim intellectuals, women quickly became men's acknowledged partners. The women, like the men, derived from the educated, privileged, and urbanized elite. For the most part, they made their case for women's educational and social advancement within the framework that the men had established, linking the nation's future to the contributions that enlightened mothers would make: "Sisters we need schools where we can get an education; we should be able to be useful to some extent to our Motherland if we can educate [properly] our children."[13] Following the revolution of 1905, in the city of Bakhchesarai in the Crimea, in Kazan, and in Baku, journals devoted to women were established, and other journals opened their pages to women contributors. Women's journals informed their readers about women's legal status, advised them of their domestic responsibilities, and presented them with information about the situation of women elsewhere. While emphasizing the need for change, advocates of women's emancipation nevertheless continued to uphold traditional Islamic values of devotion, chastity, and obedience to the will of Allah as the ideal for women. Nationalists thus embraced the values of the West selectively; as mothers especially, women would be instrumental in preserving the best of the national heritage. Muslim intellectuals, men and women alike, conceived of women's emancipation in terms of the greater good of the nation.

So did most of their Western counterparts. In the West, differing visions of what constituted the nation's greater good colored campaigns for women's emancipation. The examples of the Baltic Germans, Finns, and Ukrainians illustrate the diversity of ways that the politics of gender intersected with the politics of nationalism.

In the three Baltic provinces (Estland, Livland, and Kurland), a deeply conservative national partisanship shaped some women's involvement in public life. Germans comprised a tiny minority (6.9 percent) of the population of the Baltic region, but they enjoyed disproportionate social and political privileges. A German nationalist movement emerged in response to late

---

[12] Nayereh Tohidi, "Gender and National Identity in Post-Soviet Azerbaijan: A Regional Perspective," in *Gender and Identity*, 276.

[13] Quoted in Rohrlich, "Intersecting Discourses," 155.

nineteenth century policies of Russification, which required among other things that schools teach in the Russian language. To circumvent this requirement, Baltic Germans established semiclandestine home school circles, for which women assumed major responsibility. These and other endeavors offered an outlet for women who sought a purpose beyond the home.

The revolution of 1905 widened the sphere of activity accessible to German women. During the upheavals in the Baltic region, liberals strove to divest the Germans of their privileges and democratize politics while peasants attacked the estates of the German elite. In response, many middle- and upper-class German women joined a movement aimed at maintaining German ways and securing German privileges. Hundreds joined Women's Leagues, which aimed to "nurture and preserve Germandom" and to unite Germans across differences of class and social estate. Still larger numbers assumed significant responsibilities in the German national unions that emerged in each of the Baltic provinces. Women served as officers and conducted important organizational, fund-raising, and public relations work. Activism on behalf of their people offered women a compelling combination of tradition and emancipation. Nationalist rhetoric emphasized women's role as guardian of German culture and nurturer of Germanness, gaining widespread support for women's public activism. At the same time, national organizations provided forums from which women could argue for better educational and employment opportunities for themselves as women. Thus, for Baltic German women, the road to emancipation led through a nationalist movement that aligned them with the men of their nationality against democratic change and in defense of ethnic and social privilege.[14]

Women's activism in Finland assumed a completely different political coloration. In 1906, Finnish women became the first in Europe to gain the vote. Women's suffrage was the achievement of a broad popular movement, rather than of a women's suffrage struggle as such. An overwhelmingly agrarian society (90 percent of the people were peasants), Finnish women and men, long accustomed to cooperating, worked side by side in worker-led labor and temperance movements. The labor movement won the loyalty of tens of thousands of women, and the temperance movement, by contrast with its counterparts in Western Europe and the United States, included substantial numbers of men.

Having enjoyed an unusual degree of autonomy since their incorporation into the Russian empire in 1809, including an elected parliament (the Diet), Finns reacted angrily when, toward the end of the nineteenth century, Russia began to limit their autonomy and reduce the Diet's powers. By then,

---

[14] Anders Hendriksson, "Minority Nationalism and the Politics of Gender: Baltic German Women in the Late Imperial Era," *Journal of Baltic Studies* 27, no. 3 (Fall 1996), 213–28.

elite sponsored schools and cultural organizations had nurtured a sense of shared Finnish nationality among workers and peasants. Because the prevailing class-based electoral system disenfranchised working-class and peasant men as well as women, women and men made common cause in the political, social, and nationalist struggle. From the 1890s onward, both the labor and the temperance movements supported equal suffrage for men and women. Popular women's organizations, especially the homemaker's organization Martta (Martha), added a gendered dimension to the shared struggle by ascribing to women the role of nurturers and caretakers working for the larger national family, thereby linking social welfare and women's rights.[15] Ellen Marakowitz argues that this self-presentation afforded women a key place in the "national narrative" and an unusual degree of power in shaping the development of the Finnish state.[16] By contrast, the Finnish women's rights movement, composed primarily of highly educated upper-class women, never attained the same importance. A great national strike in October 1905, in which both sexes participated actively, forced the tsar to accede to popular demands for universal and equal suffrage, including the vote for women. Women ran for office in the very first elections, and nineteen women were selected as representatives to the Parliament, nearly 10 percent of the total, a record unequaled for decades elsewhere. Having incorporated themselves into the "national narrative," however, women in power found themselves limited by its terms. Mainly, they served in positions associated with housekeeping, broadly construed – that is, welfare and social services.

In Ukraine, the alliance between nationalists and women proved both less harmonious and less propitious for women. The Ukrainian nationalist movement was weak and fragmented, led by urban intellectual elites, a tiny minority in an overwhelmingly peasant society. Initially more cultural than political in emphasis, it arose in response to discriminatory language policies. Its aim: to enlighten, educate, and raise the national awareness of the Ukrainian people – that is, the peasantry, through *Hromady*, or "communities," cultural and political organizations with fluid membership that first emerged in the 1860s. Becoming active in their own right, women established the first Women's *Hromada* around the turn of the century. Women also set up libraries and strove to foster adult literacy in villages. After the revolution of 1905, women became very active in the Enlightenment Societies (*Prosvitas*) that aimed to link the Ukrainian intelligentsia with the common people and promote the use of the Ukrainian language. Ukrainian nationalist activities

---

[15] Irma Sulkunen, "The Women's Movement," in Max Engman and David Kirby (eds.), *Finland, People, Nation, State* (London: Hurst, Co., 1989), 178–93. For a somewhat different reading, see also Karen Offen, *European Feminisms, 1700–1950* (Stanford, Calif.: Stanford University Press, 2000), 215–6.

[16] Ellen Marakowitz, "Gender and National Identity in Finland," *Women's Studies International Forum* 19, no. 1 (1996), 55–63.

encountered vigorous repression. In participating in proscribed nationalist activities, women activists risked arrest and harassment by the police even after 1905. Almost all of the women put nationalism ahead of women-related issues. Whatever their political affiliations, women activists, including some who felt drawn to the cause of women's rights, downplayed a woman-oriented agenda.[17]

Yet despite women's manifest loyalty, tension arose between Ukrainian men and women, although it was usually kept beneath the surface. Older activists felt uncomfortable around assertive women; younger ones, like their populist counterparts of the 1870s and later, believed that feminism was irrelevant to the "liberation of the masses."[18] The Ukrainian intelligentsia "did not say a word about women." When Oleksandra Kosach tried to add the principle of equality between the sexes to a democratic constitution that intellectuals drew up in 1904, she was told that sexual equality was "implicit in the other rights."[19] Although women activists assumed important responsibilities in many Ukrainian nationalist organizations, women remained deferential in the presence of activist men, and most of them subordinated specifically feminist concerns to the cause of political and national rights. After the tsar was overthrown in February 1917, women's concerns were again submerged in the ultimately unsuccessful efforts to create and defend a new Ukrainian nation.

Jewish Women

In any assessment of the relationship between gender and nation, Jewish women occupy a unique position. Constituting about 4 percent of the empire's population around the turn of the century, Jews were regarded as "other" in Orthodox Christian Russia. Most were restricted to the Pale of Settlement and, especially after 1881, their access to education and employment was severely circumscribed. Anti-semitism was widespread. Following the assassination of Alexander II in 1881, horrific outbreaks of violence against Jews swept the towns of the Pale; another wave of anti-Jewish violence erupted during and after the revolution of 1905. Despite legal disabilities and social prejudice, or perhaps because of them, substantial numbers of Jewish women participated in intellectual and social movements of the late nineteenth century that were neither Jewish nor feminist in orientation.

---

[17] Martha Bohachevsky-Chomiak, *Feminists Despite Themselves: Women in Ukrainian Community Life, 1884–1939* (Edmonton, Alberta, Canada: Canadian Institute of Ukrainian Studies, 1998), 33–43. Sharing some of the same dilemmas, similarly emphasizing the link between motherhood and nation, some Polish feminists nevertheless proved more self-assertive. Robert Blobaum, "The Woman Question in Poland, 1900–1914," *Journal of Social History* 35, no. 4 (Summer 2002), 799–824.
[18] Bohachevsky-Chomiak, *Feminists*, 41.   [19] Quoted in Ibid., 37.

Women's pursuit of education set the stage. Striving for the learning that Jewish culture valued and seeking a passport out of the Pale of Settlement, Jewish women occupied a disproportionate share of seats in institutions of secondary and higher education as long as the government allowed it. Thus, for example, Jewish women constituted almost a third of the women enrolling in the Women's Medical Courses at the end of the 1870s. After a decree of 1887 limited the proportion of non-Christian students in Russian schools to 3 percent, hundreds of Jewish women left the country and pursued their studies abroad. At the turn of the century, about three-quarters of the thousands of Russian women who studied in Swiss universities were ethnically Jewish. When restrictions on admittance to the Bestuzhev courses were temporarily eased after 1905, the proportion of ethnically Jewish women in the entering class expanded to 19 percent.

Yet it was not their own disadvantages but those of Russia's laboring masses that initially prompted most educated Jewish women to social action. The proportion of Jewish women in movements that fought tsarist rule far exceeded their proportion in the population. In the 1870s, dozens participated in the populist movement, which accepted them as equals. The most well-known is Gesia Gelfman, who joined the terrorist People's Will and looked after the apartment where explosives were hidden. One of six sentenced to death after the assassination of Alexander II, Gelfman was spared execution, her sentence postponed and then commuted when officials learned she was pregnant. Gelfman died in prison not long after giving birth. In the early twentieth century, ethnically Jewish women streamed into the Socialist Revolutionary party, heir to populist tradition and into the Social Democratic (Marxist) parties: Jewish women comprised nearly 8 percent of female membership of the prerevolutionary Bolshevik party.

Women also joined organizations that aimed to transform the lives of fellow Jews. The Bund, the Jewish socialist organization founded in 1897, attracted substantial numbers of working as well as educated middle-class Jewish women from the Pale of Settlement. So did the Zionist movement that promoted Jewish settlement in Palestine. Like Russian radical organizations, both of these expected female participants to subordinate their own concerns as women to the goals of the larger struggle. In the words of Yelena Gelfand, "The woman question is not a separate issue, but part of the great socialist question."[20] The handful of Zionist feminists who emigrated to Palestine found their interests taking third place to those of the working-class and Jewish national brotherhood. Although some ethnically Jewish women joined feminist organizations, Jewish women in radical organizations appear to have vastly outnumbered them.

[20] Quoted Naomi Shepherd, *A Price Below Rubies: Jewish Women as Rebels and Radicals* (Cambridge, Mass.: Harvard University Press, 1993), 147; for the broader picture, 140–71.

The Impact of Revolution

After 1917, it becomes difficult to separate the fate of women of the minority peoples of the former Russian empire from that of the men of their ethnicity, region, or political grouping and, in the case of those incorporated into the Soviet Union, from the fate of ethnically Russian women. In the aftermath of World War I, some, most notably Finns, Poles, and Baltic peoples, detached themselves from the empire and established separate states. Members of other ethnic groups became incorporated into the Soviet Union, either at once or following the unsuccessful struggles for national autonomy that represented a significant component of the civil war. Subsequently, as members of their particular nationalities or ethnic groupings, they experienced the vicissitudes of Soviet nationality policies, as well as efforts to eradicate religion, modernize the "backward," and emancipate women by encouraging them to enter paid employment and the political arena. As was the case with Russians, those women who joined the triumphant Bolshevik party or were willing to take advantage of policies aimed to liberate them gained access to a range of new opportunities, although rarely so many as their male counterparts.

A Surrogate Proletariat

In some cases, however, gender itself assumed central importance. In areas the Soviets deemed "backwards," women's status served to legitimate conquest and guidance by a more advanced power, that is, the Soviet Union. Raising women's status became far more central to the Soviet civilizing mission than it was to the imperial Russian, in part because women's emancipation is important to the Marxist project, in part because gender seemed to offer a powerful strategic advantage. Where an indigenous proletariat or homegrown communist movement was lacking or weak, gender provided a spearhead of revolutionary transformation and women a kind of "surrogate proletariat," in Gregory Massell's felicitous phrase. The leadership adopted variations of this approach in Azerbaijan and toward the "small peoples" of the North (and, it has been argued, the Russian peasantry, too). The policy was pursued most intensively in Central Asia, which provides the primary focus of the discussion to follow.[21] It offered women unprecedented opportunities to participate in, even to shape, the civilizing mission.

The new Soviet leadership regarded the status of women in traditional Muslim cultures as emblematic of their cultural backwardness. As had their imperial predecessors, they condemned as evidence of women's oppression

---

[21] Soviet policy toward the Tatars of the Volga region, who lived interspersed with Russians, seems to have differed little from that adopted toward Russian peasants and to have led to similar social outcomes. See David Ransel, *Village Mothers: Three Generations of Change in Russia and Tataria* (Bloomington, Ind.: Indiana University Press, 2000).

such customary family practices as arranged and early marriage, payment of brideprice, polygamy, and seclusion of women. The cloak-like *parandzha* and the waist-length black horsehair veil (the *chachvan*) that concealed women's faces and bodies whenever they left home attracted particular Soviet opprobrium. In seeking to end such practices, the leadership in Moscow pursued a political agenda. In their view, women's oppressed status endowed them with the potential to become agents of social transformation. Once women's traditional status had been transformed in conformity with Soviet values, it was believed that grateful women would support the Soviets, undermining indigenous patriarchal cultures and resistance to Sovietization. Thus, women would substitute for the working class that was absent among the largely rural and nomadic peoples of Central Asia, making gender rather than class the foundation for socialist construction.[22]

Cautiously at first and then with more urgency the government moved to undermine traditional practices that enforced the subjection of women. In 1918, Central Asian women gained the option of seeking divorce under new Soviet laws. Between 1921 and 1923, practices such as polygamy, payment of brideprice, and marriage without the bride's consent were banned. Girls' minimum age for marriage was raised to sixteen. It became illegal to insult or mistreat a woman, especially to force her to wear a veil or remain in seclusion. Those who violated these laws were declared "enemies of the people" and became subject to severe penalties.

Gender transformation offered extensive opportunities for female activism. In Azerbaijan, where a similar emancipatory campaign proceeded, the regime relied on Azeri Bolshevik women to carry it out. Economic development in Azeri cities, Baku in particular, had already produced an industrial proletariat and a Westernized elite from which many activists derived. Dressed in Western fashion, their faces unveiled, literate and economically independent, female Azeri activists modeled the new emancipated lifestyle for their more traditional sisters. Creatively, they drew on traditional institutions; the communal bathhouse, sewing circles, women's corners, as well as more modern locations such as women's clubs and delegate meetings, literacy schools, and the like. "Through these channels, Azeri women pioneers succeeded in mobilizing tens of thousands of women, contributing to the process of modernization and nation-building of Soviet Azerbaijan, at times, beyond a mere 'surrogate proletariat.'"[23]

There were few female native supporters in Central Asia, however. One was Anna Nurkhat, raised in a Muslim and then a Russian milieu. "Before

---

[22] Gregory Massell, *The Surrogate Proletariat: Moslem Women and Revolutionary Strategies in Soviet Central Asia, 1919–1929* (Princeton, N.J.: Princeton University Press, 1974).

[23] Nayereh Tohidi, "Gender, Ethnicity and Islam in Soviet and Post-Soviet Azerbaijan," *Nationalities Papers* 25, no. 1 (1997), 149.

the October Revolution, there was, throughout the vast expanse of Russia, no human being more ignorant, more downtrodden and enslaved, than the Eastern women," Nurkhat wrote.[24] One of the first Turkic women writers, Nurkhat became an activist and organizer among Central Asian women (Fig. 16). However, the handful of Muslim women in Soviet organizations did not share her views about transforming women's roles. In any case, women from Russian, Armenian, or Jewish backgrounds vastly outnumbered indigenous female activists, their role all the more important because the seclusion of Central Asian women rendered them inaccessible to male party organizers. Working on behalf of Muslim women offered outsiders an opportunity for action and adventure as well as to act according to deeply held ideals. Most were single and in their twenties. (How many, one wonders, had read Lydia Charskaia?) Steeped in European humanist traditions, they were genuinely appalled by what they saw as Central Asian women's virtual slavery. Much as other Bolshevik feminists did, they eagerly shouldered the responsibility for their civilizing mission: liberating women from their oppression, bringing them into public life, and creating the bases of their equality with men. Indeed, *Zhenotdel* activists sought to shape state policy by pressing party and local officials to ameliorate what they saw as the "patriarchal oppression" of Central Asian women.[25] Eventually, some of them would pay with their lives.

The initial steps were modest but significant. By 1920, women activists had established women's sections in the region. They organized social clubs exclusively for women, which provided medical, legal, and educational services in a protected setting outside the home in which native women could feel at ease. They worked to raise women's literacy rates, which in some regions stood as low as 1 percent. Slowly, they began to draw native women, primarily women from poor backgrounds with the least to lose, into the party and public activity. Then Moscow shifted course. Throughout 1926, the party intensified the campaign, and at the end of the year, the party replaced this gradualist policy with an all-out assault on native customs. In Moscow's view, the goal was to produce new Soviet citizens and workers rather than to liberate women as such. There was no question of "the struggle against female enslavement [becoming] an end in itself," wrote a leading party analyst of Central Asian affairs.[26] Matters were less clear-cut for *Zhenotdel* activists on the spot.

The medium the leadership chose was the mass unveiling of native women, known as *khudzhum* (onslaught). Discarding the veil and thereby revealing the face that custom required women to conceal served as dramatic

---

[24] Quoted in Massell, *The Surrogate Proletariat*, 96.
[25] Douglas Northrup, "Subaltern Dialogues: Subversion and Resistance in Soviet Uzbek Family Law," *Slavic Review* 60, no. 1 (Spring 2001), 120.
[26] Quoted in Massell, *The Surrogate Proletariat*, 226.

16. Anna Nurkhat, from Fannina W. Halle, *Women in the Soviet East* (New York, 1938)

demonstration of a woman's conversion from native to Soviet values. The campaign focused on Uzbekistan, where people lived in settlements and the veil was ubiquitous; where the veil was absent, for example, in the nomadic regions of Turkmenistan, the campaign encountered more difficulty. But in Uzbekistan it took hold. On International Women's Day (March 8), 1927, a mass demonstration of unveiling took place, in which women threw off their *parandzha* and *chachvan* and tossed them onto huge bonfires. According to Soviet accounts, the effect on those assembled to watch was electrifying. Thousands more women were inspired to tear off and burn their veils and then move through the city streets unveiled, chanting challenges to the traditional order. The movement spread. Although official figures indicate that by May, some 90,000 women had discarded their veils, these figures are likely inflated.[27]

Pressure to unveil intensified. Male party members were pressured to unveil their wives and daughters; female party members were pressured to unveil themselves. The party instituted measures to encourage women. Those who abandoned the veil gained special privileges, whereas the husbands of those who failed to unveil might be penalized and husbands who were party members might even be forced to give up their party card. Some jobs required that a woman relinquish her veil. Indoctrination in all available media accompanied the campaign.

The response was massive resistance. Because women's seclusion and veiling was indissolubly linked with family honor, men experienced unveiling as an assault on their most fundamental social institutions – gender and family relations and the division between public and private space. Central Asian men, even party officials, sometimes refused to permit their wives to unveil or forced them to resume the veil after one demonstrative "public" unveiling. Women themselves resisted unveiling, some because they preferred to be veiled, others in response to their own fears or to public reaction. "Everybody acts as though he is busily engaged in agitating for female emancipation," a woman party member complained. "But go ahead and try to unveil: immediately everyone, including village communists, regard you as a fallen woman. This is exactly what happened to me: at one time I discarded the veil, and everyone persecuted me for this. The communists not only refused to defend me; quite the contrary, they let it be known that I was a prostitute. That's why I donned the veil again, and now people treat me with greater respect."[28] Women rioted openly in opposition to the policy of unveiling, taking advantage of the immunity that followed from the assumption that women were victims, incapable of acting on their own. Outraged men took to the streets to demand the end of unveiling and the return of women to female quarters in the home. Local courts refused to enforce the new norms or enforced them in ways that in fact upheld traditional practices.[29]

Resistance to Soviet-sponsored efforts to transform gender relations sometimes erupted in violence. In Azerbaijan, men beat and even murdered women not only for removing their veil but also for participating in social and political

---

[27] Douglas Northrup argues that resistance to these campaigns was widespread, and reports of unveiling likely exaggerated.

[28] Quoted in Massell, *The Surrogate Proletariat*, 332.   [29] Northrup, "Subversion," 127–8.

activities outside the home. In Central Asia, the violence became most extensive and extreme. In Turkmenistan, resistance was connected with the rising number of divorces initiated by women taking advantage of their new rights: husbands murdered wives who sued for divorce in Soviet courts. Elsewhere, unveiled women became targets. During the *khudzhum* of 1927, crowds of men followed unveiled women through the streets, harassing them and casting aspersions on their morality. Within days, men's behavior turned violent: bands of youths seized unveiled women and raped them. With growing frequency, unveiled women were murdered, not only on the streets but also at home, by their own kinsman, as traitors to tradition and prostitutes. By 1928, female activists had become targets as well. In the end, thousands of women were killed or wounded in connection with the unveiling campaign; only a tiny minority of assailants were ever arrested and taken to court.[30] The campaign turned the veil into an important symbol of resistance to Soviet rule.

Most of the resistance to gender transformation assumed more passive forms. In Central Asia, campaigns to emancipate women garnered almost no genuine local support. In addition to resisting unveiling, Central Asians evaded the laws that sought to reform their family practices. Prospective husbands continued to pay brideprice, for example, but instead of cattle they offered cash and called it a "wedding gift." Polygamous marriages continued, too. Central Asian officials and party members were no more compliant than the rest. Officials dragged their feet when women sought divorce. They refused to provide the kind of assistance that women who tried to break with tradition most needed: enterprises where they might find employment; credit and seeds to support women's farming ventures; schoolhouses, teachers, and books for those who sought schooling; clubs where women might meet. Even as Moscow and the *Zhenotdel* pulled out the stops in their campaign to mobilize Central Asian women, local officials did everything in their power to sabotage those efforts. Consequently, the women who did respond to the party's campaign – most of them from socially marginal groups such as widows or orphans – frequently experienced unemployment, homelessness, and destitution. In the winter of 1928–9, massive hunger riots occurred, with Muslim women demanding bread and work.

Fearful of entirely alienating Central Asian elites and horrified at the violence, in 1929 the government gave up its aggressive methods. Without abandoning its original goals, the party replaced outright assault with less dramatic and more gradual approaches to transforming native customs and family values. Nayereh Tohidi has drawn attention to a subtle bargain, an

---

[30] Shoshanna Keller, "Trapped Between State and Society: Women's Liberation and Islam in Soviet Uzbekistan," *Journal of Women's History* 10, no. 1 (Spring 1998), 26–9.

17. Tadzhik Mountain Women, from *Women in the Soviet East*

"unwritten deal," that left intact the Muslim male's domination over his private domain, that is, women and the family, not only in Central Asia but also in Azerbaijan.[31] In Azerbaijan, this arrangement followed the abolition of the *Zhenotdel* in 1930 and the closing of Azeri women's clubs in 1933, leaving the "woman question" to be solved by local or national male elites.

Efforts to bring women into public life and to transform their public image nevertheless continued. At the end of the twenties, Soviet officials intensified their efforts to raise the abysmally low level of literacy among Central Asian women. Primary schooling became compulsory. The proportion of girls among primary school students grew from about 33 percent in the late twenties to about 48 percent by 1940. Although far fewer girls than boys continued past primary school and girls were far the more likely to drop out or miss school because of their families' resistance, the numbers represent substantial progress. By the late thirties, some women had begun to pursue advanced education and professional training, especially in the fields of law, medicine, teaching, and science. Soviet schools inculcated their students with a new set of values, encouraging them to study, to take part in physical education and sports, and to perform in public settings. When the Soviet Union

[31] Tohidi, "Gender, Ethnicity and Islam," 159.

collapsed in 1991, the literacy rates of Central Asian women had become roughly equivalent to those of their counterparts elsewhere in the nation and their representation in institutions of higher education surpassed that of men. In Azerbaijan, too, some 46 percent of professionals were female.

Pressures to accommodate other Soviet standards also continued. In the late twenties, having an unveiled wife or being an unveiled woman became the lodestone of loyalty for Central Asian party members. A verification campaign of 1928–9 sought to discover all members whose family practices failed to reach the Bolshevik standard, labeling them "class-alien" and a poor example for their compatriots. "Is it possible to consider a person ideologically suited to be a Communist [if he] locks up his wife, holds her under the *paranji* [*parandzha*], [and] forbids her to go to a meeting . . . ?" rhetorically inquired a top Bolshevik official in a speech of 1929.[32] The many men who failed to live up to these standards suffered reprimands, public humiliation, expulsion from the party, even imprisonment. In Central Asia, the terror of the mid thirties acquired a distinctively gendered dimension. Among the accusations of disloyalty leveled at targeted party members, *byt* crimes, that is, keeping wives veiled and opposing women's liberation, occupied a central place. Thus, the continuing resistance to gender transformation became not only politicized but also the primary focus of the attack on alleged "enemies of the people." "Organizing a struggle for the liquidation of feudal serf survivals in relations towards women is a part of the sharpening class struggle," reads an Uzbek party resolution of 1939.[33] The terror of the mid thirties succeeded in eradicating most of the overt resistance to Soviet policies. By the end of the decade, it had become rare to see a fully veiled woman in the cities of Central Asia, although as late as the 1980s, women continued to cover their bodies and faces in rural villages of the Ferghana valley, and likely, elsewhere too.

Less sweeping efforts to "civilize" Muslim peoples proceeded as well. In addition to literacy programs and efforts to abolish customary marital practices and bring women into the workforce, the Soviets focused on maternity. Aimed at ending traditional practices that produced exceedingly high rates of both infant and maternal mortality, they sought to transform traditional women's culture and win their support for the state. This effort was particularly important in Kazakhstan, where indigenous people were nomadic or seminomadic herders. Although Kazakh women neither wore veils nor experienced seclusion and by some prerevolutionary accounts, enjoyed unusually high status, the Soviets deemed them victims. The campaign commenced at the end of the twenties. In special "women's evenings," lecturers taught women that Kazakh customs brought negative consequences for the health

---

[32] Quoted in Douglas Northrup, "Languages of Loyalty: Gender, Politics, and Party Supervision in Uzbekistan, 1927–1941," *Russian Review* 59, no. 2 (April 2000), 188–9.

[33] Ibid., 199.

and endeavored to inspire confidence in Western medicine. Physicians singled out lay midwives and native healers as targets for vicious attack, much as physicians did in the Russian countryside. The Soviet government initiated a rapid expansion of women's health care in Kazakh areas, more rapid than in Russian ones. Only at the end of the thirties, however, did these efforts bear fruit, after the Soviets created a medical infrastructure almost from the ground up. The number of hospital and clinic beds for maternity cases rose from 202 in 1929 to 14,782 in 1941. Increasingly, Kazakh women had their children in hospital settings instead of the customary familiar environment of the home. Daycare centers increased in number, too, growing from 495 in 1928 to 7,989 in 1938 in cities and from 30 to 9,000 in rural areas.[34] These facilities brought genuine health care benefits to women and children in a modern rather than traditional environment. Delivering on promises of a brighter and healthier future, these facilities convinced indigenous women of the benefits of Western medical practices. They failed however, in their central purpose: to undermine faith in traditional practices, which continued alongside modern ones, and to win women's loyalty to the Soviet regime.

Nevertheless, by the second half of the thirties, the Soviet government could, and did, claim major victories in the campaign to "liberate" Muslim women. Quotas that granted women one third of posts in government and party institutions ensured that they filled public roles. The government taught women that it was their right, as well as their responsibility, to seek work outside the home. Media celebrated women's achievements in the arts, sports, and science. Women became highly visible, serving as positive role models, for younger generations of women. For the Soviet government, women professionals, women party members and activists, and women who worked outside the home and dressed no differently than their European counterparts served as proof of Soviet success. "It has required the enormous efforts of the party and the working class to raise up the formerly degraded and enslaved woman of the East, to help her to throw off the *chador*, the *chachvan* and the *parandzha*," boasted a Soviet publication in typical self-congratulation. "Only the tireless concern of the party and Soviet power for women and children has brought women to full equality and the possibility of realizing their rights in practice."[35]

The realities were more complex. In some regions, women's workforce participation came at substantial cost. In Kazakhstan, collectivization combined with the forced resettlement of nomads led to the loss of millions of lives. Most Muslim women labored on collective farms. Where cotton

---

[34] Paula Michaels, "Medical Traditions, Kazak Women and Soviet Medical Politics to 1941," *Nationalities Papers* 26, no. 3 (1998), 499–500, 502.

[35] I. Kovaleva, "Samoderzhavie i izbiratel'nye prava zhenshchin," *Krasnyi Arkhiv* 6, no. 79 (1936), 28.

culture predominated, the majority of women were employed on a seasonal basis, performing the backbreaking job of harvesting cotton by hand. While women's public roles were transformed, their private ones remained more traditional. In Central Asia, reproduction continued to take precedence over production. There, by contrast with European Russia, the pronatalist campaign launched in the mid thirties yielded substantial results. The campaign was in accord with traditional values, and women were eager to take advantage of the stipends awarded to women bearing seven or more children, which made a genuine economic difference in this impoverished region. Birthrates in the region remained high, even as rates elsewhere steadily declined. In 1970, Central Asian women bore, on the average, more than twice as many children as their Russian compatriots. Consequently, their participation in the workforce was usually short-lived or intermittent, with women taking off years to bear and raise their children. As in the rest of the Soviet Union, the labor force in Muslim areas became sexually segregated, with women trapped in low-paid, unskilled, or semiskilled occupations.

Most important of all, within the home, gender relations remained virtually unchanged. Despite rising literacy rates and increased participation in the workforce, despite the growing availability of Western-style medical services and the reduction of infant mortality, despite greater female visibility in public life, almost everywhere Muslim men and women alike resisted change in the family. Thanks to the "unwritten deal," Muslim men could rest assured that women's employment would not interfere with their work at home. Having succumbed to Russian domination in the public realm, men became all the more adamant about their rights in private. Indeed, Shirin Akiner argues that it was the very intensity and pace of change that prompted women (and men) to embrace more firmly than ever the prerevolutionary domestic order.[36] Muslim women continued to bear the heavy burden of household responsibilities, which retarded their activity outside the home. Wrote the Azeri poet Nigar Rafibeyli:

> I feel so heartsore
> 　　in this kitchen world;
> After all,
> There is something of the poet in me.
> Some are destined to occupy high posts,
> Others to wash up dishes in the kitchen.
> But who's there to see
> That the book burning by the stove
> Doesn't turn into cinders?[37]

[36] Shirin Akiner, "Between Tradition and Modernity: The Dilemma Facing Contemporary Central Asian Women," in Mary Buckley (ed.), *Post-Soviet Women: From the Baltic to Central Asia* (New York: Cambridge University Press, 1997), 276.

[37] Quoted in Tohidi, "Gender, Ethnicity and Islam," 151.

In the home, women assumed guardianship of national identity and protected it against Soviet encroachments, maintaining the rites associated with the Muslim faith and the behaviors traditionally associated with proper woman-hood, such as self-sacrificing motherhood, docility, and subservient behavior toward men. Thus, although Muslim women of Azerbaijan and Central Asia adopted new public roles, most colluded in the preservation of traditional arrangements in private life, which became still more closely identified with national traditions as a result of Soviet assaults.

Conclusion

By the outbreak of World War II, the Soviets' civilizing mission had achieved genuine, but only partial, success. Making inroads among Muslim peoples of Central Asia and Azerbaijan, efforts to "emancipate" indigenous women failed to transform women's family roles. As was the case with Russians, women gained new rights in public life and numerous individuals bene-fited from the changes that the Soviets introduced. Women became more likely to survive childbirth and less likely to lose their infants; especially in the cities, they obtained opportunities for education and upward mobility that enabled them to live very different lives than had their mothers. Yet, changes in women's public roles were sometimes accompanied by wrenching and destructive economic and lifestyle transformations and the imposition of Russian hegemony and norms perceived as alien. Whether it was indige-nous women or *Zhenotdel* activists who fostered gendered change, women's "emancipation" was often regarded as an alien import, especially by men whose prerogatives it challenged. As a result, when formerly Soviet peo-ples began their search for a usable past and sought to forge a new national brotherhood, their rejection, especially men's rejection, of Russian-style "So-vietization" almost invariably involved a rejection of gender transformation, too. This posed a difficult dilemma for those women, particularly professional women, who treasured the new opportunities.

Suggestions for Further Reading

Blobaum, Robert. "The Woman Question in Poland, 1900–1914." *Journal of Social History* 35, no. 4 (Summer 2002), 799–824.

Bohachevsky-Chomiak, Martha. *Feminists Despite Themselves: Women in Ukrainian Community Life, 1884–1939*. Edmonton, Alberta, Canada: Canadian Institute of Ukrainian Studies, 1998.

Edgar, Adrienne. "Emancipation of the Unveiled: Turkmen Women under Soviet Rule, 1924–29," *Russian Review* 62, no. 1 (2003), 132–149.

Freeze, ChaeRan. "The Litigious Gerusha: Jewish Women and Divorce in Imperial Russia." *Nationalities Papers* 25, no. 1 (1997), 89–102. *How legal reform empowered Jewish women.*

Hendriksson, Anders. "Minority Nationalism and the Politics of Gender: Baltic German Women in the Late Imperial Era." *Journal of Baltic Studies* 27, no. 3 (1996), 213–228.

Layton, Susan. *Russian Literature and Empire*. New York: Cambridge University Press, 1994. *Explores the gendered dimension of imperial conquest.*

Marakowitz, Ellen. "Gender and National Identity in Finland." *Women's Studies International Forum* 19, no. 1 (1996), 55–63.

Massell, Gregory. *The Surrogate Proletariat: Moslem Women and Revolutionary Strategies in Soviet Central Asia, 1919–1929*. Princeton, N.J.: Princeton University Press, 1974. *The classic account of Soviet efforts to transform women's roles.*

Michaels, Paula. "Medical Traditions, Kazak Women, and Soviet Medical Politics to 1941." *Nationalities Papers* 26, no. 3 (1998), 493–509. *A study of biomedical efforts to further the Soviet imperial mission.*

Northrup, Douglas. "Subaltern Dialogues: Subversion and Resistance in Soviet Uzbek Family Law." *Slavic Review* 60, no. 1 (Spring 2001), 115–139. *Attends to local reactions and efforts to subvert and resist Soviet-style modernization.*

Rorlich, Azade-Ayşe. "Intersecting Discourses in the Press of Muslims of Crimea, Middle Volga and the Caucasus: The Woman Question and the Nation," in Feride Acar and Ayşe Güne-Ayata, eds. *Gender and Identity Construction: Women of Central Asia, the Caucasus and Turkey*. Boston: Brill, 2000, 143–161. *Assesses the role of gender in prerevolutionary Islamic nationalism.*

Tohidi, Nayereh. "Gender, Ethnicity and Islam in Soviet and Post-Soviet Azerbaijan." *Nationalities Papers* 25, no. 1 (1997), 147–67.

11

WORLD WAR II AND ITS AFTERMATH

At 4:00 in the morning on June 22, 1941, Hitler's forces launched a surprise attack on the Soviet Union. The threat of warfare had hung like a cloud over the second half of the 1930s, as the Soviet Union readied itself both materially and psychologically for conflict. "Be aware of the international situation and prepared to replace your husbands, brothers and sons in case of war," Lazar Kaganovich had urged some 200 wife activists at the end of 1936.[1] Officers' wives acquired basic military training and then trained other women in driving and nursing skills. Women were encouraged to gain military-related skills by participating in the work of the Red Cross and the Red Crescent and to keep fit by engaging in military sports. Mass programs for basic military and physical training equipped women to use gas masks and firearms. By 1941, about a quarter of a million women were prepared to assume combat roles.

Nevertheless, nothing prepared Soviet citizens for the magnitude of the conflict with Hitler's forces. The Nazi-Soviet pact of August 1939 had raised hope of avoiding war. Catching the leadership by surprise, the lightening attacks along three separate fronts proved stunningly effective, easily overrunning Soviet defenses and destroying much of the Soviet air force. Vast portions of the Western borderlands, home to some 80 million citizens, fell to Nazi occupying forces. By September 8, German forces had surrounded and placed under siege the city of Leningrad; they closed in on Moscow in early October. Millions of refugees and evacuees snarled transport. The resulting chaos was exacerbated by frantic efforts to disassemble and transfer thousands of industrial enterprises and some 25 million workers and their families from West to East, beyond the Urals and out of reach of German forces.

[1] Veronique Garros, Natalia Korenevskaia, and Thomas Lahusen (eds.), *Intimacy and Terror: Soviet Diaries of the 1930s* (New York: The New Press, 1995), 184.

During the four terrible years that the Soviets fought in World War II, the entire nation mobilized, becoming one gigantic "front" in which every action was supposed to be geared to defense and offense. Repression eased and patriotic feelings deepened, at least among Russians, nurtured by nationalist propaganda aimed at maintaining morale and combat-readiness in seemingly hopeless circumstances and by the ferocious brutality of the German occupiers. In terms of the responsibilities that citizens were summoned to fulfill, gender differences almost ceased to matter. The line separating "men's work" from "women's work" dissolved. Soviet women replaced men in heavy industry, drove tractors, fortified cities, took up arms and entered combat on an unprecedented scale. Yet in imagery, gender distinctions not only continued but even intensified as war drew to a close. Gender shaped wartime and postwar propaganda, which represented women in ways designed to bolster men's morale and facilitate their postwar healing. So compelling were the images that they could overshadow or deeply color real-life experience.

The "Home Front"

For most women, wartime experience consisted of physical toil, material deprivation, and emotional strain. To replace the labor of men called to arms, the Soviet government ordered full labor mobilization, incorporating into the labor force the "nonworking" population of towns and villages. Housewives and young girls were mobilized for labor; women already employed were transferred into war-related work, where the need was greatest. Like their U.S. counterpart "Rosie the Riveter," Soviet women produced the armaments needed for combat. They descended into mines and worked with pneumatic drills at the coalface; they operated cranes; they kept the trains running, even repairing, stoking, and driving locomotives. Women accompanied industrial plants evacuated to the East, where no dwellings had been prepared. They lived in earth shelters, holes in the ground, or derelict barracks, often working in the open air in twelve to fourteen hour shifts, with mandatory three hours overtime. By the beginning of October 1942, women comprised 52 percent of the labor force in military-related industry and 81 percent of the labor in light industry (up from 60 percent on the eve of the invasion). At the end of the war, 56 percent of the entire labor force was female.[2]

The draconian labor legislation of December 26, 1941, applied to women workers as well as men. The legislation made absence without leave from

---

[2] John Erickson, "Soviet Women at War," in John and Carol Garrard (eds.), *World War 2 and the Soviet People: Selected Papers from the Fourth World Congress for Soviet and East European Studies, Harrogate 1990* (New York: St. Martin's Press, 1993), 53–5.

defense-related industry punishable by five to eight years of prison; in mid-April 1943, workers in railway, telegraph, and water transportation were likewise placed under military discipline. Such legislation brought new recruits to forced labor camps, which contributed vitally to military production. When German forces threatened, tens of thousands of women were mobilized to dig antitank ditches, build barricades, and in other ways prepare the defense of their towns or cities. Most worked willingly, aware that their own lives and those of their compatriots depended on their labor. "Hard work. My back aches. I don't have the necessary shoes or clothing," wrote Raisa Orlova, mobilized to gather firewood in early October 1941. The firewood would ensure that Moscow did not freeze. "I didn't want to go back home. I was cold and hungry, but on the other hand it was for the front, for victory."[3]

It was women who kept the country fed, if barely: 70 percent of the agricultural labor force was female in 1943, 91.7 percent by 1945. With men off at war and childless women mobilized into war-related production, mothers, children, and the elderly were left to do the farm work, made all the heavier because the army commandeered both horses and tractors. Those tractors that remained saw endless service, driven and maintained by women who had taken short, intensive training courses in tractor driving, which had hitherto been performed almost exclusively by men. "The spring planting is also part of the 'front'" and "Female tractor drivers are soldiers on collective farm soil!" Women collective farmers were informed.[4] Between 1940 and 1944, the proportion of tractor drivers who were women rose from 4 to 81 percent. Without spare parts and with lubricants strictly rationed, driving a tractor became difficult work indeed. "We slept three or four hours a day. For a long time we warmed up the engines with naked flames – against all the rules. Lubricants and fuel were rationed. You answered with your head for every drop. . . ."[5] More difficult still was the lot of farm women without access to tractors or to draft animals; in such cases, women pulled the plow using the force of their own bodies. Paid a pittance for the work performed for collective farms, farm families subsisted mainly on what women could coax from their private plots. In village and in city, the population went hungry.

During World War II, there really was no Soviet home front, strictly speaking – no place untouched by warfare, one way or another, no ordinary person who remained unmobilized or safe from suffering and loss. The war years were a time of deprivation for all but the most pampered party leaders. The government reintroduced rationing in 1941. Provisions were based on the person's work; the highest norm was 1.2 kilos of bread a day (just over

---

[3] Raisa Orlova, *Memoirs* (New York: Random House, 1983), 110.

[4] Lynne Attwood, *Creating the New Soviet Woman: Women's Magazines as Engineers of Female Identity, 1922–1953* (New York: St. Martin's Press, Inc., 1999), 142.

[5] Erickson, "Soviet Women at War," 56.

$2^1/_2$ pounds) for workers in heavy industry; children and expectant mothers received from 300 to 400 grams – essentially, starvation rations. Mobilization into defense work could actually improve the diet of women in low-status occupations such as teaching. "Only during the war, when I began working at a defense plant, did my family finally have enough to eat. Then I wasn't restricted to the teacher's ration of 400 grams of bread per adult. . . . At the plant I received 800 grams of bread; I had a worker's ration card. And they gave me groats for the children and some other stuff. Before that, we went hungry all the time."[6] People did go hungry much of the time. Only combat soldiers and workers in war-related industry received rations substantial enough to survive on. Others foraged, mothers forced to use all their resourcefulness simply to feed their children. During the first years of war, Soviet citizens ate about two-thirds less food than they had in 1940. Life was especially grim in the winter of 1941–2, when the sight of men and women falling dead of starvation on Moscow streets became too commonplace even to attract crowds.

Life was perhaps grimmest of all for the inhabitants of Leningrad, primarily women and children (about 400,000 altogether), who endured the 900-day siege. Efforts were made to distribute scarce rations equitably (except for the party elite, who dined well throughout). But supplies quickly ran out. Less than a month after the siege began, Elena Kochina found herself unable to satisfy her starving child. At the pediatric clinic, the child immediately downed all the soy milk in her $3\frac{1}{2}$ ounce ration, then cried bitterly, stretching her hands toward the white baby bottles, and vainly shouting "more, more, more!"[7] Like countless other Leningrad mothers, Kochina watched her child sicken and lose her ability to stand or even to sit as the siege continued. Having lost parents to starvation, other children found themselves on their own. The twelve-year-old Tania Savicheva recorded the demise of her own family, first her uncles and grandmother, finally, her mother. "Everyone is dead," she wrote in her diary. "Only Tania is alive."[8] But Tania, too, did not survive the war. By the time the siege was lifted, an estimated million people had perished under artillery fire or died of hunger or hunger-related diseases.

The war was hard on women and children and corrosive of families in other ways, too. In occupied areas, rape was a fact of life. On the flimsiest pretext, the Germans might annihilate entire villages, composed mainly of women, children, and the elderly, the men having gone to war. Traumatized

---

[6] Barbara Alpern Engel and Anastasia Posadskaya-Vanderbeck (eds.), *A Revolution of Their Own: Voices of Women in Soviet History* (Boulder, Colo.: Westview Press, 1998), 170.

[7] Elena Kochina, *Blockade Diary*. Samuel Ramer (ed. and trans.) (Ann Arbor, Mich.: Ardis Press, 1990), 42.

[8] Nina Tumarkin, *The Living and the Dead: The Rise and Fall of the Cult of World War II in Russia* (New York: Basic Books, 1994), 70.

survivors would respond with sleep. "You would enter a hut, and see three or four children dead on the floor, much of the rest of the village in flames, and the children's mother sound asleep."[9] Families became separated. Millions of women and children fled the invaders on foot. Evacuated in haste, it was easy for mothers and children to become separated. Sofia Pavlova, a party member evacuated by train from Moscow separately from her children, spent days tracking them down and found them only by chance. "I went along the siding, knocking at every car and asking, 'Is my family here?' "[10] During the course of the war, about 25 million people became homeless, their towns and villages occupied, their homes burned to the ground.

Then, of course, there was the endless waiting for news: of how the Red Army was faring, of whether a family member or friend had survived combat or Nazi occupation. As casualties mounted into the millions, millions more bore the additional burden of grief.

Women in Combat

During World War II, hundreds of thousands of women took up arms. The speed of the German invasion turned home fronts into frontlines in a matter of moments. In 1941, thousands joined the hastily formed people's militia units that took on crack German troops. As the German hold solidified and the barbarity of the German occupation became all too evident, tens of thousands more joined local resistance movements and partisan bands. By 1944, around 26,000 women performed operational roles behind enemy lines, constituting 9.3 percent of partisan forces (Fig. 18). Still others risked their lives distributing leaflets or organizing underground Communist party cells and committees. There were positions for which women proved particularly suited: they could move about more easily than men and consequently proved valuable as messengers and scouts; women were also better able to procure drugs, food, ammunition, and weapons to supply resistance forces. If captured, women's punishment was the same as men's: torture then death or deportation to a concentration camp.

Tens of thousands more sought to join the fighting. They besieged registration and recruitment centers in the days after war broke out. Initially, the leadership was reluctant to admit women into combat positions; instead, women were recruited to perform traditionally female roles. With hands cracked and bloody from lye or coarse soap, women washed by hand the filthy and bloodstained clothing of the fighting forces (Fig. 19). They prepared kasha and ladled it out to soldiers. The vicious fighting and enormous casualties created particular need for women with medical skills. The

---

[9] Ibid., 69.   [10] Engel and Posadskaya-Vanderbeck, *A Revolution of Their Own*, 76.

18. Women partisans, courtesy of the Library of Congress

government drafted women medical students and established crash courses to prepare frontline medics and nurses. Most went willingly. "Naturally it was our duty to go to the front," remembered Vera Malakhova, drafted for duty immediately after her medical school graduation.[11] Forty-one percent of physicians at the front were female; so were 43 percent of all field surgeons, 43 percent of medical assistants, and 100 percent of nurses.[12]

The line between fighting and noncombatant forces often blurred. Like other women who fulfilled noncombatant roles, Vera Malakhova, a frontline physician, carried her own weapon and claimed to shoot more skillfully than the raw recruits who actually went into battle. Under constant bombardment, medical personnel daily risked their lives. Every woman who provided first aid removed hundreds of wounded men from the battlefield under fire, often crawling with the wounded on their backs or dragging them along the ground. The work demanded enormous courage. When the medic Zina Tusnolobova fell seriously wounded behind enemy lines, there was no one around to rescue her. To avoid being taken prisoner, she pretended she was dead – even when a German soldier struck her with a rifle butt. She was found and rescued by the Soviets 48 hours later, but both her arms and her legs had to be amputated because gangrene had set in.[13] Losses among women medics serving with rifle detachments were second only to those of the fighting forces.

[11] Ibid., 139.   [12] Erickson, "Soviet Women," 61–2.
[13] K. Jean Cottam, "Soviet Women in Combat in World War II: The Rear Services, Resistance Behind Enemy Lines and Military Political Workers," *International Journal of Women's Studies* 5, no. 4 (1982), 367.

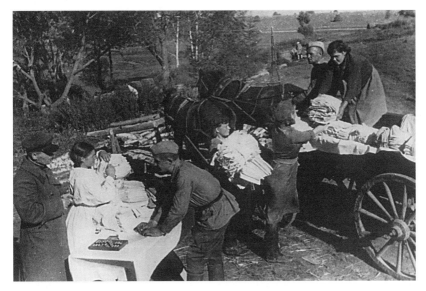

19. Laundresses, courtesy of the Library of Congress

It was women's participation in those fighting forces that renders the Soviet Union's wartime experience unique. To shore up resistance against the invaders, Communist party and *Komsomol* members, women and men alike, were mobilized for combat immediately after war broke out. Women machine gunners gave up their lives in the unsuccessful defense of Kiev in September 1941; a women's militia battalion took part in the similarly doomed defense of Odessa. In acknowledgment of the important role that women had already assumed in combat, as well as to meet the insatiable need for fresh troops, early in 1942 the Central Committee of the Communist party formally accepted women into the military. By the end of 1943, when female participation reached it height, more than 800,000 served in the armed forces and partisan units; by the war's end, more than a million had done military service. Women fought on every front and in all branches of the service, constituting about 8 percent of military personnel overall.[14]

Although Russia's women had served as armed combatants earlier in the nation's history, never before had they served in such numbers, nor had their service been as crucial to military success. About 200,000 women flew in the air defense forces, following in the footsteps of the pioneering Marina Raskova, whose achievements in long-distance flying won her the honor of Hero of the Soviet Union in 1938. Raskova convinced the Soviet Air Force in October

---

[14] K. Jean Cottam, "Soviet Women in World War II: The Ground Forces and the Navy," *International Journal of Women's Studies* 3, no. 4 (1980), 345.

1941 to accept women into mainly male air regiments and to create three all-female ones. The most well known was the 46th Guards Regiment, staffed entirely by women, from pilots and political officers to armorers and mechanics. The Germans called them *Night-Witches*. The women conducted dangerous night-bombing raids behind German lines in open cockpit biplanes, which until 1944 lacked parachutes and remained otherwise unarmed, and thus offered the crew no protection. To fly such a plane meant coming under fire from antiaircraft weapons of every caliber, facing enemy night-fighters, blinding searchlights, and often bad weather, too: "[L]ow clouds, fog, snow, ice, and gales that throw a light aircraft from one wingtip to the other and wrench the controls from your hand. . . . And all this in a Po-2, which is small, slow and as easily set alight as a match."[15] The women's casualty rate was about 27 percent of flying personnel – high, but normal for a night-bomber regiment.

Other women fought the Germans on the ground. As snipers, they "hunted" for Germans in all kinds of weather, crawling from foxholes to the neutral zone, risking bombardment or death under fire. Physically fit, cool, and resourceful, functioning alone or in pairs, the most experienced women snipers claimed credit for having shot about 300 enemy soldiers or officers apiece. Women were also numerous among communication troops, serving as radio operators, telephone operators, and telegraphers, risking their lives to maintain uninterrupted communications in field conditions. When Liubov Kozlova, telephone operator of a mortar subunit, was found dead, she was still holding the two ends of a wire she was trying to join.[16]

Even in those desperate times, women sometimes had to overcome the resistance of commanders and rank-and-file soldiers, who regarded warfare as inappropriate for women. Of their male commanding officers, women veterans had this to say: "They tried not to send us. You had to request to be sent out or earn the right, to distinguish yourself in some way."[17] The number of women in artillery and machine gun units remained low. Only women's persistence gained them permission to operate tanks. The thirty-eight-year-old Maria Oktiabrskaia, who had lost her parents, husband, and two sons in the war, offered to donate 50,000 rubles, the cost of a tank, if the authorities would permit her to drive it and name it "Amazon" (*Boevaia Podruga*). Having learned to drive and handle weapons as an army wife, she entered battle with the 26th Guards Tank Brigade in 1943 and was killed in action in 1944. Other women, most of them half Oktiabrskaia's age, fought as driver mechanics, tank commanders, even as platoon commanders in tank

---

[15] Quoted in Reina Pennington, "'Do Not Speak of the Services You Rendered': Women Veterans of Aviation in the Soviet Union," in Gerard J. DeGroot and Corinna Peniston-Bird (eds.), *A Soldier and a Woman: Sexual Integration in the Military* (Essex, England: Pearson Education, 2000), 154.
[16] Cottam, "Soviet Women in World War II," 346–8.   [17] Erickson, "Soviet Women," 67.

units. However, although female officers led platoons of men into battle and women won military awards for their bravery and distinguished service, often posthumously, they also encountered a glass ceiling. Apart from the three all-women air regiments, women exercised command only up to the platoon level and they never rose higher than the rank of colonel.

Military life offered women other difficulties particular to their gender. Although the Soviet government drafted women physicians for frontline duty and after 1942 permitted women volunteers to fight, it did not modify procedure for women's sake or initially provide uniforms appropriate for them. At first, women fought in clothing manufactured for men, wearing men's undershirts and underpants beneath men's uniforms and military greatcoats. Women clumped about in heavy boots designed for the larger feet of men. Women sometimes improvised, for example creating skirts for themselves by cutting the bottoms out of sacks. Women medics used the ribbons they were issued for the purpose of dragging away the wounded to sew themselves stockings instead; they made themselves bras from green triangular scarves intended for bandages. "The senior physicians chewed us out, but what were we supposed to do?" Vera Malakhova wondered.[18]

Women's very anatomy could prove problematic at the front. "There were those physiological needs that had to be taken care of," as Malakhova put it.

> We'd be marching along and there would be men everywhere you looked. Suddenly you'd have the urge to go, but how could you? . . . So three of [the older men] would stand up, turn their backs to us, open their greatcoats wide and say: "Dear daughters, go ahead, don't be bashful. We see that you can't march any further." And we would squat and then pee. . . .

It was much simpler for the men. "The men didn't even pay attention to us: they simply turned their backs and that was it, if you please."[19] No separate arrangements were made for women's sanitary needs. If a woman became pregnant, she had to continue serving until her seventh month; some commanders viewed the pregnancy itself as a violation of military discipline.

Sexual liaisons at the front were not uncommon. Officers and soldiers might be separated from their wives for the four long years of warfare; sexual access to dependent females had long been one of the perks of power. Competition for women's favors at the front was "fierce." Often young and inexperienced, women sometimes found it easier to choose a "protector" than to deal with importunate suitors.[20] Officers occasionally took advantage of their authority to sexually harass the women under their command. There

---

[18] Engel and Posadskaya-Vanderbeck, *A Revolution of Their Own*, 199.   [19] Ibid., 199–200.

[20] Mary Leder, *My Life in Stalinist Russia: An American Woman Looks Back* (Bloomington, Ind.: Indiana University Press, 2001), 235–6.

was one disgusting commissar who attempted to take advantage of Vera
Malakhova:

> Once he summoned me without warning in the middle of the night and said: "Sit
> down we need to talk." I replied, "Aye, aye, comrade major." I didn't sit down. He
> spread out his overcoat – it was chilly – and said: "Sit down on the coat." I replied,
> "I will stand." " 'No, no, no, you sit down." Well, I didn't have the right to disobey.
> At that time I was still in the lower ranks, and he was already a major. I sat down
> on the edge of the coat. . . . He moved closer and closer; and suddenly – bang! He
> put his hand under my skirt.[21]

Others labeled a woman who entered a sexual liaison with the derogatory
term *field campaign wife*. They applied no such label to the man.

Gendering World War II

Although gender offered no protection from the hardships of war, it did provide a potent propaganda tool. During the war, writers and propagandists
(the line between them often indistinguishable) not only drew on the gendered imagery that had evolved by the end of the thirties but also reinforced
it, even as they summoned both sexes to give their all to repel the enemy.
Women were represented first and foremost as mothers. The well-known
wartime poster, featuring a larger than life woman summoning Soviet citizens to war and entitled "The Motherland Calls," exemplifies the tendency
(Fig. 20). "We will always picture our motherland as a woman, a
mother. . . . After the battle, wiping his face, black with smoke, the soldier
thinks about his wife, his mother, his sweetheart, his Motherland," wrote
the journalist Ilya Ehrenburg.[22] Likewise, propaganda emphasized women's
relationship with men, even when women undertook "unfeminine" activity
such as work in war-related industry. Especially in the early days, women's
war work was portrayed as their special duty to men at the front, as if, un-
mediated by their relationship with a man, women's relationship to the nation
remained somehow tenuous. While "heroic Red Army soldiers fearlessly battle the perfidious and treacherous enemy . . . women and girls take the place
of brothers, husbands and fathers gone off to the army." The wartime press,
on one side of the coin, represented female tractor drivers, metalworkers,
and coalminers as taking up such work primarily *because* of their relationship to men at the front.[23] On the other side of the coin, feminized women

---

[21] Engel and Posadskaya-Vanderbeck, *A Revolution of Their Own*, 187.
[22] Quoted in Attwood, *Creating the New Soviet Woman*, 136.
[23] Lisa Kirschenbaum, " 'Our City, Our Hearths, Our Families': Local Loyalties and Private Life in
Soviet World War II Propaganda," *Slavic Review* 59, no. 4 (Winter 2000), 834–5, 840.

20. "The Motherland calls!" Courtesy of Victoria Bonnell

became embodiments of the home and family for which men risked their lives.

The emphasis on femininity was pervasive. Hava Volovich, a "serf actor" in a labor camp during the war, was outraged to portray "positive heroines" at a time when people endured such hardship. Instead of a peasant woman pulling a plow – the reality – she was required to play ladies, "vivacious and dewy eyed, the prosperous permed wives of army officers. Where had the pre-war heroines, in their shifts and short hair, gone to?" Volovich wondered.[24] Femininity preoccupied even the women who marched off to fight. Women volunteers wept when the military barber cut off their braids. They fixed up each other's hair in the bathhouse. They darkened their brows and kept mirrors handy at the front. In general, they tried as best they could to "remain women," in the words of one. "I was very fearful that I'd look ugly if they killed me," confessed Olga Vasilievna, a medic.[25] The emphasis on women's maternal role likewise complicated a woman fighter's self-image. Commented Vera Davydova, a volunteer who served for four years as a partisan behind enemy lines: "Of course, war isn't women's work. . . . A woman can't get used to that it, despite her far greater capacity to endure, and her greater adaptability . . . because she is a mother, and she must defend and preserve a child, nature herself has taught her that."[26]

Perhaps because they were so hard to square with gendered imagery, women's frontline responsibilities received relatively little attention during the war and their role as fighters, even less. Despite the enormous role of women in the struggle, the war as portrayed in *Pravda*, the Soviet Union's leading newspaper, was "largely a male experience."[27] When media did depict women soldiers, it was almost invariably as feminine and girlish, by contrast with brave and manly men. Contrasting their gentleness to the brutality of war, representations of women soldiers emphasized their "spiritual qualities rather than their actions, thus confirming their exceptional status."[28] The exception was partisans and guerrilla fighters, women who took up arms to protect their children or avenge their murdered loved ones and consequently were transformed into ferocious fighters by their feminine and maternal feelings. As Vera Ketlinskaya expressed it on the pages of *Krestianka* (Peasant Woman), "They are wives and mothers, they passionately love their

[24] Simeon Vilensky (ed.), *Till My Tale Is Told: Women's Memoirs of the Gulag* (Bloomington, Ind.: Indiana University Press, 1999), 265.

[25] Svetlana Alekseivich, *U voiny ne zhenskoe litso. Poslednie svideteli* (Moscow: Sovietskii Pisatel', 1988), 111–3; 136–48.

[26] Ibid., 61.

[27] Jeffrey Brooks, "Pravda Goes to War," in Richard Stites (ed.), *Culture and Entertainment in Wartime Russia* (Bloomington, Ind.: Indiana University Press, 1995), 21.

[28] Katharine Hodgson, "The Other Veterans: Soviet Women's Poetry of World War 2," in Garrard and Garrard (eds.), *World War 2*, 81.

children, their families, their hearths. But they do not want to rear children for captivity, they do not want to see their loved ones turned into slaves. . . . Love and motherhood . . . does not deaden their urge to fight to the end for the independence of the motherland, but fans it into a terrible flame."[29]

Prominently featuring women warriors, most of the films of the war years offered some variation of a single basic plot: "halcyon days on the eve of war turn to terrible tragedy as bestial Germans kill husband/children/parents, with the woman (mother/wife/lover) who survives transformed into avenging angel."[30] The prototype was Zoia Kosmodemianskaia. A teenaged Komsomol member from Moscow, Kosmodemianskaia joined the partisans and in November 1941 set afire a stable of German horses. Captured by the Germans, she was tortured and publicly hanged. Made into a feature film (*Zoia*) and play, Kosmodemianskaia's life story was altered to present her as secular saint and exemplar of communist youth. Representations stressed her suffering and sacrifice over her heroic action.

Wartime propaganda relegated women to a passive role sexually, too. Behind the lines, women and men sometimes became involved in wartime sexual liaisons, "some of which were very serious," even as the women might deprive themselves to send goodies to husbands at the front.[31] But wartime film, journalism, poetry, and prose portrayed women as exemplars of loyalty, chastity, endurance, and self-sacrifice. Such imagery helped to make the love poem, *Wait for me*, beloved of millions:

> Wait for me and I'll come back,
> Wait with might and main.
> Wait when you are drowned by grief
> In floods of yellow rain
> Wait amid the driving snow,
> Wait in torrid heat.
> Wait when others cease to wait
> Forgetting yesterday.[32]

As late as 1959, Grigorii Chukrai's award-winning film *Ballad of a Soldier*, about a World War II hero, upset communist censors by depicting a wife unfaithful to her soldier husband in an era when women's adultery still "officially did not exist."[33] When women were eroticized in wartime writing, it was as chaste victims, not as seductresses. "They [the Germans] rape women

[29] Quoted in Attwood, *Creating the New Soviet Woman*, 138.

[30] Denise Youngblood, "A War Remembered: Soviet Films of the Great Patriotic War," *American Historical Review* 106, no. 3 (June 2001), 842.

[31] Leder, *My Life*, 235.

[32] Quoted in Richard Stites, *Russian Popular Culture: Entertainment and Society Since 1900* (New York: Cambridge University Press, 1992), 101.

[33] "Obituary of Grigorii Chukrai," *New York Times*, October 30, 2001, A17.

in front of their children. They mock mothers by driving their daughters into brothels, trampling their maidenly honor into dirt," reads a wartime article in *Krestianka*.[34] The violated woman represented both herself and the innocence of the violated Mother Russia. Acting as a foil for the brutal German occupiers, who perpetrated ghastly crimes, her image helped to stimulate hatred and intensify the fighting fury of soldiers, whose manhood required the defense of woman's honor. These themes emerge in the following poem, which, like the preceding, was written by Konstantin Simonov, one of the most important wartime writers.

> If you do not want to have
> The Girl you courted
> But never dared to kiss
> Because your love was pure –
> If you don't want fascists to bruise and beat
> And stretch her naked on the floor
> In hatred, tears and blood
> And see three human dogs despoil
> All that you hold dear
> In the manliness of your love ...
> Then kill a German, kill him soon
> And every time you see one – kill him.[35]

The insistent sexualization of German war crimes may have contributed to the sexual violence that Soviet soldiers perpetrated on the defeated Germans in the final months of the war. Although still a controversial subject, it seems indisputable that Soviet forces occupying German territory brutally raped tens of thousands, perhaps hundreds of thousands, of German women.[36]

Restoring Order

As victory drew near and the chaos of the early wartime period gave way to order and renewed political controls, gender distinctions became newly institutionalized. Thus in 1943, coeducation, the norm since 1918, was abolished in urban secondary schools in order to give proper attention to "the different requirements of their [boys and girls] vocational training, practical activities, preparation for leadership and military service."[37] Following a "phony

---

[34] Quoted in Attwood, *Creating the New Soviet Woman*, 138.

[35] Quoted in Stites, *Russian Popular Culture*, 100.

[36] Norman Naimark, *The Russians in Germany: A History of the Soviet Zone of Occupation, 1945–1949* (Cambridge, Mass.: Harvard University Press, 1995), 69–140. Naimark does not link Soviet rape of Germans to sexualized imagery.

[37] Rudolf Schlesinger (ed.), *The Family in the USSR: Documents and Readings* (London: Routledge and Kegan Paul, 1949), 363.

nationwide discussion" similar to the one held before the ban on abortion in 1936, a new family code was issued on July 8, 1944. Intended to strengthen the family, the code reinforced marital ties by making divorce even more expensive and complicated. A person who sought divorce had to apply to the local people's court and then place an advertisement about the impending divorce in the local newspaper. The waiting time just to place the ad could be as long as two years.[38] The new law deprived people in nonregistered unions of legal benefits and access to housing. The distinction between legitimate and illegitimate children was restored. Henceforward, the child of an unwed mother would be unable to use the father's name or claim a share of his property as inheritance; the child's internal passport had a blank space instead of the father's name. Women were barred from bringing paternity suits. At the same time, the code was unabashedly pronatalist: single people were taxed, as were married couples with fewer than three children, excepting those younger than age twenty-five and attending school full-time and those who had lost children during the war. The real motive was clear: "to relieve men of financial responsibility so that they would produce more babies to replenish the population" after the war. The law also aimed "to reassure the wives of men in the armed forces that they would not be displaced by frontline liaisons."[39]

The cult of motherhood intensified. Even unmarried mothers, otherwise stigmatized by the new laws, became eligible for additional financial support from the state. In the summer of 1944, the leadership instituted military-style "Motherhood medals," almost identical to those awarded by the Nazis, and graduated according to the number of children a woman had borne and raised. A woman with five children earned a "Medal of Maternity," a woman with ten or more won the honor of "Heroine Mother," bestowed before the Supreme Soviet. After 1944, when the press began publishing the names of the women who had won these awards, mothering became "women's most systematically publicized work."[40]

In the postwar period, wives and mothers almost completely effaced the woman warrior. World War II came to occupy a key place in the nation's mythology. It was one of those transcendent times, as were the revolution and the civil war, that stood outside of ordinary time and conferred an exalted status on those who played a major role. Women were rarely eligible. They received proportionately fewer medals than did men and most of those were awarded posthumously. Women's most praiseworthy wartime activity became bearing and rearing the nation's soldiers. Even in the pages of women's magazines, women fighters now took a distant second place, with primary

---

[38] Orlova, *Memoirs*, 114.   [39] Leder, *My Life*, 255.
[40] Kirschenbaum, " 'Our City, Our Hearths,' "845.

emphasis on the maternal qualities even of them. The "mother-heroines" of wartime cinema disappeared. Most women performing military service were demobilized immediately after the war and discouraged from pursuing a military career. "Do not give yourself airs in your future practical work. Do not speak of the services you rendered, let others do it for you," President Mikhail Kalinin advised recently demobilized women soldiers in July 1945.[41]

There were additional reasons for women to remain silent about their front-line experiences. Popular opinion in the Soviet Union often regarded women who served at the front as "camp followers." Women's extraordinary achievements, their awards for bravery and heroic action under fire made no difference. "They'd look at you askance and say 'We know what you did there!'" one former servicewoman remembered.[42] Such attitudes were so widespread that many – especially unmarried – servicewomen became hesitant to appear in public in their uniforms. Arriving back home with her infant son and without her husband, Vera Malakhova found herself suspect in people's eyes. "Many people thought I, too, had been a 'W' [whore] – that's the way they referred to women who had been at the front." Some women nevertheless persisted in affirming their wartime record; others became "as silent as fish." "I tell you honestly, we hid it, we didn't want to say that we had been at the front," remembered one. "We wanted to become ordinary girls once again. Marriageable girls." The postwar experience of the women who had served at the front thus differed from that of the men who served beside them and whose exploits continued to be celebrated in the postwar period. In the words of one female veteran, the men "as victors, heroes, and marriageable men could wear their medals; they had a war, while people looked at us [women] as if we were completely different."[43]

Healing the Wounds of War

World War II utterly devastated the Soviet Union. The Germans destroyed hundreds of towns and tens of thousands of villages; some 25 million people remained homeless at the war's end. About half of railway lines were destroyed and about a third of prewar capital stock. About 9 million soldiers died; estimates of war-related civilian deaths range from 16.9 to 24 million. Some 18 million more people were wounded or mutilated. The majority of the dead were male: In 1946, the Soviet population numbered 96.2 million women and 74.4 million men. Among twenty- to forty-four–year-olds, women exceeded men by close to 13 million. In the postwar countryside, two-thirds of all

---

[41] Quoted in Pennington, "'Do Not Speak,'" 170.   [42] Alekseivich, *U Voiny*, 171.
[43] Engel and Posadskaya-Vanderbeck, *A Revolution of Their Own*, 215; Alekseivich, *U Voiny*, 85, 171, 175–6.

able-bodied collective farmers were women. It was women who bore much of the burden of postwar reconstruction.

Reconstruction began at home. Every family endured losses or welcomed back members permanently maimed. Whatever traumas women themselves might have suffered, literature assigned them the task of healing their damaged men. As war drew to a close, women's most heroic deed became preserving the private hearth for men. The home became a major locus of literary action (Fig. 21). Although virtually all women held jobs, writers rarely depicted women who worked outside the home; if they mentioned waged work, it was only in passing, "as a mere adjunct" to women's domestic responsibility. That responsibility consisted most of all of restoring men's self-esteem and faith in their own manhood. "Images of wives welcoming mutilated and traumatized husbands and fiancés home functioned as a promise and a hope for men and as a suggestion and instruction to women."[44]

The emphasis on homemaking and domesticity intensified. To an unprecedented extent, the media celebrated personal and family happiness. Love, peripheral at best in 1930s fiction, became central to the fiction of the postwar era, no doubt reflecting as well as shaping popular priorities. Media encouraged women to enhance their physical appearance. A periodical devoted completely to fashion appeared intermittently in the postwar years. Featuring mainly neat and sensible attire, it also emphasized the feminine: high-heeled shoes, makeup, hairstyles. Magazines intended for women offered advice on beautifying the home, housekeeping, skin care, exercising, gardening, and cooking. "[J]ust see what beautiful things we will make. Our women worked hard through the war, and now we will prepare a holiday for them. Let them dress up like queens!" declares a woman worker in a postwar novel.[45]

Thus, postwar longings for normalcy and material comforts became embodied in propaganda and fiction. Vera Dunham has called this the "Big Deal." With promises of upward mobility and the material goods necessary for the good life, the leadership bought the loyalty of the new middle class. The Big Deal, like so much else, rested at least partially on the shoulders of women. It was women who dusted the lampshades and tidied up, watered the geraniums, and prepared the homemade jam that symbolized the idealized home. For the majority, this was a kind of "Potemkin home" – the home as it should be and someday would be, not as it really was.

In reality, most women faced hardship. Hardship was particularly acute for widows and those women unable to find a mate due to the postwar

---

44 Anna Krylova, "'Healers of Wounded Souls': The Crisis of Private Life in Soviet Literature, 1944–1946," *Journal of Modern History* 73, no. 2 (June 2001), 324–6.
45 Quoted in Vera Dunham, *In Stalin's Time: Middleclass Values in Soviet Fiction* (Durham, N.C.: Duke University Press, 2000), 53.

21. "Happy housewarming," Courtesy of Victoria Bonnell

gender imbalance. These women faced poverty because men continued to earn far more than women, loneliness, and perhaps a sense of failure in a society that now held up the married heterosexual couple with three or more children as the most desirable social unit. "A woman born in 1927 had to consider every marriage proposal," observed Liudmila Alexeyeva.[46] But even women with husbands rarely had it easy, or dressed like queens. Clothes and consumer goods were unavailable. Millions went hungry in the years 1946–7, in the countryside as well as in the cities, because agricultural production was around half of its prewar level, and the government took from collective farmers literally everything that they grew. In 1946, Muscovites lived on potatoes and macaroni. Deaths from starvation again grew common. There was an upsurge of what came to be called "women's crime," that is, women stealing from shops in order to feed their starving children. In the fall of 1946 alone, the government prosecuted over 53,000 people for stealing bread: about three-quarters of them were sentenced to five to eight years in a corrective labor camp.[47] Rationing ceased in 1947; thereafter, the food supply improved, but most people still could afford only the basics. The average person ate less than half a pound of meat per week through the end of the decade.

Spending priorities did not help. Despite the desperate need for investment in agriculture, housing, and consumer goods, the government put most of its money and resources into heavy industry and defense. This led to scarcity everywhere else, and in ways that bore particularly heavily on women. Thus, for example, despite the government's desire for women to bear children and its genuine commitment to providing high-quality health care for them, investment priorities meant maternity clinics and hospitals were plagued by shortages of personnel and of such basic supplies as gowns, gloves, and soap. Overworked and underpaid physicians and nurses treated women patients callously even when the medical personnel themselves were women. Child care became less available in the postwar years than it had been in the final year of war.[48]

The lack of public services and consumer goods, as much the result of government priorities as of wartime devastation, added to women's burdens. The most basic household items were difficult or impossible to lay hands on after the war. Prepared foods were nonexistent. Few people owned a refrigerator, which forced women to spend hours every day waiting in lines

---

[46] Ludmilla Alexeyeva and Paul Goldberg, *The Thaw Generation: Coming of Age in the Post-Stalin Era* (Boston: Little, Brown, 1990), 36, 103.

[47] Elena Zubkova, *Russia After the War: Hopes, Illusions, and Disappointments, 1945–1957* (Armonk, N.Y.: M. E. Sharpe, 1998), 49.

[48] Greta Bucher, " 'Free and Worth Every Kopeck': Soviet Medicine and Women in Postwar Russia," in William Husband (ed.), *The Human Tradition in Modern Russia* (Wilmington, Del.: Scholarly Resources, 2000), 177–85.

at the shops, in addition to preparing food from scratch and then cleaning up. There were no clothes dryers on the market and, until the early fifties, no washing machines, either. In the absence of public laundromats, women did the laundry by hand, then hung it the kitchen of their communal apartment. In the absence of vacuum cleaners, they swept carpets with a broom and beat rugs. Clothing had to be mended because the shelves in stores were empty, and clothing could not be replaced.

In addition to doing housework, the majority of the adult female population held full-time jobs. Women were needed to rebuild the Soviet Union, thus they remained at work, unlike their counterparts in the United States who made way for men and returned to the home after the war ended. To be sure, the return of 8.5 million Soviet soldiers by early 1948 brought changes. During the war, women had risen to responsible and well-paid positions on collective farms, in factories, and in party and state institutions. After the war, women were expected to surrender these positions to demobilized men. Thanks to new entry requirements that favored male veterans, men replaced women in institutions of higher education, too. When Liudmila Alexeyeva first enrolled in Moscow State University in 1945, there were only fourteen men among the four hundred students in the Department of History. As women students flunked or dropped out, veterans (*frontoviki*) replaced them. By the end of the first year, their number had grown to fifty, by graduation, to about a hundred. "To get into the department, the girls had to overcome stiff competition. One in fourteen made it. *Frontoviki*, almost without exception, were admitted on the strength of their service records."[49] The proportion of women enrolled in higher education dropped from a wartime high of 77 percent to 52 percent in 1955, then to 42 percent in 1962. Women continued to work. To ensure that they would, food distribution was tied to the workplace. Between 1945 and 1950, the number of women in the workforce grew by more than 3 million, although the proportion of women workers dropped from 56 to 47 percent because of returning soldiers.

As had become the pattern, the pressures on women were reflected in fertility rates. True, perhaps as a response to their loneliness, perhaps because of pronatalist propaganda, roughly a quarter of a million unmarried women bore children in 1946 and sizeable numbers of single women continued to bear children into the 1950s, helping to replenish the decimated population. Nevertheless, despite the policies penalizing small families and encouraging large ones, most women continued to limit their fertility. The means they employed were the usual: abortion. In 1954, abortions numbered 6.84 per 1,000 women, according to official figures that undoubtedly underestimate them. The result of women's refusal to reproduce was that as of 1954–5, the

---

[49] Alexeyeva and Goldberg, *The Thaw Generation*, 29–30.

birthrate per thousand women remained only about 60 percent of what it had been in the prewar years.[50]

Conclusion

In addition to the Big Deal, about which Vera Dunham has written, the postwar years introduced a smaller but no less important deal, designed to win the loyalty of men. Powerless in public life, the "small deal" made men kings of their own small domain, the family. Wives became both consort and servant. Exhorted to work hard, to make a home, to comfort their shell-shocked husband, to bear children, and to be feminine, in the postwar period women were expected to be all things to all people and to enjoy it. Reflected in these contradictory demands was a genuine shift in the balance between work and home and in the rhetoric of women's emancipation. Although the Soviet government continued to proclaim the equality of men and women, women were now asked to accept the "Orwellian doctrine" that men were the more equal.[51]

The evidence suggests that women did so. Believing themselves naturally more concerned than men with domestic affairs, women did not regard the division of labor in the home as unjust. Taking pride and sometimes pleasure in their work, they wanted to be attractive, too. In the words of a mathematics professor, "Women thought, 'yes I work, but I should not forget about myself. I should dress nicely and be a woman and not only sweat as a worker.'"[52] Women drew the line, however, at bearing the desired number of children in the absence of the most basic amenities and with insufficient state support.

Media representations affected women in one more important respect. The hardships and suffering that most endured after the war were only partially reflected in the books, magazines, and newspapers that women read or in the films that they watched in moments snatched from a work-filled day. But the "Potemkin homes" that the media portrayed, featuring as they did the material accoutrements of the good life, no doubt raised women's expectations, even if reality as yet provided few means to satisfy them. When a new regime sought for the first time to court public opinion after Stalin's death, such unfulfilled desires would help to shape new political and economic priorities.

[50] Christopher Williams, "Abortion and Women's Health in Russia and the Soviet Successor States," in Rosalind Marsh (ed.), *Women in Russia and Ukraine* (Cambridge, England: Cambridge University Press, 1996), 137.

[51] Dunham, *In Stalin's Time*, 216.

[52] Greta Bucher, "Struggling to Survive: Soviet Women in the Post War Years," *Journal of Women's History* 12, no.1 (Spring 2000), 151.

Suggestions for Further Reading

Alekseivich, Svetlana. *War's Unwomanly Face*. Moscow: Progress, 1989. *Interviews with women World War II veterans.*

Bucher, Greta. "Struggling to Survive: Soviet Women in the Post War Years." *Journal of Women's History* 12, no. 1 (Spring 2000), 137–159.

Conze, Susanne and Beate Fieseler. "Soviet Women as Comrades in Arms." In Robert Thurston and Bernd Bonwetsch, eds. *The People's War: Responses to World War II in the Soviet Union*. Urbana, Ill.: University of Illinois Press, 2000. *On the representation of women at war.*

Erickson, John. "Soviet Women at War." In John Garrard and Carol Garrard (eds.), *World War 2 and the Soviet People: Selected Papers from the Fourth World Congress for Soviet and East European Studies, Harrogate 1990*. New York: St. Martin's Press, 1993, 50–76. *The best overall treatment of the contribution of women to the Soviet victory.*

Kirschenbaum, Lisa. "'Our City, Our Hearths, Our Families': Local Loyalties and Private Life in Soviet World War II Propaganda." *Slavic Review* 59, no. 4 (Winter 2000), 825–847. *On the new attention to private life.*

Kochina, Elena. *Blockade Diary*. Samuel Ramer (ed.). Ann Arbor, Mich.: Ardis, 1990. *One woman's story of surviving the Leningrad siege.*

Krylova, Anna. "'Healers of Wounded Souls': The Crisis of Private Life in Soviet Literature, 1944–1946." *Journal of Modern History* 73, no. 2 (June 2001), 307–331. *Treats postwar expectations of women.*

Pennington, Reina. "Do Not Speak of the Services You Rendered: Women Veterans of Aviation in the Soviet Union." In Gerard J. DeGroot and Corinna Peniston-Bird, *A Soldier and a Woman: Sexual Integration in the Military*. Essex, England: Pearson Education, 2000, 152–171. *Examines the postwar treatment of women who fought.*

12

───── • ─────

GRAPPLING WITH THE STALINIST LEGACY

During the war, the men went off and the women did everything themselves. After the war ended, the men came back and, realizing that the women could do everything themselves, the men never did anything again.

Liuda, 1985

I think when women were emancipated, it actually amounted to men's liberation from the family.

Liza, *Moscow Women*, p. 25

The death of Joseph Stalin on March 5, 1953, and the ascension to power of Nikita Sergeevich Khrushchev brought a shift away from the highly centralized and coercive policies of late Stalinism and toward a more "democratic," humanistic, and consensual vision of the socialist project. A product of the Stalinist system who sought to chart a different course, both Khrushchev the man and the Soviet Union under his direction (1953–64) proceeded in fits and starts, with much backtracking and concessions to conservatives in powerful positions. The episodic nature of reform resulted not only from pressures on Khrushchev but also from his contradictory motivations. Desirous yet fearful of change, under his leadership the government sought both to foster and control popular initiative. Both of these impulses can be seen in the gender politics of "the thaw" era.

The "thaw" officially began in 1956, with Khrushchev's "secret" speech condemning Stalin's terror against party members and abuses of power, and after much back-tracking, "the thaw" took on new energy in 1961–2. However inconsistently and erratically, Khrushchev directed new attention and resources to the needs of the Soviet population. He also significantly expanded what could be said in public about a variety of topics, the "woman question" among them. In Stalin's time, the question was declared to be resolved. Soviet women, went the claim since the 1930s, were the most emancipated in the world. Beginning in the mid-1950s, the leadership not only acknowledged that the Soviet Union fell short of this goal but also actually attempted to alleviate some of the worst shortcomings.

However, no one in the leadership ever tackled head-on the most fundamental women's issue of all: the extent to which the entire Soviet economy rested on women's unpaid and underpaid labor. Women performed the most poorly paid and onerous labor in the least desirable sectors of the economy; in their own homes, women toiled at night and on weekends for no pay at all. To end this situation would have required a revolution in economic priorities: institution of genuinely equal pay for equal work and shifting of resources from heavy industry and defense to the social services that the revolution had promised would liberate women from household chores. Although economic priorities changed, they did not change enough to eliminate the double burden borne by working women. Moreover, the leadership dared not challenge the "little deal" that in the postwar era, if not before, encouraged men to rule their domestic roost, which acted as a palliative for their political impotence. Never did the leadership launch a campaign to convince husbands to do their fair share of the household labor. Instead, promising but not delivering collective facilities, ideologists and experts treated domestic labor as naturally suitable for women, a function of their innate feminine qualities. Nevertheless, during the 1950s, genuine ideological differences about ways to solve "the woman question" surfaced for the first time since the 1930s. Those differences would intensify after the fall of Khrushchev in 1964, even as public discourse about other matters grew more circumscribed.

De-Stalinizing Private Life

The death of Stalin brought profound changes to Soviet political culture. Abandoning coercion and terror as methods of rule, the leadership sought to mobilize popular initiative and encourage self-discipline in order to reinvigorate the sluggish economy and increase productivity. Censorship eased; the powers of the secret police were circumscribed; local authorities, even ordinary individuals, gained new opportunities to exercise initiative. Yet much of the Stalinist legacy lived on in the new era. Conservatives refused to relinquish their prerogatives without a struggle. Old habits of mind were difficult to overcome, perhaps especially difficult in the realm of gender relations. A look at the contradictory policies affecting private life suggests that resistance to liberalization existed in many spheres besides the economic and political.

Reproductive politics provides one example of these contradictory policies. After Stalin's death, the leadership abandoned coercion in the sphere of reproduction. In 1955, abortion, illegal since 1936, became legal again. The need to protect women's health was given as the reason. During the twenty years following the prohibition of abortion, as millions of women endured underground abortions in order to control their fertility, the press had remained silent about the cost in women's lives and health. Then, in the months before publication of the 1955 decree, the media finally drew attention to the dangers these women ran, printing brief articles that described specific cases of suffering at the hands of underground abortionists. While continuing to maintain that it was women's duty to reproduce, with the decree of 1955 the government for the first time since the revolution explicitly recognized women's freedom to choose. It was up to women to decide "the question of motherhood," declared the newspaper *Izvestiia*. Instead of forbidding abortion, the state would henceforward seek to warn of its dangers and provide incentives for women to give birth and raise children.[1] In the early sixties, women who worked in state enterprises became eligible for eight weeks of fully paid leave before and after childbirth, 112 days in all. The provisions excluded collective farm women but benefited almost all other women workers. Yet no public debate accompanied the new legislation concerning abortion; the reporting was terse. Moreover, the state, which planned all production, made no effort to increase the availability of contraceptives as a substitute for abortion. As a result, abortion remained women's primary means of birth control; ordinarily, it was performed without anesthetic. By all accounts, abortions were painful and humiliating experiences.

Family policy was equally contradictory. In conformity with the new atmosphere of openness, the leadership permitted a highly critical discussion of the 1944 family law. The debate revealed a more diverse range of opinions than any heard since the early 1930s. Many of the proponents of liberalizing the law were women who had benefited from enhanced educational opportunities. Possessing the expertise to participate in policy debates, they spoke out forcefully on behalf of a more egalitarian view of marriage and the family (and a view closer to the original revolutionary vision) than the one embodied in the legislation of 1944. Among the women participating in debates were M. G. Masevich of the Kazakh Academy of Sciences and Dr. Kh. S. Sulaimanova, an outstanding Uzbek jurist and former Minister of Justice of Uzbekistan, as well as the Russians N. Ershova and N. V. Orlova of the Institute of Law, and Alexandra Pergament, a respected expert on civil and family law employed by the All-Union Institute of Juridical Sciences. In the opinion of Pergament, the family law of 1944 was a "retreat from the principle [of equality of men and women]."[2] Claiming that the 1944 law had failed to ensure family stability, reformers called for freedom of marriage and divorce and equal rights for all children, regardless of whether the biological parents

---

[1] Mary Buckley, *Women and Ideology in the Soviet Union* (Ann Arbor, Mich.: University of Michigan Press, 1989), 156–8.

[2] Quoted in Gail Warshofsky Lapidus, *Women in Soviet Society: Equality, Development and Social Change* (Berkeley, Calif.: University of California Press, 1978), 239.

were legally married. In reformers' opinion, mothers and fathers should bear equal responsibility for parenting. Reformers' stance evoked fierce opposition from conservatives, who sought to uphold the double standard and feared the threat to men and to family stability of women bringing unfounded paternity suits. A woman "is a maid only once and must guard her female honor" one of them told a Western investigator.[3] The reform debates resembled a "battle of the sexes," reported Peter Juviler, who attended the meeting.[4] On this issue, Khrushchev came down on the side of conservatives, convinced that the family law of 1944 contributed to all-important high birthrates. In his time, family law remained unreformed.

Yet, in reality, divorce became more accessible. Taking advantage of their greater freedom to exercise initiative, judges responded favorably to applications for divorce. The proportion of divorce applications resolved in favor of the plaintiff grew steadily. Perhaps in response, the number of divorce applications increased dramatically. Women initiated the majority of divorces, a sign of new assertiveness. Despite the regime's repeated admonitions to women to observe "communist morality" and subordinate individual desire to social well-being, women sought to escape unsatisfactory marriages. Between 1950 and 1965, divorce rates per thousand people quadrupled.[5]

A Man's Game

Khrushchev's reformist rhetoric notwithstanding, decision-making authority remained in the hands of men. At the Twentieth Party Congress of 1956, at which Khrushchev revealed the "Crimes of the Stalin Era," he also drew attention to women's virtually total absence from policymaking and leadership positions. That year, women constituted a mere 3.9 percent of the Central Committee of the Communist party and less than 2 percent of the leadership of the Supreme Soviets, the highest governing body of the constituent republics. Declared Khrushchev, "It should not be overlooked that many party and state organs put women forward for leadership posts with timidity. Very few women hold leading posts in the party and Soviets. . . . "[6] However, the methods he adopted to increase women's public presence in some ways exacerbated the problem. In 1961 Khrushchev revived and extended *Zhensovety*,

[3] Ibid., 239.

[4] Peter H. Juviler, "Family Reforms on the Road to Communism," in Peter H. Juviler and Henry W. Morton (eds.), *Soviet Policy-Making: Studies of Communism in Transition* (New York: Praeger, 1967), 47.

[5] Deborah Field, "'Irreconcilable Differences': Divorce and Conceptions of Private Life in the Khrushchev Era," *Russian Review* 57, no. 4 (October 1998), 599–613.

[6] Quoted in Buckley, *Women and Ideology*, 140.

or women's councils, to address issues "of concern to women," that is, either cultural issues or the problems of daily life. Activists supervised school meals and sanitation in children's institutions, helped provide after-school activities for children, organized sewing and craft circles, and the like. Created by Khrushchev to bring women into public life, women's organizations served merely to make private issues public, where they remained the province of women.[7]

High politics, on the other hand, remained a man's game, as Ekaterina Furtseva, former textile worker and the first female member of the leadership since Alexandra Kollontai, learned to her regret. In 1957, Khrushchev appointed her Minister of Culture and raised her to the presidium in gratitude for her support during a political crisis. Reportedly, she used the absence of a nearby woman's rest room to slip out of the meeting where rivals sought to oust Khrushchev, and from her office she telephoned the generals who ultimately intervened on Khrushchev's behalf. Four years later, Khrushchev removed her from the position, supposedly for having criticized him during a telephone conversation.[8] At the end of Khrushchev's rule in 1964, the proportion of women in positions of genuine political authority still barely exceeded 4 percent.

Reforming the Gendered Economy

Stalin's gendered economic legacy proved equally tenacious, despite well-intentioned efforts at reform. In a very real sense, the entire Soviet economy rested on the unpaid and underpaid labor of women. On collective farms, women comprised two-thirds of the agricultural labor force, and virtually all collective farm women engaged in manual labor. The majority of the work was seasonal, unskilled, and poorly paid; it remained difficult for women to advance. As Khrushchev himself remarked in 1961, after having observed the scarcity of women in the hall where a regional farm conference was in session: "It turns out that it is the men who do the administrating and the women who do the work."[9] Despite the campaigns of the thirties that celebrated women tractor drivers and the fact that during the war years tractor-driving became women's work, a decade after the war ended under 1 percent of tractor

---

[7] Genia Browning, "Soviet Politics – Where Are the Women?" in Barbara Holland (ed.), *Soviet Sisterhood: British Feminists on Women in the USSR* (Bloomington, Ind.: Indiana University Press, 1985), 213–22.

[8] Anton Pototskii, "Vospominaia o proshlom: Ekaterina Furtseva," *Vzgliad*, no. 385 (8–14 January, 2000), 24–25.

[9] Quoted in Norton D. Dodge and Murray Feshbach, "The Role of Women in Soviet Agriculture," in Beatrice Farnsworth and Lynn Viola (eds.), *Russian Peasant Women* (New York: Oxford University Press, 1992), 250.

drivers remained female. The most highly paid, year-round work to which rural women could aspire was dairying, which also ranked among the most arduous labor that collective farm workers performed. Dairying required a workday that lasted from 4:00 or 5:00 in the morning until 6:00 or 7:00 in the evening or even later, with breaks after each of three milking sessions, and only one day off a week.

The situation was no better in the industrial sector. There, the low wages paid to women in female-dominated trades such as textiles helped to subsidize the entire industrial economy. Almost a quarter of all women workers were employed in the textile or garment industry. Work in these light industries was as intense as industrial work ever got: women were on the job more than 95 percent of the time, with only 8 to 10 minutes of break per shift. Poorly designed machinery, inadequate ventilation, and shifting schedules exacted an enormous physical toll. The stress of the job put workers "right at the physiological limit of human capabilities." Yet workers in these industries received less annual leave than all other industrial workers, and they earned less than four-fifths of the average wage of an industrial worker and two-thirds of what a metalworker might earn. Women's low wages meant that light industry turned a profit, which the state used to subsidize investment in heavy industry and to maintain the economy. Low wages also made it "unprofitable" to invest in the costly machinery that would have lightened women's work. In addition to economic realities, gendered assumptions contributed to restricting women to the least desirable positions. Where machinery was introduced, men often took charge of it, leaving the remaining unskilled, manual labor for women to perform.[10]

To his credit, Khrushchev recognized at least some of these problems. Addressing elections to the Supreme Soviet in March 1958, he acknowledged: "We have done much to ease the labor of women, but it is still insufficient. The time has come to get to work earnestly on the mechanization of labor-intensive processes in order to lighten labor, particularly in those areas in which women work, to make it more productive, and this means more highly paid, too."[11] However, to really address the problem would have required a massive commitment of resources and systematic gender reeducation. The arrangement was simply too advantageous for the state to abandon it voluntarily, and women lacked the clout to force a change from the shop floor. Despite Khrushchev's rhetoric, women workers' economic position continued to deteriorate under his leadership.

[10] Donald Filtzer, *Soviet Workers and De-Stalinization: The Consolidation of the Modern System of Soviet Production Relations, 1953–1964* (New York: Cambridge University Press, 1992), 104, 193–4.
[11] Quoted in Susan Reid, "Masters of the Earth: Gender and Destalinization in Soviet Reformist Painting of the Khrushchev Thaw," *Gender and History* 11, no. 2 (July 1999), 292.

Addressing the Double Burden

A major cause of women's poor bargaining position was their infamous double burden, that is, keeping house as well as working full-time for wages. This was a problem they shared with their Western sisters. However, Western women did not belong to a society that claimed to have emancipated women, and they participated in the waged labor force in far less substantial proportions than Soviet women. The double burden served to maintain Soviet women's subordinate status at work while saving the government millions of rubles. In the Soviet Union, housework was usually far more time-consuming than in the contemporary United States. In 1956, two-thirds of Soviet families living in urban areas lacked running water, which had to be fetched in buckets from the communal tap or pump; less than 3 percent had access to hot water. Entire families lived in a room, or a portion of a room, in communal apartments. "We have to wash out of basins in the communal kitchen because there is no bathroom," remembered Irina Ratushinskaia, whose mother, father, grandmother, and for a while, a nanny, occupied two rooms in the southern port city of Odessa in the late 1950s. The tap in the kitchen rarely worked, requiring that water be lugged in buckets from the yard. Dirty water was poured into a bucket, which was then disposed of in the outside toilet, "a latrine surmounted by two wooden cubicles." These were the only toilet facilities for everyone in the building, year-round.[12] Almost all Soviet women did their washing by hand, there being only 300,000 washing machines among the entire urban population of the Russian republic, and using these was awkward and time-consuming. When Ratushinskaia's younger sister was born, her parents boiled her diapers in a large saucepan on the gas stove. Just over 2 percent of worker families owned a vacuum cleaner; only 3 percent had refrigerators. Scarcity of goods and poor distribution required urban women to spend at least an hour a day on shopping, then another $1\frac{1}{2}$ to two hours preparing food and cleaning up. In the countryside, running water, indoor plumbing, and central heating were almost nonexistent. Rural women, facing empty shelves in village shops, had to travel periodically to a nearby city to stock up on necessities.

Children only added to women's responsibilities. Roughly 13 percent of children aged one to six years could be accommodated in children's institutions, whereas almost eighty percent of women of childbearing age worked outside the home. Sometimes, children had simply to be left alone. "You hang the key to the apartment around the child's neck, give him hundreds of instructions about gas, electricity, matches and strange voices outside the

---

[12] Irina Ratushinskaia, *In the Beginning* (New York: A. A. Knopf, 1991), 11.

door, and send him off! The key is a two-ton weight on the mother's heart."[13] Managers were rarely sympathetic. "And I would leave my kids," remembered Irina Kniazeva, who spent the postwar period working on a collective farm. "They were such good kids. They didn't start a fire and burn the house down – [although] I had to let them light the stove by themselves." Kniazeva begged the collective farm chairman to spare her from night work for the children's sake, only to be told: "The kids aren't going anywhere. Get on with it, work."[14] If they were fortunate enough to find a place in daycare, or if their children were of school age, urban women often had to accompany them long distances in overcrowded transport and then drag them around on shopping trips after work. Men helped little, if at all, averaging half or less of the hours that their wife devoted to domestic chores daily or weekly.

Here, too, the leadership made promises. Remarked Khrushchev in 1958: "It is necessary to give some thought also to easing the housework burden of women in every possible way. For this, more creches, nurseries, boarding schools, dining rooms, laundries, and other cultural and domestic facilities have to be built."[15] The Twenty-First Party Congress of 1959 promised a shift in economic priorities away from heavy industry and defense and toward consumer goods, domestic appliances, collective services, and housing. In this realm, the leadership was as good, or almost as good, as its word. Domestic responsibilities prevented women from joining the labor force in sufficient numbers. Moreover, consumption and comfort comprised an important dimension of the socialist promise and the failure to supply them had become a source of humiliation internationally. Khrushchev redirected resources away from defense and heavy industry and toward consumer-related production for the first time since the thirties. The government undertook vast new housing projects: between 1955 and 1964, the state's housing stock nearly doubled. Many of the new structures, poorly built as most were, were nevertheless supplied with heat and water. The production of shoes, clothing, appliances, and furniture increased. The number of preschool institutions grew as well, providing spaces for 22.5 percent of eligible children by 1965 – about half of urban children, less than 12 percent of rural ones. The standard of living improved modestly, easing somewhat the strain on women's lives.

But with most women employed outside the home, their needs were infinitely greater, much greater than the regime was willing or able to satisfy. Soviet women with children continued to spend almost as much time on unpaid labor in the household as they did at paying jobs. Women had to

---

[13] Quoted in Michael Sacks, *Women's Work in Soviet Russia: Continuity in the Midst of Change* (New York: Praeger, 1976), 45.

[14] Barbara Alpern Engel and Anastasia Posadskaya-Vanderbeck (eds.), *A Revolution of Their Own: Voices of Women in Soviet History* (Boulder, Colo.: Westview Press, 1998), 128.

[15] Quoted in Reid, "Masters of the Earth," 295.

compensate with their time and energy for the many shortcomings of the Soviet production and distribution system – figuring out where to obtain scarce goods and cultivating the personal relations that provided access to them, standing on lines, performing by hand the work that Westerners performed by machine, and the like. It was only thanks to their "titanic efforts" that the Soviet system functioned at all.[16] Their onerous double burden kept women from upgrading skills and advancing on the job and kept most from even seeking more demanding and well-paid employment because such employment took more energy than most women had. As a result, many women filled positions for which they were overqualified. Ironically, such decisions confirmed people's prejudices about women's inability to perform skilled or responsible work. Women remained locked in a vicious circle.

Reviving Femininity

The voices that dominated public discourse preferred to reinforce rather than challenge this vicious circle, perpetuating the "little deal" that left men lords of their tiny domains. Rarely did anyone suggest publicly that domestic life was men's responsibility as well as women's. Economic planners were as bad as the rest. Despite Khrushchev's promise that the collective would assume responsibility for housework, planners failed to include facilities for collective services in the housing that was constructed in this era, instead promising that such facilities would come later. As a result, the burden of housekeeping was placed squarely on the nuclear family, and propaganda ensured that women felt responsible for doing it. Through the fifties and early sixties, representations of women as mothers and educators continued to crowd out images of heroic women workers, just as they had done in the postwar period.

The standards for both mothering and domesticity actually rose in this period. Between 1954 and 1961, the number of publications devoted to the family and everyday life grew almost fivefold. Psychological and pedagogical literature began to place new emphasis on the particularities of women's nature. Biology, it was agreed, determined woman's role and shaped her personality. Women's natural vocation of motherhood meant not only bearing a child but also raising that child, leading him or her "by the hand into life, into history." It was also "natural" for women to make "the home more comfortable, food more tasty, children more healthy and better brought up."[17] Women's nature affected even the kind of work that they should do outside

---

[16] Alla Sariban, "The Soviet Woman: Support and Mainstay of the Regime," in Tatyana Mamonova (ed.), *Women and Russia: Feminist Writings from the Soviet Union* (Boston: Beacon Press, 1984), 208.

[17] Reid, "Masters of the Earth," 184, 197.

22. "Women, this is for you!" *Ogonek*, no. 10, 1961

the home – "treatment of the ill, the upbringing of children and so on" – not so very different from what tsarist officials had decreed almost a century earlier.[18]

Many people became preoccupied with femininity. Male artists and writers figuratively wrung their hands over the passing of female beauty, lost to the hardships of recent history and the shortcomings of Soviet life. Popular and high culture taught women how to attain or regain femininity. Although fashionable dress and cosmetics remained inaccessible to all but the most privileged Soviet women, media encouraged women to dress well and make themselves attractive. Even *Rabotnitsa*, the magazine aimed at working women, toed the line, albeit on a modest level. After a day wearing businesslike clothing, *Rabotnitsa* advised its readers, a woman should change her appearance: "In the evening, she's femininity itself: a soft, blurred silhouette, folds, flowers, glittering embroidery."[19] Magazines intended for teenage girls instructed them to dress tastefully and behave appropriately with boys, warning them against unfeminine behavior such as swearing. Although expectations

[18] Quoted in Lynn Attwood, "The New Soviet Man and Woman – Soviet Views on Psychological Sex Differences," in Holland, *Soviet Sisterhood*, 70.

[19] Quoted in Ol'ga Vainshtein, "Female Fashion, Soviet Style: Bodies of Ideology," in Helena Goscilo and Beth Holmgren (eds.), *Russia. Women. Culture* (Bloomington, Ind.: Indiana University Press, 1996), 67.

for women in the contemporary United States were very similar, unlike the States, the Soviet Union needed women's full-time labor outside the home in addition to desiring their femininity within it. Moreover, in the Soviet Union, many of the new consumption items featured in advertising – not only low-cut gowns but also efficient washing machines – existed in the realm of fantasy and hope, not concrete and accessible reality.

Masculinity became an issue, too. Now that "father-Stalin" was dead, the sons positioned themselves to take his place while keeping women in theirs. Embracing Khrushchev's ideal of more democratic politics, pioneering artists of the "thaw" linked that ideal with a resurgent masculinity. Replacing iconographic images of Joseph Stalin with representations of virile heroes set in the typically masculine realm of industrial production, artists celebrated male workers, the embodiment of the new democratism, and crowned them the "Masters of the earth." By contrast, women's bodies became the means by which male artists claimed freedom of artistic expression. Expressing themselves through paintings of nude women, which had been rare in Stalin's time, male artists "paraded their liberated feeling and defiance of taboos over women's naked flesh."[20]

Soviet Union and the West

For several million people, consumer fantasies assumed concrete form in 1959, when the American National Exhibition opened for six weeks in Sokolniki Park outside of Moscow. The exhibit, designed to emphasize the triumphs of capitalism and to challenge the communist system, included a "typical" American home with a model kitchen, stocked with gleaming pots and pans and modern appliances, as well as a beauty salon and fashion show. Appealing to impulses the leadership itself had encouraged but was unable to satisfy, this was dangerous stuff. The Soviet government made strenuous efforts to restrict public access: limited the number of tickets, attempted to intimidate the public into staying away, and at the exhibits themselves, discouraged excessive displays of enthusiasm for the blandishments of capitalism. It even forbade the organizers to give away free cosmetic samples or build modern restrooms with flush toilets and blow-driers for the hands, constructing instead its own, far inferior, toilet facilities. This failed to stem the tide. Thousands stood in line all night for tickets; others climbed over the fence or even forced their way in. Sears-Roebuck catalogues reportedly sold for the equivalent of $20 – an enormous sum – on the Soviet black market. While men crowded the automobile exhibits, women flocked to the Helena Rubinstein beauty salon, where they watched cosmetics being applied, and

[20] Reid, "Masters of the Earth," 286.

then went off to admire kitchen appliances. At the fashion show, Soviets would plead, "Please comrade, where can we buy it?"[21] Most visitors came away enormously impressed.

Yet if Soviet citizens had begun to long for more and better consumer items, they also took pride in their own nation's achievements in science and technology, for which the lack of consumer goods and services was purportedly the price. The Soviet conquest of outer space, in particular the launching of Sputnik, the first artificial earth satellite, was a source of anxiety to the U.S. government and of pride to Soviet citizens. When in 1961 the Soviet Union sent the first manned craft in history into outer space, millions of Soviet women and men took to the streets in massive demonstrations, the first genuinely spontaneous demonstrations in many decades. On June 16, 1963, Valentina Tereshkova, daughter of a tractor driver and textile worker, became the first female cosmonaut. Having seen the progress that the government had made, most nurtured the hope that still better things were to come. Khrushchev encouraged that hope, declaring, "We will overtake the West" within a matter of decades.

This goal was never achieved. Failure brought frustration in its wake.

Trouble on the Home Front

The trends that emerged during the "thaw" continued and intensified during the following decades, a period that former Soviet citizens usually term the "Era of Stagnation." Modest improvements in the provision of consumer goods and social services continued. But expectations rose more quickly, fueled by the promises that Khrushchev had made, by increasing contact with the West and Western standards of living, and by the coming to adulthood of a generation who had not known the horrors of war, the deprivations of the postwar period, or the terrors of the Stalin era, and who were impatient for the satisfaction of their desires.

More "Stalinist" than Khrushchev on a number of other issues, under Leonid Brezhnev the leadership nevertheless went further than Khrushchev on matters that affected women. In December 1965, divorce law was reformed, the procedures simplified, and the cost reduced. A new Family Law of 1968 opened the door to paternity suits and made it possible to eliminate the blank space on the birth certificate of an out-of-wedlock child. It also contained a definition of rape that included forced sexual intercourse between spouses. Birth control became available on a limited basis, mainly barrier methods, intrauterine devices, and the condoms that men half-jokingly

---

[21] Quoted in Walter L. Hixson, *Parting the Iron Curtain: Propaganda, Culture and the Cold War* (New York: St. Martin's Press, 1997), 206.

referred to as "galoshes" and refused to use. Without abandoning the priority given to heavy industry and defense, the leadership nevertheless redirected greater resources to consumer goods. Conditions gradually improved. By the mid-1970s, about half of Soviet families owned a refrigerator and two-thirds owned a washing machine. The places available in child care centers had grown to accommodate about 45 percent of preschool children. Still, improvement was relative. Major cities, the best supplied with consumer goods, still suffered from periodic shortages and even a lack of shops. In 1973, each outlet served 363 customers in comparison with 89 customers per shop in Great Britain.[22] As a result, lengthy lines often formed wherever desirable goods appeared. In villages, where even electricity was sometimes lacking as late as the 1980s (indeed, to this very moment), one could see women doing their wash in the river and lugging water for the household from a pump or a stream.

It was women who continued to bear the heavy double burden. Most husbands refused to participate in women's work, most wives assumed the work was their responsibility. "Of course my husband has more free time," explained a woman engineer, married to an engineer and the mother of a child. "After dinner, when I'm busy with the baby and other things he sits and reads and rests. But we never argue about that. Since I have to take care of the baby I might as well do other chores as well. . . . "[23] Husbands themselves required work, as one study revealed. According to a survey conducted in 1965, a married woman with one child had eight hours less free time every week than a single mother.[24]

At the same time, women were growing more dissatisfied with such arrangements. A Moscow survey found that 50 percent of women who declared themselves unhappily married were dissatisfied with the division of labor in their household. The dilemma of the double burden became public in 1969, when Natalia Baranskaya published her short story, "A Week Like Any Other," in the liberal journal *Novyi Mir (New World)*. Featuring a harried housewife with a demanding job as well as a husband and a child, Baranskaya offered a grim portrait of what it meant to carry groceries on the crowded public transport system, a daily reality for most urban women:

> At last the train arrives at the end stop. Everyone jumps up and rushes to the narrow stairs. But I can't, I'm carrying parcels of eggs and milk. I trail along at the back. When I get to the bus stop there are lines for six buses. Shall I try to get into one that is filling up? But the bags! All the same I try to climb onto the third bus. But because of the bags in both hands I can't get a grip on the handrail, my foot

[22] Alix Holt, "Domestic Labor and Soviet Society," in Jennie Brine, Maureen Perrie, and Andrew Sutton (eds.), *Home, School and Leisure in the Soviet Union* (Boston: Allen & Unwin, 1980), 32.
[23] Carola Hansson and Karin Liden (eds.) *Moscow Women* (New York: Pantheon, 1983), 76.
[24] Lapidus, *Women in Soviet Society*, 270–3.

slips off the high step, I hit my knees very painfully, and at this moment the bus starts moving. Everyone's yelling and I scream. The bus stops, some guy by the door grabs me and pushes me in. I fall onto my shopping bag.[25]

Improved educational opportunities and the postwar emphasis on personal happiness and material well-being had made women more self-assertive. By 1975, almost 52 percent of Soviet women over age ten had received secondary or higher education. Increasingly unwilling to tolerate their difficult circumstances, women sought a solution.

Dissatisfaction spread to rural women, too. The number of rural women over age ten with secondary or higher education also increased substantially, rising to almost half of the rural female population by 1979, thanks to increased government investment in rural schools. Well-educated rural women became far less inclined than their mothers to tolerate the lack of consumer amenities and the low-paying jobs that required heavy labor. Indeed, their own mothers often encouraged them to go elsewhere, determined that their daughters would enjoy better lives than the mothers had. "You can make for anywhere you like, daughter, even if it's a thousand miles from home, but I'll not let you go into a dairy unit – I'll lie down in the road first!"[26] In the European part of the Soviet Union, the outcome was massive migration of rural women away from the countryside and to the cities in pursuit of higher education and more appealing work. Men followed. Faced with a "bride problem," young men abandoned the village, leaving behind them dying villages, where only aging women did the work.

Everywhere in the European sectors of the Soviet Union, although not in Central Asia, urbanization and women's rising expectations led to a reduction of the birthrate. It steadily dropped, from 26.7 births per 1,000 people in 1950, to 24.9 in 1960, to 23.8 in 1970, to 22.53 in 1980. "Women can't afford the luxury of two or three children," explained the mother of one child, who, like many women, swore she wanted more.[27] The rising divorce rate contributed to the decline. Divorce rates doubled between 1963 and 1974; by 1978 a third of all marriages ended in divorce, half of all marriages in Moscow and St. Petersburg. Women initiated most divorces, often citing men's alcohol abuse as the primary reason. Divorce also grew more common in the countryside, where earlier it had been comparatively rare. Younger rural women were disinclined to put up with drunken and brutal husbands. Now women wanted romance, "Love with a capital L."[28] If a marriage did

---

[25] Quoted in Alix Holt, "Domestic Labor and Soviet Society," 33.
[26] Quoted in Susan Bridger, *Women in the Soviet Countryside: Women's Roles in Rural Development in the Soviet Union* (New York: Cambridge University Press, 1987), 159, 211.
[27] Hansson and Liden, *Moscow Women*, 16.
[28] Quoted in Susan Allott, "Soviet Rural Women: Employment and Family Life," in Holland, *Soviet Sisterhood*, 190, 197–8.

not provide the emotional fulfillment that women sought, they were prepared to end it.

Troubled by these changes in the family, the leadership sought ways to address the problems. There was much talk about a "demographic crisis" by the midseventies. The declining birthrate in European Russia and family instability seemed a threat to productivity and military strength; high Central Asian birthrates raised fears that Russians would soon constitute less than half of the population of the U.S.S.R. The debate that had begun in the Khrushchev era intensified. Women as a "demographic resource" set the tone, as scholars and experts tried to figure out how to induce women in the non-Asian regions of the U.S.S.R. to bear more children. Some methods, such as encouraging women to leave the workforce, they ruled out immediately. The economy still depended on women's labor, and besides, paying homage to Lenin and Marx, everyone had to endorse the connection the two had made between women's productive labor and women's emancipation. Introducing part-time work and flexible schedules, which many women claimed to want, was discussed but never implemented. Instead, the leadership offered more legal protection and financial incentives to mothers. Thus, according to the new family code of 1968, it became illegal for a man to divorce his wife without her consent while she was pregnant or raising a child under the age of one. In addition to the already existing, fully paid maternity leave of 56 days before and after giving birth, in March 1981 the government introduced a partially paid leave for working mothers to enable them to care for a child until she reached the age of one. The decree also offered women (but not men) the option of taking an additional six months of unpaid leave, with no loss of position or job status. This replaced the previous policy, which offered the option of a year's unpaid leave. Women also gained a lump sum payment of fifty rubles for their first child, with double that amount for the second and third.

Thus, the leadership chose encouragement over coercion. Abortion remained legal and, at a cost of five rubles, inexpensive and accessible. But the leadership did little to increase the availability or attractiveness of contraceptives as an alternative means of birth control. Men remained reluctant to employ Soviet-made condoms. Nor did the leadership act to quiet women's fears about the dangers of the birth control pill, which women confused with thalidomide, the cause of serious birth defects. Instead, the medical establishment sought to raise awareness concerning the supposed danger of abortion to women's health and future childrearing. The circumstances under which most Soviet abortions were performed continued to be discouraging, too: too little or no anesthetic, insensitive and humiliating treatment of patients, and assembly-line procedures with up to six patients being operated on simultaneously. The dissident feminist Tatiana Maltseva described a tortuous procedure, during which "The faces in torment and the bloody mess flowing out of women's wombs" were visible to everyone around the patient.[29] Soviet women referred to legal abortions with fear – "They're horrible, absolutely horrible" – but abortion remained just about the only option for women who sought to limit their fertility.[30] Starting in 1960, abortions outnumbered live births every year and were the primary cause of the declining birthrate.

Having eschewed outright coercion, the leadership intensified the pronatalist propaganda barrage in order to convince women to take up their demographic burden. Books and articles designed for a popular audience insisted that maternity was not only woman's most important role but also essential to her very nature. "The character and structure of a woman's personality will be incomplete if she abstracts herself from her family functions and especially, from the functions of maternity," intoned one such article in 1979.[31] Publicists made concerted efforts to convince women to have at least two, and preferably three, children by emphasizing the psychological damage supposedly suffered by the only child. *Krestianka*, aimed at rural women, offered celebrations of "Heroine Mothers" who had borne more than ten children. In interviews, famous women insisted that their greatest joy was motherhood. To a columnist from *Krestianka* who inquired about what being modern meant to her, Ada Rogovtseva, People's Artist of the Soviet Union, responded in typical fashion: "Being first and foremost an ordinary mum.... Our emancipation never liberated us from this great female duty and never took away these great joys. In my opinion, the fear of having children and neglect of family responsibilities are signs of social laziness."[32] Literature designed for children presented women primarily as mothers and grandmothers, while showing men at work, out of doors, or in political settings. Boys spent time in shop class; girls learned the domestic arts.

Femininity to the Rescue?

In the Brezhnev era, women were allocated yet another burden: straightening up the mess left by decades of social trauma and domestic upheaval, during which neither men nor women had exercised much control over anything, including the disposition of their own bodies. The leadership began to acknowledge a range of deep-seated social ills, among them men's alcoholism and demoralization. For these ills, femininity provided both cause and cure. Descrying women's supposed loss of femininity, writers bemoaned the

---

[29] Natasha Maltseva, "The Other Side of the Coin," in Mamonova, *Women and Russia*, 116.

[30] Hansson and Liden, *Moscow Women*, 21.

[31] Jo Peers, "Workers by Hand and Womb – Soviet Women and the Demographic Crisis," in Holland, *Soviet Sisterhood*, 138.

[32] Quoted in Allott, "Soviet Rural Women," in Holland, *Soviet Sisterhood*, 194–5.

feminization of men. Ever since women began to work outside the home, men had lost "the title of family breadwinner," experts declared. This was the role that helped a man "to feel significant to those closest to him"; without it, "the very earth slips from beneath his feet." Newly publicized social problems, such as hooliganism and alcoholism, were blamed on the failure of women to be yielding and feminine. "Yesterday's proud groom gets used with difficulty to subordination and dependence. The nerves weaken, different stresses appear. And the medicine against stress is well-known – twenty drops of valerian or 200 drops of a more popular expedient [alcohol]." When marriages broke down, the woman bore the blame. A truly feminine woman, by contrast, could cure the problems of men: "Marriage with a really feminine girl instills in a man two things. On the one hand, he becomes more masculine from the need to protect and defend her, and on the other hand, sharp traits in his character soften; gradually, he becomes more tender and kind." To avoid marital discord, articles warned young rural women to avoid jealousy or possessiveness, and most of all, not to nag: "Men really value women's indulgence . . . their talent for forgiveness."[33] The media thus implored women to heal the social order and as an antidote to men's feelings of powerlessness, sought further to reinforce men's lordship of the domestic realm.

Occasionally, women raised their voices in public to offer a different opinion. "Nowadays all the work and all the worry about the family lie in the main on women. Men have no sense of responsibility either towards their family, or towards their children or towards their work," reads one typical outburst, published in *Krestianka* in 1982.[34] The most dramatic dissent appeared on the pages of *An Almanac: Woman and Russia*, a *samizdat* (self-published) journal that appeared in the fall of 1979. The government did everything possible to suppress this independent, feminist critique of the Soviet system. The K.G.B. summoned the editors and demanded that they cease publication. The women refused. After two more issues appeared, the four leaders were deprived of their citizenship and deported. By then, the editorial collective had split into two groups, one of which adopted a secular outlook close to Western socialist feminism, the other of which embraced the Russian Orthodox faith as a meaningful moral alternative to the system. While arousing considerable interest among Western feminists, neither group exerted much influence in the Soviet Union.[35]

---

33 Quoted in Attwood, "The New Soviet Man and Woman," in Holland, *Soviet Sisterhood*, 73; Marianne Liljestrom, "The Soviet Gender System: The Ideological Construction of Femininity and Masculinity in the 1970s," in Marianne Liljestrom, Eila Mantysaari, and Arja Rosenholm (eds.), *Gender Restructuring in Soviet Studies. Conference Papers – Helsinki, August 1992* (Tampere, Finland: University of Tampere Press, 1993), 171; Allott, "Soviet Rural Women," in Holland, *Soviet Sisterhood*, 194.

34 Ibid., 196.

35 Alix Holt, "The First Soviet Feminists," in Holland, *Soviet Sisterhood*, 237–62.

Neither did those writers who proposed more woman-oriented policies within official publications. Specialists, many of them women, took advantage of increased freedom of discussion to propose ways to resolve the purported demographic crisis that would ease rather than intensify women's burden. A few even questioned whether a crisis existed at all. In scholarly publications, they suggested approaches more in keeping with the original Marxist vision. Writers criticized men for their failure to share housework; they attacked "the old, patriarchal point of view" that domestic work is uniquely women's work. They demanded that men adopt a "new, genuinely communist attitude toward women."[36] To alleviate the double burden, they called on the state to improve public services, mechanize housework, and upgrade and expand daycare. Drawing attention to the concentration of women in low-paying, low-skilled jobs, they proposed better preparation for young women and on-the-job training for those who lost skills during maternity leaves. However, their writing seems to have had little, if any, impact on government policy. Cold war strains, the increasingly stagnant and inefficient economy, and the patriarchal attitudes of the leadership combined to uphold the gendered status quo. Through the mid-1980s, women's situation failed to improve.

Conclusion

In the post-Stalin years, women remained "workers by hand and by womb." The massive loss of life during the war years, the declining birth rate, and the lack of a reserve labor force prompted intensive pressures on women not only to participate in the labor force but also to assume their reproductive burden. Many of the policy changes of the period can be seen as efforts to coax women into the desired reproductive behavior after coercion had palpably failed. At the same time, in pursuit of demographic aims, the leadership betrayed the Marxist vision that they claimed to fulfill. Pronatalist propaganda and woman-blaming essentialized women's maternal and feminine qualities and, in a most un-Marxist fashion, treated women's biology as if it were their destiny.

The pronatalist campaign reinforced rather than challenged the prevailing gender order. It became convenient to blame women for social ills not of their making, such as the emasculation that allegedly plagued men. The efforts of experts, substantial numbers of them female, to offer an approach more in keeping with the original revolutionary vision made little difference to policy makers. Other women rejected the revolutionary vision itself. Believing their government's propaganda, they became convinced that their difficult lives

---

[36] Gail Warshofsky Lapidus (ed.), *Women, Work and Family in the Soviet Union* (Armonk, N.Y.: M.E. Sharpe, 1982), 258.

were the result not of incomplete emancipation but of the much-vaunted emancipation itself.

Suggestions for Further Reading

Baranskaya, Natalya. *A Week Like Any Other: Novellas and Stories*. Translated by Pieta Monk. Seattle, Wash.: Seal Press, 1989. *The short story that disclosed the cost to women of their double burden.*

Bridger, Susan. *Women in the Soviet Countryside: Women's Roles in Rural Development in the Soviet Union*. New York: Cambridge University Press, 1987.

Hansson, Carola and Karin Liden, eds. *Moscow Women*. New York: Pantheon, 1983. *Revealing interviews with Soviet women.*

Holland, Barbara, ed. *Soviet Sisterhood: British Feminists on Women in the USSR* Bloomington, Ind.: Indiana University Press, 1985. *Essays covering diverse aspects of Soviet women's lives.*

Lapidus, Gail Warshofsky. *Women in Soviet Society: Equality, Development and Social Change*. Berkeley, Calif.: University of California Press, 1978. *A pioneering study of the Soviet effort to emancipate women.*

Mamonova, Tatyana, ed. *Women and Russia: Feminist Writings from the Soviet Union*. Boston: Beacon Press, 1984. *Selections from feminist* samizdat.

Reid, Susan. "Cold War in the Kitchen: Gender and the De-Stalinization of Consumer Taste in the Soviet Union Under Khrushchev." *Slavic Review* 61, no. 2 (Summer 2002), 211–252.

Reid, Susan. "Masters of the Earth: Gender and Destalinization in Soviet Reformist Painting of the Khrushchev Thaw." *Gender and History* 11, no. 2 (July 1999), 276–312. *Gender and the art of the thaw era.*

13

———— • ————

NEW RUSSIANS, NEW WOMEN?

Secretary/personal assistant required with knowledge of English, pretty girl under 25.

Russian job ad, 1994

In March 1985, Mikhail Gorbachev assumed leadership of the Communist party and of the Soviet Union. Comparatively young at age fifty-four, well-educated, familiar with Western ways, and married to an independent and articulate professional woman, Raisa, whom he obviously adored, Gorbachev clearly differed from his aging and colorless predecessors. A believer in the fundamental correctness of the Soviet system as were they, he proved far more ready than they to undertake substantive changes aimed at ending economic stagnation, a source of growing popular discontent. Toward this goal, he initiated the policies of *glasnost'* (openness) and *perestroika* (restructuring), which spiraled out of control, culminating in the collapse of the Soviet Union. Encouraging hard-hitting discussions of the Soviet system's shortcomings, including its failure to resolve "the woman question," *glasnost'* and *perestroika* offered no ready-made solutions. Neither did Gorbachev. Prepared at the end to relinquish the centralized, command economy, the Communist party's monopoly over politics, and Moscow's hegemony over the Eastern European and Soviet empire – three of the pillars of the Soviet order – Gorbachev proved more conservative in his approach to a fourth pillar, the subordination of women at home and at work.

Gorbachev and "The Woman Question"

Glasnost' elicited unprecedented challenges to the Soviet claim to have emancipated women. Whereas many topics had remained off limits during the previous three decades, by the end of the 1980s, virtually anything went. However, even as proponents of women's emancipation emphasized the many ways that the Soviet Union fell short of that goal, for the first time, powerful opposition emerged against the emancipatory project itself.

The lid came off in January 1987, when the Soviet Women's Committee launched a biting critique of numerous party policies. An officially sponsored organization that had since its inception loyally celebrated the party's achievements, the Women's Committee turnabout offered a clear sign of the times. The occasion was the All Union Conference of Women. In a hard-hitting speech, Valentina Tereshkova, the first female astronaut in history and the outgoing chair of the committee, touched on a range of sensitive topics. For instance, referring to the well-known fact that women performed up to 98 percent of the unmechanized agricultural labor, some of it exceedingly heavy – lugging 120-pound sacks of animal feed is one example – Tereshkova accused the leadership of disregarding women workers' health. Tereshkova also noted the underrepresentation of women in mechanized work. This, she observed, resulted from the production of machinery, such as tractors and industrial equipment, designed for men not women: "It is paradoxical but a fact: institutions and organizations responsible for the production of new technology gear themselves only to the average working man." Tereshkova implied that men in positions of authority blocked the advance of women. She even questioned the different patterns of socialization that had become a cornerstone of the school system and that contributed to a labor force segregated by gender. "It is important to instill from school days an interest in technology in girls, not only in boys," she asserted.[1] Finally, Tereshkova and other speakers referred to infant mortality, a topic so sensitive that for decades, no statistical information about it had been published. Noting that infant mortality rates in the Soviet Union exceeded rates in capitalist countries, they blamed the inadequacies of Soviet medical care and environmental pollution.

Their statements prepared the way for still more radical critiques. For the first time since 1930, the accusation that the Soviet Union was a patriarchal society appeared in print. Investigative journalists offered grim depictions of women's work. They revealed, for example, that enterprises routinely ignored the labor legislation that restricted the weight of objects lifted by women to 10 kilograms and to a total of no more than 7 tons during a shift; in fact, women workers were lifting as much as 30 tons a shift. Dairy women and shop assistants hefted sacks weighing 30 kilograms; women railroad bed repairers lifted supports that weighed up to 200 kilograms apiece. Investigators found that a substantial proportion of women workers labored under the most

---

[1] Quoted in Mary Buckley, *Women and Ideology in the Soviet Union* (Ann Arbor, Mich.: University of Michigan Press, 1989), 200–03.

hazardous conditions: amidst filth, noise, toxic fumes, and dangerous equipment. The annual yearbook *Women in the USSR*, having hitherto celebrated
Soviet success in emancipating women, in 1990 offered instead a depressing
summary of women's working conditions: "[P]hysically heavy, monotonous
and wearing work, unsatisfactory sanitary and hygienic conditions of work,
inconvenient hours, the lack of rhythm to the work, (involuntary and unpaid)
overtime, and also the unsatisfactory size of the pay packet."[2] Most women
had no way of escaping their situation. A survey conducted in 1990 showed
that of women workers who had raised their qualifications in the expectation
of improving their position, 90 percent received neither a promotion nor an
upgrade of their work classification; 81 percent claimed they earned exactly
what they had before.[3]

Gorbachev himself acknowledged the inequities that women faced in the
workplace, attributing them to the legacy of war. However, when it came to
solving the problem, Gorbachev proved indecisive. Sometimes, Gorbachev
parroted the conservative views of the Brezhnev period, rather than the
revitalized "Leninism" that he often claimed as his model. Thus, in his
book *Perestroika*, published in 1987, Gorbachev praised Soviet achievements
in emancipating women and noted what he regarded as the shortcomings.
Among these was the failure to attend to "women's specific rights and needs
arising from their role as mother and home-maker and their indispensable
educational function as regards children." Engaged full-time in the workforce, "women no longer have enough time to perform their everyday duties
at home – housework, the upbringing of children and the creation of a good
family atmosphere." Thus, experts were now debating how to enable women
to "return to their purely womanly mission," that is, to home and family.[4]
However, at other times, Gorbachev seemed more of a "Leninist." At the
Nineteenth Party Congress in 1988, for example, he referred to the "daily
cares" that still prevented women from "enjoying their rights fully." Regret-
ting that this situation had continued for years, he attributed it to the fact that
"women's opinions were not duly reckoned with," mainly because women
were not sufficiently represented in government bodies. Gorbachev stressed
the importance of opening to women "a wide door" into governing bodies at
all levels, so that women would be able to participate in decisions concerning
their interests.[5] A few months later, Alexandra Biriukova was appointed a
candidate (nonvoting member) of the Politburo, which made her the most

---

[2] Quoted in Judith Shapiro, "The Industrial Labor Force," in Mary Buckley (ed.), *Perestroika and
Soviet Women* (New York: Cambridge University Press, 1992), 19.

[3] Donald Filtzer, *Soviet Workers and De-Stalinization: The Consolidation of the Modern System of
Soviet Productive Relations, 1953–1964* (New York: Cambridge University Press, 1992), 218.

[4] Mikhail Gorbachev, *Perestroika: New Thinking for Our Country and the World* (New York: Harper
and Row, 1987), 117.

[5] Quoted in Buckley, *Women and Ideology*, 199.

powerful Soviet woman since the eclipse of Ekaterina Furtseva. Nevertheless, Gorbachev failed to advocate strongly and consistently on behalf of the
"Leninist" vision.

Anti-Feminist Backlash

In the absence of such leadership, the conservative position easily prevailed.
Beginning in the 1970s, some conservatives had argued that women's participation in the workforce was too high, a view that reflected mounting
concern about the declining population in the European U.S.S.R. relative
to that of Central Asia. The conservative argument accorded well with the
radical reform policy that Gorbachev adopted in 1987, a policy premised
on the idea that the Soviet economy required not more but fewer industrial
workers, working more productively. Projecting a slimmed down labor force,
most economists assumed that it was women who would lose jobs. Many
welcomed the idea. The emerging "back to the home" movement gained
momentum. Male candidates in the election campaign of 1989 repeatedly
called for the "emancipation" of women from the double burden by returning them to the home. Even the sociologist Tatiana Zaslavskaia, a member
of the first Congress of People's Deputies and by no means an opponent of
women's work, expressed a version of this view: "It would seem that the high
level of employment of women in social production is socially unjustified,"
she declared. "It has had a negative effect both on the birthrate and on the
upbringing of children."[6] Increasingly, political leaders, the media, and even
the general public embraced the idea that women should withdraw from the
workforce.

The moral crisis that seized the country likewise fostered the "back to the
home" movement. During the *glasnost'* era, the media disclosed a plethora
of demoralizing facts about Soviet society. Such previously forbidden topics
as crime, drug abuse, sexual promiscuity, and prostitution were depicted in
graphic detail. In the late eighties for example, the media dwelt lovingly on
the salacious aspects of prostitutes' lifestyle, even as it treated prostitution
as the prostitutes' moral failure. Prostitutes "have chosen to walk the streets
not out of hunger or because they are homeless or unemployed. Chosen is
exactly what they have done – leaving behind families that are economically
secure, giving up their jobs."[7] To a public accustomed to being buffered by
censorship from such unseemly realities, the avalanche of negative images
offered shocking proof of national degeneration, for which the authorities

---

[6] Quoted in Shapiro, "The Industrial Labor Force," 20.
[7] Quoted in Elizabeth Waters, "Restructuring the 'Woman Question': Perestroika and Prostitution,"
Feminist Review 33 (Autumn 1989), 10.

blamed the usual suspect – women. The cure? Strengthening the family and within it, women's role. Concluded a sociologist: "It is obvious that in these conditions we must rethink the stereotypes that have developed and realize that, for the future of the country and for socialism, the most important form of creative work for women is the work of motherhood."[8]

The "back to the home" movement proved equally well-suited to the worldview of nationalists, whose voices grew increasingly insistent in Russia as well as the other states of the Soviet Union. In their view, women's primary mission was to preserve and transmit to her children the culture of her people. According to the populist-nationalist writer Valentin Rasputin, writing in 1991:

> Women have been led astray by their "public significance." They became liberated ... from their "quiet duty" which they had been performing since ancient times, the one of nurturing people culturally ... like the cuckoo, they've developed the habit of placing their chicks in the "collective nests" of child-care centers. ...[9]

In Ukraine, where a movement for national independence gained momentum on the eve of Soviet collapse, women's emancipation became part of the rejected Soviet legacy. "We should restore her [woman's] role in society as the main carrier of the genetic code and hereditary information about traditions, customs, culture, etc. ..." proclaimed a deputy of the Ukrainian Supreme Soviet.[10] In Azerbaijan and Central Asia, conservative nationalists and the new Islamic movement blamed the Soviet system for "super-employment" and "abuse" of Muslim women, for forcing women to perform work "disrespectful" of their femininity, and for dishonoring motherhood as women's "primary duty."[11]

In Russia, the "back to the home" movement was usually couched in the language of women's choice. Instead of exhorting women to be both exemplary workers and outstanding mothers, as the leadership had for decades, shifting the emphasis as necessary, the new motto was "realism." Women could be *either* workers *or* mothers; it was up to them to choose. In the course of the eighties, writer after writer in the Soviet press propounded the idea of "choice." The new generation of television journalists on the most politically exciting shows did the same. "Men in comfortable studios shook their heads ruefully at footage of women manual laborers and offered women 'choice' as a

---

[8] Quoted in Sue Bridger, Rebecca Kay, and Kathryn Pinnick, *No More Heroines? Russia, Women and the Market* (New York: Routledge, 1996), 24.

[9] Valentin Rasputin, "Women Mirror Our Entire Culture," *Perestroika* no. 3 (1991), 39.

[10] Quoted in Solomea Pavlychko, "Between Feminism and Nationalism: New Women's Groups in the Ukraine," in Buckley, *Perestroika and Soviet Women*, 88.

[11] Shirin Akiner, "Between Tradition and Modernity: The Dilemma Facing Contemporary Central Asian Women," in Mary Buckley (ed.), *Post-Soviet Women: From the Baltic to Central Asia* (New York: Cambridge University Press, 1997), 256.

new form of chivalry."[12] Women found the notion of "choice" appealing, too, especially when presented in terms of part-time work or extended maternity leave. Mothers of young children regarded as liberating the opportunity to spend more time at home, to provide more care for their children, and to be less harried in the evening because they had to accomplish less.

"Choice" was all the more appealing because contact with the West, through television programs, magazines, films, and in Moscow and St. Petersburg, an increased tourist presence, influenced people's notions of what constituted the "good life." As barriers to Western-style advertising eroded, images of glamorous, scantily clad models selling cars replaced those of women workers in overalls or of mothers tending small children. Foreign fashion magazines appeared on newsstands in 1987; even Soviet magazines started devoting more space to fashion and care of the body. In 1988, the Soviet Union witnessed its first beauty contest, ever – the Miss Moscow contest. Small towns across the Soviet Union followed Moscow's lead. Especially for the young, femininity came to mean not only being naturally nurturing, gentle, and understanding but also being attractive, slim, and well-dressed.

To accomplish this, a woman needed time to devote to herself. Men wanted more of women's time, too. According to public opinion polls conducted at the end of the 1980s, most men believed that women should devote more time to their family responsibilities. "What's it like for us men?" one complained. "We come home from work tired and hungry and there's no one at home – the wife is at work or queuing for food. . . . Everything's empty – both your home and your heart. I think that only a family where there's a strong man supported by the angelic generosity of a woman, his wife, the mother of his children, can form the foundation of our country's power."[13] Men wanted to feel "like men" again, which meant the wife waiting to greet them at day's end.

Lured by promises of opulence and expanded choices and by hope for a "normal life," in the language of the times, many of the younger generations of women and men regarded the market economy and capitalism as more enticing than the socialist endeavor. They became more enticing still at the end of the eighties, as Gorbachev's attempt to reform the command economy foundered badly. Productivity declined; shortages intensified; lines lengthened. Women spent yet more time providing for the family. Early in 1991, rationing was reintroduced for many basic consumer items, sugar and vodka among them.

But if choice was the language, policy pointed in a different direction. Virtually every policy initiative aimed to encourage women to bear and raise

[12] Quoted in Bridger, Kay, and Pinnick, *No More Heroines?*, 26.   [13] Ibid., 34.

children, rather than to help them advance on the job or combat discrimination at the workplace. In 1987, two weeks were added to the period of fully paid maternity leave, extending it from fifty-six to seventy days from the birth of the baby, and the period of partially paid maternity leave was extended from one year to eighteen months. Women also gained up to fourteen days paid leave a year to care for a sick child. Making the pronatalist intent of such legislation clear, its provisions were introduced gradually, starting in the regions with the lowest birth rates. In the context of Gorbachev's economic reforms, this legislation disadvantaged working women. Generous in principle, the legislation failed to obligate the government to pay for the leaves it decreed. Instead, the cost of funding maternity-related leaves continued to fall on the enterprise for which the woman worked. Previously, the expense had hardly mattered because economizing on labor costs was of little concern to management. But the expense mattered a lot when enterprises had to watch their budgets carefully, as they did during Gorbachev's reforms.[14] When enterprises laid off workers, women with children were often the first let go. The Soviet Women's Committee and various women's magazines were deluged with complaints from women who had lost their job or been prevented from resuming work after maternity leave. Anticipating substantial unemployment for the first time since the 1920s, economic planners projected still worse to come.

Women Respond

The Gorbachev era saw positive developments, too. For the first time since the revolution, the state permitted independent movements, some of which sought explicitly to advance the interests of women, ending the monopoly of the Soviet Women's Committee. In Leningrad, Olga Lipovskaia began publishing *Zhenskoe Chtenie* (*Reading for Women*); in Moscow, three academics, Natalia Zakharova, Anastasia Posadskaia, and Natalia Rimashevskaia, published an article entitled "How We Solve the Woman's Question" in *Kommunist*, the official journal of the Communist party of the Soviet Union. Instead of returning women to the home, the authors advocated "genuine equality," meaning an end to all forms of discrimination and a redefinition of men's family responsibilities.[15] In 1990, they formed the Moscow Center for Gender Studies, the first institution of its kind in the Soviet Union. Unofficial women's groups emerged in Ukraine, Latvia, and Lithuania as well as elsewhere in Russia.

[14] Shapiro, "The Industrial Labor Force," 26.
[15] N. Zakharova, A. Posadskaia, and N. Rimashevskaia, "Kak my reshaem zhenskii vopros," *Kommunist* no. 4 (1989), 56–65.

Women also became active in independent movements that pursued a wide range of goals, many unrelated to the advancement of women as such. They were especially drawn to ecological movements and campaigns related to child welfare. In Ukraine, women worked to protect children from exposure to radiation in the Chernobyl region following the disastrous explosion of a power plant in 1986. In Kazakhstan, women protested nuclear testing in one of the first such demonstrations to occur in Soviet times. The group that exercised the most political clout was the Organization of Soldiers' Mothers (not, as Solomea Pavlychko observes, fathers or parents).[16] Foreshadowed by women's groups opposed to the war in Afghanistan and then by Baltic women seeking to prevent local conscripts from having to serve outside their region, the Organization of Soldiers' Mothers formed in 1989. It aimed to end the brutal treatment of conscripts in the Soviet army, who were sometimes driven to suicide by the beatings and personal indignities they were forced to suffer. The Mothers demanded that such incidents be investigated and the details fully disclosed. Using the court system and the media to press their concerns, the Mothers also took to the streets to end questionable recruitment practices, to expand opportunities for alternative service and, in the post-Soviet period, to oppose the war in Chechnya. Acting as mothers rather than as women, the Organization of Soldiers' Mothers nevertheless raised a serious challenge to authoritarian, male-dominated institutions such as the army.[17] Their presence in the public sphere also went against the grain of new intellectual trends, which held that a woman's (meaning, a mother's) place was exclusively in the home.

After Gorbachev

Having passed much of the years since the 1930s in economic autarky and behind an iron curtain, in the decade following the fall of Gorbachev, Russia became part of the global economy and U. S.-dominated cultural system with astonishing rapidity. However, at least in the short run, the introduction of a market economy gave few the promised choices. Most of those tempted by the capitalist paradise dangled before them in advertising and foreign-made television serials encountered massive hardship instead. The relative, if bare-bones equality that had characterized Soviet life disappeared. A relative few, mostly men, became extravagantly wealthy; many more, the majority of them women, became desperately poor. The end of the U.S.S.R. also ended the unified state policy toward women. Social supports melted away. Life became

---

[16] Pavlychko, "Between Feminism and Nationalism," 94.
[17] Brenda Vallance, "The Rule of Law and Russian Military Reform: The Role of Soldiers' Mothers in Russian Society," *The Carl Beck Papers*, no. 1407, 10–20.

more dangerous. Violence, including violence against women, escalated. Although the lived experience of women varied enormously according to age, family status, geography, and nationality, everywhere in the former Soviet Union, women encountered a gender backlash that intensified following the collapse of the Soviet Union. The remainder of this chapter focuses on the changes that occurred in Russia.

For the majority of Russia's women, the end of the Soviet system brought a dramatic decline in standard of living. Millions lost their jobs. There is disagreement concerning the precise figures; most estimates concur that women constituted around 70 percent of the unemployed in the mid nineties; however, figures from 1998 show roughly equal proportions of male and female unemployed (13.7 percent and 13.3 percent, respectively).[18] Unfortunately, such figures tell us nothing about the changes that may have occurred since 1990 in the character of the work that women do or the level of its remuneration. The first round of firings affected women employed in defense industries, research institutes, and ministries, who were approaching retirement age or raising young children. Highly educated women, engineers and economists, suffered disproportionately; as of 1995, such women constituted about a third of women registered as jobless. When they sought new professional positions, highly qualified women encountered blatant gender and age prejudice. The majority of employers openly voiced a preference for hiring men. On the other hand, most of the vacancies for which employers did seek women – secretarial work, cleaning, and sales, for example – not only required far less skill than these women possessed but also were clearly earmarked for the young. Advertisements stated explicitly that an applicant must be under age thirty or at most, under thirty-five.

Loss of child care services raised a serious obstacle to women's work outside the home. In the final decades of the Soviet era, women had complained endlessly about child care institutions, first privately and then, during *glasnost'*, in public. Overcrowded and understaffed, child care institutions had long waiting lists and provided unsatisfactory care. Yet, whatever their shortcomings, millions of women depended on them. In the post-Soviet period, the spaces available for children decreased while drastically increasing in price. Enterprises had often provided child care and summer camps as benefits for workers. When profitability became the major goal, both were discontinued. In 1990, responsibility for child care establishments was transferred from the federal to the local level, with no provision made for funding. Between 1990 and 1995, the number of children in nurseries and kindergartens declined from 9 to 6 million; that year, the number of children attending summer

---

[18] Sarah Ashwin (ed.), *Gender, State and Society in Soviet and Post-Soviet Russia* (New York: Routledge, 2000), 19.

camp was half of what it had been in the late 1980s. The cost of existing places escalated. As of May 1993, a parent who sought to place her child in a kindergarten or child care center paid over a quarter of her average wage; it cost almost two-thirds of the average wage to send the child to summer camp.[19] No wonder, then, that it seemed such a good idea to return women to the home. At home, women could look after the children abandoned by the disintegrating social support system.

But women proved far from eager to return home. Many simply could not afford it. Male unemployment and underemployment and the rising cost of everyday life made it necessary even for married women to continue to earn money. But most women actually preferred to remain on the job. Survey after survey showed that even if their husband earned enough to support a family, only a miniscule percentage of women wanted to cease working altogether. Work occupied an important place in their lives. Thanks to seventy years of Soviet propaganda, women viewed participation in social production as valuable in itself as well as important to their self-development, even after their government began singing a different tune. Work also provided membership in a "labor collective" that offered companionship and emotional support. "We all know each others' problems here. The collective is your second family. You come to work and you can express your feelings, talk about your problems and then you'll feel better." Many women viewed work in the home as less rewarding: "you cook a meal, it gets eaten and then what have you got to show for it?"[20] Consequently, women's loss of employment brought emotional in addition to economic hardship. Women who had spent many years obtaining education or skills now deemed unnecessary found the changes particularly difficult. Declared one former engineer: "We are nothing now, we are nobody.... All these women, they were better than the men – not better scientists necessarily, but more intellectual, on a different level. They were interested in art and music and literature. Now they're all working as cleaners and traders. We don't exist any more, no one is interested in us."[21]

But most of all, economic change brought hardship and for the first time a "feminization of poverty." People who remained formally employed were put on indefinite, unpaid, or poorly paid leave; others failed to receive wages for months on end. In the service sectors where women predominated, wages rose more slowly than in male-dominated sectors, so that women's earnings, on average 70 percent of men's in the late Soviet period, had dropped to

[19] Bertram Silverman and Murray Yanowitch, *New Rich, New Poor, New Russia: Winners and Losers on the Russian Road to Capitalism* (Armonk, N.Y.: M. E. Sharpe, 1997), 73.

[20] Quoted in Sarah Ashwin and Elain Bowers, "Do Russian Women Want to Work?" in Buckley, *Post-Soviet Women*, 28, 30.

[21] Bridger, Kay, and Pinnick, *No More Heroines?*, 86.

40 percent of men's by 1994. Prices rose sixfold in 1992; by March 1995, the average Russian salary was worth a third less than the year before. Hyperinflation drastically reduced the buying power of pensions too; close to three-quarters of pensioners were female. Life grew more difficult in the countryside, as well. No longer politically dangerous, protest had become economically disadvantageous. Rural women accepted uncomplainingly their deteriorating working and living conditions, for example, because farm managers were virtually all-powerful and controlled access to paid employment and housing. As the value of their wage declined, rural women took on additional jobs and intensified their work on their private plots in order to feed their family. By the late 1990s, at least a quarter and perhaps as much as half of the Russian population qualified as poor or very poor and over two-thirds of those poor were female.

Other measures of social welfare make these figures look still grimmer. In the early nineties, the rate of marriage dropped because young people could not afford to begin family life. Divorce rates rose, as did mortality rates. Between 1990 and 1997, women's life expectancy at birth dropped from 74.3 to 72.8, and men's, from 63.8 to 60.9.[22] By 2000, the life expectancy of Soviet men had declined to 57.6, more than sixteen years less than that of U.S. men. The birthrate declined as well, from 13.4 per 1,000 in 1990 to 8.6 per 1,000 in 1997. Between 1991 and 2000, the population of Russia declined by 3 million. It is projected to fall by an additional 11 million by 2015.[23] Malnutrition and poor health among women contributed to a drop in the weight of newborns and an increase in babies born sick: from one in eight in 1989, the proportion of sick babies rose to one in five by 1993. Infant mortality rose to 19 per 1,000 by 1993, then decreased to 16.6 by 1998, still more than twice the rate of the United States and Western Europe. Environmental pollution produced birth defects, from which 6 to 8 of every 100 newborns in Russia suffered. Motherhood itself became more dangerous as a result of maternal ill health and the drastic deterioration of the public health system. Between 1987 and 1993, the number of mothers who died during pregnancy or in childbirth rose from 49.3 to 70 for every 100,000 births; by 1998, the number had dropped to 50, still more than twice the average European level of 22. "Women in Russia are afraid to give birth and do not want to go through it," maintained the journalist Elena Shafran, "because of their distrust of doctors, women's clinics and maternity hospitals,"[24] the result of antiquated equipment, unhygienic conditions, and poorly trained personnel.

[22] For 1990 figures, Silverman and Yanowitch, *New Rich, New Poor*, 25; Marina Kiblitskaya, "Once We Were 'Kings': Work and Men's Loss of Status," in Ashwin, *Gender, State and Society*, 95.

[23] "Russians Vanishing," *New York Times*, (December 6, 2000), 8.

[24] Elena Sargeant, "The 'Woman Question' and Problems of Maternity in Post-Communist Russia," in Rosalind Marsh (ed.), *Women in Russia and Ukraine* (New York: Cambridge University Press, 1996), 270–4.

One of the few positive notes in this otherwise depressing picture involves contraception. To reduce dependence on abortion, in 1993 the Russian Public Health Ministry began a family planning program, opening more than 200 clinics around the country; retraining doctors, midwives, and nurses; and providing information and advice on sex, pregnancy, and birth. The new market economy vastly increased the availability of a range of contraceptive devices. Efforts to convince women to use them as a substitute for abortion bore fruit: from a high of 4.6 million in 1988, the number of abortions in the Russian Republic dropped to 2.5 million in 1997. Some 66 percent of married couples practiced some form of birth control, up from 30 percent in 1990.

Engendering the "New Russian"

Mainly, however, the benefits of the new market economy accrued to a relatively small group of men. The economy became a cutthroat place, where laws were routinely broken, and bribery and corruption rife; where bankers and big businessmen might be blown up by a car bomb or gunned down on the streets; and where Russian mafia offers of protection were backed with threats of retributive violence in the event of refusal. Highly successful businesspeople employed bodyguards twenty-four hours a day. Initially, most of the newly wealthy were well-placed Soviet officials and factory directors, who took advantage of privatization to acquire formerly state-owned industrial enterprises and the rights to natural resources on the cheap. Because men occupied the most important positions in the Soviet system, the beneficiaries of perhaps the biggest giveaway in human history were virtually all male. Most women lacked the resources to start up a business, and in an economic climate characterized by aggressive masculinity, women who sought loans had difficulty making their case to bankers. Two years after the collapse of the Soviet Union, over 80 percent of new businesspeople were male. Indeed, entrepreneurship itself was coded male. According to Russian psychologists, the personal qualities required for success, such as competitiveness, aggressiveness, boldness, and independence, belonged naturally to men, not women. In Lynne Attwood's incisive phrase, "the market has a male face."[25]

Some women succeeded against the odds, gaining powerful and well paying positions. They became far more prominent than before in journalism and the media. They have taken advantage of computer and linguistic skills to enter the modern sector of the economy and foreign owned businesses; a few even became directors of commercial banks. Younger women, in particular, sometimes adapted more successfully than men to the new conditions,

---

[25] Lynne Attwood, "The Post-Soviet Woman in the Move to the Market: A Return to Domesticity and Dependence?" in Marsh, *Women in Russia and Ukraine*, 255.

becoming well-to-do entrepreneurs and businesswomen. Most women who entered commerce, however, did so on a more basic and less profitable level. They traveled to Europe, China, and Turkey to buy up cheap goods for sale back in Russia; others sold goods in kiosks owned by others; and still others stood on urban streets all day, whatever the weather, peddling cigarettes, kittens, or items that they had purchased elsewhere, grown at their dacha or manufactured themselves. These low-level entrepreneurs included highly skilled women and former female professionals with advanced degrees as well as working-class women. Increasing numbers of women sold themselves as well.

The Sexual Marketplace

The commodification of sex was one of the very first fruits of the new economic freedom. The early 1990s witnessed a veritable explosion of pornographic literature, most of it imported from abroad and much of it sold near subway entrances by elderly women supplementing their pensions. No film appeared without at least one graphic, frequently brutal and sadistic, sexual encounter, sometimes entirely unrelated to the plot. Although this pornographic flood began to recede by the end of the nineties, having lost its edge of novelty, pornographic-style imagery has seeped into other commercial realms to a far greater degree than even in the contemporary United States. Russian advertisements feature women's semiclothed bodies draped over cars and lounging by computers, just as do ads virtually everywhere in the capitalist world. But in Russia, naked or semiclothed women's bodies appear in places (as yet) unthinkable in the West. For example, in 1991 the economic journal *Ekonomika* showed a bare-breasted woman on one of its covers; the journal *Ogonek* used bare breasts and fleshy buttocks as leads to stories that had nothing to do with either. A television show entitled *The Naked Truth* aired on a major Moscow channel in the fall of 2000, featuring young women either undressed, undressing, or in the process of being undressed, delivering the latest news in straightfaced fashion. In a highly competitive market, where funds were scarce and the rate of failure high, seasoning a product with women's sexuality boosted sales.

Women's sexuality figured prominently in the expectations of many potential employers. Job advertisements often specified not only the preferred age of potential female hires but also the preferred appearance: "Secretaries required: attractive girls with office experience," a typical advertisement might read. Taking advantage of women's economic vulnerability, some advertisements explicitly required women's sexual availability, by specifying, for example, that to be successful, a job candidate would have to be "without complexes." Sexual harassment, which had existed unacknowledged in Soviet times, intensified. Wrote one reader to the journal *Business Woman* (*Delovaia zhenshchina*): "Nothing has changed since then, only the added fear of losing your job. This particularly affects women who are the sole breadwinners for their families. It is these women who are transformed into office prostitutes. Those who refuse any proposition are simply chucked out."[26]

Women with the requisite physical qualities sometimes sought to turn the commodification of their bodies to their advantage. Flaunting their assets, even professionally trained women donned bikinis and entered beauty contests or pursued careers in modeling in an effort to expand their options. However, success often came at the price of sexual favors sometimes indistinguishable from outright prostitution. "Models get paid, not laid!" proclaimed placards carried by demonstrating fashion models in August of 1993. The models declared their aim to be regulating minimum rates of pay and combating what they called "sexual terror."[27] Others sought to locate, perhaps even marry, a rich protector, a "New Russian," for whom an attractive, sexually available woman had become a key attribute. Women whom age or nature had disqualified for such roles sought instead to wed a foreigner. Dating agencies, newsletters, and an exponentially increasing number of websites emerged to cater to this new trade, bringing planeloads of middle-aged, often divorced men seeking brides to provincial towns as well as to Moscow. And finally, an unknown number of women simply sold themselves, at home or abroad, prostitution having become the most attractive of a range of unsavory options. At a bar in southern Spain, a Russian named Liuda explained the lure of the sex trade simply: "One-zero-zero-zero instead of one-zero-zero," that is, the chance to earn $1,000 rather than $100 a month.[28]

Some of these prostitutes became involved unwillingly. The traffic in women from the former Soviet Union to Asia, Europe, Israel, the Middle East (especially the Gulf States), and the United States exploded after 1989 and had become an international cause célèbre by the turn of the twenty-first century, eliciting the concern of international funding and humanitarian agencies. Every year, men linked to criminal networks, promising a better life or a better-paid job in a foreign country and offering a plane ticket and a visa, entice tens of thousands, perhaps as many as hundreds of thousands of women without a visible future in Russia's depressed towns and villages. The case of "Lena" was typical: a nineteen-year-old from the Russian Far East, she responded to a newspaper ad for a work and study program in China. After arrival, the sponsors confiscated the passports of "Lena" and her companions and informed them that they would each have to pay $15,000 to retrieve

[26] Quoted in Bridger, Kay, and Pinnick, *No More Heroines?*, 178–9.   [27] Ibid., 171.
[28] Roger Cohen "The Oldest Profession Seeks New Market in West Europe," *New York Times* (September 19, 2000), 1.

their documents. Subjected to beatings, imprisonment, and hunger, "Lena" and her companions had to work as "entertainers" in local restaurants, hotels, and nightclubs. They received little help from the Russian Consulate, to whom they appealed for assistance. Even women who initially entered the sex trade voluntarily might become subject to similar treatment. Terrorized and beaten, locked into apartments, they were forced into debt bondage.[29]

The Crisis of Masculinity

The impact of these massive, primarily negative changes on Russia's public was nothing short of shocking, and all the more so because until the mid-1980s, almost everyone had been cut off from both bad news about domestic matters and contact with the larger world. The old communist values may have rung hollow, but they had once provided order and rules for public life. By the mid nineties, many had ceased to believe in them altogether. Authority had broken down and lawlessness and violence raged in the streets, or so the media suggested. Much of the public trudged stoically onward, trying to make ends meet. In some respects, change brought a return to an older way of life: the family, not the workplace, became the source of economic survival. For the majority of women, the changes meant that they visited dozens of shops to find the lowest prices, ate bread instead of meat, if necessary stinting on their own nourishment to provide for others, made over old clothing, networked with friends and neighbors, and employed a range of economic strategies to keep food on the table and a roof over their family's heads.

The change was even harder on most men. Whereas their family responsibilities provided an important component of women's self-image, men's self-image derived almost exclusively from their work and ability to provide. Now millions had lost their jobs or found themselves, like women, unable to support their family in the positions for which they had prepared for years, their education and skills having lost their value and their workplace no longer serving as a source of goods or services. Accustomed to defining themselves through their nondomestic roles, husbands found it more difficult than their wives to adopt family-based survival strategies. More women than men embraced religion, but more men than women took up serious drinking. Men's high rates of mortality were the result of alcohol abuse and stress, as well as the deterioration of the health care system and the astronomical price of medicines.

The crisis was often experienced as a crisis of masculinity on both the political and the personal levels. From being the center of the Soviet Union,

[29] "TED Case Studies: Trafficking in Russian Women," *http://www.american.edu/TED/traffic.htm.*

one of the two most powerful nations on this earth, Russia had been reduced to a beggar at international financial tables and a provider of sexual services. Because national prowess had always been presented as male, national humiliation was experienced as a loss of masculinity. The way that economic change was presented made that loss all the more painful. The introduction of the market economy brought a celebration of masculinity. The old Soviet system, Russian psychologists intoned, had deprived men of appropriate outlets for their naturally masculine behavior. By contrast, the market required and rewarded such masculine traits as competitiveness and aggressiveness. But in this new environment, where what you could buy determined who you were, most men were losers, not winners. Even if the earning power of employed men exceeded that of employed women, which it usually did, most men's earnings purchased far less than before. And by contrast with women, whose family responsibilities, however onerous and debilitating, also served as a source of satisfaction, men had only their role as provider, now newly emphasized as the very measure of their manhood. Emasculated in the marketplace, deprived of authority in the family, men found one outlet for the resulting anger in the aggressive, often violent masculinity of pulp literature and film, and they found another in the more hidden domestic violence, acknowledged for the first time in the post-Soviet period and evidently, on the rise.

New Possibilities

Women faced an uphill battle when they sought to counter the post-Soviet backlash and growing feminization of poverty and to ensure a place for women in the new civil society. In the early 1990s, the economic crisis and collapse of social benefits stimulated a fresh wave of organizing. Most of the new groups offered self-help or employment training/retraining and tried to fill the void left by the retreating state. Even the venerable Soviet Women's Committee joined the trend. Transforming itself into the Union of Russian Women in 1991, it began to offer free training courses to women officially registered as unemployed. By early 1994, more than 300 women's groups had registered with Russia's Ministry of Justice; countless more operated unofficially. Professional women, their thinking stimulated by foreign travel and by contact with Western feminists, led many of the organizations with a feminist orientation. They included a wide variety of organizations, some of them small and grassroots, others extending across the nation with local branches but headquartered in Moscow. Those who shared a commitment to improving the lot of women adopted a range of approaches. They organized conferences, they campaigned for women candidates, they organized charity events to assist women and children, they set up support groups for single mothers or women artists, they established rape crisis centers and domestic violence hotlines, they published journals and newsletters, and much, much more. The movement scored one of its greatest victories in 1992, when the Supreme Soviet considered a bill – "Protection of the Family, Motherhood, Fatherhood and Childhood" – that would have seriously eroded women's rights in public life. Had the bill passed, the family rather than the individual would have become the basis of many civil rights, such as owning an apartment or a plot of land. The law would have required women with children under fourteen to work no more than 35 hours a week. The women's movement successfully mobilized to defeat the bill, lobbying parliamentary deputies, publishing critiques, and organizing "a barrage of approximately 400 negative appraisals in the form of letters, faxes and telegrams."[30]

But such clear-cut victories were few. Women experienced difficulty placing woman-oriented concerns on the political agenda. Once quotas for female representation ended, the number of women elected to governing bodies declined precipitously. From over 34 percent of delegates to Republic-level Supreme Soviets in the 1970s and 1980s, the proportion of women dropped to 5.4 percent in Russia and 7 percent in Ukraine.[31] A centrist women's party, Women of Russia, which did well in the elections of 1993, lost significant popular support just two years later. Those women who succeeded in being elected often encountered patronizing, even hostile treatment from men that hindered their participation in debates. Galina Starovoitova, elected to the State Duma in 1995, recalled an incident when the woman deputy Bella Denisenko tried to speak. The Speaker Ruslan Khasbulatov turned off the microphone at which she was standing. Turning the microphone back on after the other deputies demanded it, Khasbulatov then asked her rudely: "Well, and what else did you want to say." Taken aback, she responded, "That was below the belt." To which Khasbulatov retorted, "I don't have anything to do with what's below your belt" and turned off the microphone again.[32] Also in 1995, the populist fascist politician Vladimir Zhirinovsky punched deputy Evgenia Tishkovskaia in the face and later excused the act by claiming that he had been "fending off her sexual advances."[33] Despite the efforts of feminists and other women activists, politics has remained a man's game, even as the arena has expanded.

[30] Valerie Sperling, *Organizing Women in Contemporary Russia: Engendering Transition* (New York: Cambridge University Press, 1999), 114.
[31] Mary Buckley, "Adaptation of the Soviet Women's Committee: Deputies' Voices from 'Women of Russia,'" in Buckley, *Post-Soviet Women*, 162.
[32] Galina Starovoitova, "Being a Woman Politician in Contemporary Russia," in *Feminist Theory and Practice: East – West. Papers Presented of [sic] International Conference. St. Petersburg, Repino. June 9–12, 1995* (St. Petersburg, Russia, 1997), 25. Thanks to Olga Lipovskaya for providing me with this publication.
[33] Quoted in Sperling, *Organizing Women*, 138.

Activists on behalf of women encountered innumerable difficulties. They lacked even a language with which to press women-oriented demands, the words having already been "hijacked" by Soviet leadership. "Emancipation, liberation, equality were dirty words from the Stalinist past, only to be employed with heavy irony." Most equated feminism with "fighting against men." "Feminism in Russia was a curse word, a term of abuse."[34] Moreover, even when they shared similar goals, women's organizations experienced difficulty coordinating their efforts. Most organizations operated on a shoestring. Their need for financial resources led to fierce, often divisive competition for foreign assistance. Structuring projects according to the requirements of foreign funding organizations, they sometimes neglected local needs.

In the post-Soviet era, the more successful women's organizations often had little in common with feminism. The Organization of Soldiers' Mothers, which expanded greatly after the Soviet Union's collapse, remained the most important. Operating on a shoestring, it continued to campaign on behalf of the human rights of soldiers and played a leading role in protests against the war in Chechnya. Its efforts won the organization a nomination for the Nobel Peace Prize in 1996 and that year gained it the "Right Livelihood Award," known as the "Alternative Nobel Prize," for its "courageous and exemplary initiative" on behalf of the common humanity of Russians and Chechens and in opposition to militarism and violence.[35]

The presence of women's groups on the political scene, new possibilities for foreign travel, and contacts, together with the proliferation of new models of female behavior, were among the signs of hope in an economic and cultural environment that was, in many ways, depressing. Women's organizations provided services and raised issues forbidden in the Soviet era. They provided women with opportunities to actively shape, rather than simply to be victimized by, the changes occurring in their society. Women established shelters for battered women, offered counseling for victims of rape, and taught computer and other skills to help women survive in the new economy. Gender and women's studies centers generated women-oriented scholarship; young scholars have begun to explore hitherto neglected realms of women's experience. Collaboration with foreign scholars became more common. Women writers experimented with new forms of expression. Everywhere, the end of the state's monopoly on media has meant the end of its monopoly on images of women, too. Women artists, filmmakers, journalists, television personalities, and writers, more visible than before, present the public with a profusion of images of women: "in contrast to the unified 'ideal mother and worker' of the Soviet period, there are now a myriad of masculine and feminine types."[36]

---

[34] Ibid., 65. [35] Vallance, "Rule of Law," 9.
[36] Hilary Pilkington, *Gender, Generation and Identity in Contemporary Russia* (New York: Routledge, 1996), 16.

These new images, which complicate and enrich notions of what it is to be a woman and offer alternatives to the essentialist notions of womanhood left over from the late Soviet era, are very encouraging.

Nevertheless, essentialist notions remain powerful. Not least among the ironies of the Soviet legacy is the intensely gendered nature of the backlash. Rejecting the "emancipation" that Stalinism celebrated, many post-Soviet Russians nevertheless embraced the domesticity that became its counterpart. A blend of Soviet and prerevolutionary gender discourses, firmly melded to dreams of national revival, these ideas have assumed new life in the vacuum left by communism.

Suggestions for Further Reading

Ashwin, Sarah, ed., *Gender, State and Society in Soviet and Post-Soviet Russia*. New York: Routledge, 2000.

Bridger, Sue, Rebecca Kay, and Kathryn Pinnick. *No More Heroines? Russia, Women and the Market*. New York: Routledge, 1996. *Outstanding examination of women's situation in post-Soviet society.*

Buckley, Mary, ed. *Perestroika and Soviet Women*. New York: Cambridge University Press, 1992. *Essays surveying women's status during the Gorbachev era.*

Buckley, Mary, ed. *Post-Soviet Women: From the Baltic to Central Asia*. New York: Cambridge University Press, 1997. *Includes changes in the lives of non-Russians as well as Russians.*

Kagal, Ayesha and Natasha Perova, eds. *Present Imperfect: Stories by Russian Women*. Boulder, Colo.: Westview Press, 1996. *A selection of post-Soviet women's writing.*

Sperling, Valerie. *Organizing Women in Contemporary Russia: Engendering Transition*. New York: Cambridge University Press, 1999.

INDEX